THE 👁 EYEWITNESS

ATLAS
OF THE
WORLD

THE ◉ EYEWITNESS

ATLAS
OF THE
WORLD

DK PUBLISHING, INC.

CONSULTANTS

Consultant editor
Dr. David R. Green, Department of Geography, King's College

Digital mapping consultant
Professor Jan-Peter A. L. Muller, Professor of Image Understanding and Remote Sensing,
Department of Photogrammetry and Surveying, University College London

Digital base map production
Department of Photogrammetry and Surveying, University College London:
Philip Eales (Producer) • Kevin Tildsley • David Rees •
James Pearson • Peter Booth • Tim Day • Planetary Visions Ltd

Contributors
Peter Clark, Former Keeper, Royal Geographical Society, London •
Martin McCauley, Senior Lecturer in Politics,
School of Slavonic and East European Studies, University of London

Dorling Kindersley would also like to thank
Dr. Andrew Tatham, Keeper, and the Staff of the Royal Geographical Society, London,
for their help and advice in preparing this Atlas

Project art editor: Nicola Liddiard
Project editors: Elizabeth Wyse and Caroline Lucas
Project cartographer: Julia Lunn

Editorial: Jayne Parsons • Phillip Boys • Chris Whitwell • Donna Rispoli •
Margaret Hynes • Ailsa Heritage • Sue Peach • Laura Porter

Design: Lesley Betts • Rhonda Fisher • Paul Blackburn • Jay Young

Cartography: Roger Bullen • Michael Martin • James Mills-Hicks • James Anderson •
Yahya El-Droubie • Tony Chambers • Simon Lewis • Caroline Simpson

Illustrations: John Woodcock • Kathleen McDougall • Mick Gillah • David Wright

Photography: Andy Crawford • Tim Ridley • Steve Gorton

Picture research: Clive Webster • Charlotte Bush •
Sharon Southren • Frances Vargo • Caroline Brook

Editorial director: Andrew Heritage
Art director: Chez Picthall
Production: Susannah Straughan
U.S. Editor: Charles A. Wills

A DK PUBLISHING BOOK

Revised Edition
2 4 6 8 10 9 7 5 3

Published in the United States by DK Publishing, Inc.,
95 Madison Avenue, New York, NY 10016

Published in Great Britain by Dorling Kindersley Limited.

Library of Congress Cataloging-in-Publication Data
DK Publishing, Inc.
The eyewitness atlas of the world. – Revised edition
p. cm.
Includes index

1. Atlases. I. Title. II. Title: Atlas of the world
G1021.D65 1993 <G&M>
912-dc20   93-18572 CIP MAP

CONTENTS

THE EARTH IN SPACE

THE EARTH IS ONE OF NINE PLANETS that orbit a large star – the Sun. Together they form the solar system. All life on Earth – plant, animal, and human – depends on the Sun. Its energy warms our planet's surface, powers the wind and waves, drives the ocean currents and weather systems, and recycles water. Sunlight also gives plants the power to photosynthesize – to make the foods and oxygen on which organisms rely. The fact that the Earth is habitable at all is due to its precise position in the solar system, its daily spin, and its annual journey around the Sun at a constant tilt. Without these, and the breathable atmosphere that cloaks and protects the Earth, it would be as barren as our near-neighbors Venus and Mars.

Asteroid belt

Uranus 84 years *Mercury 88 days* *Mars 687 days* *Jupiter 12 years*

Venus 225 days *Earth 365 days (1 year)*

Neptune 165 years *Saturn 29 years*

Pluto 248 years

THE SOLAR SYSTEM
Although the planets move at great speeds, they do not fly off in all directions into space because the Sun's gravity holds them in place. This keeps the planets circling the Sun. A planet's "year" is the time it takes to make one complete trip around the Sun. The diagram shows the length of the planet's year in Earth-days or Earth-years.

THE SUN
The Sun is 865,000 miles (1,392,000 km) across. It has a core temperature of 25 million°F (14 million°C).

Venus 870°F (465°C)

Mars -9.5°F (-23°C)

Mercury Day: 806°F (430°C) Night: -292°F (-180°C)

Earth 60°F (15°C)

Jupiter -238°F (-150°C)

Saturn -292°F (-180°C)

Uranus -346°F (-210°C)

Neptune -364°F (-220°C)

Pluto -382°F (-230°C)

YOU CAN USE THIS SENTENCE TO REMEMBER THE SEQUENCE OF PLANETS: MANY VERY EAGER MOUNTAINEERS JOG SWIFTLY UP NEW PEAKS.

Above: The relative sizes of the Sun and planets, with their average temperature.

Venus 67,200,000 miles (108,200,000 km)
Jupiter 483,000,000 miles (778,330,000 km)

Mercury 36,000,000 miles (57,910,000 km)
Earth 92,900,000 miles (149,500,000 km)
Mars 141,600,000 miles (227,940,000 km)
Saturn 886,700,000 miles (1,426,980,000 km)
Uranus 1,783,000,000 miles (2,870,990,000 km)
Neptune 2,800,000,000 miles (4,497,070,000 km)
Pluto 3,670,000,000 miles (5,913,520,000 km)

Above: The planets and their distances from the Sun.

THE LIFE ZONE: THE EARTH SEEMS TO BE THE ONLY HABITABLE PLANET IN OUR SOLAR SYSTEM. MERCURY AND VENUS, WHICH ARE CLOSER TO THE SUN, ARE HOTTER THAN AN OVEN. MARS, AND PLANETS STILL FARTHER OUT, ARE COLDER THAN A DEEP FREEZE.

Huge solar flares, up to 125,000 miles (200,000 km) long, lick out into space

THE FOUR SEASONS
The Earth always tilts in the same direction on its 590 million-mile (950 million-km) journey around the Sun. This means that each hemisphere in turn leans toward the Sun, then leans away from it. This is what causes summer and winter.

DECEMBER 21ST (SOLSTICE)
Summer in the Southern hemisphere; winter in the Northern hemisphere. At noon, the Sun is overhead at the Tropic of Capricorn. The South Pole is in sunlight for 24 hours, and the North Pole is in darkness for 24 hours.

MARCH 21ST (EQUINOX)
Spring in the Northern hemisphere; autumn in the Southern hemisphere. At noon, the Sun is overhead at the Equator. Everywhere on Earth has 12 hours of daylight, 12 hours of darkness.

The Earth travels around the Sun at 66,600 miles per hour (107,244 km per hour).

It takes 365 days, 6 hours, 9 minutes, and 9 seconds for the Earth to make one revolution around the Sun. This is the true length of an Earth "year."

To North Star

The Earth takes 23 hours, 56 minutes, and 4 seconds to rotate once. This is the true length of an Earth "day."

Sun

JUNE 21ST (SOLSTICE)
Summer in the Northern hemisphere; winter in the Southern hemisphere. At noon, the Sun is overhead at the Tropic of Cancer. The North Pole is in sunlight for 24 hours, and the South Pole is in darkness for 24 hours.

SEPTEMBER 21ST (EQUINOX)
Autumn in the Northern hemisphere; spring in the Southern hemisphere. At noon, the Sun is overhead at the Equator. Everywhere on Earth has 12 hours of daylight, 12 hours of darkness.

South Pole

24 HOURS IN THE LIFE OF PLANET EARTH
The Earth turns a complete circle (360°) in 24 hours, or 15° in one hour. Countries on a similar line of longitude (or "meridian") usually share the same time. They set their clocks in relation to Greenwich Mean Time (GMT). This is the time at Greenwich (London, England), on longitude 0°. Countries east of Greenwich are ahead of GMT. Countries to the west are behind GMT.

Noon everywhere on this meridian

 0° *15°W* *30°W* *45°W* *60°W* *75°W* *90°W* *105°W* *120°W* *135°W* *150°W* *16*

Noon at:	*Greenwich*	*Dakar*	*E. Greenland*	*Rio de Janeiro*	*Caracas*	*New York*	*Mexico City*	*Calgary*	*Los Angeles*	*E. Alaska*	*Honolulu*	*(Pacific Oce*
Greenwich time:	*1200 hrs*	*1100 hrs*	*1000 hrs*	*0900 hrs*	*0800 hrs*	*0700 hrs*	*0600 hrs*	*0500 hrs*	*0400 hrs*	*0300 hrs*	*0200 hrs*	*0100 hrs*

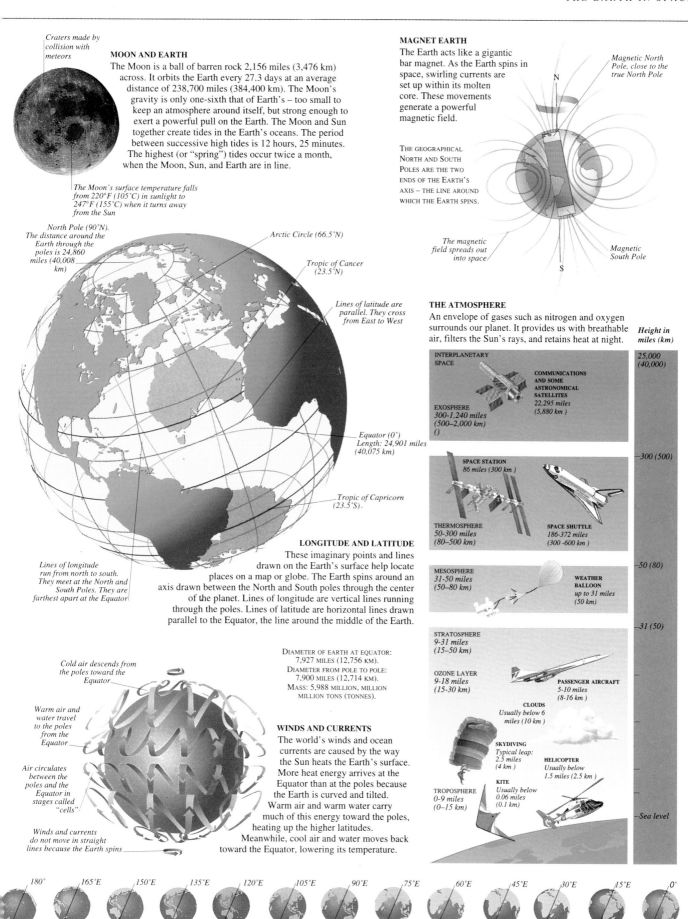

Craters made by collision with meteors

MOON AND EARTH

The Moon is a ball of barren rock 2,156 miles (3,476 km) across. It orbits the Earth every 27.3 days at an average distance of 238,700 miles (384,400 km). The Moon's gravity is only one-sixth that of Earth's – too small to keep an atmosphere around itself, but strong enough to exert a powerful pull on the Earth. The Moon and Sun together create tides in the Earth's oceans. The period between successive high tides is 12 hours, 25 minutes. The highest (or "spring") tides occur twice a month, when the Moon, Sun, and Earth are in line.

The Moon's surface temperature falls from 220°F (105°C) in sunlight to 247°F (155°C) when it turns away from the Sun

MAGNET EARTH

The Earth acts like a gigantic bar magnet. As the Earth spins in space, swirling currents are set up within its molten core. These movements generate a powerful magnetic field.

Magnetic North Pole, close to the true North Pole

THE GEOGRAPHICAL NORTH AND SOUTH POLES ARE THE TWO ENDS OF THE EARTH'S AXIS – THE LINE AROUND WHICH THE EARTH SPINS.

The magnetic field spreads out into space

Magnetic South Pole

North Pole (90°N). The distance around the Earth through the poles is 24,860 miles (40,008 km)

Arctic Circle (66.5°N)

Tropic of Cancer (23.5°N)

Lines of latitude are parallel. They cross from East to West

Equator (0°) Length: 24,901 miles (40,075 km)

Tropic of Capricorn (23.5°S).

Lines of longitude run from north to south. They meet at the North and South Poles. They are farthest apart at the Equator

THE ATMOSPHERE

An envelope of gases such as nitrogen and oxygen surrounds our planet. It provides us with breathable air, filters the Sun's rays, and retains heat at night.

Height in miles (km)

INTERPLANETARY SPACE

COMMUNICATIONS AND SOME ASTRONOMICAL SATELLITES 22,295 miles (5,880 km)

EXOSPHERE 300-1,240 miles (500–2,000 km) ()

25,000 (40,000)

SPACE STATION 86 miles (300 km)

THERMOSPHERE 50-300 miles (80–500 km)

SPACE SHUTTLE 186-372 miles (300 -600 km)

300 (500)

MESOSPHERE 31-50 miles (50–80 km)

WEATHER BALLOON up to 31 miles (50 km)

50 (80)

STRATOSPHERE 9-31 miles (15–50 km)

OZONE LAYER 9-18 miles (15-30 km)

PASSENGER AIRCRAFT 5-10 miles (8-16 km)

31 (50)

CLOUDS Usually below 6 miles (10 km)

SKYDIVING Typical leap: 2.5 miles (4 km)

HELICOPTER Usually below 1.5 miles (2.5 km)

KITE Usually below 0.06 miles (0.1 km)

TROPOSPHERE 0-9 miles (0–15 km)

Sea level

LONGITUDE AND LATITUDE

These imaginary points and lines drawn on the Earth's surface help locate places on a map or globe. The Earth spins around an axis drawn between the North and South poles through the center of the planet. Lines of longitude are vertical lines running through the poles. Lines of latitude are horizontal lines drawn parallel to the Equator, the line around the middle of the Earth.

DIAMETER OF EARTH AT EQUATOR: 7,927 MILES (12,756 KM). DIAMETER FROM POLE TO POLE: 7,900 MILES (12,714 KM). MASS: 5,988 MILLION, MILLION MILLION TONS (TONNES).

Cold air descends from the poles toward the Equator

Warm air and water travel to the poles from the Equator

Air circulates between the poles and the Equator in stages called "cells"

Winds and currents do not move in straight lines because the Earth spins

WINDS AND CURRENTS

The world's winds and ocean currents are caused by the way the Sun heats the Earth's surface. More heat energy arrives at the Equator than at the poles because the Earth is curved and tilted. Warm air and warm water carry much of this energy toward the poles, heating up the higher latitudes. Meanwhile, cool air and water moves back toward the Equator, lowering its temperature.

180°	165°E	150°E	135°E	120°E	105°E	90°E	75°E	60°E	45°E	30°E	15°E	0°
Wellington 2400 hrs	(Pacific Ocean) 2300 hrs	Sydney 2200 hrs	Tokyo 2100 hrs	Manila 2000 hrs	Jakarta 1900 hrs	Dacca 1800 hrs	Karachi 1700 hrs	Muscat 1600 hrs	Baghdad 1500 hrs	Cairo 1400 hrs	Berlin 1300 hrs	Greenwich 1200 hrs

THE EARTH'S STRUCTURE

IN SOME WAYS, the Earth is like an egg, with a thin shell around a soft interior. Its hard, rocky outer layer – the crust – is up to 45 miles (70 km) thick under the continents, but less than 5 miles (8 km) thick under the oceans. This crust is broken into gigantic slabs called "plates," in which the continents are embedded. Below the hard crust is the mantle, a layer of rocks so hot that some melt and flow in huge swirling currents. The Earth's plates do not stay in the same place. Instead, they move, carried along like rafts on the currents in the mantle. This motion is very slow – usually less than 2 in (5 cm) a year – but enormously powerful. Plate movement makes the Earth quake and volcanoes erupt, causes immense mountain ranges such as the Himalayas to grow where plates collide, and explains, how over millions of years, whole continents have drifted across the face of the planet.

Pangaea

DRIFTING CONTINENTS
Currents of molten rock deep within the mantle slowly move the continents. Over time, they appear to "drift" across the Earth's surface.

200 MILLION YEARS AGO
All of today's continents were joined in one supercontinent, called Pangaea. It began to break up about 180 million years ago.

"Africa" *"India"* *"Atlantic Ocean" opening up*

120 MILLION YEARS AGO
The Atlantic Ocean splits Pangaea into two. India has broken away from Africa.

"North America" *"Asia"* *"India"*

"Australia" *North America* *Europe* *Asia* *Ind...*

"Antarctica"

40 MILLION YEARS AGO
India is moving closer to Asia. Australia and Antarctica have separated.

South America *South America* *Austra...* *Africa* *Antarctica*

TODAY
India has collided with Asia, pushing up the Himalaya Mountains.

Great Rift Valley, now sea

50 MILLION YEARS IN THE FUTURE?
If today's plate movements continue, the Atlantic Ocean will be 775 miles (1,250 km) wider. Africa and Europe will fuse, the Americas will separate again, and Africa east of the Great Rift Valley will be an island.

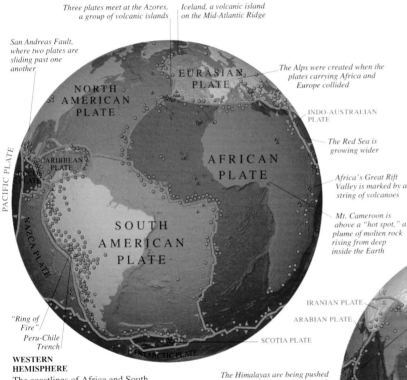

Three plates meet at the Azores, a group of volcanic islands

Iceland, a volcanic island on the Mid-Atlantic Ridge

San Andreas Fault, where two plates are sliding past one another

The Alps were created when the plates carrying Africa and Europe collided

NORTH AMERICAN PLATE

EURASIAN PLATE

INDO-AUSTRALIAN PLATE

The Red Sea is growing wider

CARIBBEAN PLATE

AFRICAN PLATE

Africa's Great Rift Valley is marked by a string of volcanoes

PACIFIC PLATE

Mt. Cameroon is above a "hot spot," a plume of molten rock rising from deep inside the Earth

SOUTH AMERICAN PLATE

NAZCA PLATE

"Ring of Fire," Peru-Chile Trench

SCOTIA PLATE

ANTARCTIC PLATE

The "Ring of Fire" passes through Japan.

Mariana Trench, 6.8 miles (11,033 m) deep, where an ocean plate dives into the mantle

EURASIAN PLATE

IRANIAN PLATE

ARABIAN PLATE

PHILIPPINE PLATE

PACIFIC PLATE

The Himalayas are being pushed up by the collision of India with the rest of Asia

AFRICAN PLATE

INDO-AUSTRALIAN PLATE

ANTARCTIC PLATE

The Java Trench, 4.6 miles (7,450 m) deep, runs parallel to a long chain of active volcanoes in Southeast Asia

The Hawaiian islands lie over a "hot spot"

Highly volcanic New Zealand lies on the "Ring of Fire"

WESTERN HEMISPHERE
The coastlines of Africa and South America "fit" one another like huge jigsaw pieces. This is because they were once joined. About 180 million years ago, a crack appeared in the Earth's crust. Hot liquid rock (magma) rose through the crack and cooled, forming new oceanic crust on either side. As the ocean grew wider, the continents moved apart. The process continues today.

EASTERN HEMISPHERE
Most earthquakes and volcanoes occur around the edges of crustal plates (or plate margins). Australia, in the middle of the Indo-Australian plate, has no active volcanoes and is rarely troubled by earthquakes. Things are very different in neighboring New Zealand and New Guinea, which lie on the Pacific "Ring of Fire". The ring is an area of intense volcanic activity which forms a line all the way round the Pacific rim, through the Philippines, Japan, and North America, and down the coast of South America to New Zealand.

KEYBOX	
△	Major active volcano
⊙	Major earthquake
⊢⊣	Colliding plates
▽	Sliding plates
⊢⊣	Spreading plates

THE ATLANTIC OCEAN IS GROWING WIDER BY 1 IN (2.5 CM) A YEAR – ABOUT THE SAME SPEED THAT FINGERNAILS GROW. THE NAZCA PLATE IS SLIDING THREE TIMES FASTER UNDER SOUTH AMERICA, PUSHING UP THE ANDES.

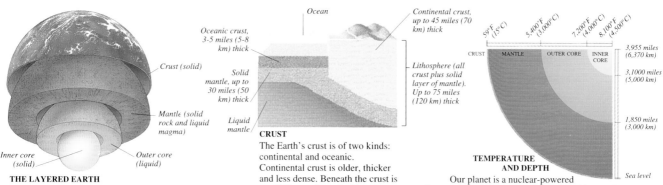

Ocean

Oceanic crust, 3-5 miles (5-8 km) thick

Solid mantle, up to 30 miles (50 km) thick

Liquid mantle

Continental crust, up to 45 miles (70 km) thick

Lithosphere (all crust plus solid layer of mantle). Up to 75 miles (120 km) thick

Crust (solid)

Mantle (solid rock and liquid magma)

Inner core (solid)

Outer core (liquid)

59°F (15°C) 5,400°F (3,000°C) 7,200°F (4,000°C) 8,100°F (4,500°C)

CRUST | MANTLE | OUTER CORE | INNER CORE

3,955 miles (6,370 km)

3,1000 miles (5,000 km)

1,850 miles (3,000 km)

Sea level

THE LAYERED EARTH
The Earth has layers, like an egg. The core is made of metals such as iron and nickel. This is surrounded by a rocky mantle and a thin crust.

CRUST
The Earth's crust is of two kinds: continental and oceanic. Continental crust is older, thicker and less dense. Beneath the crust is a solid layer of mantle. Together, these form the lithosphere, which is broken into several plates. These float on the liquid mantle layer.

TEMPERATURE AND DEPTH
Our planet is a nuclear-powered furnace, heated from within by the breakdown of radioactive minerals such as uranium. Temperature increases with depth: 60 miles (100 km) down it is 2,460°F (1,350°C), hot enough for rocks to melt.

Magma rising along center of ridge

Ocean

Magma from molten mantle

Solid mantle

Deep ocean trench opens where plate dives

Mountain

Volcano

Oceanic plate dives into mantle

Valley *Mountain*

Continent A *Continent B*

Line of collision

Continental crust crumples

Fault

Plate *Plate*

SPREADING PLATES
When two plates move apart, molten rock (magma) rises from the mantle and cools, forming new crust. This is called a constructive margin. Most are found in oceans.

COLLIDING PLATES THAT DIVE
When two ocean plates or an ocean plate and a continent plate collide, the denser plate is forced under the other, diving down into the mantle. These are destructive margins.

COLLIDING PLATES THAT BUCKLE
When two continents collide, their plates fuse, crumple, and push upward. Mountain ranges like the Himalayas and the Urals have been formed in this way.

SLIDING PLATES
When two plates slide past one another, intense friction is created along the "fault line" between them, causing earthquakes. These are called conservative margins.

ICELAND, MID-ATLANTIC RIDGE
Most constructive margins are found beneath oceans, but here in volcanic Iceland one comes to the surface.

VOLCANO, JAVA
Diving plates often build volcanic islands and mountain chains. Deep ocean trenches form offshore.

FOLDING STRATA, ENGLAND
The clash of continental plates may cause the Earth to buckle and twist far from the collision zone.

SAN ANDREAS FAULT
A huge earthquake may one day occur somewhere along California's San Andreas Fault, seen here.

EXPLOSIVE VOLCANO
About 50 of the world's 600 or so active volcanoes erupt each year. Explosive pressure is created by the buildup of magma, gases, or superheated steam.

Crater

Cloud of ash, gases, and steam

Lava flows

Main vent (opening)

Cone of ash and lava from old eruptions

SOME MAJOR QUAKES AND ERUPTIONS
This map shows some of the worst natural disasters in recorded history. Over one million earthquakes and about 50 volcanic eruptions are detected every year. Most are minor or occur where there are few people, so there is no loss of human life or great damage to property. But crowded cities and poorly-constructed buildings are putting ever-greater numbers at risk.

Direction of ocean plate movement

HOT SPOT, HAWAII
Hawaii is on a "hot spot" in the Earth's crust. This is a plume of hot magma that rises from the mantle and breaks through the thin ocean crust to feed a volcano. As the crust moves, the volcano is carried away, but the hot spot stays, forming a new volcano.

Maui

Chain of older islands, now eroded to below sea level

Oahu: no longer sits over the hot spot. No volcanic eruptions for over 2 million years

Hawaii rises more than 33,000 ft (10,000 m) from the ocean floor

Hot spot

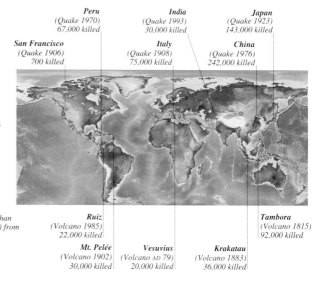

Peru (Quake 1970) 67,000 killed

India (Quake 1993) 30,000 killed

Japan (Quake 1923) 143,000 killed

San Francisco (Quake 1906) 700 killed

Italy (Quake 1908) 75,000 killed

China (Quake 1976) 242,000 killed

Ruiz (Volcano 1985) 22,000 killed

Tambora (Volcano 1815) 92,000 killed

Mt. Pelée (Volcano 1902) 30,000 killed

Vesuvius (Volcano AD 79) 20,000 killed

Krakatau (Volcano 1883) 36,000 killed

SHAPING THE LANDSCAPE

LANDSCAPES ARE CREATED AND CHANGED – even destroyed – in a continuous cycle. Over millions of years, constant movements of the Earth's plates have built up continents, islands, and mountains. But as soon as new land is formed, it is shaped (or "eroded") by the forces of wind, water, ice, and heat. Sometimes change is quick, as when a river floods and cuts a new channel, or a landslide cascades down a mountain slope. Usually, however, change is so slow that it is invisible to the human eye. Extremes of heat and cold crack open rocks and expose them to attack by wind and water. Rivers and glaciers scour out valleys, the wind piles up sand dunes, and the sea attacks shorelines and cliffs. Eroded materials are blown away or carried along by rivers, piling up as sediments on valley floors or the seabed. Over millions of years, these may be compressed into rock and pushed up to form new land. As soon as the land is exposed to the elements, the cycle of erosion begins again.

☐ **ICE ACTION, ALASKA**
Areas close to the North Pole are permanently covered in snow and ice. Glaciers are rivers of ice that flow toward the sea. Some glaciers are more than 40 miles (60 km) long.

☐ **SEA ACTION, CAPE COD**
Cape Cod, a sandy peninsula 65 miles (105 km) long, juts out like a beckoning finger into the Atlantic Ocean. Its strangely curved coastline has been shaped by wave action.

KEYBOX

☐ Area covered in ice today	☐ Area drained by major river
☐ Ice and snow 18,000 years ago	☐ Protected coastline
☐ Desert	☐ Coast affected by tidal swell
☐ Wind direction (simplified)	☐ Coast affected by storm waves

Keybox applies to all maps opposite

THE "ROOF OF NORTH AMERICA"
Steeply sloping Denali (also called Mt. McKinley), Alaska, is North America's highest mountain at 20,320 ft (6,194 m). It is a fairly "young" mountain, less than 70 million years old. The gently sloping Appalachians in eastern North America are much older. Once, they were probably higher than Denali is today. But more than 300 million years of ice, rain, and wind have ground them down.

THIS SECTION OF THE GLOBE SHOWS NORTH AMERICA AND THE DIFFERENT FORCES WORKING ON ITS LANDSCAPE. THE LANDSCAPE IN EVERY PART OF THE WORLD IS CHANGED BY THE ACTION OF ICE, RUNNING WATER, SEA WAVES, AND WIND.

☐ **WIND ACTION, DEATH VALLEY**
Death Valley is the hottest, driest place in North America. Its floor is covered in sand and salt. Winds sweeping across the valley endlessly reshape the loose surface.

☐ **WATER ACTION, MISSISSIPPI**
The Mississippi River and its many tributaries frequently change course. Where two loops are close together, the river may cut a new path between them, leaving an "oxbow lake."

Ice floats because it is less dense than seawater

Only one-ninth of an iceberg is above sea level

A GLACIER REACHES THE SEA
When a glacier enters the sea, its front edge, or "snout," breaks up and forms icebergs – a process called calving. These "ice mountains" are then carried away by ocean currents.

ICE COVER *See keybox opposite*

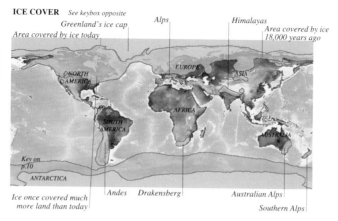

Greenland's ice cap

Area covered by ice today

Alps

Himalayas

Area covered by ice 18,000 years ago

NORTH AMERICA

EUROPE

ASIA

SOUTH AMERICA

AFRICA

AUSTRALIA

Key on p.10

ANTARCTICA

Ice once covered much more land than today

Andes   Drakensberg

Australian Alps

Southern Alps

NORDFJORD, NORWAY
One sign of glacial action on the landscape is the fjord. These long, narrow, steep-sided inlets are found along the coasts of Norway, Alaska, Chile, and New Zealand. They mark the points where glaciers once entered the sea.

Rock eroded here

Rock fragments and sand deposited here

Hard rock headland broken into small sections

Advancing sea waves

Bay

Headland

COASTAL ATTACK
The ceaseless push and pull of waves on a shore can destroy even the hardest rocks. The softest rocks are eroded first, leaving headlands of hard rock that survive a little longer.

COASTAL EROSION *See keybox opposite*

Northwest Europe's shorelines are heavily eroded by Atlantic storms

Permanent ice protects Antarctica's shores

Key on p.10

The southern tip of South America is notorious for its devastating storms

The Mediterranean Sea is enclosed by land, so there is little coastal erosion

Islands help protect Asia's mainland from advancing waves

WAVE POWER
The powerful action of waves on an exposed coast can erode a coastline by several feet a year.

The sheltered slope is steeper than the slope facing the wind

Dunes advance when sand particles are blown over the top of the dune

Wind direction

DESERT DUNE
Dunes are slow-moving mounds or ridges of sand found in deserts and along some coastlines. They form only when the wind's direction and speed is fairly constant.

THE GREAT DESERTS *See keybox opposite*

Great Basin

Sahara   Arabian

Kara Kum

Takla Makan

Key on p.10

Atacama

Namib

Kalahari   Thar   Gobi

Great Victoria

NAMIB DESERT, SOUTHERN AFRICA
The sand dunes seen in the center of the picture are about 160 ft (50 m) high. Winds are driving them slowly but relentlessly toward the right. Not all deserts are sandy. Wind may blow away all the loose sand and gravel, leaving bare rock.

This crescent-shaped oxbow lake was once a meander

Old river channel, now filled with sand and gravel

New river channel

Direction of flow

Sand and gravel deposited here so bank grows

Swift currents on outer bends cut steep banks

MEANDERS
River banks are worn away most on the outside of bends, where water flows fastest. Eroded sand and gravel are built up into banks on the inside of bends in slower-moving water.

THE LARGEST RIVER BASINS *See keybox opposite*

Mackenzie   Mississippi

Ob'   Yenisey

Lena   Amur

Key on p.10

Amazon

Paraná   Niger

Congo

Nile   Ganges

Yangtse

WINDING RIVER, ALASKA
The more a river meanders across a plain, the longer it becomes and the more slowly it flows.

CLIMATE AND VEGETATION

THE EARTH IS the only planet in our solar system which supports life. Most of our planet has a breathable atmosphere and sufficient light, heat, and water to support a wide range of plants and animals. The main influences on an area's climate are the amount of sunshine it receives (which varies with latitude and season), how close it is to the influence of ocean currents, and its height above sea level. Since there is more sunlight at the Equator than elsewhere, and rainfall is highest here, too, this is where we find the habitats which have more species of plants and animals than anywhere else: rain forests, coral reefs, and mangrove swamps. Where rainfall is very low, and where it is either too hot, such as in deserts, or too cold, few plants and animals can survive. Only the icy North and South Poles and the frozen tops of high mountains are practically without life of any sort.

WEATHER EXTREMES
Weather is a powerful influence on how we feel, the clothes we wear, the buildings we live in, the plants that grow around us, and what we eat and drink. Extreme weather events – heat waves, hurricanes, blizzards, tornadoes, sandstorms, droughts, and floods – can be terrifyingly destructive.

TORNADO
Tornadoes are whirlwinds of cold air that develop when thunderclouds cross warm land. They are extremely violent and unpredictable. Windspeeds often exceed 180 miles (300 km) per hour.

TROPICAL STORMS
These devastating winds develop when air spirals upward above warm seas. More air is sucked in and the storm begins to move. They bring torrential rain, thunder and lightning, and destruction.

DROUGHT
Long periods without water kill plants. Stripped of its protective covering of vegetation, the soil is easily blown away.

North Pacific current · Equatorial currents · California current · Labrador current · E. Greenland current · Gulf Stream · Canaries current · Benguela current · Monsoon Drift · Oya Shio current

NORTH AMERICA · EUROPE · ASIA · AFRICA · SOUTH AMERICA · AUSTRALIA · ANTARCTICA

Brazil current · Peru current · Antarctic circumpolar current · Agulhas current · W. Australia current

OCEAN CURRENTS
Currents are a powerful influence on climates. They are like great rivers in the ocean that carry warm water (orange) away from the Equator and cold water (blue) toward the Equator.

Tropical storms · Hurricanes, August to October · Blizzards · Blizzards, November to March · Typhoons, April to December

Areas prone to flooding · Cyclones, May to December · Williwaws, December to April

MAIN STORM ZONES
Storms combine very high winds with heavy rainfall (tropical storms) or driving snow (blizzards). Typhoons, cyclones, hurricanes, and williwaws are regional names for tropical storms.

TEMPERATURE
Average temperatures vary widely around the world. Areas close to the Equator are usually hot (orange on the map); those close to the Poles are usually cold (deep blue). The hottest areas move during the year from the Southern to the Northern hemispheres.

Arctic Circle · Tropic of Cancer · Equator · Tropic of Capricorn · Antarctic Circle

Average January temperature

Average July temperature

Highest: (136°F) 58°C Saharan Libya

Lowest: -129°F (-89°C), Antarctica

Average January rainfall

Average July rainfall

RAINFALL
The wettest areas (gray) lie near the Equator. The driest are found close to the tropics, in the center of continents, or at the poles. Elsewhere, rainfall varies with the season, but it is usually highest in summer. Asia's wet season is known as the monsoon.

Arctic Circle · Tropic of Cancer · Equator · Tropic of Capricorn · Antarctic Circle

Highest in 1 year: 460 in (11.68 m), Hawaii

Lowest: No rain in more than 14 years, Atacama

■ BROADLEAF FOREST
Temperate climates have no great temperature extremes, and drought is unusual. Forests usually contain deciduous (broad-leaved) trees, such as beeches or oaks, that shed their leaves in autumn.

TRAVELING SOUTHWARD FROM THE NORTH POLE, A NUMBER OF DISTINCT LIFE ZONES OR "BIOMES" CAN BE SEEN. PLANT AND ANIMAL LIFE IS CLOSELY ADAPTED TO LOCAL CLIMATE.

□ TUNDRA
As long as frozen soil melts for at least two months of the year, some mosses, lichens, and ground-hugging shrubs can survive. They are found around the Arctic Circle and on mountains.

■ NEEDLELEAF FOREST
Forests of coniferous (needleleaf) trees, such as pines and firs, cover much of northern North America, Europe, and Asia. They are ever-green and can survive long frozen winters. Most have tall, straight trunks and down-pointing branches. This reduces the amount of snow that can settle on them. The forest floor is dark because leaves absorb most of the incoming sunlight.

□ MEDITERRANEAN
The hot dry summers and warm wet winters typical of the Mediterranean region are also found in small areas of Southern Africa, the Americas, and Australia. Mediterranean-type vegetation can vary from dense forest to thinly spread evergreen shrubs like these.

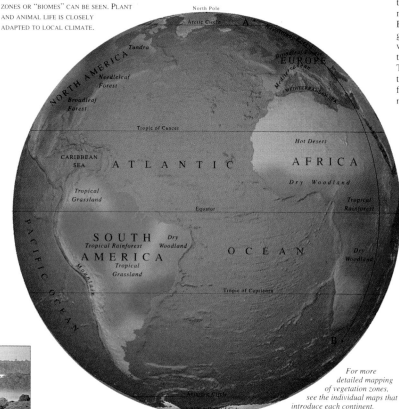

For more detailed mapping of vegetation zones, see the individual maps that introduce each continent.

□ MOUNTAIN
Vegetation changes with height because the temperature drops and wind increases. Even on the Equator, mountain peaks can be covered in snow. Although trees may cloak the lower slopes, at higher altitudes they give way to sparser vegetation. Near the top, only tundra-type plants can survive.

■ TROPICAL RAIN FOREST
The lush forests found near the Equator depend on year-round high temperatures and heavy rainfall. Worldwide, they may contain 50,000 different kinds of trees, and support several million other plant and animal species. Trees are often festooned with climbing plants, or covered with ferns and orchids that have rooted in pockets of water and soil on trunks and branches.

■ DRY WOODLAND
Plants in many parts of the tropics have to cope with high temperatures and long periods without rain. Some store water in enlarged stems or trunks, or limit water losses by having small, spiny leaves. In dry (but not desert) conditions, trees are widely spaced, with expanses of grassland between, called savannah.

□ HOT DESERT
Very few plants and animals can survive in hot deserts. Rainfall is low – under 4 in (10 cm) a year. Temperatures often rise above 104 °F (40°C) during the day, but drop to the freezing point at night. High winds and shifting sands can be a further hazard to life. Only specially adapted plants, such as cacti, can survive.

NORTH-SOUTH CROSS-SECTION THROUGH EUROPE AND AFRICA

The line running between points 'A' and 'B' on the map is the line of the cross-section

PEOPLE AND PLANET

SOON, THERE WILL BE 6 billion people on Earth, and numbers are rising at the rate of about 1 million every week. The Earth's population is not distributed evenly. Some areas, such as parts of Europe, India, and China, are very densely populated. Other areas – particularly deserts, polar regions, and mountains – can support very few people. Almost half of the world's people now live in towns or cities. Until 1800, most people lived in small villages in the countryside and worked on the land. But since then, more and more people have lived and worked in much larger communities. A century ago, most of the world's largest cities were in Europe and North America, where new industries and businesses were flourishing. Today, the most rapidly growing cities are in Asia, South America, and Africa. People who move to these cities are usually young adults, so the birth rate among these new populations is very high.

A CROWDED PLANET?
If the 5.5 billion people alive today stood close together, they could all fit into an area no larger than the small Caribbean island of Jamaica. Of course, so many people could not live in such a small place. Areas with few people are usually very cold, such as land near the poles and in mountains, or very dry, such as deserts. Areas with large populations often have fertile land and a good climate for crops. Cities can support huge populations because they are wealthy enough to import everything they need.

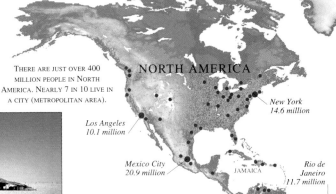

THERE ARE JUST OVER 400 MILLION PEOPLE IN NORTH AMERICA. NEARLY 7 IN 10 LIVE IN A CITY (METROPOLITAN AREA).

NORTH AMERICA

New York 14.6 million

Los Angeles 10.1 million

Mexico City 20.9 million

JAMAICA

Rio de Janeiro 11.7 million

SOUTH AMERICA

São P. 18.7 millio

Buenos Aires 11.7 million

THERE ARE ABOUT 300 MILLION PEOPLE IN SOUTH AMERICA. MORE THAN 7 IN LIVE IN A CITY.

KEYBOX

Orange represents towns and cities

● City with more than 1 million people.

● City with more than 10 million people

MILLIONAIRE CITIES 1900
Less than a century ago there were only 13 cities with more than 1 million people living in them. All the cities were in the Northern hemisphere. The largest was London, with 7 million people.

MILLIONAIRE CITIES 1950
By 1950, there were nearly 70 cities with more than one million inhabitants. The largest was New York City.

WORLD POPULATION GROWTH 1500–2020
Each figure on the graph represents 500 million people.

SAHARA, AFRICA
The Sahara, like all deserts, is thinly populated. The Tuareg of the northern Sahara are nomads. They travel in small groups because food sources are scarce. Their homes have to be portable.

MONGOLIA, ASIA
Traditionally, Mongolia's nomadic people lived by herding their animals across the steppe. Today, their felt tents, or *gers*, are often set up next to more permanent houses.

AMAZONIA, SOUTH AMERICA
The Yanomami people gather plants in the rain forest and hunt game, but they also grow crops in small forest gardens. Several families live together in a "village" under one huge roof.

MALI, AFRICA
The Dogon people of Mali use mud to construct their elaborate villages. Every family has its own huts and walled areas in which their animals are penned for the night.

The world's population in 1500 was about 425 million

The world's population in 1600 was about 545 million

The world's population in 1700 was about 610 million.

1500

1600

1700

POOR SUBURB
Densely-populated "shantytowns" have grown on the fringes of many cities in the developing world. Houses are usually built from discarded materials.

RICH SUBURB
Cities are often surrounded by areas where the richest people live. Population densities are low, and the houses may be luxurious, with large gardens or swimming pools. People in these suburbs rely on their cars for transportation. This allows them to live a great distance from places of work and leisure in the city center.

Land covers less than a third of the Earth's surface.

OCEAN 71%

LAND 29%

Only one-tenth of the total land area can grow crops.

TOO COLD 17%

TOO DRY 24%

POOR SOILS 49%

SUITABLE FOR CROPS 10%

CULTIVATION
Only a small portion of the Earth's surface can grow crops. It may be possible to bring more land – such as deserts – into production, but yields may be costly.

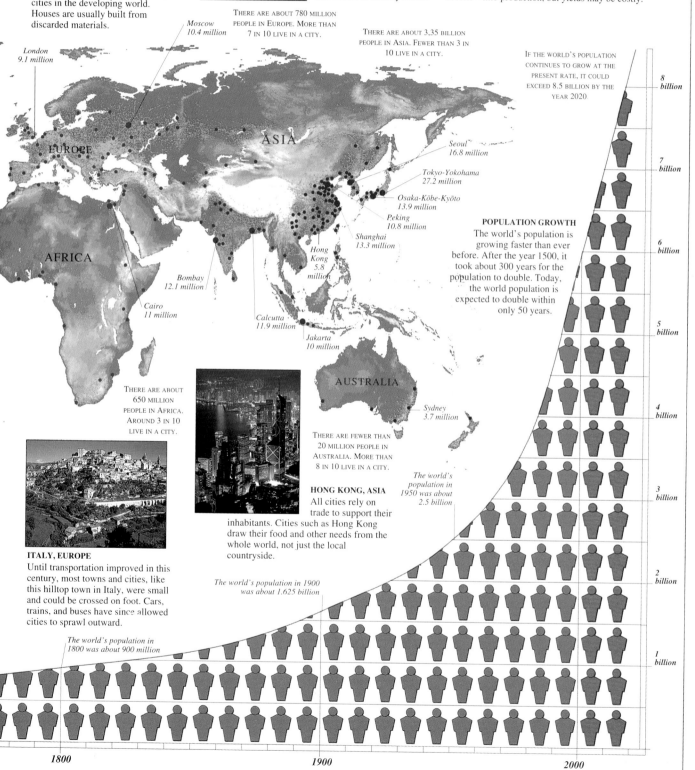

London 9.1 million

Moscow 10.4 million

THERE ARE ABOUT 780 MILLION PEOPLE IN EUROPE. MORE THAN 7 IN 10 LIVE IN A CITY.

THERE ARE ABOUT 3,35 BILLION PEOPLE IN ASIA. FEWER THAN 3 IN 10 LIVE IN A CITY.

EUROPE

ASIA

Seoul 16.8 million

Tokyo-Yokohama 27.2 million

Osaka-Kōbe-Kyōto 13.9 million

Peking 10.8 million

Shanghai 13.3 million

AFRICA

Bombay 12.1 million

Hong Kong 5.8 million

Cairo 11 million

Calcutta 11.9 million

Jakarta 10 million

THERE ARE ABOUT 650 MILLION PEOPLE IN AFRICA. AROUND 3 IN 10 LIVE IN A CITY.

AUSTRALIA

Sydney 3.7 million

THERE ARE FEWER THAN 20 MILLION PEOPLE IN AUSTRALIA. MORE THAN 8 IN 10 LIVE IN A CITY.

HONG KONG, ASIA
All cities rely on trade to support their inhabitants. Cities such as Hong Kong draw their food and other needs from the whole world, not just the local countryside.

ITALY, EUROPE
Until transportation improved in this century, most towns and cities, like this hilltop town in Italy, were small and could be crossed on foot. Cars, trains, and buses have since allowed cities to sprawl outward.

IF THE WORLD'S POPULATION CONTINUES TO GROW AT THE PRESENT RATE, IT COULD EXCEED 8.5 BILLION BY THE YEAR 2020

8 billion

7 billion

POPULATION GROWTH
The world's population is growing faster than ever before. After the year 1500, it took about 300 years for the population to double. Today, the world population is expected to double within only 50 years.

6 billion

5 billion

4 billion

3 billion

The world's population in 1950 was about 2.5 billion

2 billion

The world's population in 1900 was about 1.625 billion

1 billion

The world's population in 1800 was about 900 million

1800

1900

2000

THE WORLD TODAY

THERE ARE 192 INDEPENDENT countries in the world today. With the exception of Antarctica, every land area of the Earth's surface belongs to, or is claimed by, one country or another. In 1950, there were only 82 countries. Since then, many former colonies of the European countries have gained independence. The final stage in this process was the breakup of the Soviet Union after 1990. The world's nations vary enormously in size and shape. The largest country in the world is the Russian Federation; the smallest is Vatican City.

ENCLAVES
If part of a country's territory has become separated from the rest of the country and is surrounded by foreign territory, it is called an enclave. Kaliningrad is part of the Russian Federation, but is cut off from it by the Baltic States.

RIVER BORDERS
Over one-sixth of the world's national borders are formed by rivers. Long stretches of the Danube form borders in south-eastern Europe. It is also an important navigable waterway for over 1,000 miles (1,600 km).

KEY TO EUROPE

1 SLOVENIA
2 CROATIA
3 BOSNIA/HERZEGOVINA
4 YUGOSLAVIA
5 MACEDONIA
6 ALBANIA
7 BELGIUM
8 LUXEMBOURG
9 LIECHTENSTEIN
10 SWITZERLAND
11 MOLDAVIA
12 ANDORRA
13 MONACO
14 SAN MARINO
15 VATICAN CITY
16 NETHERLANDS

STRAIGHT-LINE BORDERS
The borders of many countries in Africa and other former colonial territories are straight lines. This was the simplest solution for colonial administrators, who often knew little of the country's geography or population.

IN 1884, AN INTERNATIONAL AGREEMENT CONNECTED EACH COUNTRY'S TIME TO THE TIME AT GREENWICH, UK. THE TIME ALONG THE LINE OF LONGITUDE WHICH PASSES THROUGH GREENWICH IS CALLED GREENWICH MEAN TIME.

LAKE BOUNDARIES
Countries which lie next to lakes usually fix their borders in the middle of the lake. Complicated agreements between colonial powers led to the awkward division of Lake Nyasa.

BORDER DISPUTES
There are many disputed territories and borders in the world today. China, for example, controls part of northern India. It rejects the 19th-century border drawn up by Britain which incorporated the region into India. Look for ✴.

THE CHANGING MAP
Borders between nations can change dramatically during their history. In 1500, Poland was Europe's largest nation; between 1772 and 1795 it was absorbed into Prussia, Russia, and Austria. After World War I, it again became an independent country, but its borders changed again in 1945 following German and Russian invasions.

In 1634, Poland was Europe's biggest nation.

MILITARY BORDERS
At the end of World War II, Korea was occupied by Soviet and American troops. In 1950, after the troops were withdrawn, the communist north attempted to invade the south. In 1953, North and South Korea were divided along the 38° line of latitude. This border has remained heavily fortified.

THE LONGEST BORDER
The border between the USA and Canada is the longest in the world. It cuts through the center of the Great Lakes. To the west of Michigan, the border runs along the 49° line of latitude. The border slices through the American territory of Point Robert, separating it from the rest of the USA.

CANADA
Strait of Georgia
Point Robert
USA

ARCTIC OCEAN

International Date Line

BEAUFORT SEA

Greenland (Denmark)

Baffin Bay

Alaska (USA) Yukon

Mackenzie

Great Slave L.

Hudson Bay

BERING SEA

Gulf of Alaska

CANADA

ATLANTIC OCEAN

PACIFIC OCEAN

UNITED STATES OF AMERICA

Missouri

Mississippi

St Pierre and Miquelon (France)

KEY TO CARIBBEAN

17 CAYMAN IS. (UK)
18 NAVASSA (USA)
19 ARUBA (Neth.)
20 NETHERLANDS ANTILLES (Neth.)
21 ST. VINCENT AND GRENADINES
22 MARTINIQUE (Fr.)
23 TURKS AND CAICOS IS. (UK)
24 ST. KITTS AND NEVIS
25 MONTSERRAT (UK)
26 BRITISH VIRGIN IS. (UK)
27 VIRGIN IS. (USA)
28 ANTIGUA AND BARBUDA
29 ANGUILLA (UK)
30 GUADELOUPE (Fr.)

MIDWAY IS. (USA)

Bermuda (UK)

Hawaii (USA)

BAHAMAS

Revillagigedo Islands (Mexico)

CUBA

JOHNSTON ATOLL (USA)

WAKE I. (USA)

NORTHERN MARIANAS IS. (USA)

MARSHALL ISLANDS

MEXICO

Gulf of Mexico

DOMINICAN REPUBLIC

HAITI

CAYMAN IS.
BELIZE JAMAICA PUERTO RICO (USA)
GUATEMALA
EL SALVADOR HONDURAS CARIBBEAN SEA
NICARAGUA
COSTA RICA PANAMA

DOMINICA
SAINT LUCIA
BARBADOS
GRENADA
TRINIDAD & TOBAGO

ICRONESIA

KINGMAN REEF (USA)

PALMYRA ATOLL (USA)

HOWLAND I. (USA)
BAKER I. (USA)

Jarvis Island (USA)

Clipperton Island (France)

Galapagos Is. (Ecuador)

VENEZUELA GUYANA SURINAME FRENCH GUYANA (Fr.)

COLOMBIA

ECUADOR

Amazon

NEW GUINEA

NAURU

KIRIBATI

TOKELAU (NZ)

TUVALU

COOK ISLANDS (NZ)

AMERICAN SAMOA (USA)

Purus

Claimed by Argentina

PERU

BRAZIL

SOLOMON ISLANDS

CORAL SEA

CORAL SEA IS. (Australia)

VANUATU

WALLIS & FUTUNA (Fr.)

WESTERN SAMOA

NIUE (NZ)

FRENCH POLYNESIA (Fr.)

BOLIVIA

PARAGUAY

NEW CALEDONIA (Fr.)

FIJI

TONGA

PITCAIRN IS. (UK)

San Ambrosio Island (Chile) San Felix I. (Chile)

Easter Island (Chile)

Parana

Pilcomayo

Uruguay

MOUNTAIN BORDERS
Mountain ranges such as the Pyrenees, Alps, and Himalayas form natural borders between many countries. In the Andes, border disputes between Chile and Argentina centered on finding the highest point in the mountain range which divided them.

NORFOLK I. (Australia)

Lord Howe Island (Australia)

NEW ZEALAND

Juan Fernandez Islands (Chile)

ARGENTINA

CHILE

PACIFIC OCEAN

TASMAN SEA

Chatham Island (NZ)

Bounty Island (NZ)

Antipodes Islands (NZ)

Auckland Islands (NZ)

Campbell Island (NZ)

MacQuarie Island (Australia)

THE WORLD IS DIVIDED INTO 24 TIME ZONES. THE 180° LINE OF LONGITUDE IS CALLED THE INTERNATIONAL DATE LINE. PLACES JUST WEST OF THIS LINE ARE 24 HOURS AHEAD OF PLACES TO THE EAST, SO BY TRAVELING EAST ACROSS THE DATE LINE YOU CAN GO BACK A WHOLE DAY.

FALKLAND IS. (UK)

SOUTH GEORGIA (UK)

SOUTH SANDWICH IS. (UK)

International Date Line

Peter the First Island (Norway)

PRUSSIA RUSSIA
Moscow
Warsaw
Kiev
AUSTRIA

POLAND
Warsaw
Moscow
Kiev

POLAND
Warsaw
Moscow
Kiev

KEYBOX

Present-day countries established before 1990.

New countries created since 1990.

International borders   Disputed borders

From 1772, Poland was part of Austria, Russia, and Prussia.

After World War I, Poland became a nation again.

After World War II, the Polish borders were again redrawn.

HOW TO USE THIS ATLAS

THE MAPS IN THIS ATLAS are organized by continent: North America; Central and South America; Europe; Africa; North and West Asia; South and East Asia; Oceania. Each section of the book opens with a large double-page spread introducing you to the physical geography – landscapes, climate, animals, and vegetation – of the continent. On the following pages, the continent is divided by country or group of countries. These pages deal with the human geography; each detailed map is supplemented by photographs, illustrations, and landscape models. Finally, a glossary defines difficult terms used in the text, and the index provides a list of all place names in the Atlas and facts about each country.

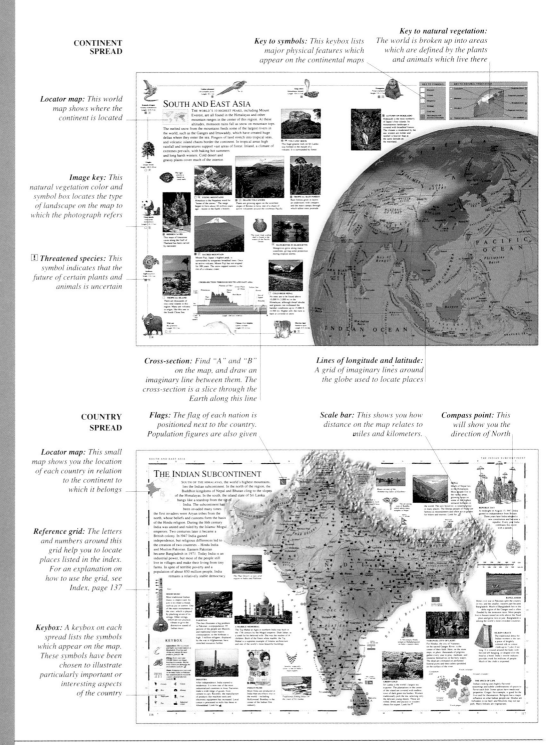

CONTINENT SPREAD

Locator map: *This world map shows where the continent is located*

Image key: *This natural vegetation color and symbol box locates the type of landscape on the map to which the photograph refers*

⚠ Threatened species: *This symbol indicates that the future of certain plants and animals is uncertain*

Key to symbols: *This keybox lists major physical features which appear on the continental maps*

Key to natural vegetation: *The world is broken up into areas which are defined by the plants and animals which live there*

Cross-section: *Find "A" and "B" on the map, and draw an imaginary line between them. The cross-section is a slice through the Earth along this line*

Lines of longitude and latitude: *A grid of imaginary lines around the globe used to locate places*

COUNTRY SPREAD

Locator map: *This small map shows you the location of each country in relation to the continent to which it belongs*

Reference grid: *The letters and numbers around this grid help you to locate places listed in the index. For an explanation on how to use the grid, see Index, page 137*

Keybox: *A keybox on each spread lists the symbols which appear on the map. These symbols have been chosen to illustrate particularly important or interesting aspects of the country*

Flags: *The flag of each nation is positioned next to the country. Population figures are also given*

Scale bar: *This shows you how distance on the map relates to miles and kilometers.*

Compass point: *This will show you the direction of North*

HOW THIS ATLAS WAS MADE

MAKING UP-TO-DATE and accurate maps of the world is a complicated process which draws upon the skills of geographers, researchers, cartographers (or map-makers), and designers. The maps in *The Eyewitness Atlas of the World* are completely new. They have been created using the latest computerized techniques. At the heart of this process was the development of a computerized model of the Earth. Computers store vast amounts of information. Cartographers used this technology to create precise maps, which may be regarded as the most accurate representation of the Earth's surface achieved in atlas form.

MAPS AND PROJECTIONS

Mapmakers have a problem: the Earth is round, but a map is flat. In order to represent a curved surface on a flat page, the image of the Earth's surface needs to be stretched and distorted. The mathematical way of achieving this is by using a projection. There are three main types of projection used in this atlas.

CYLINDRICAL PROJECTION
This is most commonly used to make maps of the whole world. The image is rolled out to form a rectangular shape. The image becomes distorted as it moves away from the Equator toward the poles.

CONIC PROJECTION
This is useful for making regional maps and is most often used in this atlas. Distortion occurs as lines converge as they move away from the center of the map.

ORTHOGRAPHIC PROJECTION
This kind of projection is useful for mapping polar regions. The image appears as though you were looking at the Earth from Space. Distortion increases as you move away from the center of the map.

THE EARTH MODEL

To create a faithful representation of the Earth's relief – the shape of coastlines, mountains, valleys, and plains – an enormous model of the Earth (called a "terrain model") was constructed using a computer. This was achieved by combining and processing various sets of data. Then other features, such as roads, railroads, place names, and colored vegetation areas, were added to complete each map.

Points on the grid represent height values

HEIGHT DATA
A grid was created which covers the whole of the Earth's surface. Each point on the grid has an accurate height value. The grid was fed into the computer to form the basic framework for the terrain model.

Data record the height of individual hills and mountains

LARGE SCALE MAPS
For large-scale maps, this basic framework was combined with a data set of land heights, which record the height of the summit of every hill and mountain. This produced a much more detailed framework for the terrain model.

Lines join the height points to create a model

PRODUCING THE TERRAIN MODEL
The computer then transformed these elevation points into a basic terrain model known as a wire-frame model. The computer does this by joining the individual height points with lines, creating a realistic image of the Earth's surface.

Color is added to the wire-frame model

THEMATIC MODELS
Models such as these appear on various pages throughout the Atlas. By adding various layers of extra information and annotations, they are a useful diagrammatic way of showing how the landscape of a particular region works.

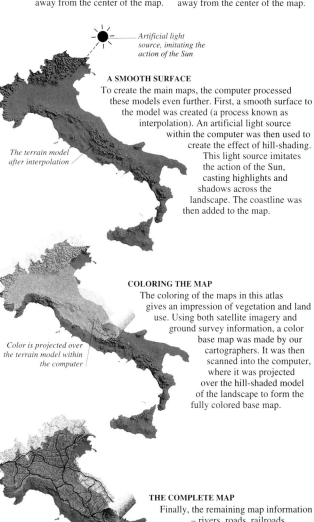

Artificial light source, imitating the action of the Sun

A SMOOTH SURFACE
To create the main maps, the computer processed these models even further. First, a smooth surface to the model was created (a process known as interpolation). An artificial light source within the computer was then used to create the effect of hill-shading. This light source imitates the action of the Sun, casting highlights and shadows across the landscape. The coastline was then added to the map.

The terrain model after interpolation

COLORING THE MAP
The coloring of the maps in this atlas gives an impression of vegetation and land use. Using both satellite imagery and ground survey information, a color base map was made by our cartographers. It was then scanned into the computer, where it was projected over the hill-shaded model of the landscape to form the fully colored base map.

Color is projected over the terrain model within the computer

THE COMPLETE MAP
Finally, the remaining map information – rivers, roads, railroads, borders, place names, and other symbols – were carefully compiled from the most up-to-date sources. These were traced into the computer and combined with the colored landscape image to create the finished map.

Roads and railroads are added to the colored terrain model

Raccoon
Procyon lotor
Length: 26 in (66 cm)

Desert swallowtail
Papilio coloro
Wingspan: 3 in (7 cm)

Collared lizard
Crotaphytus collaris
Length: 14 in (35 cm)

NORTH AMERICA

NORTH AMERICA LOOKS LIKE a gigantic downward-pointing triangle out of which two bites have been taken – Hudson Bay and the Gulf of Mexico. Huge parallel mountain chains run down the eastern and western sides. The oldest are the Appalachians to the east, which have been worn away by wind and rain for so long that they are now considerably lower than the younger Rockies to the west. The vast landscape between the mountain chains is mostly flat. There are large forests in the north, while the central Great Plains are covered by grasslands on which huge herds of buffalo once roamed. North America is a continent of climatic extremes. In the farthest north, temperatures drop to a freezing -87°F (-66°C), and a dome of ice up to 2 miles (3 km) thick covers Greenland. In the hot deserts of the southwest, temperatures can soar to 134°F (57°C).

Triceratops, a vegetarian dinosaur that lived in western North America 70 million years ago.

Douglas fir cone
Pseudotsuga menziesii
Length: 3 in (8 cm)

Road runner
Geococcyx californianus
Length: 2 ft (60 cm)

Loggerhead turtle
Caretta caretta
Length: 4 ft (1.2 m)

AUTUMN IN ALASKA
Only short grasses, low shrubs, and small trees can survive the climate of the northern tundra. In the brief Alaskan summer, plants burst into bloom, changing color in autumn.

THE ROOF OF AMERICA
When water-laden ocean air rises over the Alaska Range, moisture freezes and falls as snow. It is so cold that mountain slopes as low as 3,000 ft (900 m) are always snow-covered.

Eutrephoceras, which lived in North America 100 million years ago. It swam by squirting water out of its body cavity.

VOLCANIC ACTIVITY
The volcanic island of Iceland lies above the Mid-Atlantic Ridge. Intense heat generated deep underground creates bubbling hot mud pools and hot springs.

Coast redwood
Sequoia sempervirens
Height: 330 ft (100 m)

Priscacara, a perch that swam in North America's lakes and rivers 50 million years ago.

RAIN FORESTS
Temperate rain forests thrive between the Pacific and the Coast Ranges. Heavy rainfall carried inland by moist ocean winds makes their lush growth possible.

RIVERS, TREES, AND GRASSLAND
For millions of years, rivers flowing east from the Rockies have deposited silt on the Great Plains. This has helped to create a deep and very fertile soil which supports huge areas of grassland.

NORTHERN FORESTS
Forests grow across most of the northern region and on cold mountain slopes. These contain mostly coniferous trees which are well suited to growing in cold conditions.

Bald eagle
Haliaeetus leucocephalus
Wingspan: 7 ft (2.2 m)

DRY WINDS AND SAND DUNES
Dry winds blowing from the center of the continent, combined with the lack of rain, are responsible for the extensive deserts in the southwest. Because the climate is so dry, vegetation is sparse.

DESERT RIVER
The brown silt-laden waters of the Colorado River have cut a spectacular gorge through solid rock – the Grand Canyon – nearly 6,135 ft (2 km) deep.

OKEFENOKEE SWAMP
The Okefenokee Swamp is part of the complex river system of the southeast. This large wetland area has a warm climate, providing a haven for reptiles such as alligators and snakes. It is also an important resting place for many migratory birds.

American beaver
Castor canadensis
Length: 5 ft (1.6 m)

KEY TO SYMBOLS

▲	Mountain
△	Volcano
	Mangroves
	Wetlands
	Coral reef
	Plate margins showing direction of movement

DESERT TREES
With searing temperatures and low rainfall, deserts are home to plants which are adapted to conserve water, like cacti and the Joshua trees shown here.

CROSS-SECTION THROUGH NORTH AMERICA

Great Basin
Lake Michigan
Coast Ranges
Mississippi
Lake Erie
Pacific Ocean
Great Plains
Appalachian Mts.
Rocky Mts.
Cape Cod
Atlantic Ocean

9,843 (3,000)
Sea level 0
-14,764 (-4,500)
Feet (meters)

A
Length: 3,600 miles (5,800 km)
B

KEY TO NATURAL VEGETATION

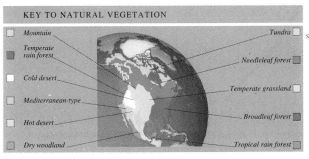

Mountain
Temperate rain forest
Cold desert
Mediterranean-type
Hot desert
Dry woodland

Tundra
Needleleaf forest
Temperate grassland
Broadleaf forest
Tropical rain forest

Hooded seal
Cystophora cristata
Length: 10 ft (3 m)

Moose
Alces alces
Shoulder height: 7 ft (2 m)

WESTERN CANADA AND ALASKA

THOUSANDS OF YEARS AGO, the first people to settle in North America crossed the Bering Strait and arrived in present-day Alaska. Their descendants – peoples such as the Inuit (Eskimos) – still inhabit this region. European immigrants began to arrive in large numbers in the 19th century. Alaska was bought by the USA from Russia for $7.2 million in 1867. Many Americans thought this was a waste of money until gold was discovered there in 1896 and then oil in 1968. Canada is a huge country with a small population, most of which lives in cities within about 100 miles (160 km) of the Canada-US border. The fertile plains and dense forest in the south give way to tundra and icefields farther north.

ALASKAN OIL
The USA's largest oilfield is at Prudhoe Bay in Alaska. But drilling is made difficult by temperatures as low as -110° F (-79° C), ground that is frozen for most of the year, and long periods of darkness in winter. Look for ⚒

LOGGING
About 40 percent of Canada is covered by forests. Until recently, there were no controls on logging, and huge areas of forest were cut down. Trees like this one are used to make lumber or plywood. Look for ⌐

UNITED STATES
POP: 263,563,000
(ALASKA)
POP 587,000

PIPELINE
When the 795 mile (270 km) long Trans-Alaskan pipeline from Prudhoe Bay to the ice-free port of Valdez was constructed, it was feared it would harm the environment and wildlife of this remote and beautiful region. To prevent disruption to the moose and caribou migration routes, and to stop the pipeline from freezing, it was raised above ground. The pipeline crosses plains, mountain ranges, and several rivers on its journey south.

KEYBOX

Oil: *Alberta is rich in oil, but new sources are being sought, such as the tar sands near Athabasca, where oil has to be separated from sand. Look for* ⚒

Border: *The world's longest undefended border runs between Canada and the USA. People and goods can cross it with few restrictions. Look for* ⇄

Radar: *The joint Canada-US Distant Early Warning system has been a key component in the defense of the North American continent since 1957. Look for* ⊙

🐂	Cattle	⛏	Mining
🌾	Cereals	⚒	Coal
⌐	Lumber	⌀	Gas
⚓	Fishing	🏭	Industrial center

CALGARY STAMPEDE
The city of Calgary in Alberta started life as a center for the cattle trade. Although today it is an oil center, its cowboy traditions are continued in the Stampede, a huge rodeo held every July. For ten days, spectators watch events that include bronco-busting, bull-riding, and chuck-wagon racing.

VANCOUVER
This city began as a small settlement for loggers and is now a major port. Grain from Canada's prairies and timber from its forests are shipped from Vancouver's ice-free harbor to countries across the Pacific. The city has attracted many immigrants; at first from Europe, then Asia and, most recently, from Hong Kong.

Brilliant autumn colors in British Columbia.

Mountains are mirrored in Lake Louise, Alberta.

Caribou roam the northern parts of Canada and Alaska.

TRANSPORTATION

In a country as vast as Canada, transportation is vital. When the Canadian Pacific Railway was completed in 1885, the country's east and west coasts were linked for the first time. Roads like the Trans-Canada Highway also helped to open up the country, especially the wilderness areas. Here, a highway crosses a spectacular part of Alberta.

SALMON FISHING

The main fish caught on Canada's west coast is the Pacific salmon. The bulk of the catch is canned. The cans are made at aluminum smelting plants like the one at Kitimat; the plant is powered by hydroelectricity produced by the damming and reversing of the Nechako River. Look for ⌁

Pacific salmon

Edmontonia, a dinosaur once found in Alberta.

CANADA
POP: 29,248,000
(WESTERN CANADA)
POP: 8,062,000

KWAKIUTL

The Kwakiutl were skilled artisans and among the first peoples to settle along Canada's west coast. Families displayed their wealth and prestige in totem poles carved with animal and human figures. Other carved pieces were created for the potlatch, a celebration of gift-giving. When this was banned in 1884, many artifacts were destroyed. Since the 1950s, native artists have revived the traditional techniques.

SNOWSHOES

Snowshoes, made from wooden frames strung with animal gut or leather strips, were once essential for winter travel. They are still used in areas where vehicles, such as snowmobiles, cannot maneuver.

THE PRAIRIES

Grain production on the vast prairies of western Canada is highly mechanized; one farmer can harvest several hundred hectares single-handed. After the grain is cut, it is stored in huge grain elevators like these before being sent by rail to cities or ports. Railroads were the key to the development of farming on the prairies. Look for ⍦

Harvesting grain on the fertile prairies of Saskatchewan.

EASTERN CANADA

THE VIKINGS WERE THE FIRST Europeans to visit eastern Canada, in about AD 986. Then, in the 15th and 16th centuries, two expeditions, one from England and one from France, reached Canada and each claimed it. Traders and fur trappers from the two countries followed, setting up rival trading posts and settlements. The struggle for territory led to war between Britain and France. The French were forced to give up their Canadian territories to Britain in 1763, but the French language is still spoken in the province of Quebec today. Canada eventually achieved effective independence from Britain in 1867. Today, southern Quebec and Ontario form eastern Canada's main industrial region, containing most of its population and two of its largest cities – Montreal and Toronto. The Hudson Bay area, while rich in minerals, is a wilderness of forests, rivers, and lakes. Snowbound for much of the year, it is sparsely inhabited except by Inuit in the far north.

The Toronto Sky Dome, a huge stadium which seats 50,000.

FRENCH / ENGLISH
Most Canadians speak English, but the country is officially bilingual – as can be seen from the use of both French and English on this stamp which commemorates the province of New Brunswick.

The sap of the sugar maple tree is made into syrup and sugar. The maple leaf is Canada's national symbol.

CANADA
POP: 29,248,000
(EASTERN CANADA)
POP: 19,738,000

Evergreen and silver birch forests in southern Quebec.

Thousand Island salad dressing

Salad dressing, named after the islands in the St. Lawrence River.

INDUSTRY
Ontario is Canada's most important industrial province and produces about 55 percent of the country's manufactured goods. Electronics, steel, and food processing are among the major industries, but cars are Ontario's main manufacturing industry and largest export. Many of the factories are owned by U.S. multinational companies.
Look for

TORONTO
The CN tower – the world's tallest free-standing structure – dominates the skyline of Toronto, seen here across the waters of Lake Ontario. Toronto is Canada's biggest city, the main commercial and industrial center, and an important port. Its wealthy, multicultural population includes Italians, Chinese, Greeks, and Poles.

HOCKEY
In winter, Canadians play or watch their favorite sport: hockey. The country produces some of the best players in the world.

The Canadian or Horseshoe Falls at Niagara.

KEYBOX

Potatoes: The Atlantic provinces, especially Prince Edward Island, grow some of North America's finest potatoes – seed potatoes in particular. Look for

Mining: Canada is rich in iron ore, nickel, gold, silver, and other minerals and is the world's leading uranium exporter – mainly from Ontario. Look for

High-tech industry: Ottawa has most of the electronics and computer companies in Canada, centered on an area known as Silicon Valley North. Look for

Mixed fruits		Shellfish	
Timber		Hydro-electricity	
Fishing		Industrial center	

THE MOUNTIES
The Royal Canadian Mounted Police – the Mounties – were established in 1873 during the opening of the vast areas in the west to trade and industry. Today, they are one of the world's most efficient and sophisticated police forces, with their headquarters in Ottawa.

OTTAWA
The Parliament Buildings in Ottawa, Canada's capital city, were inspired by the British Houses of Parliament. Many older buildings reflect the city's British origins. Others, such as the National Gallery, are thoroughly modern.

K   L   M   N   O   P   Q   R   S   T

A polar bear mother and cubs on the ice in Hudson Bay.

JAMES BAY
Canada uses its rivers to produce more hydroelectric power than any other nation. In the remote James Bay region of Quebec, five hydroelectric power complexes are planned to utilize the area's powerful rivers. So far, only the Grande Rivière complex has been completed. Look for

NEWFOUNDLAND
Until recently, Newfoundland's economy was largely dependent on fishing. Now, however, the mining and timber industries are being developed, and the island boasts two of Canada's largest paper mills. Oil is also a major industry.

Sawn log

FOREST PRODUCTS
Wood and other products from its forests earn Canada twice as much as agriculture does. Newsprint is a major export in Ontario, Quebec, and the Atlantic provinces. It is made from wood pulp. Look for

FISHING
Off Canada's eastern coast is a shallow continental shelf called the Grand Banks, which is one of the world's richest fishing areas. Many types of fish are caught there, the most valuable being cod. However, the area has been overfished, and stocks of fish must now be carefully conserved. Canada has taken control of all fishing within 200 miles (320 km) of its coastline and hardly any commercial cod fishing is allowed. Look for

Atlantic cod

FRUIT GROWING
The Niagara Peninsula is the strip of land between Lake Erie and Lake Ontario. These huge lakes affect the climate in this area, making it milder. The peninsula has rich soils, so a wide range of fruit can be grown, including peaches, cherries, apples, and grapes. Look for

Apple *Cherry* *Peach*

N

ST. LAWRENCE SEAWAY
This 2,200 mile (3,500 km) long waterway follows the St. Lawrence River and the Great Lakes to the heart of Canada's industrial region. Oceangoing ships of many nations pass through the 16 locks which climb 600 ft (183 m) from sea level to the level of Lake Ontario.

0   50   100   150   200   250   300   350   400 KM
0   50   100   150   200 MILES

Map labels:
Salisbury I.
Nottingham I.
Hudson Strait
C. Chidley
Akpatok I.
Ungava Bay
LABRADOR SEA
Inukjuak
Rivière aux Feuilles
Kuujjuaq
Nain
Hopedale
Makkovik
NEWFOUNDLAND
Cartwright
Port Hope Simpson
Belle I.
Grande Rivière de la Baleine
Caniapiscau Res.
Scheffville
LABRADOR
Smallwood Reservoir
Goose Bay
Strait of Belle Isle
La Grande Rivière
La Grande Rivière HEP Project
Churchill Falls
Ross Bay Junction
Iron
Labrador City
Iron
Newfoundland
Gander
Grand Falls
Clarenville
Corner Brook
ST JOHN'S
QUEBEC
CANADA
Eastmain
Rivière de Rupert
Manicouagan Res.
L. Mistassini
Havre-Saint-Pierre
Sept-Îles
Île d'Anticosti
Gulf of St. Lawrence
Placentia Bay
Grand Banks
C. Race
ST PIERRE
ST PIERRE & MIQUELON (France)
Channel-Port-aux-Basques
Cabot Strait
Copper
Silver
Zinc
Gold
Silver
Copper
Chibougamau
Gold
Gouin Res.
L. Saint-Jean
Jonquière
Chicoutimi
St. Lawrence
Gaspé
Îles de la Madeleine
PRINCE EDWARD ISLAND
Sydney
ATLANTIC OCEAN
Abitibi
Silver
Gold
Val-d'Or
La Tuque
QUEBEC
Trois-Rivières
Drummondville
Copper
Silver
Zinc Lead
Bathurst
NEW BRUNSWICK
Grand Falls
Moncton
FREDERICTON
CHARLOTTE-TOWN
Truro
NOVA SCOTIA
HALIFAX
Ottawa
North Bay
Gatineau
Laval
Montreal
Sherbrooke
OTTAWA
St. Lawrence Seaway (Canal)
Trans-Canada Highway
Saint John
Bay of Fundy
Liverpool
Yarmouth
C. Sable
Barrie
Peterborough
Kingston
TORONTO
Hamilton
Niagara Falls
Lake Ontario
UNITED STATES OF AMERICA
Niagara Peninsula

(Northwest Territories)
Belcher Is.
Kuujjuarapik

25

NORTHEASTERN UNITED STATES

THE MOST DENSELY populated, heavily industrialized, and ethnically diverse region of the USA, the Northeast can be divided into New England – Maine, New Hampshire, Vermont, Massachusetts, Rhode Island, and Connecticut – and the Mid-Atlantic states – New York, New Jersey, Pennsylvania, and Delaware. The terrain of the region ranges from the near-wilderness of New York's Adirondack Mountains to the rocky coastline of northern New England and the rolling hills of Pennsylvania; climate is temperate, with cold winters and warm summers. First settled in the early 1600s, the region's good harbors, mineral resources, fast-flowing rivers, and rich coastal fishing grounds contributed to its early economic development; by the American Revolution, New York City, Boston, and Philadelphia were leading cities. Rapid industrialization after about 1800 brought millions of immigrants from Europe and elsewhere. In recent decades, a decline in manufacturing and a population shift toward the "Sun Belt" states of the South and West has weakened the Northeast's economy, but high-tech and service industries have taken up some of the slack. Today, New York is the nation's largest city and a financial, communications, and artistic center for the world.

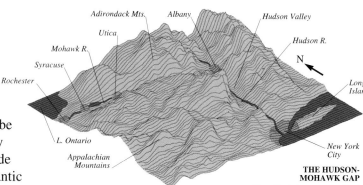

THE HUDSON-MOHAWK GAP
New York became the East Coast's leading port thanks to its fine harbor and its location at the mouth of the Hudson River. The Hudson connects with the Mohawk River, giving the city access to the continent's interior; mineral resources and industrial products were transported along this route.

THE AMISH
This isolated Amish farm near Lancaster, Pennsylvania, is run without any modern technology. The Amish are a Protestant sect who came to America from Switzerland in the 18th century. They live by farming, make all their own clothes and use horses for transport.

The spectacular Niagara Falls near Buffalo, New York.

PUMPKINS
Pumpkins are grown all over New England, and pumpkin pie is a favorite American dish. Pumpkins are also hollowed out to make Jack-O'-Lanterns for Halloween.

TOMATO SOUP
Many of the fruits and vegetables for the region's big cities, especially New York, are grown on the fruit and vegetable farms, called market gardens, of New Jersey (known as "the Garden State"). Tomatoes are grown in huge quantities, and made locally into canned tomato soup. Look for ➤

Severe winter weather is common in New England.

NEW ENGLAND BERRIES
Cranberries and blueberries both came from New England and large quantities are grown there. Cranberries are used in sauces, especially to go with roast turkey at Thanksgiving. Blueberries are sweeter and are often used in pies.

Blueberries

Cranberries

KEYBOX

Sailing: Yachting is a popular pastime on New England's Atlantic coast. The Bermuda Race starts from Rhode Island. Look for ▲

Universities: There are more centers of further education and research and development in New England than in any other part of the USA. Look for ▤

Maple syrup: Both sugar and syrup are obtained from the sap of maple trees. Vermont is the USA's main producer. Look for ❀

🐂	Cattle	⛴	Fishing port
🐓	Poultry	⛏	Coal
🛒	Market gardening	🏭	Industrial center
🐟	Fishing	💻	High-tech industry

UNITED STATES
POP: 263,563,000
(NORTHEASTERN STATES)
POP: 51,806,000

0	25	50	75	100	125	150	175	KM
0		25		50		75	100	MILES

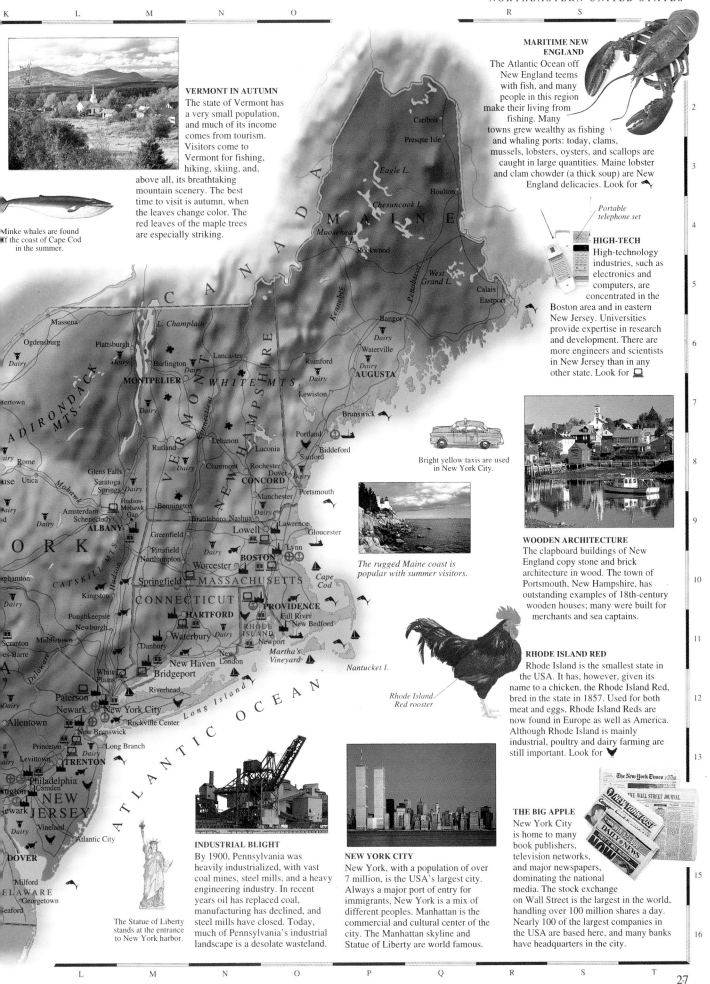

MARITIME NEW ENGLAND
The Atlantic Ocean off New England teems with fish, and many people in this region make their living from fishing. Many towns grew wealthy as fishing and whaling ports: today, clams, mussels, lobsters, oysters, and scallops are caught in large quantities. Maine lobster and clam chowder (a thick soup) are New England delicacies. Look for

VERMONT IN AUTUMN
The state of Vermont has a very small population, and much of its income comes from tourism. Visitors come to Vermont for fishing, hiking, skiing, and, above all, its breathtaking mountain scenery. The best time to visit is autumn, when the leaves change color. The red leaves of the maple trees are especially striking.

Minke whales are found off the coast of Cape Cod in the summer.

Portable telephone set

HIGH-TECH
High-technology industries, such as electronics and computers, are concentrated in the Boston area and in eastern New Jersey. Universities provide expertise in research and development. There are more engineers and scientists in New Jersey than in any other state. Look for

Bright yellow taxis are used in New York City.

The rugged Maine coast is popular with summer visitors.

WOODEN ARCHITECTURE
The clapboard buildings of New England copy stone and brick architecture in wood. The town of Portsmouth, New Hampshire, has outstanding examples of 18th-century wooden houses; many were built for merchants and sea captains.

RHODE ISLAND RED
Rhode Island is the smallest state in the USA. It has, however, given its name to a chicken, the Rhode Island Red, bred in the state in 1857. Used for both meat and eggs, Rhode Island Reds are now found in Europe as well as America. Although Rhode Island is mainly industrial, poultry and dairy farming are still important. Look for

Rhode Island Red rooster

INDUSTRIAL BLIGHT
By 1900, Pennsylvania was heavily industrialized, with vast coal mines, steel mills, and a heavy engineering industry. In recent years oil has replaced coal, manufacturing has declined, and steel mills have closed. Today, much of Pennsylvania's industrial landscape is a desolate wasteland.

The Statue of Liberty stands at the entrance to New York harbor.

NEW YORK CITY
New York, with a population of over 7 million, is the USA's largest city. Always a major port of entry for immigrants, New York is a mix of different peoples. Manhattan is the commercial and cultural center of the city. The Manhattan skyline and Statue of Liberty are world famous.

THE BIG APPLE
New York City is home to many book publishers, television networks, and major newspapers, dominating the national media. The stock exchange on Wall Street is the largest in the world, handling over 100 million shares a day. Nearly 100 of the largest companies in the USA are based here, and many banks have headquarters in the city.

THE SOUTHERN STATES

THE SOUTH'S GEOGRAPHY includes the Tidewater along the Atlantic coast, the Piedmont extending to the coal-rich Appalachian Mountains, the Mississippi River Valley, and the subtropical coastal belt along the Gulf of Mexico. The region was settled mostly by British colonists, beginning with the founding of Jamestown, Virginia, in 1607. The South soon developed an agricultural economy based on tobacco, rice, indigo, and especially cotton, grown by African-American slaves. The American Civil War (1861-65) left the region devastated. The war ended slavery, but a system of legal segregation (separation by race) lasted into the 1960s in much of the South. Today, the South's economy is more varied, thanks to the discovery of oil reserves in the Gulf region and the development of industry. Florida, first colonized by Spain in 1565, has experienced great growth in recent years, becoming the fourth-largest state in the 1980s. Its population includes retirees from other states and refugees from Cuba, the Caribbean, and Latin America.

Horses graze on a Kentucky farm in the Bluegrass country.

ATLANTA
The commercial center of the region is Atlanta, which is the hub of the South's transport network, and has one of the world's busiest airports. Raw materials flood into Atlanta and manufactured goods pour out: clothes, books, iron and steel products, and Coca-Cola are all made here.

DERBY DAY
Kentucky is called the "Bluegrass State" after the grasslands around the city of Lexington, which provide superb grazing for livestock. This area has the world's greatest concentration of stud farms for breeding thoroughbred horses. The Kentucky Derby, held at Louisville, is one of the world's most famous horse races.

KEYBOX

Soybeans: The main crop in the South is the soybean. Used for oil, margarine, and livestock feed, it has found both domestic and export markets. Look for ◖

Coal: Coal, mined from the rich reserves of the Appalachian Mountains, is being overtaken by oil and gas. Look for ◗

High-tech industry: The South, with its skilled labor force and good communications, is attracting many high-tech industries. Look for ▭

Space center: The Space Shuttle is launched from the Kennedy Space Center, the launch site of the U.S. Space program. Look for ♁

⚘	Cereals	🐬	Fishing
✿	Citrus fruit	⛽	Oil
🥜	Peanuts	⚒	Mining
❀	Cotton	🏭	Industrial center
🪈	Tobacco	✈	Tourism

JAZZ
Jazz saxophone
Jazz developed in New Orleans in the early 1900s. Originally it was the music of the bands who marched through the streets, playing at funerals and weddings. Jazz combined many influences – blues and spirituals (sung by slaves) and popular songs. Wind instruments are accompanied by drums, piano, and double bass.

Orange *Lemon* *Grapefruit* *Lime*

Florida produces three-quarters of the USA's oranges and grapefruits.

BOURBON
Corn is one of Kentucky's major crops. It is used for making Bourbon whiskey, which is a worldwide export.

MISSISSIPPI
Steamboats carry tourists on scenic trips along the Mississippi, one of the world's busiest waterways. Barges transport heavy cargoes from the industrial and agricultural regions near the Great Lakes to the Gulf Coast.

KING COTTON
Cotton, grown on large plantations using slave labor, was once the basis of the Southern economy. Today, it is still grown on farms in some parts of the South. Look for ❀

Okra *Shrimp*

Gumbo is a spicy seafood and vegetable stew from Louisiana.

RETIREMENT STATE
Nearly 30 percent of Florida's inhabitants are over 55 years old. Large numbers of people retire to Florida, lured by its climate and sports facilities. Many settle in retirement developments or in the coastal cities.

## Map labels

MISSOURI · OKLAHOMA · Fayetteville · BOSTON MTS · White R. · Black R. · Fort Smith · ARKANSAS · L. Ouachita · North Little Rock · LITTLE ROCK · Hot Springs · Aluminum · Pine Bluff · Ouachita · Arkansas · Mississippi · Corn · Greenville · TEXAS · Shreveport · Red R. · Monroe · Yazoo · LOUISIANA · JACKSON · Alexandria · Mississippi · MISSISSIPPI · Corn · Pearl · Lake Charles · Lafayette · BATON ROUGE · L. Pontchartrain · Gulfport · Biloxi · Marsh I. · New Orleans · Sulfur · Breton Sound · Mississippi Delta

K L M N O R S T

1

PENNSYLVANIA

INDIANA OHIO

Covington Ohio Morgantown
Parkersburg

ILLINOIS Louisville FRANKFORT WEST
Owensboro Corn VIRGINIA Huntington WASHINGTON D.C. Baltimore ANNAPOLIS
Corn Lexington CHARLESTON Alexandria MARYLAND DELAWARE
Paducah KENTUCKY Charlottesville
Corn Hopkinsville Green R. Corn VIRGINIA Chesapeake Bay
Corn Bowling Cumberland RICHMOND
Clarksville Green Kentucky Roanoke Lynchburg Petersburg
Corn NASHVILLE Johnson City Danville Newport News C. Charles
Murfreesboro Knoxville Lead Norfolk
TENNESSEE Zinc Winston-Salem Greensboro Durham Corn
Phosphates Chattanooga Asheville RALEIGH Roanoke
Florence Copper Gastonia Charlotte Wilson C. Hatteras
Corn Huntsville Greenville Spartanburg Corn
Lewis Smith L. Corn Rome Fayetteville NORTH
umbus Gadsden SOUTH Corn CAROLINA
Tuscaloosa Birmingham Athens CAROLINA Morehead City
Chattahoochee ATLANTA COLUMBIA Florence Wilmington
ALABAMA Pee Dee
MONTGOMERY Selma L. Marion Santee C. Fear ATLANTIC OCEAN
Corn Corn Augusta Corn
Aluminum Columbus Savannah Charleston
Corn Macon Oconee Corn
Dothan Corn Corn Savannah
Pensacola GEORGIA Albany Alapaha
Flint Brunswick

Fields of ripening tobacco in
North Carolina.

Panama City TALLAHASSEE Okefenokee Valdosta Swamp
Gulf of Mexico Phosphates UNITED STATES
POP: 263,563,000
(SOUTHERN STATES)
POP: 66,586,000 The Everglades – a
vast tropical marsh
in southern Florida.

Jacksonville AMERICAN CAPITAL
Gainesville The city of Washington, also known as
the District of Columbia, became the
USA's capital and seat of the federal
government in 1800. This picture shows
FLORIDA Daytona the lighted dome of the Capitol Building.
Beach Kennedy
Orlando Space Center
Disney World The elegant
Clearwater C. mansions of cotton
Tampa Melbourne Canaveral plantation owners
St. Petersburg can still be seen in
Phosphates the South.

DISNEY WORLD
In 1971, Disney World opened near
Orlando, Florida. Millions of visitors
each year come to this vast fantasy Fort Myers
land. It occupies a huge area of L. Okeechobee West Palm
reclaimed swamp, lake, and forest. The Everglades Beach
Tourists also come to Florida to visit Hollywood Fort
the Epcot Center – a trip through Hialeah Lauderdale
a vision of the future – and the Miami
Kennedy Space Center. Straits of Florida
Key West Florida Keys

Peanut
butter

TOBACCO
The Southern states grow high-quality
tobacco. The leaves are cured for 4-6
days in controlled temperatures before Peanut
being moistened and sorted. Tobacco
factories can produce up to 450 million **PEANUTS**
cigarettes a day. Look for Georgia
grows nearly half
the USA's total crop of
peanuts. Half the crop is used
for making peanut butter, the
rest for edible oil and animal
feed. Look for

THE GREAT LAKES

THE FIVE GREAT LAKES of North America – Ontario, Erie, Huron, Michigan, and Superior – together form the largest area of fresh water in the world. The states of Indiana, Illinois, Michigan, Ohio, Wisconsin, and Minnesota, all of which border on one or more of the lakes, are often called the industrial and agricultural heartland of the United States. This region is rich in natural resources, including coal, iron, copper, and timber, and there are large areas of fertile farmland on the flat plains of the prairies. First explored by French traders, fur trappers, and missionaries in the 17th century, the region began to attract large numbers of settlers in the early 1800s. Trading links were improved by the opening of the Erie Canal in 1825, which connected the region to the Atlantic Coast, while the Mississippi and other rivers gave access to the Gulf of Mexico and the rest of the continent. When railroads reached the region in the 1840s, cities such as Chicago grew and prospered as freight-handling centers. Steel production and the car industry later became the main industries in the region. In recent years, a decline in these traditional industries has led to high unemployment in some areas.

Walleyes live in the Great Lakes, but their numbers are falling due to pollution.

HOG

In the 19th century, huge numbers of animals from all over this region were sent to the stockyards in Chicago for slaughter and processing. Rearing livestock is still important in Illinois. Corn and soybeans, both grown locally, are used as animal feed. Look for 🐷

HAMBURGERS

Hamburgers are America's own fast food, first produced on a massive scale in Illinois in the 1950s. It has been calculated that in every second of the day, 200 Americans are eating a hamburger. American-style hamburgers and fast food can now be found all over the world.

Cherries: One-third of the world cherry crop is grown along the shores of Lake Michigan. Look for 🍒

Iron ore: Iron ore deposits are found around the shores of Lake Superior. It is mined, processed, then shipped to industrial centers in pellet form. Look for ⬤

🐂	Cattle	🫘	Soybeans
🐖	Hogs	⛏	Coal
🌾	Cereals	🛢	Oil
🌱	Sugar beets	🏭	Industrial center
🛒	Market gardening	🚗	Vehicle manufacture

MILWAUKEE BEER

The Great Lakes region has attracted many immigrants, especially from Germany, the Netherlands, and the Scandinavian countries. Milwaukee, where many Germans settled, is home to several of the USA's largest breweries.

Baseball and fielder's glove. Baseball is the USA's national game.

COLD WINTERS

The Great Lakes region has severe winters, and Minnesota, in particular, suffers from heavy snowstorms. Parts of the Great Lakes themselves can freeze over in winter, and lakeside harbors can be frozen from December to early April.

THE WINDY CITY

Chicago is situated at the southern tip of Lake Michigan. It gets its nickname – the Windy City – from the weather conditions in this area. Chicago was ideally positioned for trading with the Midwest region and quickly became a wealthy modern city. By 1900 it had vast complexes of lumber mills, meat processing factories, railroad yards, and steel mills.

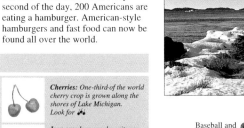

PRAIRIE LANDS

The fertile soil and hot, humid summers make the flat expanses of the Midwestern prairies ideal for farming. Nearly half of the world's corn crop is grown on the huge farms in this region.

An isolated farm on the open prairies of Illinois.

CORNFLAKES

Food processing is a major industry throughout this agricultural region. Wisconsin, for example, is the major producer of canned peas and sweet corn in the USA. Corn and wheat-based breakfast cereals are exported all over the world from Battle Creek, Michigan. Look for 🌾

## Map labels

CANADA

Lake of the Woods

NORTH DAKOTA

MINNESOTA

Wheat · Wheat · Red Lake R. · Upper Red L. · Lower Red L. · Iron · Bemidji · Iron · Iron · Virginia · Hibbing · Wheat · Leech L. · Moorhead · Mississippi · Duluth · Superior · Chequa · Manganese · Brainerd · Fergus Falls · Wheat · Iron · Mille Lacs L. · Chippewa · Dairy · Dairy · WISCO · Wheat · St Cloud · Wheat · Willmar · Minneapolis · Stillwater · Beef · Corn · ST PAUL · Bloomington · Dairy · Eau Claire · Red Wing · Marshfiel · Corn · New Ulm · Dairy · Faribault · Iron · Mankato · Owatonna · Winona · Dairy · Rochester · Wheat · La Crosse · Corn · Fairmont · Albert Lea · Austin · Dairy · Dairy · Wiscon.

SOUTH DAKOTA

IOWA

Be

MISSOURI

ILL · Macomb · Quincy · Jackson · Galesburg · K

A wooded island in Minnesota.

LAKESIDE VACATIONS
The lakes attract millions of visitors a year. Summer holiday homes line accessible parts of the shores, and huge marinas have been built for the pleasure craft that sail on the lakes.

Over 10,000 loons, the state bird of Minnesota, spend the summer on its lakes.

Parts of the shores have been eroded by water, endangering buildings

UNITED STATES
POP: 263,563,000
(GREAT LAKES STATES)
POP: 47,233,000

LAKES UNDER THREAT
Heavy industry around the shores of the Great Lakes has caused disastrous water pollution. In some regions, fish are now unsafe to eat and swimming is dangerous. In addition, changes to the weather, such as heavy rainfall and cooler temperatures, have led to much higher water levels. Lakeside holiday towns are often flooded, threatening tourism. Many houses, perched precariously on the lakes' crumbling shores, are under threat.

Model of a 1956 Ford Fairlane

THE MOTOR CITY
In the early 20th century Detroit became the center of a revolution in transport when two engineers, Henry Ford and Ransom Olds, began mass-producing cars there. Today, Detroit is still the center of the American car industry, with several of the USA's biggest car manufacturers based in the city. Look for

TAMLA MOTOWN
In 1961 Berry Gordy, a worker from the Ford factory in Detroit, launched the Tamla Motown record label to promote local black talent. Motown artists, such as Smokey Robinson, the Supremes and Stevie Wonder, perfected the unique style of "soul" music.

A farmhouse and barn in the rich farm country of Indiana.

OPEN HIGHWAYS
The Great Lakes states have benefited from their central location and well-developed rail and water transport systems. The region is also well served by roads – Indianapolis has more major highways than any other American city.

Robie House, Chicago (built 1910), was designed by the world-famous US architect, Frank Lloyd Wright.

0   50   100   150   200   250   KM
0   25   50   75   100   125   150   MILES

**Map labels:**

Lake Superior · Isle Royale · Keweenaw Bay · Marquette · Iron · Dairy · Escanaba · Beaver I. · Straits of Mackinac · Cheboygan · Sault Sainte Marie · CANADA · Lake Huron · Alpena · Saginaw Bay · MICHIGAN · Traverse City · Manistee · Muskegon · Midland · Mount Pleasant · Bay City · Dairy · Saginaw · Port Huron · Flint · Owosso · Muskegon · Grand Rapids · Holland · LANSING · Pontiac · Sterling Heights · St. Clair Shores · Detroit · Wolf · Marinette · Green Bay · Appleton · Manitowoc · Oshkosh · L. Winnebago · Fond du Lac · Sheboygan · Dairy · Wauwatosa · MADISON · Milwaukee · Dairy · Janesville · Racine · Kenosha · Rockford · Evanston · Waukegan · Kalamazoo · Battle Creek · Ann Arbor · Jackson · Dairy · Lake Erie · Monroe · Lake Ontario · PENNSYLVANIA · Ashtabula · Dairy · Cleveland · Warren · Youngstown · Akron · East Liverpool · Canton · Massillon · Steubenville · Elyria · Huron · Toledo · Chicago · Aurora · Joliet · Gary · Michigan City · South Bend · Niles · Benton Harbor · Corn · Maumee · Findlay · Mansfield · Marion · Ottawa · Kankakee · INDIANA · Fort Wayne · Logansport · Kokomo · Marion · Muncie · Lima · Scioto · OHIO · Corn · Newark · Piqua · COLUMBUS · Zanesville · Beef · Springfield · Richmond · Anderson · Frankfort · Danville · Champaign · INDIANAPOLIS · Dayton · Lancaster · Chillicothe · Ohio · Terre Haute · Columbus · Bloomington · Cincinnati · Portsmouth · White R. · Bedford · Vincennes · Wabash · Kaskaskia · Carlyle L. · Corn · Centralia · Mount Vernon · New Albany · Rend L. · Evansville · Lead · Carbondale · Zinc · KENTUCKY · WEST VIRGINIA

M N O P Q R S T

CENTRAL AND MOUNTAIN STATES

THIS REGION INCLUDES the lowlands on the west bank of the Mississippi River, the vast expanses of the Great Plains, and the majestic Rocky Mountains. In climate, it is a region of extremes: hot summers alternate with cold winters, and hailstorms, blizzards, and tornadoes are frequent events. Once home to large numbers of Native Americans and great herds of buffalo, the plains were settled in the 19th century; the Native Americans were pushed onto reservations and the buffalo slaughtered. Originally dismissed as a desert because of low rainfall and lack of trees, the Great Plains proved to be one of the world's great agricultural regions; today, vast amounts of cereals are grown on mechanized farms, and cattle are grazed on huge ranches. The Rockies are rich in minerals, and reserves of coal, oil, and natural gas are being exploited.

The foothills of the snow-covered Rockies in Montana.

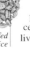

Shredded wheat

AGRICULTURAL INDUSTRIES

A great range of cereals are grown in the Midwest and transported to local cities for processing. Iowa has the largest cereal processing factory in the world, and it is in the cities of this region that many cereals are prepared for the world's breakfast tables. Cities also provide storage facilities for grain and cereals, as well as markets for grain, livestock, and farm machinery.

Corn flakes *Oats* *Puffed rice*

COWBOYS

Cattle are raised on the Great Plains and foothills of the Rocky Mountains. Ranches often have thousands of cattle. In summer, mounted cowboys herd cattle to upland pastures and drive them back to the ranch for the winter. Cattle are then taken to markets in nearby towns for cattle auctions. Look for 🐂

WYOMING COAL

Wyoming now leads the USA in coal production. Coal from the West is in demand because it has a lower sulfur content than coal mined in the East and causes less pollution when burned. Shallow coal reserves are extracted from open-pit mines, like this one, which spoil the landscape. Look for 🔨

Fossils of dinosaurs, such as *Tyrannosaurus*, have been found in the foothills of the Rockies.

KEYBOX

Aerospace industry: Both Wichita and St. Louis are centers of aircraft production. They have recently been hit by a slowdown in the US economy. Look for ✈

Irrigated agriculture: The Ogallala Aquifer is a vast underground reserve of water, which is tapped to water crops in this dry region. Look for 🌿

🐂	Cattle	⚒	Coal
🌾	Cereals	🛢	Oil
🌱	Potatoes	⬭	Gas
⛏	Mining	🏭	Industrial center

Railroad towns are now surrounded by agricultural land

A central route over the Rockies links mining towns

Main east-west railroad route

To Minnesota and Chicago

N ↑

Snake River valley: potato farming on fertile floodplain

MODEL OF ROCKY MOUNTAINS

The Rocky Mountains divide the North American continent in two; rivers to the west of the range flow toward the Pacific, while those to the east drain into the Arctic and Atlantic oceans and the Gulf of Mexico. First explored by fur trappers and traders in the 19th century, the mountain passes were used by settlers on their way west. Miners followed the settlers, and the mining towns of Montana were established. By 1869, the Transcontinental railroad had crossed the Rockies, linking the Pacific Coast with the rest of the country.

FARMING

Corn is the main crop in Iowa, while wheat is more important in the center of this region. Nearer the Rockies, the rainfall decreases and wheat farming gives way to cattle ranching. Farming in the Midwest is large-scale and mechanized. These vast wheat fields in Nebraska stretch to the far horizon. Farmers often produce more than they can sell. Look for 🌾

### Map labels

CAN[ADA]

WASHINGTON OREGON NEVADA UTAH

MONTANA IDAHO WYOM[ING]

Wheat Shelby Barley
Zinc Lead Coeur d'Alene Beef L. Elwell Havre
Kalispell Flathead L. Barley Wheat Missouri
Silver Silver Beef Great Falls
Missoula Great Falls
Lewiston Canyon Ferry L. Beef
HELENA Copper Beef Beef
Anaconda Butte Beef
Salmon Bozeman Billings Yellowstone
Dillon Beef Bighorn
Beef Beef
Beef Cody
BOISE Yellowstone L. Worland
Nampa Jackson L. GRAND TETON MTS.
Snake Wheat Uranium
Idaho Falls WIND RIVER RANGE Iron
Phosphate Snake
Beef Pocatello
Twin Falls Beef Rock Springs Rawli[ns]
Beef Wheat Green R[iver]
Flaming Gorge Res. Path[?]

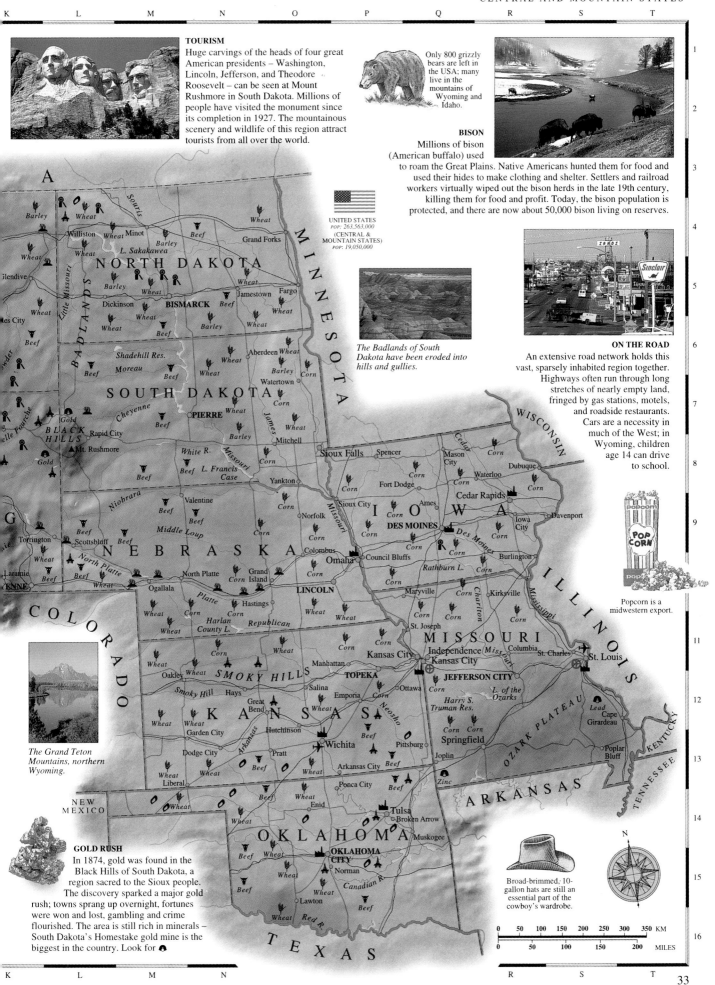

TOURISM

Huge carvings of the heads of four great American presidents – Washington, Lincoln, Jefferson, and Theodore Roosevelt – can be seen at Mount Rushmore in South Dakota. Millions of people have visited the monument since its completion in 1927. The mountainous scenery and wildlife of this region attract tourists from all over the world.

Only 800 grizzly bears are left in the USA; many live in the mountains of Wyoming and Idaho.

BISON

Millions of bison (American buffalo) used to roam the Great Plains. Native Americans hunted them for food and used their hides to make clothing and shelter. Settlers and railroad workers virtually wiped out the bison herds in the late 19th century, killing them for food and profit. Today, the bison population is protected, and there are now about 50,000 bison living on reserves.

UNITED STATES
POP: 263,563,000
(CENTRAL & MOUNTAIN STATES)
POP: 19,050,000

The Badlands of South Dakota have been eroded into hills and gullies.

ON THE ROAD

An extensive road network holds this vast, sparsely inhabited region together. Highways often run through long stretches of nearly empty land, fringed by gas stations, motels, and roadside restaurants. Cars are a necessity in much of the West; in Wyoming, children age 14 can drive to school.

Popcorn is a midwestern export.

The Grand Teton Mountains, northern Wyoming.

GOLD RUSH

In 1874, gold was found in the Black Hills of South Dakota, a region sacred to the Sioux people. The discovery sparked a major gold rush; towns sprang up overnight, fortunes were won and lost, gambling and crime flourished. The area is still rich in minerals – South Dakota's Homestake gold mine is the biggest in the country. Look for 🔨

Broad-brimmed, 10-gallon hats are still an essential part of the cowboy's wardrobe.

THE SOUTHWESTERN STATES

THE SOUTHWESTERN USA is a region of deserts and high tablelands, broken by the ridges of the southern Rocky Mountains. Many different Native American peoples lived in the Southwest. The region still has the country's largest concentration of Native Americans. The first Europeans to settle in this region were the Spanish who came north from Mexico. This mixed Spanish and Native American heritage is reflected in the region's folk art, architecture, and foods. American settlers in Texas rebelled against Mexican rule in 1836, and Texas was annexed to the USA a decade later. The rest of the region became part of the USA after the Mexican War of 1846-48. Gold and silver mining and cattle ranching attracted settlers to the region in the late 19th century, and oil became a major part of Texas's economy in the 20th century. The region's natural beauty draws tourists from all over the world.

Jordan Mormon Temple, Utah

MORMON CITY
Salt Lake City in Utah is the headquarters of the Latter-day Saints, or Mormons. They settled in Utah in the 1840s, after fleeing from the eastern states, where they had been persecuted for their beliefs. There are now more than six million Mormons worldwide.

NAVAJO RUGS
Many Navajo people live on a vast reservation in Arizona and New Mexico. They still practice weaving, pottery, silverworking, and other traditional crafts. Navajo rugs are woven into geometric patterns, and colored with natural dyes such as juniper and blackberry.

The Saguaro cactus thrives in the deserts of Arizona.

An 11th-century pottery bowl, made by the Mogollon people.

KEYBOX

	High-tech industry: The space program has attracted high technology industries to the area. Look for 💻
	Irrigated agriculture: Sprinklers fixed on central pivots create circular oases of green fields in the arid landscape. Look for 🌿
	Dams: Acute water shortages are being remedied by the construction of dams on the region's rivers. Look for 🌉
	Military bases: The first nuclear bombs were tested in New Mexico and Nevada. Military installations are common in the region. Look for III

Symbol		Symbol	
🐂	Cattle	🛢️	Oil
🌾	Cereals	🔷	Gas
⚓	Cotton	🏭	Industrial center
⛏️	Mining	⛷️	Skiing

THE GREAT OUTDOORS
Riding, hiking, canoeing, skiing, and fishing are just some of the outdoor activities which draw tourists to the Southwest. But the region's main attraction is the Grand Canyon. About 10,000 visitors each year navigate the Canyon's dangerous waters on rubber rafts, and many others explore it on foot or by donkey.

TAOS
The *pueblo*, or village, of Taos in New Mexico is built of unbaked clay brick, called *adobe*. This style of building dates back to the Pueblo people, who lived in the region a thousand years ago, farming corn, cotton, beans, and squash.

These strangely shaped rocks in Monument Valley, Arizona, have been carved by the wind.

THE GRAND CANYON
Over the last million years, the Colorado River has cut its way through the rocky plateaus of northern Arizona. At the same time, the plateaus have risen. This combined action has formed the largest land gorge in the world – the Grand Canyon. It is more than 1 mile (1.6 km) deep, and 220 miles (350 km) long. Some of the oldest rocks in North America have been found at the base of the canyon.

Bright Angel Point

Colorado River

To Lake Powell

Grand Canyon

Eroded sediment carried down rivers creates fertile plains

To Lake Mead

N

Map labels: OREGON, IDAHO, BLACK ROCK DESERT, Mercury, Beef, Bear, Winnemucca, GREAT, Beef, Great Salt L., Brigham City, Logan, Rye Patch Res., Gold, Humboldt, Elko, Ogden, Pyramid L., BASIN, Bountiful, SALT LAKE CITY, Reno, Sparks, Tooele, Zinc, L. Utah, Orem, Provo, CARSON CITY, L. Tahoe, NEVADA, Copper, Silver, Walker L., Ely, UTAH, Beef, Sevier L., Salina, CALIFORNIA, Nellis Air Force Range, Beef, Bryce Canyon, Uranium, Iron, L. Po., Nevada Test Site, Glen Canyon Dam, North Las Vegas, L. Mead, Grand Canyon, Bright Angel Point, COLORADO PLATEAU, PAINTED DESERT, Las Vegas, Henderson, Hoover Dam, Davis Dam, Flagstaff, ARIZONA, Colorado, Parker Dam, Prescott, Theodore Roosevelt L., Salt, SONORAN, Glendale, PHOENIX, Scottsdale, Copper, Imperial Dam, Mesa, Central Arizona Project, Yuma, Colorado Project, Casa Grande, Luke Air Force Range, Copper, DESERT, Copper, Tucson, Santa Cruz, Beef

N

| 0 | 50 | 100 | 150 | 200 | 250 | 300 | 350 | KM |
| 0 | 25 | 50 | 75 | 100 | 125 | 150 | 175 | 200 | MILES |

SKI COUNTRY

Colorado gets lots of light, dry snow for skiing. The state has many ski resorts set in superb mountain scenery. Former gold rush towns, such as Aspen, are now the glamorous holiday haunts of the rich and famous. Look for 🎿

SPICY PEPPERS

Many hot, spicy foods are eaten in this region – a legacy of the Southwest's Hispanic settlers. Chili peppers are a vital ingredient in these dishes, and New Mexico is the USA's main chili producer, with Texas not far behind.

GATEWAY TO THE ROCKIES

Denver is a thriving city situated at the point where the plains end and the Rockies begin. Today, it is a center for big corporations and high-tech industries, but when it grew up in the mid-19th century it was a gold rush boomtown and a railroad junction.

The Appaloosa horse, a favorite mount of Native Americans.

The Rockies rise to 14,432 ft (4,000 m).

OIL BOOM

The huge East Texas oilfield was discovered in the early 1900s, bringing great wealth to the state. Texas produces more oil than any other American state except Alaska. Pipelines, tankers, and trains carry the crude oil from East Texas to refineries around the Gulf coast. Houston is the capital of the oil industry. Look for ⚓

UNITED STATES
POP: 263,563,000
(SOUTHWESTERN STATES)
POP: 29,679,000

COWBOYS

The plains of Texas are ideal for grazing cattle. Cattle ranching started in the mid-19th century, when there was a huge demand for beef from the rapidly growing cities of the East. Cattle were driven to market by cowboys. Cattle ranching is still big business in Texas today.

Bolo tie

Stetson

Spur

Cowboy boot

Bandana

LAS VEGAS

Las Vegas is a glittering, neon-lit, 24-hour city set in the middle of the arid desert. Over 10 million visitors come to Las Vegas every year, drawn by the city's many gambling casinos and nightclubs.

SPACE AGE

The great empty spaces and clear air of the Southwest are used for military and space technology tests. Telescopes probe outer space from observatories in New Mexico. The US space program is based in Houston, Texas.

WYOMING
NEBRASKA
KANSAS
OKLAHOMA
ARKANSAS
LOUISIANA
COLORADO
NEW MEXICO
TEXAS
MEXICO
Gulf of Mexico

ROCKY MOUNTAINS
SANGRE DE CRISTO MTS.
SAN JUAN MTS.
SAN ANDRES MTS.
DAVIS MTS.
EDWARDS PLATEAU
NAVAJO INDIAN RESERVATION

Yampa
White R.
South Platte
Fort Collins
Greeley
Longmont
Boulder
Sterling
DENVER
Lakewood
Aurora
Vail
Aspen
Colorado Springs
Grand Junction
Blue Mesa Dam
Pueblo
Telluride
Arkansas
Durango
Purgatoire
Farmington
Rio Grande
Navajo Dam
Uranium
Taos
NAVAJO
Gallup
Uranium
Los Alamos
SANTA FE
Albuquerque
Canadian R.
Borger
Pampa
Amarillo
Clovis
Portales
Plainview
Vernon
Wichita Falls
Gila
Elephant Butte Res.
Caballo Res.
Roswell
White Sands Missile Range
Lubbock
Copper
Alamogordo
Pecos
Artesia
Conchas L.
Hobbs
Snyder
Eagle Mountain L.
Red R.
L. Ray Hubbard
Fort Worth
Dallas
L. Tawakoni
Sabine
Tyler
Las Cruces
Fort Bliss Military Reservation
Potassium
Carlsbad
Sweetwater
Abilene
El Paso
Red Bluff L.
Odessa
Midland
Big Spring
Brazos
Waco
Pecos
Colorado
San Angelo
L. Livingston
Amistad Res.
Pecos
L. Travis
AUSTIN
Nitrate
Beaumont
Port Arthur
Del Rio
Medina L.
San Antonio
Houston
Pasadena
Texas City
Galveston
Eagle Pass
San Antonio
Nitrate
Freeport
Sulfur
Laredo
Sulfur
Corpus Christi
Rio Grande
McAllen
Brownsville
Toledo Bend Res.

THE PACIFIC STATES

THE PACIFIC COAST STATES boast some of the most varied scenery in the USA. California, for example, contains the snow-capped peaks of the Sierra Nevada Mountains and the lowest point in North America – Death Valley. Much of California is arid, with farming dependent on irrigation, while vast forests and well-watered fertile valleys are characteristic of Washington and Oregon. American settlers began to cross the Rockies to the Pacific Coast in the 1840s. California became part of the USA as a result of the Mexican–American War (1846–48), and the discovery of gold in 1848 led to its rapid settlement. All three states are now major agricultural producers and centers of high-technology industry. In the early 1960s, California became the USA's most highly populated state. Despite recent problems, the state's economy rivals those of many wealthy nations.

TIMBER
Oregon and Washington are the USA's major timber producers. The region's cedar and fir forests supply one-third of the country's softwood timber. The trees are cut into logs at one of the thousands of sawmills in the forests and then floated down rivers on rafts to the large coastal cities. Some of the wood is made into paper at pulp mills like the one pictured here. Much of the region's timber is exported to Japan. Logging has reduced the region's stocks of mature trees; efforts are now being made to plant more trees. Look for �껴

Boeing 767 aircraft

AEROSPACE
The Boeing Corporation, the world's largest aircraft manufacturer, is based in Seattle.

Boeing is the city's main employer, and any decline in orders can result in unemployment. California is a major producer of military aircraft; cuts in U.S. defense spending have badly affected this region. Look for ✈

AGRICULTURE
California alone produces half of the USA's fruit and vegetables. Fertile soils and a warm climate have contributed to the state's success, but dry conditions mean that much of the state's farmland has to be irrigated. California's main crops are cotton and grapes. Look for 🍇

Almond

Avocado

Peach

Plum

Washington's Mount Rainier is permanently snow-covered.

California redwoods are evergreen trees which can reach 330 ft (100 m).

Fortune cookie served in San Francisco's Chinese restaurants

IMMIGRATION
California attracts many immigrants from Asia and South America. Many Chinese immigrants have settled in San Francisco's Chinatown.

This area of the city is a magnet for the Chinese community and is famous for its shops and restaurants. Immigrants from Latin America, especially Mexico, make up a growing part of the state's population.

SILICON VALLEY
Santa Clara Valley south of San Francisco has one of the largest concentrations of high-technology industry in the world. Over 3,000 area firms specialize in micro-electronics and computer hardware and software. U.S. manufacturers face increasing competition from Asia. Look for 💻

Computer disks capable of storing vast amounts of information

Waves batter the rugged Pacific coast of Oregon.

SAN FRANCISCO
San Francisco is located on one of the world's finest natural harbors and is the West Coast's trade and shipping center. The city is built on a hilly peninsula, with some of the steepest streets in the world. San Francisco suffers from frequent earthquakes because it is situated on the San Andreas Fault. The city's large skyscrapers are specially designed to withstand earthquakes.

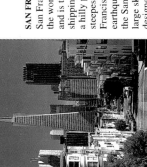

CANADA

IDAHO

WASHINGTON

OREGON

BLUE MOUNTAINS

Spokane
Uranium
La Grande
Baker City
Walla Walla
Gold
Moses Lake
Richland
Pendleton
Burns
Malheur L.
Banks L.
Kennewick
Yakima
John Day
Ross L.
Ellensburg
The Dalles
L. Chelan
Bend
Columbia
Bellingham
Everett
Snohomish
Edmonds
Bellevue
Seattle
Tacoma
OLYMPIA ▲Mt. Rainier
Vancouver
Longview
Portland
SALEM
Springfield
San Juan Is.
Riffe L.
Hillsboro
Albany
Port Angeles
Olympic National Park
Aberdeen
Corvallis
Eugene
Astoria
Newport
Coos Bay
Strait of Juan de Fuca

P

DESERT ENERGY

The resources of the California landscape – wind and sun – are being tapped to provide new sources of energy. This has become necessary because strict laws now forbid the building of power plants near Los Angeles. "Wind farms" have been built in the San Gorgonio Pass area. Solar energy is harnessed by complexes of mirrors. These force reflected light onto a central boiler, converting water to steam, which is used to generate electricity.

The sand dunes of Death Valley in eastern California.

UNITED STATES:
POP: 265,563,000
(PACIFIC STATES)
POP: 38,083,000

DREAM CITY

Hollywood in Los Angeles is the world capital of the film and television industry. Although most major studios are no longer based here, the glamor of Hollywood's heyday – 1915 to 1950 – lingers on: many movie stars still live here.

White grapes

WINE

Raisins (discovered when grapes withered on the vine) and grapes are major crops in California. The wide range of wines made here reflects the varied climates in the state. Look for 🌿

Raisins

Denim jeans were first made in the 1850s for miners during the California gold rush.

TOURISM

More than 100 million visitors a year come to California. The state offers a wide range of activities: spectacular national parks; attractions such as Disneyland and Hollywood; and the superb Pacific coastline. Venice Beach in Los Angeles draws many visitors. Jugglers, mime artists, folk-singers and bodybuilders throng the boardwalk. Fads such as rollerblading and skateboarding have spread from Venice Beach across the country. Look for 📷

Green abalone shells found off the California coast are used to make jewelry.

LOS ANGELES

Los Angeles is a vast, sprawling city stretching for 60 miles (100 km) along the Pacific coast. The city has grown rapidly over the last 100 years and is a focus for immigrants from the rest of the USA. Today, it consists of many separate residential centers, linked by an extensive road system, built in the 1930s. Most residents are dependent on cars for transportation. The city suffers from pollution as it is surrounded by mountains which stop exhaust fumes escaping.

KEYBOX

Mixed fruit: *Washington produces one-third of the USA's apple crop, grown in irrigated valleys east of the Cascade Range. Look for* 🍎

Irrigated agriculture: *Fertile but dry land in central California is irrigated, via canals and dams, by water from the mountains to the west. Look for* 🌾

Borders: *Millions of Mexicans cross the border into California, many illegally. The border is patrolled by mounted guards and helicopters. Look for* ✈

Military bases: *San Diego has the largest concentration of naval bases in the USA. Deserts in California are also used for weapons testing. Look for* ✈

🌿 Wine	🛢 Oil
🌾 Cotton	🏭 Industrial center
🌲 Timber	✈ Aerospace industry
🐟 Fishing	💻 High-tech industry
⛏ Mining	📷 Tourism

### Map labels

PACIFIC OCEAN

ARIZONA
SONORAN DESERT
MEXICO
Colorado
Brawley
San Diego
Miramar Naval Air Station
San Clemente
Oceanside
Palm Springs
Salton Sea
Riverside
San Bernardino
San Gorgonio Pass
Santa Ana
Huntington Beach
Long Beach
Pasadena
Glendale
Los Angeles
Hollywood
Edwards Air Base
Barstow
China Lake Naval Weapons Center
Mojave
MOJAVE DESERT
Death Valley
Potassium
Ventura
Oxnard
Santa Barbara
Vandenburg Air Force Base
Santa Maria
San Luis Obispo
Bakersfield
Fresno
San Joaquin
Tulare L.
Merced
Modesto
Yosemite National Park
SIERRA NEVADA
NEVADA
CALIFORNIA
Mono L.
Bishop
Salinas
Monterey
Santa Cruz
Santa Clara Valley
San Jose
Oakland
San Francisco
Novato
Petaluma
Santa Rosa
Napa Valley
Vacaville
Concord
Stockton
SACRAMENTO
McClellan Air Base
Gold
Chico
Redding
Shasta L.
Eagle L.
Weed
Clair Engle L.
Alturas
Klamath Falls
Goose L.
Ashland
Eureka
Crescent City
COAST RANGES
EAST RANGES

N

KM / MILES
0 50 100 150 200 250

MEXICO

THE LAND OF MEXICO consists of a dry plateau crossed by broad valleys and enclosed to the west and east by mountains, some of which are volcanic. Baja California, the Yucatan Peninsula, and the country's coasts are the main low-lying areas. Mexico was once home to civilizations such as the Maya and Aztec, who built magnificent cities containing plazas, palaces, and pyramids. Lured by legends of fabulous hoards of gold and silver, Spanish conquistadores invaded Mexico in 1519 and destroyed the Aztec Empire. For 300 years the Spanish ruled the country, unifying it with their language and the Roman Catholic religion. Mexico succeeded in winning its independence from Spain by 1821. Today, most Mexicans are *mestizo* – which means they are descendants of the native peoples and the Spanish settlers. Although half the population lives in towns, many people still inhabit areas only accessible on horseback, but rail and air transport are improving. So much of the country is mountainous or dry that only 12 percent of the land can be used for farming. Mexico has vast oil reserves and mineral riches, but suffers from overpopulation and huge foreign debts. The North American Free Trade Agreement (NAFTA) adopted in 1993 promised to strengthen Mexico's economy.

MEXICO
POP: 95,365,000

Cedros Island, off the northwest coast of Mexico.

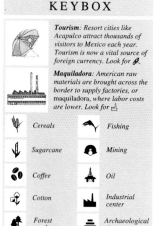

Skeleton made of papier-mâché

THE DAY OF THE DEAD

Mexicans believe that life is like a flower; it slowly opens and then closes again. During the annual festival of the Day of the Dead, the streets are decorated with flowers, and ghoulish skeletons are everywhere.

TEXTILES

Although many fabrics are now machine-made, some Mexicans still practice their traditional art of handweaving colorful textiles. This *sarape*, part of the traditional Mexican dress for men, is worn over the shoulder.

Teeth made of shell

Aztec mask, inlaid with turquoise, depicting a god.

AGRICULTURE

Although Mexico is rapidly industrializing, over half the working population still makes its living from farming. They grow crops like corn, beans, and vegetables, and raise cattle, sheep, pigs, and chickens.

Cacti growing on Mexico's dry central plateau.

SPIKED DRINKS

The desert and dry regions of Mexico are home to many varieties of the spiny-leaved *agave* plant. Juice from two varieties is used to make the alcoholic drinks *tequila* and *mezcal*. The *agave* plant is grown on plantations, then cooked, crushed, and fermented. The drink is exported worldwide.

KEYBOX

Tourism: Resort cities like Acapulco attract thousands of visitors to Mexico each year. Tourism is now a vital source of foreign currency. Look for 🏖

Maquiladora: American raw materials are brought across the border to supply factories, or maquiladora, where labor costs are lower. Look for 🏭

🌾	Cereals	🐟	Fishing
🌾	Sugarcane	⛏	Mining
☕	Coffee	⚙	Oil
🌿	Cotton	🏭	Industrial center
🌲	Forest products	⚖	Archaeological site

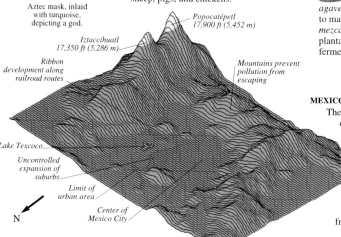

Popocatépetl 17,900 ft (5,452 m)

Iztaccíhuatl 17,350 ft (5,286 m)

Ribbon development along railroad routes

Mountains prevent pollution from escaping

Lake Texcoco

Uncontrolled expansion of suburbs

Limit of urban area

Center of Mexico City

N

MEXICO CITY

The Aztec capital, Tenochtitlán, was built on islands in Lake Texcoco. The city was destroyed by the Spanish, but modern-day Mexico City is built on the ruins. By AD 2000 it is expected to be the world's largest city, containing over 20 million people. Mexico City is very polluted because it is surrounded by a ring of mountains which trap polluted air from cars and factories.

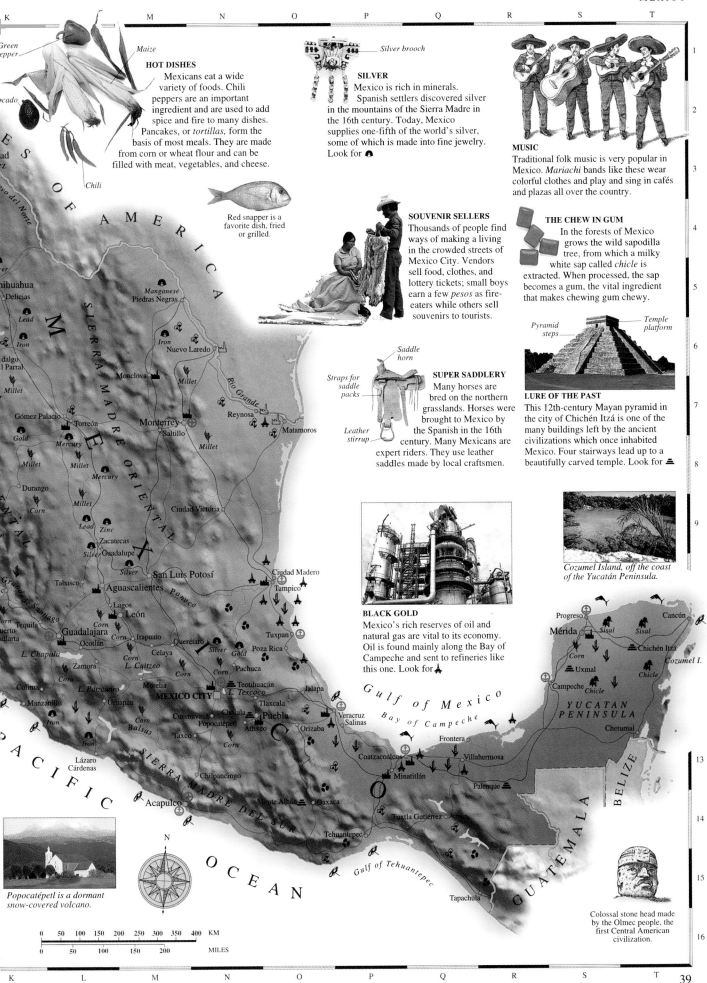

K   M   N   O   P   Q   R   S   T

HOT DISHES

Green pepper

Maize

Chili

cado

Mexicans eat a wide variety of foods. Chili peppers are an important ingredient and are used to add spice and fire to many dishes. Pancakes, or *tortillas,* form the basis of most meals. They are made from corn or wheat flour and can be filled with meat, vegetables, and cheese.

Red snapper is a favorite dish, fried or grilled.

Silver brooch

SILVER

Mexico is rich in minerals. Spanish settlers discovered silver in the mountains of the Sierra Madre in the 16th century. Today, Mexico supplies one-fifth of the world's silver, some of which is made into fine jewelry. Look for ⚇

MUSIC

Traditional folk music is very popular in Mexico. *Mariachi* bands like these wear colorful clothes and play and sing in cafés and plazas all over the country.

SOUVENIR SELLERS

Thousands of people find ways of making a living in the crowded streets of Mexico City. Vendors sell food, clothes, and lottery tickets; small boys earn a few *pesos* as fire-eaters while others sell souvenirs to tourists.

THE CHEW IN GUM

In the forests of Mexico grows the wild sapodilla tree, from which a milky white sap called *chicle* is extracted. When processed, the sap becomes a gum, the vital ingredient that makes chewing gum chewy.

Pyramid steps

Temple platform

Saddle horn

Straps for saddle packs

Leather stirrup

SUPER SADDLERY

Many horses are bred on the northern grasslands. Horses were brought to Mexico by the Spanish in the 16th century. Many Mexicans are expert riders. They use leather saddles made by local craftsmen.

LURE OF THE PAST

This 12th-century Mayan pyramid in the city of Chichén Itzá is one of the many buildings left by the ancient civilizations which once inhabited Mexico. Four stairways lead up to a beautifully carved temple. Look for ▲

Cozumel Island, off the coast of the Yucatán Peninsula.

BLACK GOLD

Mexico's rich reserves of oil and natural gas are vital to its economy. Oil is found mainly along the Bay of Campeche and sent to refineries like this one. Look for 🛢

Popocatépetl is a dormant snow-covered volcano.

Colossal stone head made by the Olmec people, the first Central American civilization.

UNITED STATES OF AMERICA

Chihuahua
Delicias
Lead
Iron
dalgo
Parral
Millet
Gómez Palacio
Torreón
Gold
Mercury
Millet
Millet
Mercury
Durango
Millet
Corn
Lead
Zinc
Zacatecas
Silver
Guadalupe
Silver
Tabasco
San Luis Potosí
Aguascalientes
Lagos
León
Tequila
Guadalajara
Corn
Irapuato
Ocotlán
Celaya
Querétaro
Silver
Gold
L. Chapala
Corn
Zamora
L. Cuitzeo
Corn
Corn
Colima
L. Pátzcuaro
Morelia
Manzanillo
Uruapan
Corn
Iron
Balsas
Taxco
Corn
Lázaro Cárdenas
Iron
Chilpancingo
Acapulco

Manganese
Piedras Negras
Iron
Nuevo Laredo
Monclova
Millet
Rio Grande
Reynosa
Monterrey
Saltillo
Millet
Matamoros
Ciudad Victoria
Ciudad Madero
Tampico
Pánuco
Tuxpan
Poza Rica
Pachuca
Teotihuacán
MEXICO CITY
L. Texcoco
Jalapa
Tlaxcala
Cholula
Puebla
Cuernavaca
Popocatépetl
Atlixco
Orizaba
Veracruz
Salinas
Frontera
Coatzacoalcos
Minatitlán
Villahermosa
Monte Albán
Oaxaca
Tuxtla Gutiérrez
Tehuantepec
Tapachula

Gulf of Mexico
Bay of Campeche

Gulf of Tehuantepec

PACIFIC OCEAN

Progreso
Cancún
Mérida
Sisal
Sisal
Chichén Itzá
Cozumel I.
Corn
Chicle
Uxmal
Campeche
Chicle
Chetumal
YUCATAN PENINSULA

Palenque

GUATEMALA

BELIZE

N

0 50 100 150 200 250 300 350 400 KM
0 50 100 150 200 MILES

K   L   M   N   O   P   Q   R   S   T

Toco toucan
Ramphastos toco
Length: 24 in (60 cm)

Emerald tree boa
Corallus caninus
Length: 6 ft (1.8 m)

**Geoffroy's
spider monkey**
Ateles geoffroyi
Length: 5 ft (1.5 m)

CENTRAL AND SOUTH AMERICA

SOUTH AMERICA is shaped like a giant triangle that tapers southward from the Equator to Cape Horn. A huge wall of mountains, the Andes, stretches for 4,500 miles (7,250 km) along the entire Pacific coast. Until 3 million years ago, South America was not connected to North America, so life there evolved in isolation. Several extraordinary animal groups developed, including sloths and anteaters. Many unique plant species originated here, too, such as the potato and tomato. South America has the world's largest area of tropical rain forest, through which run the Amazon River and its many tributaries. Central America is mountainous and forested.

TROPICAL TOBAGO
Coconut palms grow along the shores of many Caribbean islands. Palms have flexible trunks that enable them to withstand tropical storms.

Mahogany
Swietenia macrophylla
Height: 82 ft (25 m)

VOLCANIC ISLANDS
One of the extinct volcanic craters of the Galápagos island group breaks the surface of the Pacific Ocean. Like other isolated regions of the world, many unique species have evolved here, such as the giant tortoise 4 ft (1.2 m) long.

SEA-DWELLING TREES
Mangroves grow along tropical coastlines. The tangled roots of Pinuelo mangroves create ideal homes for tiny aquatic species.

PAMPAS
Giant grasses up to 10 ft (3 m) high grow on Argentina's dry southern Pampas. Here, further north, more plentiful rainfall supports a few scattered trees.

Alpaca
Lama pacos
Height: 5 ft (1.5 m)

Archaeogeryon, a crab that lived in this region 20 million years ago.

VOLCANIC ANDES
Steam and smoke rises from Villarrica, an active volcano. Many peaks in the Andes are active or former volcanoes. Despite the intense heat within these lava-filled mountains, the highest are permanently covered in snow – even those on the Equator.

THE FOREST FLOOR
Tropical rain forest trees form such a dense canopy that little sunlight or rain can reach the ground 200 ft (70 m) below. Rain forest soils are easily washed away when the trees and plants are removed.

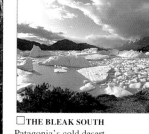

THE BLEAK SOUTH
Patagonia's cold desert environment contrasts starkly with the lush hot forests of Amazonia. Plants take root in the cracks of bare rock and grow close to the ground to survive icy winds.

DRY ATACAMA DESERT
The Atacama Desert is the world's driest place outside Antarctica. Rain has not fallen in some areas for hundreds of years. Winds that pass over cold coastline currents absorb no moisture.

Passionflower
Passiflora caerulea
Across bloom:
6 in (15 cm)

BIRTH OF A RIVER
The snow-capped peaks of the Andes are the source of the Amazon, the world's second longest river. It is 4,080 miles (6,570 km) long.

CROSS SECTION THROUGH SOUTH AMERICA

Peru-Chile Trench
Andes
Selvas
Guiana Highlands
Barbados
Pacific Ocean
Amazon Basin
Amazon
Atlantic Ocean
14,764 (4,500)
0 Sea level
-19,686 (-6,000)
Feet (meters)
A
Length: 2,700 miles (4,400 km)
B

Giant anteater
Myrmecophaga tridactyla
Length: 7 ft (2 m)

Galápagos fur seal
Arctocephalus galapagoensis
Length: 6 ft (1.8 m)

Ocelot
Felis pardalis
Length: 6 ft (1.7

The triton shell can be found from Central America to Brazil.

GREAT WATERS
The Iguaçu Falls in Brazil are spectacular. Water thunders over the rim from November to March, but at other times slows to almost a trickle.

Common Chilean tarantula
Grammostola spatulatus
Length: 4 in (10 cm)

KEY TO SYMBOLS

- ▲ Mountain
- △ Volcano
- ✱ Mangroves
- Wetlands
- Coral reef
- Plate margins and direction of movement

KEY TO NATURAL VEGETATION

- Tropical grassland
- Mountain
- Mediterranean-type
- Broadleaf forest
- Cold desert
- Tropical rain forest
- Dry woodland
- Temperate rain forest
- Temperate grassland
- Hot desert

CENTRAL AMERICA AND THE CARIBBEAN

THE TROPICAL REGION OF Central America and the Caribbean was settled by hunters and farmers many thousands of years ago. By 300 BC the Maya had established a sophisticated civilization on the mainland – ruins of their pyramids and temples can still be seen deep in the forests of Guatemala. The Maya, as well as the native peoples who lived on the Caribbean islands, were almost wiped out by European explorers who arrived in the 15th century. From this time, European nations, in particular the British, French, Spanish, and Dutch, competed for control of the region and some countries did not gain independence until recently. Europeans brought slaves from Africa to work on vast sugar plantations. In the last few decades, tourism has enriched the Caribbean, but in Central America, poverty and civil wars are still major problems.

A Jamaican beach devastated by a hurricane.

The ancient Maya temple of Altun Ha is hidden deep in the rain forest of Belize.

Swamps near the Honduran coast.

Conches from the shallow waters of the Caribbean are edible.

KEYBOX

Archaeological sites: Great civilizations, such as the Maya, flourished in Central America from 300 BC. They built temples, palaces, and cities. Look for ⚏

Shellfishing: Shrimp and lobsters thrive in the mangrove swamps on the coasts of Central America, which provide rich feeding grounds. Look for ➡

Shipping registry: Ships from all over the world fly Panama's flag. They register there because of low fees and limited controls on the labor force. Look for 🏴

↓ Sugarcane		🚬 Tobacco	
Bananas		🎋 Timber	
Coffee		⛏ Mining	
Cocoa		🏭 Industrial center	
⚓ Cotton		🖌 Tourism	

NICARAGUA
Since Nicaragua became independent in 1838 it has been devastated by civil war and foreign interference. During the 1980s, a desperate conflict took place between the Marxist government and the right-wing *Contras*, supported by the USA. Although democracy has now been restored, little progress has been made in fighting the huge problems of poverty, ill-health, and homelessness.

RURAL MARKETS
Many Guatemalans live in small villages, growing corn and beans and making brightly colored cloth, baskets, pottery, and wood carvings. These goods, as well as fruit and tobacco, are sold at local markets.

Hot pepper sauce, with spicy chilis, is used all over the region

### Map labels

MEXICO

GUATEMALA POP: 10,000,000

BELIZE POP: 200,000

EL SALVADOR POP: 5,400,000

HONDURAS POP: 5,600,000

NICARAGUA POP: 4,100,000

COSTA RICA POP: 3,300,000

PANAMA POP: 2,600,000

CUBA POP: 11,172,000

JAMAICA POP: 2,572,000

HAVANA (LA HABANA) · Matanzas · Copper · Pinar del Río · I. de la Juventud (I. of Pines) · Cienfuegos · Santa Clara · Camagüe · Jardines de la Reina · GREATER · Little Cayman · Cayman Brac · Guacan · GEORGETOWN · Grand Cayman · CAYMAN ISLANDS (UK) · Savanna-la-Mar · Mont Bay · JAMAICA · Spanish · CARIBBEAN · Great Ban

GUATEMALA · Altun Ha · Tikal · Belize City · Flores · BELMOPAN · Belize · San Ignacio · BELIZE · Cobán · Nickel · L. Izabal · Gulf of Honduras · Huehuetenango · Quezaltenango · Sololá · Mazatenango · Puerto Barrios · Puerto Cortés · Zacapa · San Pedro Sula · La Ceiba · Trujillo · GUATEMALA CITY · Copán · Santa Rosa · Escuintla · HONDURAS · Santa Ana · La Esperanza · Comayagua · Caratasca Lagoon · SAN SALVADOR · Juticalpa · TEGUCIGALPA · Patuca · La Libertad · Coco · EL SALVADOR · San Miguel · San Lorenzo · Choluteca · Gold · Somoto · Copper · Puerto Cabezas · Chinandega · Corinto · Estelí · Jinotega · León · Matagalpa · Río Grande · L. Managua · Boaco · MANAGUA · Juigalpa · NICARAGUA · Granada · L. Nicaragua · Rivas · Bluefields · San Carlos · San Juan · Liberia · COSTA · Puntarenas · Alajuela · Gulf of Nicoya · SAN JOSÉ · Cartago · Puerto Limón · RICA · Bocas del Toro · Mosquito Gulf · Colón · PANAMA · David · Panama Canal · Penonomé · Copper · PANAMA CITY · Gulf of Chiriquí · Santiago · Gulf of Panama · Coiba I. · Chitré · San José I. · Isla del Rey · Gulf of Darien · Las Tablas · La Palma · COLOMBIA

PACIFIC OCEAN

N

| 0 | 50 | 100 | 150 | 200 | 250 | 300 | 350 | 400 | KM |
| 0 | | 50 | | 100 | | 150 | | 200 | MILES |

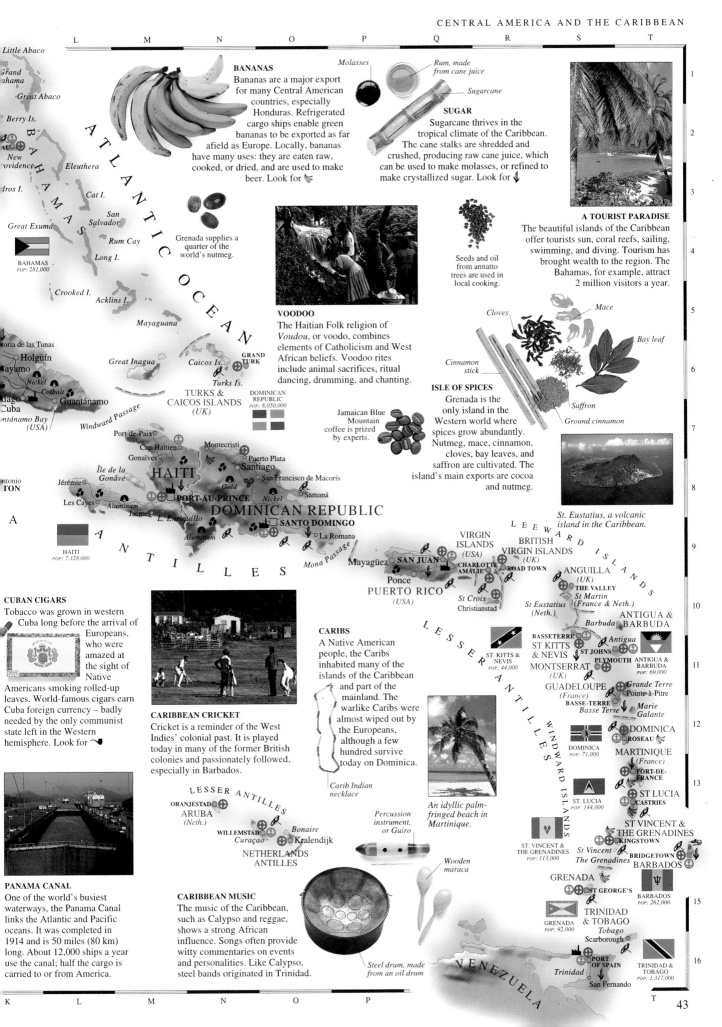

BANANAS

Bananas are a major export for many Central American countries, especially Honduras. Refrigerated cargo ships enable green bananas to be exported as far afield as Europe. Locally, bananas have many uses: they are eaten raw, cooked, or dried, and are used to make beer. Look for 🍌

Molasses

Rum, made from cane juice

Sugarcane

SUGAR

Sugarcane thrives in the tropical climate of the Caribbean. The cane stalks are shredded and crushed, producing raw cane juice, which can be used to make molasses, or refined to make crystallized sugar. Look for ⬇

A TOURIST PARADISE

The beautiful islands of the Caribbean offer tourists sun, coral reefs, sailing, swimming, and diving. Tourism has brought wealth to the region. The Bahamas, for example, attract 2 million visitors a year.

Grenada supplies a quarter of the world's nutmeg.

Seeds and oil from annatto trees are used in local cooking.

VOODOO

The Haitian Folk religion of *Voudou*, or voodo, combines elements of Catholicism and West African beliefs. Voodoo rites include animal sacrifices, ritual dancing, drumming, and chanting.

Cloves   *Mace*

Bay leaf

Cinnamon stick

Saffron

Ground cinnamon

ISLE OF SPICES

Grenada is the only island in the Western world where spices grow abundantly. Nutmeg, mace, cinnamon, cloves, bay leaves, and saffron are cultivated. The island's main exports are cocoa and nutmeg.

Jamaican Blue Mountain coffee is prized by experts.

St. Eustatius, a volcanic island in the Caribbean.

CUBAN CIGARS

Tobacco was grown in western Cuba long before the arrival of Europeans, who were amazed at the sight of Native Americans smoking rolled-up leaves. World-famous cigars earn Cuba foreign currency – badly needed by the only communist state left in the Western hemisphere. Look for 🚬

CARIBBEAN CRICKET

Cricket is a reminder of the West Indies' colonial past. It is played today in many of the former British colonies and passionately followed, especially in Barbados.

CARIBS

A Native American people, the Caribs inhabited many of the islands of the Caribbean and part of the mainland. The warlike Caribs were almost wiped out by the Europeans, although a few hundred survive today on Dominica.

Carib Indian necklace

An idyllic palm-fringed beach in Martinique.

PANAMA CANAL

One of the world's busiest waterways, the Panama Canal links the Atlantic and Pacific oceans. It was completed in 1914 and is 50 miles (80 km) long. About 12,000 ships a year use the canal; half the cargo is carried to or from America.

CARIBBEAN MUSIC

The music of the Caribbean, such as Calypso and reggae, shows a strong African influence. Songs often provide witty commentaries on events and personalities. Like Calypso, steel bands originated in Trinidad.

Percussion instrument, or Guiro

Wooden maraca

Steel drum, made from an oil drum

BAHAMAS
POP: 281,000

TURKS & CAICOS ISLANDS (UK)

DOMINICAN REPUBLIC
POP: 8,050,000

HAITI
POP: 7,328,000

ARUBA (Neth.)

NETHERLANDS ANTILLES

VIRGIN ISLANDS (USA)

BRITISH VIRGIN ISLANDS (UK)

ANGUILLA (UK)

ST. KITTS & NEVIS
POP: 44,000

MONTSERRAT (UK)

GUADELOUPE (France)

ANTIGUA & BARBUDA
POP: 69,000

DOMINICA
POP: 71,000

MARTINIQUE (France)

ST. LUCIA
POP: 144,000

ST. VINCENT & THE GRENADINES
POP: 113,000

GRENADA
POP: 92,000

BARBADOS
POP: 262,000

TRINIDAD & TOBAGO
POP: 1,317,000

Map labels: Little Abaco, Grand Bahama, Great Abaco, Berry Is., New Providence, Eleuthera, Cat I., San Salvador, Rum Cay, Long I., Crooked I., Acklins I., Mayaguana, Great Exuma, Great Inagua, Caicos Is., Turks Is., GRAND TURK, ATLANTIC OCEAN, BAHAMAS, Holguín, Bayamo, Nickel, Cobalt, Guantánamo, Cuba, Guantánamo Bay (USA), Windward Passage, ANTILLES, Port-de-Paix, Cap-Haïtien, Gonaïves, Jérémie, Île de la Gonâve, Les Cayes, Jacmel, Montecristi, Puerto Plata, Santiago, San Francisco de Macorís, HAITI, PORT-AU-PRINCE, L. Enriquillo, Aluminum, Gold, Nickel, Samaná, DOMINICAN REPUBLIC, SANTO DOMINGO, La Romana, Mona Passage, Mayagüez, Ponce, SAN JUAN, PUERTO RICO (USA), St Croix, Christianstad, CHARLOTTE AMALIE, ROAD TOWN, THE VALLEY, St Martin (France & Neth.), St Eustatius (Neth.), LEEWARD ISLANDS, Barbuda, Antigua, ANTIGUA & BARBUDA, BASSETERRE, ST KITTS & NEVIS, ST JOHNS, PLYMOUTH, BASSE-TERRE, Basse Terre, Grande Terre, Pointe-à-Pitre, Marie Galante, DOMINICA, ROSEAU, MARTINIQUE, FORT-DE-FRANCE, ST LUCIA, CASTRIES, ST VINCENT & THE GRENADINES, KINGSTOWN, St Vincent, The Grenadines, BRIDGETOWN, BARBADOS, GRENADA, ST GEORGE'S, LESSER ANTILLES, WINDWARD ISLANDS, ORANJESTAD, WILLEMSTAD, Curaçao, Bonaire, Kralendijk, TRINIDAD & TOBAGO, Tobago, Scarborough, PORT OF SPAIN, Trinidad, San Fernando, VENEZUELA

NORTHERN SOUTH AMERICA

THIS REGION IS DOMINATED BY the volcanic peaks and mountain ranges of the Andes. The powerful Incas ruled much of this area in the 15th century, and large numbers of their descendants still live in Peru, Bolivia, and Ecuador today. In the 16th century, Spanish *conquistadores* reached South America, swept the Incas and other native peoples aside, and colonized the region from Venezuela to Bolivia. Areas to the east were later settled by the French, Dutch, and British. Although all the countries except French Guiana are now independent republics, independence has brought many problems, such as military dictatorships, high inflation, organized crime, the illegal drug trade, and huge foreign debts. Many of the cities are overcrowded, but large numbers of people still flock there from the countryside, looking for jobs.

SHRIMP

Shrimp living in the muddy waters of Ecuador's mangrove swamps have become the country's second most important source of foreign currency, after oil. But as the industry expands, it is destroying the mangroves – the shrimps' natural habitat. Look for 🦐

MARKET DAY

Brightly dressed in their traditional Andean clothes and hats, local people display their wares in the market of the Peruvian town of Pisác. They sell fruit and vegetables, together with pottery and clothes produced for the tourist trade.

CARACAS

The discovery of oil in 1917 made Venezuela the richest country in the region. Its capital, Caracas, was built with oil money. Modern highways and skyscrapers dominate the city, but many people live in shantytowns on the surrounding hillsides.

The lush Caribbean coastline of northern Venezuela.

Hammered gold

A figure made by ancient Colombian craftsmen.

SURINAME
POP: 470,000

VENEZUELA
POP: 20,490,000

GUYANA
POP: 843,000

COLOMBIA
POP: 35,624,000

ECUADOR

EMERALDS

Some of the world's finest emeralds are mined near Bogotá, the capital of Colombia. Long before the Spanish invaded the country in search of gold, native peoples mined the emeralds for their gold jewelry and

Emerald

Cinchona leaves

Quinine from the bark of the Peruvian *cinchona* tree is used to treat malaria.

KM
MILES

FRENCH GUIANA *(France)*
CAYENNE
Kourou
Iracoubo
St Laurent-du-Maroni
Gold

SURINAME
PARAMARIBO
New Amsterdam
Albina
Marowijne
Brokopondo
Kabalebo Res.
Aluminum
Courantyne
Gold
Nickerie
Fort Wellington
Aluminum

GUYANA
GEORGETOWN
Bartica
Mabaruma
Suddie
Lethem
Beef
Mazaruni
Essequibo
Gold
Diamonds
Berbice
Aluminum
Gold

VENEZUELA
Margarita I.
La Asunción
Cumaná
Barcelona
Maturín
Tucupita
Orinoco
Ciudad Guayana
Ciudad Bolívar
Guri Res.
Aluminum
Gold
Diamonds
Santa Elena
Iron
Beef
San Fernando de Apure
Puerto Ayacucho
Puerto Carreño
Puerto Infrida
La Guaira
CARACAS
Maracay
Valencia
San Juan de los Morros
Puerto Cabello
San Felipe
Barquisimeto
San Carlos
Coro
Guanare
Trujillo
Barinas
Apure
Meta

CARIBBEAN SEA
Gulf of Venezuela

Maracaibo
L. Maracaibo
Cabimas
Mérida
San Cristóbal
Cúcuta
Arauca
Bucaramanga

COLOMBIA
BOGOTÁ
Santa Marta
Barranquilla
Cartagena
Riohacha
Valledupar
Sincelejo
Montería
Medellín
Bello
Quibdó
Gold
Manizales
Pereira
Armenia
Ibagué
Buenaventura
Cali
Palmira
Popayán
Pasto
Neiva
Florencia
Mocoa
Villavicencio
San José del Guaviare
Mitú
Leticia
Magdalena
Cauca
Emeralds
Tunja
Yopal
Guaviare
Caquetá
Amazon
Putumayo
Napo

ECUADOR
QUITO
Ibarra
Esmeraldas
Santo Domingo de los Colorados
Portoviejo
Manta
Montecristi
Babahoyo
Guayaquil
Gulf of Guayaquil
Machala
Loja
Cuenca
Riobamba
Ambato
Latacunga
Milagro
Iquitos
Aguarico

Gulf of Darién
PANAMA

PACIFIC OCEAN

BRAZIL

Beef

N

HIGHEST RAILROAD

Peru's railroads are the highest in the world. The single-track railroad from Lima to Huancayo in the Andes zigzags through tunnels and over wooden bridges, reaching an altitude of 15,885 ft (4,843 m) where it crosses one of the passes.

Rug decorated with llamas, the traditional Andean pack animals

OTAVALO PEOPLE

Woolen rugs woven by the Otavalo people from Ecuador are sold all over the Americas and Europe. The Otavalo have developed new techniques, such as replacing traditional natural dyes with synthetic ones.

Strap handle

Clay body

Water jar, found at the ancient Inca city of Cusco in Peru.

COCAINE

The steep slopes of the Andes are ideally suited to growing the coca bush. The native peoples have always chewed coca leaves to protect themselves against cold and altitude sickness. But the drug cocaine, made from the leaves, is now a major world problem. Today, Colombia's economy is virtually dependent on the illegal export of cocaine.

Coca leaves

Llamas grazing on the high plains of the Andes in Bolivia.

BRAZIL

BOLIVIA POP: 8,256,000

PERU POP: 24,374,000

Iron

PARAGUAY

San Miguel

Santa Cruz

Beef

Beef

Beef

Trinidad

Beef

Beef

Beef

Mamoré

Tarija

BOLIVIA

ARGENTINA

Cochabamba

Silver

Oruro

Tin

Sucre

Beni

Beef

Madre de Dios

Cobija

Zinc

Lead

L. Titicaca

LA PAZ

Potosí

Silver

Silver

Tin

Uyuni

Tungsten

L. Poopó

CHILE

A N D E S

Juliaca

Ollantaytambo

Pisac

Cusco

Machu Picchu

Copper

Puno

Arequipa

Tacna

Mollendo

ANDEAN CULTIVATION

On the steep hillsides of the Andes, every scrap of soil must be made to work efficiently. Like their Inca ancestors, Andean farmers suit the crop to the temperature, which gets lower higher up the mountains. This region is the original home of the potato, which can be grown successfully at high altitudes.

Permanent snow and ice

Inland river valleys: sugar, coffee

9,850 ft (3,000 m)

6,550 ft (2,000 m)

3,280 ft (1,000 m)

Peru-Chile Trench: c.19,686 ft (6,000 m) below sea level

Altiplano: high plateaus between mountains used for grazing animals

Highland areas: barley, potatoes, wheat

Temperate zone: coffee, tobacco, corn

Coastal lowland: sugar, cacao, bananas, rice

Sea level

N

Pacific Ocean floor

LAKE TITICACA

Stretching across the border between Bolivia and Peru is the world's highest lake, Lake Titicaca, 13,000 ft (4,000 m) above sea level. The Uru people sail on the lake in boats of woven reeds.

The native peoples of the Andes were the first to grow potatoes.

The Andes are the world's longest chain of mountains.

CORPUS CHRISTI

Every town commemorates its patron saint with a festival. Events such as this colorful procession on Corpus Christi Day in Cusco, Peru, combine the religious beliefs of the native peoples with Christian ceremonies.

P E R U

Ucayali

Pucallpa

Huánuco

Zinc

La Oroya

Huancayo

Ayacucho

Cajamarca

Trujillo

Silver

Copper

Yungay

Chimbote

Cerro de Pasco

Silver

Lead

Callao

LIMA

Ica

Nazca

San Juan

Beef

Trout

LIMA

Pizarro, a leader of the Spanish *conquistadores*, founded Peru's capital city in the 16th century, and his bones are buried in the cathedral on the Plaza de Armas, the main square in the city's center.

Lima Cathedral

PANAMA HATS

Panama hats are made of fiber from a palm tree that grows in the coastal forests of Ecuador. One hat can take up to three months to make.

PACIFIC OCEAN

KEYBOX

Bananas: Bananas are grown as a cash crop in Ecuador's tropical lowlands. Ecuador is now the world's main exporter. Look for 🍌

Oil: Oil is vital to Venezuela's economy; today the country's oil revenues account for 80 percent of its export earnings. Look for ♦

Archaeological sites: The remains of many magnificent ancient cities and temples can still be seen in the Andes. Look for ⛺

Space center: The European Space Agency launches its rocket, Ariane, from its rocket base at Kourou, French Guiana. Look for 🚀

🐂 Cattle	🌾 Rice	➤ Sugarcane
🌿 Coffee	🌲 Timber	🦐 Shellfishing
⛏ Mining	⚒ Industrial center	

45

BRAZIL

OCCUPYING NEARLY HALF of South America, Brazil possesses the greatest river basin in the world. The Amazonian rain forest, which covers some two-thirds of the country, is a vast storehouse of natural riches, still largely untapped. But land is needed for agriculture, ranching, and new roads, and each year vast tracts of forest are cleared. The Portuguese colonized the country in the 16th century, intermarrying with the local population. They planted sugar in the northeast, working the plantations with slaves brought from Africa. With a further influx of Europeans, Brazil is now one of the world's most populous and ethnically diverse democracies. A land of opportunity for some – like those in the industrial region around São Paulo – it is one of poverty and deprivation for many, especially in the northeast. In spite of improved industrial output, Brazil still has high unemployment and huge foreign debts.

Nuts fit into shell, like segments of an orange

Shelled nut

BRAZIL NUTS

Sometimes known as the *inferno verde*, or green hell, Brazil's vast rain forest is home to an astonishing variety of animals and plants from which products – such as chemicals, drugs, and rubber – can be made. Scattered through the forest are Brazil nut trees. Their nuts can be eaten or crushed to make an oil used in cosmetics. Look for 🌴

SOCCER

Soccer is an all-consuming passion for millions of Brazilians. It is played in every back street and on every open space, even on the beach at Rio. Sometimes the ball is only a coconut. During the World Cup, Brazil comes to a standstill.

NATIVE PEOPLES

There were once some two million native people in Amazonia. Today only about 240,000 survive. This Xingu girl is fortunate: she was born into a tribe which lives in a protected area of the Amazon rain forest. The well-being of many peoples is threatened by the ever-shrinking rain forest and by disease, logging, farming, and gold prospecting.

DANCE MUSIC

Transported to the northeastern region of Brazil to work on the sugar plantations, African slaves brought the musical rhythms of their homelands with them. Their music has blended with other musical influences to produce the music for dances, such as the *samba* and the *lambada*. The instruments include this drum, called a *conga*.

Conga drum

Grandillas, one of the many exotic fruits found in Brazil.

A huge tree trunk deep in the Brazilian rain forest.

A stretch of coast near Salvador in the northeast.

BRAZIL
POP: 163,577,000

ATLANTIC OCEAN

PERU

COLOMBIA

VENEZUELA

GUYANA

SURINAME

FRENCH GUIANA (France)

A M A Z O N I A

B R A Z I L

SERRA GRANDE

SERRA PELADA

Rio Negro

Amazon

Madeira

Purus

Juruá

Tapajós

Teles Pires

Xingu

Jari

Araguaia

Tocantins

Paranaíba

Natal
João Pessoa
Recife
C. de São Roque
Campina Grande
Mossoró
Fortaleza
Quixeró
Parnaíba
São Luís
Teresina
Picos
Sobradinho Res.
Carolina
Palmas
Belém
Macapá
Santarém
Manaus
Balbina Res.
Tucuruí Res.
Boa Vista
Pôrto Velho
Rio Branco
Cruzeiro do Sul

Gold
Aluminum
Manganese
Iron
Tin
Rubber
Brazil Nuts
Sisal
Tungsten
Beef

46

COLONIAL LEGACY

When the Portuguese arrived in Brazil in the 16th century, they brought their distinctive style of architecture. At the heart of many towns and cities in modern Brazil lie cobbled streets, squares, and churches. The historic town of Ouro Prêto – center of the 18th-century gold rush – remains today as a perfect example of a 16th-century town.

CARNIVAL

Every year, just before Lent, Rio de Janeiro erupts into carnival. Often called "The Biggest Party on Earth," carnival involves five days of music and dance. The main event is the competition to find the most outrageous costumes and best decorated floats as they parade through the city to the sound of *samba* music.

The huge statue of Christ the Redeemer which towers over Rio de Janeiro.

RIO DE JANEIRO

Once the capital of Brazil, the beautiful city of Rio de Janeiro sprawls among the bays, islands, and hills around Guanabara Bay. The city acts like a magnet, drawing people from poor rural areas who come in search of work. A severe lack of housing has given birth to endless shanty towns, called *favelas*, which creep up the hillsides and crowd every piece of land unfit for other development.

Guanabara Bay provides access to the sea

Suburbs have grown rapidly

Rio-Niterói Bridge

Rio de Janeiro

Favelas lacking sanitation and other amenities

Favelas on steep slopes vulnerable to heavy rain

From Rio, good road and rail routes lead inland

STEEL

Attracted by Brazil's steel industry, cheap labor, and plentiful electricity, several multinational companies have invested money in the country. US and European car manufacturers have established successful factories around São Paulo. Look for 🚗

Brazilian-made Fiat sedan

BRASÍLIA

In the mid-1950s, the government of Brazil decided to build a new capital city in the sparsely inhabited central plateau region. Built in the shape of an airplane, the futuristic city of Brasília became the country's official capital in 1960. The wide boulevards and open spaces contain spectacular buildings like this cathedral.

ORANGE JUICE

Oranges are grown in the region around São Paulo, where the climate is frost-free. Over a million tons are picked each year. Most of it is processed into orange juice concentrate. Brazil now supplies 85 percent of the world's orange juice, exporting it mainly to the USA and Europe. Look for 🍊

The Iguaçu River as it drops over the Iguaçu Falls.

COFFEE

Coffee originated in Africa, but Brazil is now the world's largest producer. When the trees have shed their white blossoms, the green berries ripen into red "cherries." Each cherry contains two seeds, or coffee beans, which are washed, dried, and roasted. Look for 🫘

The wings of the Morpho butterfly are often used to decorate jewelry.

GOLD MINING

Brazil has vast mineral reserves. This huge human anthill is the result of a gold rush which began in the 1980s near the Serra Pelada. Thousands of prospectors – called *garimpeiros* – burrow into the hillsides hoping to find gold. Look for 🪙

KEYBOX

Cattle: Vast areas of Brazilian rain forest have been destroyed to clear the land for cattle ranching. Look for 🐂

Sugar cane: In the 1970s Brazil began to make an alternative to gasoline out of sugar cane, but now falling oil prices have made this uneconomic. Look for ⚓

Aerospace industry: In recent years Brazil has been successful in developing an aerospace industry, designing planes that are sold worldwide. Look for ✈

Bananas	Tobacco
Citrus fruits	Timber
Coffee	Forest products
Cocoa	Mining
Soybeans	Industrial center
Cotton	Vehicle manufacture

KM
MILES
0
100
200 100
300 200
400 300
500
600

N

BRAZILIAN HIGHLANDS
SERRA DOS PARECIS
BOLIVIA
PARAGUAY
ARGENTINA
URUGUAY
ATLANTIC OCEAN

São Francisco
Paraguay
Paraná
Uruguay
Iguaçu

BRASÍLIA
Belo Horizonte
Vitória
C. de São Tomé
Rio de Janeiro
Ouro Prêto
Juiz de Fora
São José
Campos
Santos
São Paulo
Campinas
Ribeirão Prêto
Uberlândia
Goiânia
Curitiba
Joinville
Florianópolis
Londrina
Porto Alegre
Rio Grande
Pelotas
Passo Fundo
Santa Maria
Campo Grande
Cuiabá
Corumbá
Patos Lagoon
Mirim Lagoon

Furnas Res.
Itaipú Res.
Solteira Res.
Ilha
Iguaçu Falls

Gold, Beef, Iron, Zinc, Lead, Diamonds, Nickel, Uranium, Manganese, Copper

SOUTHERN SOUTH AMERICA

ALL FOUR COUNTRIES in this region were colonized in the 16th century by Spain. With the exception of Argentina, their populations are almost entirely *mestizo* – people of mixed Spanish and Native American descent. In Argentina, 85 percent of the population is descended from European settlers, as the native peoples were killed or driven out by the immigrants. Argentina falls into three regions: the hot, damp lands of the Gran Chaco in the north, the grasslands of the Pampas in the center, and the barren plateau of Patagonia in the south. Argentina gets its wealth from the rich soil of the Pampas, where cereals are grown and vast herds of sheep and cattle graze. The Pampas spills into neighboring Uruguay, where sheep provide the country with its main export, wool. Paraguay's economy is mainly dependent on agriculture. Chile lies stretched like a snake along the western side of the Andes, its head in the mineral-rich Atacama Desert and its tail in the icy wastes of the south. These countries all suffer from high inflation, unstable governments, and poverty.

THE PEOPLES OF THE CHACO
Only five percent of Paraguay's population live in the grasslands and swamps of the Gran Chaco. The main people still living there are the Guaraní, the first inhabitants of Paraguay. A smaller group, the Macá, make money by selling colorful hand-woven cloth and goods, like this bag, to tourists.

ASUNCION
Plaza Constitución is just one of many squares where beautiful Spanish buildings still stand in Asunción, Paraguay's capital and only large city.

PARAGUAY
POP: 4,576,000

ITAIPU DAM
On the mighty Paraná River is one of the world's largest hydro-electric projects, the Itaipú Dam. This joint venture between Brazil and Paraguay boosted Paraguay's economy, creating jobs for thousands of people. Look for

MAINLY MEAT
In the late 19th century, processing and packing meat became an important industry in Uruguay. Today, canned meats, such as corned beef, are still a major export. Look for

Tomatoes were first grown in South America.

URUGUAY
POP: 3,240,000

COPPER
Near Calama, Chile, shining orange metal is extracted from the largest open-pit copper mine in the world. Giant trucks remove thousands of tons of ore a day. However, the world price of copper is now falling, causing severe economic

The Atacama Desert in Chile is the driest place on earth.

48

TEXTILES

Uruguay is covered by flat plains which provide grazing land for vast flocks of sheep. The country is a major world exporter of wool. Some articles, like this scarf, are still handmade. Look for ∨

Handmade woolen scarf

ARGENTINA
POP: 35,298,000

The rolling plains and grasslands of Uruguay.

BUENOS AIRES

Argentina's capital, Buenos Aires, is one of the largest cities in South America and one of the world's great ports. Situated on the La Plata River estuary, it has a large population which includes many people of Italian descent. The tree-lined avenues, theaters, and cafés reflect the city's European heritage.

The leaves of the ilex tree are used to make a refreshing hot drink called yerba maté.

One of the windswept islands of Tierra del Fuego.

THE END OF THE WORLD

Ushuaia in Argentina is one of the world's southernmost towns. It is situated in Tierra del Fuego, the chain of islands at the tip of South America. The name means "land of fire" in Spanish. Ushuaia was once a port for whaling ships. It is now a modern town and busy center for tourists.

CHILEAN WINE

The Spanish first brought wine to Chile. Their vines thrived in the Mediterranean climate of the valleys near Santiago. Later, French and German settlers imported vines. Look for ❧

Rock containing calcite, pyrite, and blue lazurite

Silver and lapis lazuli necklace

in jewelry for thousands of years. The world's most important sources of this stone are many miles apart – near Ovalle in Chile and in Afghanistan. Look for ◐

THE PAMPAS

In the heart of Argentina lie vast areas of grassland – the Pampas – where great herds of sheep and cattle roam. Their hides, meat, and wool are all exported, but *gauchos*, the Argentinian equivalent of the US cowboy, are fast disappearing. Look for ▼

RAINFALL IN THE SOUTH

The contrasting climates of this region are caused by the Andes. Damp winds from the Pacific Ocean are forced up over the mountains. The air cools as it rises, and rain falls. As the air descends on the eastern side of the mountains, it is dry, and warms up. So the west is wet, the east is dry.

Spectacular peaks of the Torres del Paine in Chile.

CHILE
POP: 14,436,000

Over 80 inches (2,000 mm)
60-80 inches (1,500-2,000 mm)
20-60 inches (500-1,500 mm)
10-20 inches (250-500 mm)
10 inches (under 250 mm)

Andes
Valdés Peninsula
Continental shelf
6,560 ft (c.2,000 m) below sea level
Tierra del Fuego

prevailing winds

PACIFIC OCEAN
ATLANTIC OCEAN

KEYBOX

Cereals: These are grown in the rich soils and ideal climate of the Pampas. Argentina is one of the world's great cereal exporters. Look for ❧

Mennonites: Large areas of the Chaco in Paraguay are farmed by members of this Protestant sect who originally came from Germany. Look for ✚

Cattle	Cotton	Tobacco
Sheep	Fishing	Mining
Sugarcane	Oil	Industrial center
Wine		

### Map labels

Corn
Necochea
Mar del Plata
Olavarría
Oats
Beef
Beef
Tres Arroyos
Wheat
Santa Rosa
Beef
Bahía Blanca
Wheat
Colorado
Wheat
Viedma
Barley
Beef
San Antonio Oeste
Negro
Neuquén
Zapala
L. Nahuel Huapí
San Carlos de Bariloche
Esquel
Chubut
L. Colhué Huapí
L. Buenos Aires
Perito Moreno
Coihaique
Puerto Aisén
Cochrane
Chile Chico
TORRES DEL PAINE
Puerto Natales

Bahía Blanca
Gulf of San Matías
Valdés Peninsula
Rawson
Puerto Madryn
Trelew
Gulf of San Jorge
Comodoro Rivadavia
Caleta Olivia
Puerto Deseado
Deseado
Puerto Santa Cruz
Viedma
Calafate
Río Gallegos
Bahía Grande
Río Grande
Ushuaia
Puerto Williams
Punta Arenas
Porvenir
Strait of Magellan
TIERRA DEL FUEGO
Beagle Channel
Cape Horn

Cuneo
Talca
Linares
Cauquenes
Chillán
Talcahuano
Los Angeles
Concepción
Tomé
Coronel
Lebu
Angol
Temuco
Valdivia
Osorno
Puerto Montt
Chiloé I.
Castro
Chaitén
Wheat
Dairy

ATLANTIC OCEAN
PATAGONIA
ANDES
CHILE
ARGENTINA

N

KM
MILES
0 100 200 300 400 500
0 50 100 150 200 250 300

Uranium
Bío Bío

THE ANTARCTIC

THE CONTINENT OF ANTARCTICA has such a cold, harsh climate that no people live there permanently. The land is covered by a huge sheet of ice up to 1.2 miles (2 km) thick, and seas around Antarctica are frozen over. Even during the short summers, the temperature barely climbs above freezing, and the sea ice only partly melts; in winter, temperatures can plummet to -112° F (-80° C). Few animals and plants can survive on land, but the seas around Antarctica teem with fish and mammals. The only people on the continent are scientists working in the Antarctic research stations and tourists, who come to see the dramatic landscape and the unique creatures that live here. But even these few people have brought waste and pollution to the region.

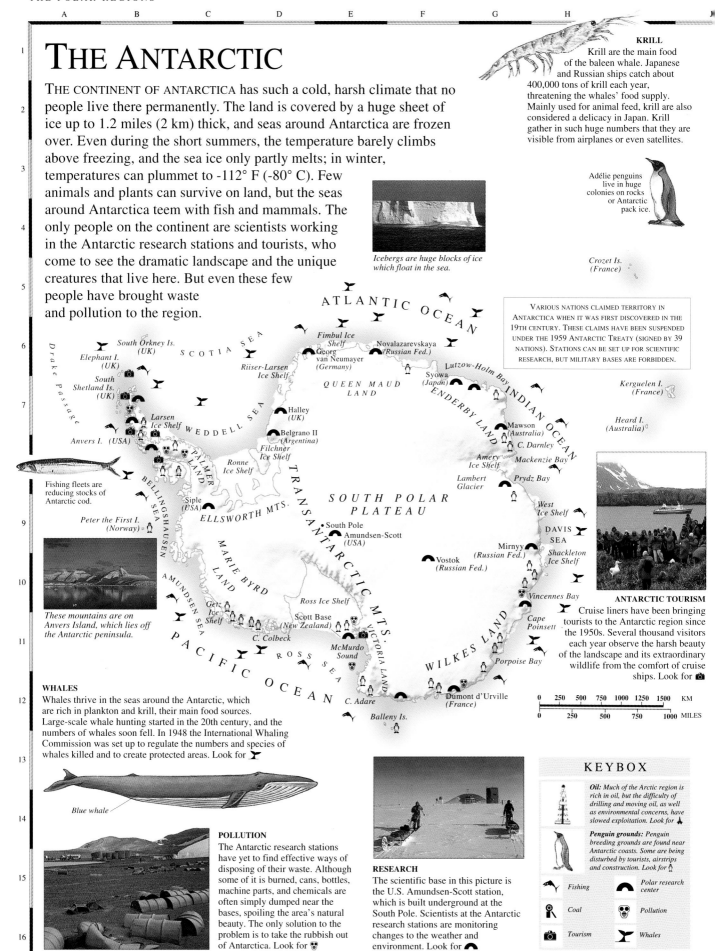

KRILL
Krill are the main food of the baleen whale. Japanese and Russian ships catch about 400,000 tons of krill each year, threatening the whales' food supply. Mainly used for animal feed, krill are also considered a delicacy in Japan. Krill gather in such huge numbers that they are visible from airplanes or even satellites.

Adélie penguins live in huge colonies on rocks or Antarctic pack ice.

Icebergs are huge blocks of ice which float in the sea.

Crozet Is. (France)

VARIOUS NATIONS CLAIMED TERRITORY IN ANTARCTICA WHEN IT WAS FIRST DISCOVERED IN THE 19TH CENTURY. THESE CLAIMS HAVE BEEN SUSPENDED UNDER THE 1959 ANTARCTIC TREATY (SIGNED BY 39 NATIONS). STATIONS CAN BE SET UP FOR SCIENTIFIC RESEARCH, BUT MILITARY BASES ARE FORBIDDEN.

Kerguelen I. (France)

Heard I. (Australia)

Fishing fleets are reducing stocks of Antarctic cod.

These mountains are on Anvers Island, which lies off the Antarctic peninsula.

ANTARCTIC TOURISM
Cruise liners have been bringing tourists to the Antarctic region since the 1950s. Several thousand visitors each year observe the harsh beauty of the landscape and its extraordinary wildlife from the comfort of cruise ships. Look for 📷

WHALES
Whales thrive in the seas around the Antarctic, which are rich in plankton and krill, their main food sources. Large-scale whale hunting started in the 20th century, and the numbers of whales soon fell. In 1948 the International Whaling Commission was set up to regulate the numbers and species of whales killed and to create protected areas. Look for ⅄

Blue whale

| 0 | 250 | 500 | 750 | 1000 | 1250 | 1500 | KM |
| 0 | 250 | 500 | 750 | 1000 | MILES |

POLLUTION
The Antarctic research stations have yet to find effective ways of disposing of their waste. Although some of it is burned, cans, bottles, machine parts, and chemicals are often simply dumped near the bases, spoiling the area's natural beauty. The only solution to the problem is to take the rubbish out of Antarctica. Look for 👥

RESEARCH
The scientific base in this picture is the U.S. Amundsen-Scott station, which is built underground at the South Pole. Scientists at the Antarctic research stations are monitoring changes to the weather and environment. Look for ◖

KEYBOX

Oil: Much of the Arctic region is rich in oil, but the difficulty of drilling and moving oil, as well as environmental concerns, have slowed exploitation. Look for ⚒

Penguin grounds: Penguin breeding grounds are found near Antarctic coasts. Some are being disturbed by tourists, airstrips and construction. Look for ☖

⅄ Fishing	◖ Polar research center
℞ Coal	👥 Pollution
📷 Tourism	⅄ Whales

THE ARCTIC

THE ARCTIC OCEAN IS covered by drifting ice up to 98 ft (30 m) thick, which partially melts and disperses in the summer. Much of the surrounding land is tundra – plains and moorlands that are carpeted with moss and lichens, but permanently frozen beneath the surface. People have lived around the Arctic for thousands of years, hunting the mammals and fish that live in the ocean. This region has large deposits of oil, but the harsh climate makes it difficult to extract from the ground.

FISH STICKS
Large numbers of cod, haddock, halibut, and other fish live in the Arctic Ocean. Cod and haddock are taken to fish-processing factories in Greenland. Here they are frozen, canned or – in the case of cod – made into fish sticks and exported to the markets of the USA and Europe. Look for 🐟

ARCTIC PEOPLES
Traditionally, the people of the Arctic survived by hunting animals. They used sealskin for boats and clothing and seal fat (blubber) for fuel. Today, tools, clothes, and buildings are made from modern materials. Rifles now replace harpoons and snowmobiles are used for transport.

The northern lights can be seen over the Arctic at night.

Polar bears spend summers on the Arctic ice. They move farther south in winter.

ICE-BREAKER
About half the Arctic Ocean is covered with ice in winter, but special ships called icebreakers can still sail across it. In 1969, a large tanker, the *SS Manhattan*, penetrated the pack ice of the Northwest Passage from eastern Canada to Alaska for the first time.

GREENLAND
The first Europeans to explore and settle Greenland were Vikings, who arrived in about 986. Greenland later came under Danish rule and is now a self-governing part of Denmark.

The Arctic tern migrates every year between the Arctic and Antarctica.

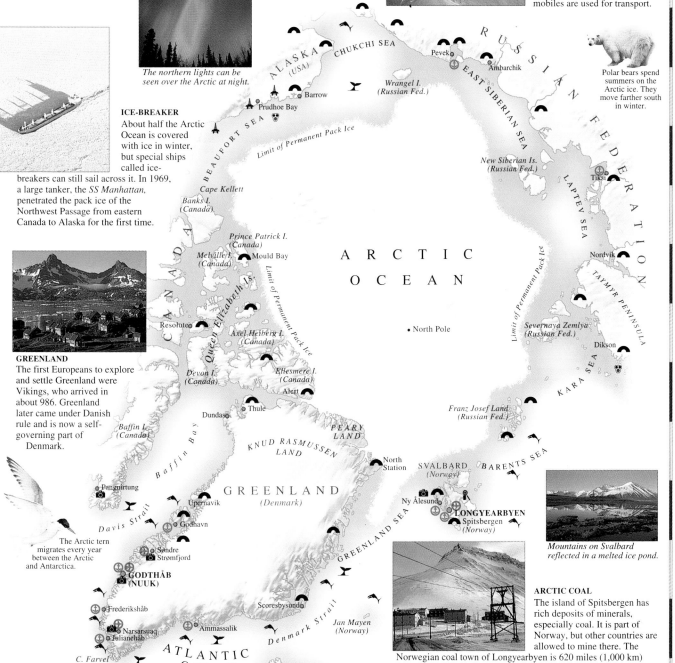

Mountains on Svalbard reflected in a melted ice pond.

ARCTIC COAL
The island of Spitsbergen has rich deposits of minerals, especially coal. It is part of Norway, but other countries are allowed to mine there. The Norwegian coal town of Longyearbyen is 620 miles (1,000 km) from the mainland. It can be reached by sea for only eight months a year, making it difficult and expensive to ship coal out. Coal screes and long, severe winters make this a desolate place. Look for 🪓

THE ATLANTIC OCEAN

THE WORLD'S OCEANS cover almost three-quarters of the Earth's surface. Beneath the surface of the Atlantic Ocean lie vast, featureless plains and long chains of mountains called ridges. The Mid-Atlantic Ridge is one of the world's longest mountain chains; some of its peaks are so high that they pierce the surface as volcanic islands, such as the Azores. A huge rift valley 15-30 miles (24-48 km) wide runs down the ridge's center. The deepest part of the Atlantic is 5 miles (8 km) below the surface. On average, the Atlantic has the warmest and saltiest waters of any ocean. Before regular shipping routes were established, the Atlantic isolated the Americas from the countries of Europe, but today it is crossed by some of the world's most important trade routes. The North Atlantic has always been one of the world's richest fishing grounds, but it has been overfished, and fish stocks are now dangerously low.

Puffins breed on rocky islands, like the Faeroes.

FISHING

Catches of cod, herring, and haddock in the North Atlantic have been severely reduced by overfishing. Fishing fleets must now travel long distances and remain at sea for months at a time. The fish are processed on the fleet's factory ship to keep them fresh. Look for ➤

LAND OF ICE AND FIRE

There are more than 100 volcanoes on Iceland. Many of them are still active. Beneath the island's harsh, rocky surface lie vast natural heat reserves. This energy is used to provide hot water and central heating for much of the population. Iceland's economy is based on fishing, which accounts for about 70 percent of its exports.

WHALING

Whaling has been going on in the world's oceans for hundreds of years. But with the invention of the explosive-tipped harpoon, catches increased rapidly. Today some species of whales are threatened with extinction. Attempts are being made to ban whaling worldwide until numbers recover. Look for ➤

TIDAL ENERGY

Electricity can be generated from the sea in areas where there is a big difference between high and low tide levels. A barrage, like this one at La Rance in France, has to be built across the estuary. Water passing backward and forward through the barrage drives the turbines. Look for ⚡

Tomatoes and other fruit are grown in the warm climate of the Canary Islands.

ICELAND
POP: 300,000

CAPE VERDE
POP: 400,000

NATO

The North Atlantic Treaty Organization (NATO) is an association of North American and European countries established in 1949 to defend its members – principally against the former Soviet Union. Look for ⚔

British aircraft carrier

An extinct volcano on an island in the West Indies.

ARCTIC OCEAN

Greenland

EUROPE

GREENLAND SEA

ICELAND
Reykjavik

FAEROE ISLANDS
(Denmark)

Rockall
(UK)

NORTH
SEA

Murmansk

Tromsø
Narvik

Kristiansund
Ålesund
Bergen
Haugesund
Stavanger
Skagen
Esbjerg
Grimsby
Aberdeen

Rotterdam
Boulogne
La Rance
Lorient
Marseille

BALTIC SEA
Liepāja

Bremerhaven

Genoa
Livorno
Naples

Gibraltar
Casablanca
Safi

Porto

Azores
(Portugal)

Madeira
(Portugal)

Canary Islands
(Spain)

BLACK SEA

MEDITERRANEAN SEA

Algiers
Annaba
Sfax

Port Said
Nile

AFRICA

NORTH AMERICA

Hudson Bay

Baffin Bay

Davis Strait

Denmark Strait

LABRADOR SEA

C. Farewell

Newfoundland
St John's
Newfoundland Basin
Grand Banks
Halifax

Bay of Fundy
Saint John
Portland
Gloucester
New York City
Baltimore

St. Lawrence

New Orleans

Gulf of Mexico

Mississippi

Bermuda
(UK)

North American Basin

West Indies

ATLANTIC OCEAN

North-Eastern Atlantic Basin

Mid-Atlantic Ridge

SARGASSO SEA

Canary Basin

TOURISM

A number of islands in the Atlantic, including the Canaries and Madeira, are great tourist attractions, especially during winter in the Northern Hemisphere. The Canaries are a chain of seven mountainous islands; some areas are green and lush, others volcanic. The volcanic lava produces dramatic black landscapes. Look for 🏖

SAILING

Areas of the Atlantic have become pleasure grounds. Sailing is one of the main activities, especially in the warm seas of the Caribbean. Long-distance races are increasingly popular, some of them transatlantic. Boats range from yachts sailed single-handed to ships like this tea clipper, sailed by large crews.

CABLES

Cables snake across the ocean floor carrying many forms of modern communication, such as telephone calls and fax messages. The first transatlantic cable was laid in 1866. The cables are laid by special ships, like this one in the North Atlantic.

Lobsters are caught in lobster pots baited with dead fish.

Massive icebergs drift among the pack ice, a threat to shipping in the Atlantic.

SARGASSO SEA

At the center of three great North Atlantic currents lies the Sargasso Sea – an area of calm water, covered with *sargassum* weed. Sailors once believed their ships would be trapped by the weeds.

Fish like these live among the sargassum weed

POLLUTION

There are very few laws to control the way the world's oceans are used. The North Atlantic is one of the busiest and most polluted oceans. Many ships discharge oil and chemicals and dump radio-active waste. Some stretches of the northeast coast of America are so polluted that signs warn people not to swim. Plastic containers litter the world's coasts. International action to control this pollution is long overdue. Look for 🗑

An isolated settlement on the island of West Falkland in the South Atlantic.

SALMON

The early years of an Atlantic salmon are spent in the river where it was born. Then it swims down-river to the ocean. It rapidly gains weight in the rich feeding grounds of the North Atlantic. When it is ready to breed, the salmon's amazing homing ability enables it to return to its native river. Here, on their long, hard journey upriver, salmon negotiate a waterfall. Few salmon survive this endurance test to breed a second time.

KEYBOX

Underwater wrecks: Marine archaeology and location of wrecks was greatly advanced by the development of deep-sea diving equipment. Look for ⚓

Pollution: Oil rig blowouts and spills from oil tankers along the coastlines and around the Gulf of Mexico are a major problem in the Atlantic. Look for 🗑

Hurricane: The warm Atlantic waters off the north coast of Brazil are the gathering grounds for hurricanes, which then sweep northwestward. Look for 🌀

⚡	Alternative power
🎣 Fishing	🏖 Tourism
🚢 Fishing ports	‖‖ Military bases
⚓ Oil	🐋 Whales
◖ Gas	

Wild boar
Sus scrofa
Height: 3 ft (1 m)

Stag beetle
Lucanus cervus
Length: 3 in (8 cm)

European badger
Meles meles
Length: 3ft (1 m)

EUROPE

EUROPE, THE SMALLEST CONTINENT after Australia, is less than half the size of North America and a quarter that of Asia. Yet it has a remarkable variety of climates, landforms and types of vegetation. Europe's main mountain ranges, including the Pyrenees and the Alps, roughly divide the continent north and south. They form a barrier that protects the south from the cold winds that blow from the north during winter. As a result, the south is much warmer and drier than the cool, wet, heavily forested north. Europe has an irregular shape, with many interlocking fingers of land and sea. Because much of the land is close to the sea, coastal areas have fewer temperature extremes. Currents also affect the climate. Thanks to the powerful Gulf Stream, which brings immense amounts of warm water northward from the Equator, even seas within the Arctic Circle stay ice-free throughout the year.

The Trunk murex is found throughout the Mediterranean region.

ARCTIC OCEAN

Nansen Basin

Franz Josef Land

80°

Svalbard

EURASIAN PLATE
NORTH AMERICAN PLATE

Norwegian Basin

BARENTS SEA

KARA SEA

Novaya Zemlya

Murmansk Rise

Pechora

KOLA PENINSULA

URAL MOUNTAINS

Arctic Circle

Voring Plateau

6,959ft

N. Dvina

Faeroe Shelf

Faeroe Is.

Shetland

60°

Orkney

L. Vanern

Gulf of Finland

L. Onega

L. Ladoga

NORWEGIAN SEA

SCANDINAVIA

KJOLEN MTS.

Gulf of Bothnia

BALTIC SEA

NORTH EUROPEAN PLAIN

ATLANTIC

4,410ft
GRAMPIAN MTS.

NORTH SEA

JUTLAND

Dvina

Volga

Ural

Ireland

2,930ft

Britain

Thames

Vistula

Oder

Don

Celtic Shelf

English Channel

Seine

Loire

Rhine

Meuse

Danube

Elbe

E U R O P E

Dnieper

Volga Delta

8,211ft
CARPATHIANS

CASPIAN

SEA OF AZOV

Biscay Plain

A

Bay of Biscay

Garonne

ALPS

L. Constance

L. Geneva
Mont Blanc
15,771ft
MASSIF CENTRAL

Dom 14,912ft
Monte Rosa 15,204ft
Matterhorn
14,689ft

Rhône

Po
Delta
Po

L. Balaton

HUNGARIAN PLAIN

Tisza

TRANSYLVANIAN ALPS

8,261ft

Danube

CRIMEA

B

Kerch Strait

El'brus
18,511ft

CAUCASUS MTS.

BLACK SEA

C. Finisterre

CORDILLERA CANTABRICA

8,088ft

PYRENEES

11,168 ft

Ebro

Rhône Delta
Gulf of Lions

Corsica

DINARIC ALPS

APENNINES

ADRIATIC SEA

9,554ft

BALKAN MTS.
8,274ft

RHODOPE MTS.

7,796ft
9,597ft

PINDUS MTS.

AEGEAN SEA

ANATOLIA

40°

Douro

IBERIA

Tagus MESETA

Guadalquivir

C. St. Vincent

C. Trafalgar

Strait of Gibraltar

Balearic Is.

Sardinia

TYRRHENIAN SEA

Vesuvius
4,190ft

Sicily
Stromboli
3,038ft
Etna
11,054ft

Strait of Messina

IONIAN SEA

2,054ft

Santorini
1,857ft

Crete

Cyprus

Madeira Ridge

MEDITERRANEAN

EURASIAN PLATE
AFRICAN PLATE

SEA

AFRICA

0°

Gulf of Sirte

20°

Siberian tit
Parus cinctus
Length: 5 in (13 cm)

Green toad
Bufo viridis
Length: 4 in (10 cm)

Osprey
Pandion haliaetus
Wingspan: 5 ft (1.6 m)

BOGLANDS
Bogs cover many of northern
Europe's wettest areas. Mosses and
reeds are among the few plants that
grow in waterlogged soils. Wetlands
take thousands of years to develop,
because plants grow so slowly there.

WAVE POWER
Waves can wear away the
shore, creating odd land-
forms. This seastack off the
Orkneys in the British Isles
is 450 ft (135 m) high.

Ammonites, fossil
relatives of today's
octopus, were once found
in Europe. They died out
65 million years ago.

PIONEERING BIRCH
Light-loving birches are
often the first trees to appear
on open land. Although quick
to grow, they are short-lived.
After a few years, birches are
replaced by trees that can
survive shade, such as oaks.

English oak
Quercus robur
Height: 130 ft (40 m)

BARE MOUNTAIN
Ice, rain, wind, and gravity strip
steep slopes of all soil. Rocks pile
up at the foot of peaks, where
plants can take root.

FJORDS
Glaciers have cut hundreds of narrow
inlets, or fjords, into Scandinavia's
Atlantic coastline. The water in the
inlet is calmer than in the open sea.

NEEDLELEAF FOREST
Cone-bearing trees such as
pines, larches, and firs cover
Scandinavia. Most are
evergreen: they keep their
needlelike leaves even when
covered in snow for many
months of the year.

TREELESS TUNDRA
Arctic summers are so cool
that only the topmost layer of
frozen soil thaws. Only
shallow-rooted plants can
survive in the tundra.

Pine marten
Martes martes
Length: 20 in (52 cm)

ANCIENT WOODLANDS
Relics of Europe's ancient forests,
such as these oaks stunted by the
rain and wind, are found only in a
few valleys in southwest Britain.

This fossil of *Stauranderaster*,
a starfish once found in
this region, dates from
around 70 million
years ago.

DRY SOUTH
Crete is a mountainous
Mediterranean island
with hot dry summers.
Many plants survive the
summer as underground
bulbs, blooming briefly
in the wet spring.

YOUNG MOUNTAINS
The Alps include some of western Europe's
highest mountains. They are part of an almost
continuous belt that stretches from the Pyrenees
in the west to the Himalayas in Asia. The Alps
are still rising because of plate movements in
the Mediterranean region.

Sweetbriar
Rosa rubiginosa
Height: 10 ft (3 m)

CROSS-SECTION THROUGH EUROPE

Massif Central
Bay of Biscay
Atlantic Ocean
Alps
Dinaric Alps
Adriatic Sea
Hungarian Plain
Transylvanian Alps
Black Sea
Crimea
Kerch Strait

9,843 (3,000)
0 Sea level
-14,764 (-4,500)
Feet (meters)

A
Length: 4,500 km (2,800 miles)
B

KEY TO SYMBOLS

▲ Mountain
△ Volcano
Mangroves
Wetlands
Coral reef
Plate margins showing
direction of movement

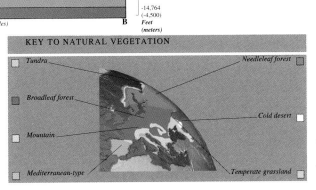

KEY TO NATURAL VEGETATION

Tundra
Needleleaf forest
Broadleaf forest
Cold desert
Mountain
Mediterranean-type
Temperate grassland

Spanish lynx
Felis lynx
Length: 4 ft (1.3 m)

SCANDINAVIA AND FINLAND

THE SCANDINAVIAN COUNTRIES of Norway, Sweden, and Denmark and neighboring Finland are situated around the Baltic Sea in northern Europe. During past ice ages, glaciers gouged and scoured the land, leaving deep fjords, lakes, and valleys in their wake. Much of Norway and Sweden and nearly two-thirds of Finland is covered by dense forests of pine, spruce, and birch trees. In the far north, winters are long and dark, and snow falls for about eight months of the year. Most Swedish people live in the central lowlands. Norway's economy depends on its shipbuilding, fishing, and merchant fleets. Denmark is flat and low-lying, with abundant rainfall and excellent farmland. The Finnish people originally came from the east, via Russia, and consequently differ from the Scandinavians both in language and culture. All four countries have small populations, are highly industrialized, and enjoy some of the highest standards of living in the world.

A NORWEGIAN FJORD
Norway is so mountainous that only three percent of the land can be cultivated. Long inlets of sea, called fjords, cut into Norway's west coast. The best farmland is found around the head of the fjords and in the lowland areas around them. Over 70 percent of Norway's population lives in cities, many in towns situated along the sheltered fjords.

Deep water enables ships to reach far inland

Fish farming of salmon sheltered waters

Rough upland grazing for sheep and goats

Coastal fish communities are declinin

Meadow crops grown for livestock

Cultivation limited to warm, south-facing slopes

Coastal islan form natural breakwaters

NORWAY
POP: 4,382,000

The still waters a Norwegian fjord.

FISHING
Because Norway has little farmland, fishing has always been a vital source of food. Today, about 95 percent of the total catch is processed; about half is made into fishmeal and oil. Fish farming is on the increase, especially of salmon in the fjords. Look for

Vast schools of herring gather in the seas around Scandinavia

LAPLAND
Lapland is a land of tundra, forests, and lakes. Here the *Samer*, or Lapps, still herd reindeer for their meat and milk. Development in the north now threatens their way of life.

Fantoft Church, Bergen

STAVE CHURCHES
The wooden stave churches of Norway were built between AD 1000 and 1300. There were once 600 of them, but today only 25 are still standing. A stave church has a stone foundation with a wooden frame on top. The four wooden corner posts are called staves. Further wooden extensions can be added to the basic framework.

Lego building blocks were invented in Denmark.

SKIING
For thousands of years skiing has been the most efficient way of crossing deep snow on foot. This region is often thought to be the original home of skiing – in fact, "ski" is the Norwegian word for a strip of wood. Long-distance cross-country skiing, or *langlaufen*, is a popular sport in Norway, Finland, and Sweden.

SMÖRGÅSBORD
Smörgåsbord means "sandwich table" in Swedish. Other countries in this region have their own versions, but the idea is the same: a great spread of local delicacies, served cold on bread, which can include dishes such as reindeer, fish, cheese, and salad.

Scrambled eggs
Prawns
Caviar
Asparagus
Smoked salmon

KEYBOX

Hydroelectric power The region's mountainous terrain enables the majority of its electricity to be supplied by HEP. Look for

Bridges: Tunnels and bridges now link the Danish islands of Fyn and Sjaelland. Linking Denmark and Sweden is under discussion. Look for

🐂	Cattle		Fishing
🐷	Pigs		Fishing port
🌾	Cereals		Mining
🌲	Timber		Industrial center

COPENHAGEN
Copenhagen's fine natural harbor and position at the main entrance to the Baltic Sea helped it become a major port and Denmark's capital city. The city's tiny shops, cobbled streets, museums, and cafés attract more than a million tourists each year.

DANISH AGRICULTURE
Two-thirds of the total area of Denmark is used for farming. Denmark exports agricultural products all over the world. The main products are bacon, dairy products, cereals, and beef. Cereals are widely grown, but mainly as fodder for pigs. Look for

Danish bacon for export

DENMARK
POP: 5,203,000

Hitra
Smøla
Vanadium
Trondhei
Molde
Iron
Ålesund
Nordfjord
Sogne Fjord
Hermansverk
Bergen
Gjøvik
L. Mjøsa
Hardanger Fjord
Oats
Haugesund
Honefoss
OSL
Bokna Fjord
Drammen
Kongsberg
Stavanger
Ora
Porsgrunn
Dairy
Fredri
Sandnes
Titanium
Dairy
Iron
Arendal
Oslo Fjord
Hø
Kristiansand
D
Skagerrak
Uddevalla
Trollhätt

DENMARK
Hjørring
Frederikshavn
Ålborg
Kattegat
Holstebro
Dairy
Rye
Randers
Halmst
Ringkøbing
JUTLAND
Århus
Hälsingborg
Barley
Horsens
Helsingor
Esbjerg
Vejle
COPENHAGEN
Ribe
Odense
Slagelse
Abenrå
Fyn
Naestved
Sjaellar
Sønderborg
Nakskov
Barley
Nykøbing
GERMANY

A B C D E F

## Map labels

ARCTIC OCEAN
WEGIAN SEA
RUSSIAN FEDERATION
BALTIC SEA
Gulf of Bothnia
Gulf of Finland

North Cape
Magerøy
Sørøya
Hammerfest
Vardø
Vadsø
Varanger Fjord
Kirkenes
Porsangen
Karasjok
L. Inari
Ringvassøy
Tromsø
Senja
Tana
Ivalo
Harstad
Hinnøya
Lofoten Vesterålen
Narvik
Sodankylä
Vestfjorden
L. Torne
Muonio
Ounas
Kemijärvi
Bodø
Copper
Kiruna
Torne
Iron
Rovaniemi
Mo i Rana
Iron
Gällivare
Iron
Kuusamo
Donna
Iron
Lead
Jokkmokk
Chromium Kemi
Kemi
Vanadium
Zinc
L.Uddjaur
Tornio
Lule
Vindel
Arvidsjaur
Lulea
Oulu
Storuman
Piteå
Oulu
Zinc
Copper
Silver
L. Oulu
Kajaani
Lead
Pite
Skellefteå
Vanadium
Gold
Zinc
Copper
Umeå
Iron
Titanium
Kokkola
Copper
Iisalmi
Jakobstad
L. Pielinen
Östersund
Örnsköldsvik
Vaasa
Kuopio
Cobalt
Lake Stor
Seinäjoki
Joensuu
Uranium
Härnösand
Nickel
L. Ori
Sundsvall
Varkaus
Jyväskylä
Savonlinna
Hudiksvall
L. Saimaa
Mora
Mikkeli
Pori
Tampere
Imatra
Rauma
Valkeakoski
Kuusankoski
Lappeenranta
Falun
Hameenlinna
Borlänge
Sandviken
Gävle
Riihimäki
Kouvola
Åland Is.
Hyvinkää
Barley
Kotka
Salo
Järvenpää
Turku
Maarianhamina
Kimito
Wheat
HELSINKI
Oats
Iron
Uppsala
Barley
Västerås
Norrtälje
Dairy
Örebro
STOCKHOLM
Huddinge
Lead
Zinc
Wheat
Motala
Nyköping
Norrköping
Linköping
L. Vatter
nköping
Fårö
Västervik
Oats
Visby
Oskarshamn
Gotland
Växjö
Öland
Kalmar
Karlskrona

SWEDEN
POP: 8,700,000

FINLAND
POP: 5,059,000

MIDNIGHT SUN
This may look like an ordinary sunset, but this photo of Bodø in Norway was taken at midnight. In the far north of this region, the sun never sets in midsummer. The farther north you travel, the longer the period of midnight sun. In winter, in Lapland, the sun remains below the horizon for a week; in the far north, this period of darkness lasts two months.

SAUNA BATHS
Ladle
Wooden bucket
Some 1,000 years ago the Finns invented the steam bath, or *sauna*, as a way of cleansing and relaxing the body. The steam is produced by throwing water over hot stones. A plunge in an icy pool or snowdrift completes the process. The *sauna* has become a national institution.

TIMBER
Finland, Norway, and Sweden are heavily forested. The timber is used in many ways, such as building, furniture, and crafts. All three countries have large wood-pulp, paper, and board industries. Finland and Sweden are now among the world's largest exporters of these products. This Swedish child's chair is cleverly designed to grow with the child. Look for ⌐

SCANDINAVIAN DESIGN
Glass fig from Finland
Glass pear from Finland
Glass eggplant from Sweden
Scandinavians have a highly developed sense of design which extends to everyday objects like stereo equipment, furniture, and glass. Sweden and Finland are well known for their glassware, and the industry attracts many famous artists who create new designs.

Trolls are characters in Scandinavian folklore.

A forest bordering one of Finland's many lakes.

CAR MANUFACTURE
A classic Volvo sedan
For its size, Sweden has a large number of highly successful multinational companies. Two examples are the motor manufacturers, Volvo and Saab-Scania, whose cars and trucks are widely exported. Volvo workers build cars in teams. The company pioneered this system to improve working conditions.

Stockholm, Sweden's capital and an important seaport.

The carved prow of a Viking ship found in Norway.

NORWEGIAN OIL
Since oil was discovered in the North Sea in the 1970s, Norway has become self-sufficient in natural gas and oil. These account for over half the country's export earnings. It is also a world leader in drilling platforms and tankers.

THE BRITISH ISLES

THE BRITISH ISLES CONSIST OF TWO large islands – Great Britain and Ireland – surrounded by many smaller ones. They are divided into two countries: the United Kingdom (UK), often known as Britain, and Ireland. At the end of the 18th century, the UK became the first country in the world to undergo an industrial revolution. It became the world's leading manufacturing and trading nation and built up an empire that covered more than a quarter of the world. The UK's traditional industries, including coal mining, textiles, and car manufacturing, have declined in recent years, but service industries such as banking and insurance have been extremely successful. Ireland, which became independent from the UK in 1921, is still a mainly rural country, and many Irish people make their living from farming. However, tourism and high-tech industries like computers and pharmaceuticals are increasingly important. The UK and Ireland still have close trading links, and many Irish people go to the UK to find work.

OIL

Rich reserves of both oil and natural gas were found under the North Sea in the 1960s. By the late 1970s, natural gas was being piped to most homes, factories and businesses in the UK. Massive oil rigs were moored in the North Sea, and wells were dug by drilling into the ocean bed below the platforms. Oil rigs and onshore refineries brought employment to many areas, especially in eastern Scotland. But oil reserves are being steadily used up, and oil production is now in decline. Look for ▮

Bright red letter boxes are a common sight on British streets.

FISHING

The waters of the north-east Atlantic are among the world's richest fishing grounds, well stocked with mackerel, herring, cod, haddock, and shellfish. The British Isles has many fishing ports, like this one in northeastern England. But EU regulations, designed to reduce catches and conserve fish stocks, are causing widespread discontent amongst fishermen. Look for ⚓

INDUSTRY

Many Japanese companies, car and electronics manufacturers in particular, are now based in the UK, attracted by a skilled labor force and access to European markets. Britain's traditional industries – such as textiles, steel, and pottery – have been joined by newer, high-tech industries. Look for ✈

AEROSPACE

UK firms design and build a wide range of civil and military aircraft. Perhaps the most famous is Concorde, a supersonic jet created in partnership with France. Recently, the aerospace industry has been badly hit by world recession, and UK companies have had to develop products in other areas, such as electronics and telecommunications. Look for ✈

The Concorde supersonic jet

TARTAN TOURISM

Tourism is an important source of income for Scotland. People come to enjoy the beautiful highland scenery and visit the ancient castles. For centuries, Scotland was dominated by struggles between rival families, known as clans. Today one of the most popular tourist souvenirs is tartan – textiles woven in the colors of the clans.

Tartan scarf

Scottish shortbread

A deep inlet of water – or loch – in northern Scotland.

"THE TROUBLES"

When British Protestants settled in Ireland in the 17th century, they came into conflict with Irish Catholics, whose land they had seized. In 1921, the Protestant North (Ulster) refused to join the independent South. Catholics were discriminated against in jobs and housing, and violence erupted in the 1960s. British troops were sent to police the province.

AGRICULTURE AND INDUSTRY

Farming has always been Ireland's principal source of income. Dairy products, beef, and potatoes are still important, but recently the number of high-tech industries has increased.

Irish butter

Shetland
Lerwick

Orkney
Kirkwall
Stromness
Thurso

C. Wrath
Ullapool
Loch Shin
Loch Ness
Inverness
Moray Firth
Elgin
Fraserburgh
Peterhead
Aberdeen
Dee

Beef
Barley
Oats

SCOTLAND

Dundee
Perth
Firth of Forth
Edinburgh
Tweed

Loch Lomond
Grangemouth
Glasgow
Clyde
Greenock

Fort William
Mallag
Loch Linnhe
Oban

Lewis
Stornoway
Harris
North Minch
Little Minch
North Uist
South Uist
Benbecula
Barra

Outer Hebrides

Skye
Canna
Rum
Eigg
Muck
Coll
Tiree
Mull
Colonsay
Jura
Islay
Kintyre
Arran

ATLANTIC OCEAN

Lough Foyle

NORTH SEA

LONDON

The Romans founded the town they called Londinium on the Thames River in AD 43. The UK's capital is now a huge, sprawling city with seven million inhabitants. London is the country's center of finance, politics, law, and culture, and contains many famous historical buildings, shops, museums, and theaters.

Big Ben

The Houses of Parliament, London

MULTICULTURAL BRITAIN

Since the 1960s, the UK has become an increasingly multicultural society. Large numbers of immigrants have come to the UK from former colonies in Africa, the Caribbean, and Asia and have greatly enriched British culture with their own traditions.

HIGH FINANCE

The skyscrapers and office blocks that surround St. Paul's Cathedral in the City of London are home to one of the world's biggest financial centers. City companies specialize in banking and insurance and lead the world in foreign currency deals. The City covers only a small area, but every day it is filled with more than half a million office workers.

Tea, served with milk, is Britain's national drink.

FARMING

About three-quarters of the land in the UK is used for farming. The crops vary from region to region and reflect the country's varied climate and soils. Barley, wheat, vegetables, and sugar beets are the main crops in the east of the country, while beef and dairy farming is a specialty in the west.

SPORT

Many sports which are now played all over the world originated in the UK. Rugby, cricket, and golf were all British inventions, while the rules of modern soccer were established on the sports fields of English schools.

Soccer ball

Cricket ball

Rugby ball

The rocky coast of Cornwall in southwest England.

Isles of Scilly

Dublin's fine O'Connell bridge over the Liffey R.

English beers are made from barley, malt, and hops.

UNITED KINGDOM
POP: 58,395,000

IRELAND
POP: 3,462,000

NORTH SEA

ENGLISH CHANNEL

IRISH SEA

St George's Channel

KEYBOX

High-tech industry: Companies making scientific instruments, electronics, and computers are based in southern England, Scotland and Ireland. Look for ▢

Tourism: Millions of visitors come to the UK each year to see palaces, castles, ancient monuments, cathedrals, and museums. Look for ▨

Tunnel: The Channel Tunnel, linking England and France, is 31 miles (50 km) long. Passenger and freight trains use the tunnel.

Airport: Heathrow, 12 miles (20 km) from London, is the world's busiest international airport. It handles 38 million passengers a year. Look for ✈

Cattle		Coal	
Sheep		Industrial center	
Cereals		Oil refining	
Market gardening		Aerospace industry	
Fishing port		Vehicle manufacture	

MILES

KM

N

SPAIN AND PORTUGAL

SPAIN AND PORTUGAL are located on the Iberian Peninsula, which is cut off from the rest of Europe by the Pyrénées. This isolation, combined with the region's closeness to Africa and the Atlantic Ocean, has shaped the history of the two countries. The Moors, an Islamic people from North Africa, occupied the peninsula in the 8th century AD, leaving an Islamic legacy that is still evident today. In 1492 the Moors were finally expelled from Catholic Spain. The oceangoing Spanish and Portuguese took the lead in exploring and colonizing the New World, and both nations acquired substantial overseas empires. During this era, Portugal was ruled by Spain from about 1580 to 1640. Eventually, both nations lost most of their colonies, and their once-great wealth and power declined. Spain was torn apart by a vicious civil war from 1936-39, and right-wing dictators ruled both Spain and Portugal for much of the 20th century. In the 1970s, both countries emerged as modern democracies and have since experienced rapid economic growth, benefiting from their membership in the European Union. Today, their economies are dominated by tourism and agriculture, although Spanish industry is expanding rapidly.

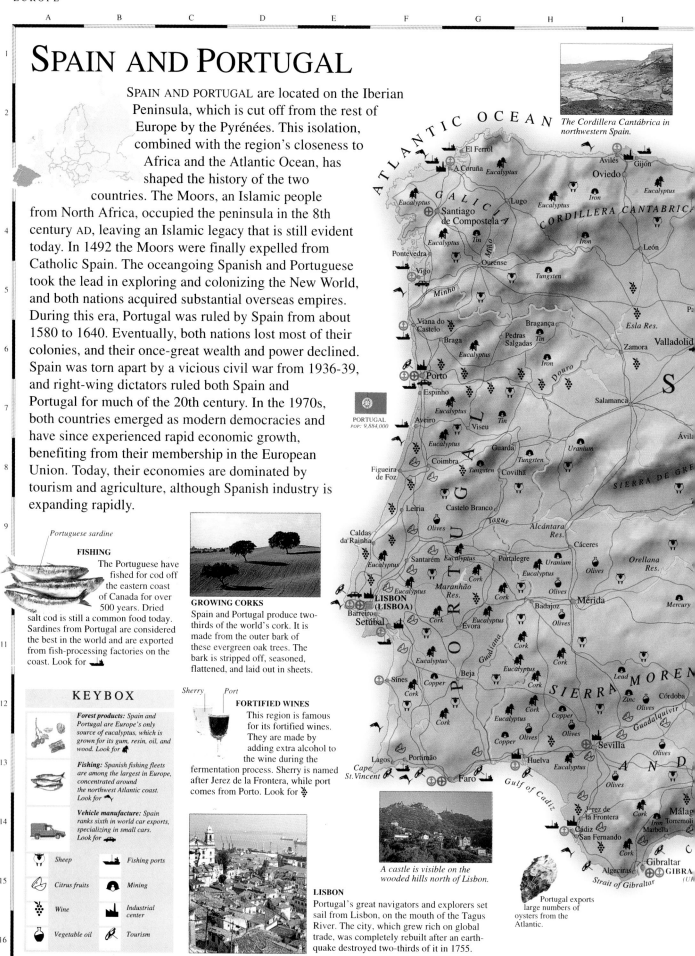

The Cordillera Cantábrica in northwestern Spain.

PORTUGAL
POP: 9,884,000

FISHING

Portuguese sardine

The Portuguese have fished for cod off the eastern coast of Canada for over 500 years. Dried salt cod is still a common food today. Sardines from Portugal are considered the best in the world and are exported from fish-processing factories on the coast. Look for

GROWING CORKS

Spain and Portugal produce two-thirds of the world's cork. It is made from the outer bark of these evergreen oak trees. The bark is stripped off, seasoned, flattened, and laid out in sheets.

FORTIFIED WINES

Sherry   Port

This region is famous for its fortified wines. They are made by adding extra alcohol to the wine during the fermentation process. Sherry is named after Jerez de la Frontera, while port comes from Porto. Look for

KEYBOX

Forest products: *Spain and Portugal are Europe's only source of eucalyptus, which is grown for its gum, resin, oil, and wood. Look for*

Fishing: *Spanish fishing fleets are among the largest in Europe, concentrated around the northwest Atlantic coast. Look for*

Vehicle manufacture: *Spain ranks sixth in world car exports, specializing in small cars. Look for*

🐑	Sheep	⛴	Fishing ports
	Citrus fruits		Mining
	Wine	🏭	Industrial center
	Vegetable oil		Tourism

LISBON

Portugal's great navigators and explorers set sail from Lisbon, on the mouth of the Tagus River. The city, which grew rich on global trade, was completely rebuilt after an earth-quake destroyed two-thirds of it in 1755.

A castle is visible on the wooded hills north of Lisbon.

Portugal exports large numbers of oysters from the Atlantic.

OLIVES

The deep fertile soils and warm climate of parts of Spain, especially Jaén in the southeast, are ideal for olive cultivation. Spain is one of the world's leading olive producers. Look for

IBERIAN INDUSTRY

Spain's industries are concentrated around the northern ports such as Bilbao and around the cities of Madrid and Barcelona. The main industries are shipbuilding, iron, steel, and petrochemicals, although food processing and textiles are also important. Spain is the fourth-largest steel exporter in the world. Look for

The classical guitar is Spain's national instrument.

FISH DISHES

Paella is a classic Spanish dish from the Valencia region, where rice is grown. It consists of a variety of meat, fish, fresh vegetables, and saffron-flavored rice, simmered in a stock. The Spanish eat a lot of fish, and fish stew is another popular dish. Spain is also famous for its cured meats, especially ham, or *jamón serrano*.

ORANGES

Oranges were introduced to Spain by the Moors in about the 9th century AD. They are grown along the Mediterranean coast and are an important export. The best Spanish oranges come from Valencia. Oranges from Seville are used for making fine marmalade. Look for

Many tourists visit the beautiful Balearic Islands.

TOURISM

Fifty million visitors a year visit Spain's Mediterranean coast alone, and tourism accounts for 10 percent of Spain's income. But large numbers of high-rise hotels have spoiled some stretches of the coastline, and popular beaches are often overcrowded. Look for

FLAMENCO

Flamenco music and dance, developed by the Andalusian gypsies, are the major folk arts of Spain. Flamenco songs deal with the entire range of human emotion, from despair to ecstasy, and are performed with a passionate intensity. Dancers dress in traditional costume and accompany themselves on castanets and guitars.

Castanets

Flamenco dancer's fan and comb

CATHOLICISM

Like the Portuguese, the Spanish blend Roman Catholicism with customs and traditions dating back to pre-Christian times. Their *fiestas* combine religious ceremonies with music and dancing.

THE ALHAMBRA

The Alhambra, at Granada in southern Spain, is a Moorish palace and fortress built during the 13th and 14th centuries. It was the Moors' last stronghold in Spain. It is a beautiful example of Moorish architecture, famous for its delicately carved stone, brilliantly patterned mosaics and tiles, and alabaster fountains.

BULLFIGHTING

In Spain, bullfighting is a national sport. During a bullfight, brightly colored capes are fluttered to tempt the bull to charge. When it charges, the matador sticks long, pointed barbs into the bull's shoulders. Once it is exhausted, the matador uses his sword to kill the bull, exposing himself to mortal danger.

ibraltar has been a British ·lony sine the 18th century.

SPAIN
POP: 39,664,000

FRANCE

FOR CENTURIES FRANCE has played a central role in European civilization. Reminders of its long history can be found throughout the land: prehistoric cave dwellings, Roman amphitheaters, medieval cathedrals and castles, and the 17th- and 18th-century palaces of the powerful French monarchs. The French Revolution of 1789 swept away the monarchy and changed the face of France forever. The country survived the Napoleonic Wars and occupation during World Wars I and II, and now has a thriving economy based on farming and industry. France is a land of varied scenery and strong regional traditions – the only country which belongs to both northern and southern Europe. Farming is still important, but many people have moved from the country to the cities. France still administers a number of overseas territories, all that remain of its once widespread empire. Today, France's population includes immigrants from its former colonies, especially Muslims from North Africa. France is one of the most enthusiastic members of the European Union.

PARIS

Paris, the capital of France, is the largest and most important city in the country. It lies on both banks of the Seine River. One of the world's great cities, Paris contains magnificent buildings, art treasures, and elegant shops. The wrought-iron Eiffel Tower, the symbol of Paris, looms above the city.

A cyclist in the *Tour de France*, the world's most famous bicycle race.

FRANCE
POP: 57,800,000

AGRICULTURE

France is a mainly rural country producing a wide range of farm products. Some farms still use traditional methods, but modern technology has transformed regions like the Paris Basin, where cereals are grown on a large scale. Look for ✿

THE AIRBUS

Developing new aircraft is so costly that sometimes several countries form a company together to share the costs. One example is Airbus Industrie: the main factory is at Toulouse, but costs are shared by France, Germany, the UK, and Spain. With successful aircraft already flying, Airbus Industrie is planning a jumbo jet. Look for ✈

KEYBOX

Market gardening: In the northwest, the mild climate and sheltered conditions are ideal for growing early vegetables, called primeurs. Look for ☙

Nuclear power: Lacking its own energy sources, France has developed its nuclear power industry. It now produces 70% of its electricity. Look for ▬

Tourism: In the underdeveloped Mediterranean region, tourism has been encouraged by the construction of attractive holiday resorts. Look for ☂

Rail routes: France has Europe's largest rail network. Intercity trains (TGVs) travel at speeds of up to 186 miles (300 km) per hour. Look for 🚆

🧀	Cheese	⛏	Coal
🌾	Cereals	🏭	Industrial center
🍠	Sugar beets	✈	Aerospace industry
🍇	Wine	🚗	Vehicle manufacturing
⛏	Mining	⛷	Skiing

CHATEAUS

France has many beautiful historic buildings. Along the banks of the Loire River and its tributaries are royal palaces, or chateaus, built by the royalty of France from the 15th-17th centuries. Chambord, once a hunting lodge, has 440 rooms and 85 staircases. Fairy-tale palaces like these attract thousands of visitors each year.

Fields of sunflowers can be seen in many areas of France.

Head of garlic

Snail

Clove of garlic

Snails, served with butter and garlic, are a great French delicacy.

Camembert

CHEESE

France is famous for its cheese. Over 300 different varieties are made. Many, like Camembert, Roquefort, and Brie, are world famous and copied in many other countries. Each region has its traditional way of making and packaging its cheeses. Goat's and sheep's milk are used as well as cow's. Look for 🧀

Brie

The principality of Andorra is situated in the Pyrenees.

Cherbourg · Le Havre · St. Lô · Caen · Channel Islands (UK) · ENGLISH CHANNEL · Île d'Ouessant · Brest · St. Brieuc · St. Malo · Wheat · Oats · TGV · BRITTANY · Quimper · Barley · Oats · Wheat · Rennes · Laval · Iron · Lorient · Vannes · Barley · Angers · Loire · Belle Île · St. Nazaire · Nantes · ATLANTIC OCEAN · La Roche-sur-Yon · Wheat · Poitie · Les Sables d'Olonne · Wheat · TGV · La Rochelle · Charente · Wheat · Saintes · Angoulême · Barley · Dord · Bordeaux · Arcachon · Garonne · TGV · Corn · Mont-de-Ma · Bayonne · Corn · Pau · Corn · PYRE · NORMANDY

WINE

When the Romans occupied France 2,000 years ago, they planted vines. From these early beginnings, France became the center of world wine making. The wine's quality depends on the region, soil, and climate, and on the producer's skillful blending and fermentation. Champagne is produced in the area around Rheims. Look for ❦

Bottle of Champagne

A circular poster display, a common sight in Paris.

CAFÉ LIFE

In the late 17th century, when cafés first became fashionable in Paris, they were used as places to meet for a snack and to exchange news and gossip. The word café means "coffee" in French. Two centuries later, cafés have become popular throughout the world.

Perfume spray

FRENCH STYLE

The 14th-century French kings and their courts established a tradition of elegance and style which the French have maintained ever since. Paris is still the world's capital of haute couture – high fashion. French clothes designs, perfumes, and cosmetics are a major influence on the world's fashion industry.

FRENCH FOOD

The French place enormous importance on food and wine. Food can be just as delicious in small provincial restaurants as in Parisian ones. French cooks have created many great dishes which are widely imitated.

Fillet de Boeuf

French sedan

MOTOR VEHICLES

France has the second-largest vehicle industry in western Europe, producing about 3 million cars a year. Paris is the center of production, although companies are encouraged to open factories in other cities. Look for 🚗

An Alpine peak in southeastern France.

MONACO

Monaco is a tiny country situated on the Mediterranean coast. Its orchestra is larger than its army. Many people have settled in Monaco because of the lenient tax laws and the gambling facilities of Monte Carlo.

MONACO
POP: 31,000

The rugged landscape of the French island of Corsica.

Corsica
(France)

ANDORRA
LA VELLA

ANDORRA
POP: 58,000

0 25 50 75 100 125 150 KM
0 25 50 75 100 MILES

THE LOW COUNTRIES

BELGIUM, THE NETHERLANDS, and Luxembourg are the most densely populated countries in Europe. They are known as the "Low Countries" because much of the land is flat and low-lying. In the Netherlands, much of the land lies below sea level, and has been reclaimed from the sea over the centuries by ingenious technology. The marshy, drained soils are extremely fertile. All three countries enjoy high living standards, with well-developed industries and excellent rail, road, and waterway communications with the rest of Europe. During the course of their history, the Low Countries have often been the battleground between warring nations, and Belgium and Luxembourg only achieved independence in the 19th century. Belgium is still divided by language – Dutch is spoken in the north, while the Walloons in the south speak French. The northern Netherlands are mainly Protestant; the rest of the region is basically Roman Catholic. Today, the Low Countries are unswerving supporters of the European Union. The cities of Brussels, The Hague, and Luxembourg are all headquarters of important European institutions.

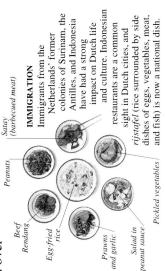

FLOWERS
The Netherlands is Europe's largest producer of flowers, and spectacular fields of spring flowers in full bloom are a major tourist attraction. Cut flowers are flown daily from the Netherlands to cities all over the world. Cultivation of bulbs such as crocuses, hyacinths, daffodils, and tulips is a speciality. Tulips have been grown here since about 1600, when they were introduced from Turkey and the Middle East. Look for 🌷

Tulip

IMMIGRATION
Immigrants from the Netherlands' former colonies of Surinam, the Antilles, and Indonesia have had a strong impact on Dutch life and culture. Indonesian restaurants are a common sight in Dutch cities, and *rijstafel* (rice surrounded by side dishes of eggs, vegetables, meat, and fish) is now a national dish.

Satay (barbecued meat)
Peanuts
Beef Rendang
Egg-fried rice
Prawns and garlic
Salad in peanut sauce
Pickled vegetables

The rind of Dutch Edam cheese is colored with anato dye.

FLOOD CONTROL
Much of the Netherlands lies below sea level, and is constantly at risk of flooding. Over the centuries, land has been painstakingly reclaimed from the sea. Barriers called dykes are built to keep the sea out, and water is drained and pumped into canals. Originally the water was pumped out by windmills, but now electric pumps are used. Sluice-gates control the flow of excess water.

DELFT TILE
Delft pottery has been made in the Netherlands since the 17th century. The technique of glazing pottery with tin, used in Delft, came to the Netherlands from the Middle East via Spain and Italy. This Delft tile is decorated with a windmill, a familiar sight in the Netherlands. There are about 1,000 windmills still standing today, dating mainly from the 18th and 19th centuries.

CITY OF CANALS
The Dutch capital, Amsterdam, is a city of islands built on swampy land. It is criss-crossed by 160 canals. Many of the city's finest gabled houses date from the 16th-18th centuries, when merchants grew rich from trade and exploration. Amsterdam is not only the country's historic center, it is also its second-largest port.

ROTTERDAM
Rotterdam is one of the world's largest ports, lying within a massive built-up and industrialized area called Randstad Holland. Rotterdam is situated near the mouth of the Rhine River, an important trade route. Imported oil is refined locally. The port also handles minerals, grain, timber, and coal.

Both Belgium and the Netherlands are major beer exporters.

NETHERLANDS
POP: 15,012,000

Map labels: GERMANY, Delfzijl, Winschoten, Beef, Wheat, Emmen, Assen, Groningen, Dairy, Hoogeveen, Almelo, Hengelo, Enschede, Schiermonnikoog, Leeuwarden, Drachten, Heerenveen, Meppel, Deventer, Ameland, IJssel, Zwolle, Harlingen, Apeldoorn, West Frisian Is., Terschelling, Flevoland, Lelystad, Harderwijk, Vlieland, WADDEN ZEE, IJSSELMEER, Hilversum, Hoorn, AMSTERDAM, Amstelveen, Texel, Purmerend, Zaanstad, Den Helder, Alkmaar, Velsen, IJmuiden, Haarlem, Leiden

DAIRY PRODUCTS

More than one-third of Dutch farmland is used for dairy production. Black-and-white Friesian cattle, which graze on the low-lying fertile land, are one of the finest dairy breeds in the world. The Netherlands exports more cheese than any other country. Cheese was originally made on a small scale in farmhouses, but today cheesemaking is highly mechanized. Look for ▼

HIGH TECHNOLOGY

All three countries have well-established electronics industries, making everything from razors to X-ray machines. Their position at the heart of Europe, good transport links, easy access to European markets and raw materials, and large pools of skilled labor, have helped to make high-technology industry a success.

LUXEMBOURG BANKING

Luxembourg is a center of international banking and finance. It is the headquarters of the European Investment Bank, and more than 100 major banks are based there. Financial services are fast becoming more important than Luxembourg's traditional steel-manufacturing industry.

The picturesque fortress of Vianden overlooking the Our River in Luxembourg.

DIAMONDS

Diamonds from Africa and Australia are cut, polished, and sold in the cities of Antwerp and Amsterdam. Most of the diamonds are used in industry for sawing, drilling, and grinding.

The medieval city of Bruges is famous for its canals and fine houses.

Flax, which is used to make linen, is grown on the flat plains of northern Belgium.

The medieval town hall at Leuven in Belgium.

Belgium, especially Brussels, is famous for its rich chocolates.

The EU flag is a symbol of unity in Europe

COMMUNITY CAPITAL

The EU (European Union) was set up in 1957 to encourage free trade between member nations and administer shared economic, social, and legal policies. There are 15 member nations. Brussels is the administrative capital of the EU, and Luxembourg is the headquarters of the Court of Justice and Investment Bank.

KEYBOX

Gas: Offshore reserves in the North Sea are the fifth largest in the world. Gas is the main domestic fuel in the Netherlands.

Dams: The Netherlands' Delta Project is the world's largest water control project. Five dams prevent flooding and provide fresh water. Look for ▥

Shipping canals: Most of Belgium's main inland industrial centers are linked with the North Sea ports and Antwerp by canals. Look for

Market gardening

Flowers

Industrial center

Cattle

Cereals

Sugar beet

BELGIUM POP: 10,042,000

LUXEMBOURG POP: 384,400

GERMANY

BELGIUM

FRANCE

LUXEMBOURG

Nijmegen
Venlo
Maas
Roermond
Oss
's-Hertogenbosch
Helmond
Eindhoven
Weert
Tilburg
Waalwijk
Breda
Roosendaal
Bergen-op-Zoom
Turnhout
Baarle-Hertog (Belgium)
Albert Canal
Antwerp
Dordrecht
Rotterdam
Overflakkee Delta Project
Oosterschelde
Westerschelde
Terneuzen
Flushing
Middelburg
Zeebrugge
Ostend
Bruges
Torhout
Roeselare
Ieper
Veurne
Ghent
Sint-Niklaas
Scheldt
Aalst
Ronse
Ath
Kortrijk
Mouscron
Tournai
Mechelen
BRUSSELS (BRUXELLES)
Leuven
Nivelles
Soignies
Mons
La Louvière
Gosselies
Charleroi
Samber
Hasselt
Tienen
Genk
Hasselt
Maastricht
Heerlen
Eupen
Verviers
Liège
Herstal
Seraing
Huy
Namur
Dinant
Meuse
Philippeville
Malmédy
St. Vith
Amblève
Ourthe
Marche-en-Famenne
Lesse
Bastogne
Neufchâteau
Arlon
Esch-sur-Alzette
LUXEMBOURG
Diekirch
Vianden
Our
Sûre
Moselle
Alzette

N

MILES
KM
0 10 25 50 75
0 25 40

65

GERMANY

SITUATED IN THE CENTER OF EUROPE, Germany is now the continent's leading economic power. In the past it has been an area of great conflict; it was not until 1871 that a patchwork of independent states, which had fought bitterly for centuries, were united under Prussian leadership to form Germany. In this century, Germany was defeated in two world wars. By 1945 the economy was shattered and the country divided between a Soviet-dominated communist East and a democratic West. The postwar years saw an amazing recovery in West Germany's economy. Natural advantages – a central position in Europe, large reserves of coal and iron, along with the construction of an efficient transportation system and the determination to succeed – have all helped to create a dynamic economy. The East, on the other hand, lagged behind. In 1989, the Soviet Union began to disintegrate, and communism collapsed throughout Eastern Europe. The two halves of Germany were reunified in 1990, but problems soon became apparent. West Germans resented the huge amounts of money invested in the East to bring it up to their standards. East Germans became impatient with the slow pace of change. These resentments have led to violence against refugees, immigrants, and "guest workers," many of whom have lived in Germany for most of their lives.

CARS
Germany is Europe's largest vehicle producer, specializing in high-quality cars. American and Japanese car companies are based here, too, attracted by the skilled workforce. Look for

BERLIN
At the end of World War II, Germany's capital city, Berlin, was divided between the four victorious Allies. In 1961, the Berlin Wall was built to separate the Russian sector from the other three. In 1989, the wall came down; East Germans streamed through this gate into West Berlin.

Brandenburg Gate

AGRICULTURE
Germany produces all its own food and is one of the world's main growers of sugar beets, barley, and rye. Oats, rye, and barley thrive in the mild, wet north, while wheat is grown in the warmer south. Look for

This decorated *stein*, or mug, is used for beer.

Green pastures and woodland on the flat Baltic coast.

DRESDEN
Once Dresden was a beautiful old city, with many 18th-century buildings. But in World War II it was devastated by Allied bombing. After extensive reconstruction, the city's historic buildings have now been restored to their former state.

Peppered salami

Salami

SAUSAGES
Sausages are Germany's favorite snack. There are many regional variations; Frankfurt has even given its name to the Frankfurter sausage. Germany also has over 200 varieties of bread.

A windmill in the fertile farmland of the northeast.

Many German towns have half-timbered buildings dating back to the Middle Ages.

NORTH SEA
BALTIC SEA
DENMARK
POLAND
NETHERLANDS
GERMANY
SAXONY
North Frisian Is.
East Frisian Is.
Sylt
Föhr
Nordstrand
Helgoland
Rügen
Fehmarn
Mecklenburg Bay
Kiel Bay

Stralsund
Greifswald
Rostock
Wismar
L. Schwerin
Schwerin
L. Müritz
Neubrandenburg
BERLIN
Potsdam
Brandenburg
Magdeburg
Dessau
Wittenberg
Frankfurt an der Oder
Cottbus
Kiel
Schleswig
Husum
Neumünster
Lübeck
Hamburg
Lüneburg
Celle
Hanover
Braunschweig
Wolfsburg
Salzgitter
Hildesheim
Cuxhaven
Bremerhaven
Bremen
Minden
Bielefeld
Paderborn
Osnabrück
Münster
Oldenburg
Wilhelmshaven
Emden

Kiel Canal
Mittelland Canal
Dortmund-Ems Canal
Oder
Elbe
Weser
Ems
Rhine

Wheat, Rye, Oats, Beef, Dairy, Potassium

66

OPTICAL SKILLS

Germany has a large number of optical instrument manufacturers who make cameras, microscopes, and telescopes. East Germany led the former Soviet bloc in this field. Since reunification, however, many of these companies in the East have closed down, as they were overstaffed and heavily subsidized and now cannot compete without government support.

BROWN COAL

In eastern Germany, large amounts of lignite (brown coal) are mined from vast open pits. Lignite is used for generating electricity. When burned, it causes severe pollution. Look for 🖤

PRECISION ENGINEERING

While heavy industry tends to be concentrated in north Germany, the south has become a center for the manufacture of special steels, cutlery, and precision instruments. This region lacks coal, so industry could not develop here until gas was piped in from the Netherlands. Look for ▫️

Flask used in chemical experiments

CHEMICALS

Over half a million people are employed in Germany's chemical industry. Germany is the leading chemical producer in Europe and still dominates world markets, despite competition from Asia. Raw materials for the chemical industry are transported along the Rhine River. Chemicals are widely used in industry to produce paints, detergents, cosmetics, and medicines.

The Bavarian Alps are popular for winter sports.

BEER FESTIVALS

Many small Bavarian towns have annual beer festivals. Local people wear traditional costume and spend several days drinking beer, dancing, and singing to the accompaniment of brass bands.

BAVARIA

The Bavarian Alps rise behind the Catholic church of St. Koloman, near Hohenschwangau. Bavaria is mainly Catholic, with a strong regional identity. The beautiful scenery and historic towns all make Bavaria a popular tourist destination.

RHINE BARGES

The Rhine River stretches from the North Sea deep into the German industrial heartland. Freight, such as coal, grain, and timber, is often carried by barges like these. Many tourists also travel on the southern part of the Rhine to see the beautiful scenery, vineyards, and castles on its banks.

Ludwig van Beethoven, Germany's most famous composer, wrote many pieces for the piano.

KEYBOX

Shipbuilding: *Once a major industry in Germany's North Sea ports, shipbuilding is now in decline, and unemployment is growing. Look for* ⚓

Castles: *The Rhine trade route was protected by castles, which are now a popular sight on tourist cruises. Look for* 🏰

Pollution: *The Rhine is polluted by industry, especially chemical factories. Companies are beginning to find ways of cleaning up plants. Look for* ☠️

🐄 Cattle	⛏️ Mining
🌾 Cereals	⚒️ Coal
🥬 Sugar beets	🏭 Industrial center
🍇 Wine	🚗 Vehicle manufacture
🌾 Hops	💻 High-tech industry

GERMANY
POP. 80,100,000

150 KM
125
100
75
50
25
0

MILES
75
50
25

N

AUSTRIA AND SWITZERLAND

RUNNING THROUGH the middle of Austria and Switzerland are the Alps, the highest mountains in Europe. Both countries lie on Europe's main north-south trading routes, with access to the heart of Europe via the great Danube and Rhine waterways.

Switzerland was formed in the Middle Ages when a number of Alpine communities united in defensive leagues against their more powerful neighbors. Modern Switzerland is a confederation of 23 separate provinces, called cantons. The country has three main languages – German, French, and Italian. Austria was once the center of the Hapsburg Empire, which had vast territories in Central Europe. When the empire collapsed in 1918, Austria became an independent country. Austria has mineral resources, especially iron, and thriving industries. With few natural resources, Switzerland has concentrated instead on skilled high-technology manufacturing.

Gold bar

BANKING
Switzerland is one of the world's main financial centers. People from all over the world put their money into Swiss bank accounts as the country is well known for its political stability. Liechtenstein is also a major banking center. Look for 🪙

DAIRY FARMING
Swiss dairy cattle spend the winter in the Alpine valleys and in summer are taken up to the Alpine pastures for grazing. The milk is used to make many varieties of cheese, including Gruyère. Look for ▼

FALSE TEETH
Liechtenstein is the headquarters of world dental manufacture. False teeth, filling materials, and plastic for crown and bridge dental work are exported to more than 100 countries.

Porcelain teeth

Liechtenstein is famous for its beautiful stamps.

The castle at Vaduz, the capital of Liechtenstein.

GENEVA
Switzerland has not been at war for 150 years and is therefore seen as a neutral meeting place. Many international organizations have their headquarters in the city of Geneva.

KEYBOX

Hydroelectric power: The Swiss pioneered hydroelectricity. Today, Austria is an important producer, tapping the potential of the Danube. Look for ▣

Climbing: Mountaineers first started climbing the Alps in the 19th century. Some of the peaks are still thought to be the world's toughest climbs. Look for ⊤

Tunnels: There are only a few road passes through the Alps, but railroad routes through tunnels are helping to ease the traffic. Look for ⌒

Pollution: Tourism in the Alps, especially the heavy use of roads, is causing environmental problems. Look for ☣

🌾	Cereals	🕐	Watchmaking
🐂	Cattle	💉	Pharmaceuticals
🍇	Wine	🪙	Financial center
🏭	Industrial center	⛷	Skiing

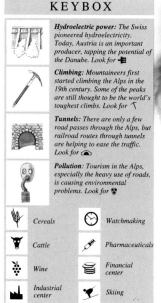
St. Bernard dogs were trained to rescue travelers lost in the Alps.

SWITZERLAND
POP: 6,995,000

LIECHTENSTEIN
POP: 31,500

The Swiss consume more chocolate than any other nationality in the world.

GERMANY

Schaffhausen
Büsingen (Germany)
Frauenfeld
Sankt Gallen
Bregenz
Dornbirn
Basle
Rhine
Liestal
Winterthur
Herisau
Appenzell
Feldkirch
St. Anton
Delémont
Olten
Aarau
Zurich
L. of Zurich
L. of Wallenstedt
VADUZ
LIECHTENSTEIN
Arlberg Tunnel
La Chaux de Fonds
Biel
Aare
Rye
Lucerne
Zug
Schwyz
Glarus
Chur
Neuchâtel
Beef
L. of Lucerne
L. of Uri
St. Moritz
L. of Neuchâtel
BERN
Stans
Sarnen
Altdorf
San Bernadino Tunnel
Yverdon
Fribourg
Thun
L. of Brienz
RHAETIAN ALPS
Wheat
L. of Thun
Interlaken
Bellinzona
Locarno
Lausanne
Gstaad
Lötschberg Tunnel
Mt. Eiger
Jungfrau
St. Gotthard Tunnel
LEPONTINE ALPS
Montreux
BERNESE ALPS
Sierre
Brig
Simplon Pass
Simplon Tunnel
Lugano
L. Maggiore
L. Lugano
Geneva
L. of Geneva
Sion
Rhône
PENNINE ALPS
Martigny
Matterhorn
Great St. Bernard Tunnel
ITALY
FRANCE
SWITZERLAND
ALPS

Mount Eiger can be glimpsed through clouds.

N

Rhône Valley offers route into the heart of the Alps

Bernese Alps

Brig

Simplon rail tunnel, built in 1906

Simplon Pass, built 1801-06, open to cars all year round

ALPINE PASSES
Although the Alps are a formidable obstacle to communications, mountain passes have been used since prehistoric times. Since the 19th century, major engineering feats have made the Alps more accessible: bridges cross gorges and deep valleys, and tunnels pass under the mountains.

Heavily used trans-Alpine routes are congested and difficult to cross in winter

VIENNA

For many centuries, Austria was ruled by the Hapsburg family. Their empire included Hungary; their capital was Vienna. The city contained many grand buildings and elegant palaces such as this one, the Schönbrunn Palace, which was the Hapsburg family's summer residence. The Hapsburg empire finally collapsed in 1918.

Cowbells help farmers locate animals in remote Alpine pastures.

AUSTRIA
POP: 7,884,000

PHARMACEUTICALS

One of Switzerland's main industries is pharmaceuticals (drugs and medicines). The industry has benefited from the Swiss emphasis on the importance of research and product development, the latest technology, and a highly skilled workforce. Perfumes, cosmetics, and drugs are all made in the Basel area. Look for

WATCHMAKING

Watches and clocks have been made in Switzerland since the 16th century. Recently, however, Swiss companies have been under pressure from the Japanese and Americans, who developed quartz technology. The Swiss have saved their industry by making certain of their more famous watches less expensive. Look for ⊙

AUSTRIAN INDUSTRY

Iron ore

Hydroelectric power from the Austrian Alps is a major source of energy for heavy industry. Iron ore deposits around Linz and Donawitz fuel the Austrian steel industry. Some Austrian steel plants have been forced to close by lower world steel prices. Look for

The abbey at Melk in Austria was built in the 18th century.

Edelweiss is a rare Alpine flower.

COFFEE AND CAKES

Sachertorte

The Ottoman Turks, who besieged Vienna in 1529 and 1683, first brought coffee to the city. It was in Vienna that the first coffee shop in Western Europe was opened. There are still many cafés in Vienna, where people drink coffee and eat Austria's famous chocolate cakes. *Sachertorte* is named after the Viennese pastry shop where it is made.

SKI CENTER

The Alps are visited by over 100 million people each year. But ski runs, improved roads, and expanding resorts are all having a harmful effect on the environment. Huge numbers of trees have been cut down to make way for ski runs, but this can provide routes for avalanches. Look for ☇

AUSTRIAN TOURISM

Austria's tourist industry is booming due to the attractions of its beautiful scenery, historical towns, picturesque villages, and winter sports facilities. Tourism is now one of Austria's most profitable industries. A quarter of Austria's tourists visit during the winter; many of the visitors come from nearby Germany.

SWISS FOLK TRADITIONS

Alpine accordion

Swiss folk traditions are very much alive: among the annual events are carnivals during Lent, cheese and wine-makers' festivals, and celebrations marking the change of the seasons, such as the return of the cows from Alpine pasture. Colorful costumes and traditional musical instruments are used at these events.

CENTRAL EUROPE

IN 1989 THE COMMUNIST governments of Central Europe collapsed and the region entered a period of momentous change. All four countries of Central Europe only became independent states earlier this century. After World War II, they were incorporated into the Soviet bloc and ruled by communist governments. These states started to industrialize rapidly, but they were heavily dependent on the former Soviet Union for their raw materials and markets. When communism collapsed in 1989, the new, democratically elected governments were faced with many problems: modernizing industry, huge foreign debts, soaring inflation, rising unemployment, and terrible pollution. In 1993 the former state of Czechoslovakia was split into two countries, the Czech Republic and Slovakia.

Grudziądz, a medieval Polish town on the Vistula River.

POLAND
POP: 38,500,000

POLLUTION
The Czech Republic is Europe's most polluted country. The pollution comes from its own industry, but also from factories in Germany. Forests are dying because of acid rain, rivers are poisoned and the scarred landscapes will take decades to recover. Look for 😷

PUPPETS
Puppet shows are popular throughout Central Europe, but the former Czechoslovakia is acknowledged as the original home of European puppetry. Today, over a thousand Czech Republic and Slovak puppet companies perform plays.

Wooden puppet

GLASS
The Czech Republic's glass industry is centuries old. Glassware, such as this decanter and glasses, is often intricate and brightly colored. The industry uses local supplies of sand to make the glass. Bohemian crystal is manufactured principally in the northwest around Karlovy Vary and is also popular with the ever-increasing number of tourists.

PRAGUE
The Czech Republic's capital, Prague, has some of the most beautiful and well-preserved architecture in Europe. Since 1989, when the country was opened to tourists, thousands of people have flocked to the city Look for 📷

CZECH REPUBLIC
POP: 10,302,215

KEYBOX

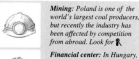

Mining: Poland is one of the world's largest coal producers, but recently the industry has been affected by competition from abroad. Look for 👤

Financial center: In Hungary, the Budapest stock exchange opened in 1990, and many new banks have now opened in the city. Look for 💰

Dam: The dam built by the Slovaks on the Danube at Gabčíkovo has caused a major dispute between Hungary and Slovakia. Look for 🎛

🌾	Cereals	🏭	Industrial center
🥕	Sugar beets	🗑	Shipbuilding
🍱	Mixed fruits	📷	Tourism
7	Timber	🌱	Spas
👤	Mining	😷	Pollution

HUNGARIAN INDUSTRY
Since the end of World War II, Hungary has industrialized rapidly. It manufactures products such as aluminum, steel, electronic goods, and vehicles, especially buses. When the Soviet Union disintegrated, Hungarian manufacturers lost many of the traditional markets for their products – especially in heavy industry – and now face many problems. Look for 🏭

BEER
Some of Europe's finest beers are brewed in the Czech Republic. Pilsener lager originated in the town of Plzeň; Budweiser beer has been brewed at České Budějovice for over a century. Huge quantities of beer, the Budweiser beer in particular, are exported, principally to European countries such as Germany and the UK.

Beautifully painted eggs are sold in the Czech Republic and Slovakia at Easter.

CZECH REPUBLIC
POP: 10,302,215

HUNGARY
POP: 10,518,000

N

| 0 | 50 | 100 | 150 | 200 | KM |
| 0 | 25 | 50 | 75 | 100 | MILES |

Map labels: BALTIC, Pomeranian Bay, POMERANIA, Szczecin, Rega, Koszalin, Odra, Drawa, Wheat, Gorzów Wielkopolski, Rye, Warta, Zielona Góra, Bóbr, Rye, Poznań, Copper, Wheat, Legnica, Copper, Wrocław, SILESIA, SUDETEN, Liberec, Wałbrzych, Ústí nad Labem, Ohře, Karlovy Vary, Wheat, Jizera, Labe, Wheat, Hradec Králové, PRAGUE (PRAHA), Pardubice, Tin, Plzeň, CZECH REPUBLIC, Zinc, Lead, L. Vltava, Tábor, Jihlava, Uranium, Vltava, Uranium, Blanice, Lužnice, České Budějovice, Jihlava, MORA, AUSTRIA, BRATIS, Szombathely, Zalaegerszeg, SLOVENIA, Nagykanizsa, CR

K L M N O P Q R S T

SEA

Gulf of Danzig

Gdynia

Gdańsk

RUSSIAN FEDERATION (KALININGRAD OBLAST)

LITHUANIA

Elbląg

L. Mamry

Suwałki

Wheat

L. Jeziorak

Olsztyn

Ełk

L. Śniardwy

BELARUS

Grudziądz

Rye

Rye

Rye

Rye

Białystok

Bydgoszcz

Barley

Rye

Ostrołęka

PODLASIE

Toruń

Rye

KUJAWY

Wheat

Włocławek

Bug

Wheat

L. Włocławskie

Płock Płońsk

P O L A N D

WARSAW (WARSZAWA)

Krzna

Wheat

Łódź

Wheat

Rye

Wisula

Rye

Radom

Lublin

Kalisz

Rye

Rye

Chelm

Rye

Piotrków Trybunalski

Barley

Warta

Rye

Barley

Rye

Częstochowa

Kielce

Wheat

Opole

Iron

Sulfur

Wheat

Zinc

Bytom

MAŁOPOLSKA

Barley

Gliwice

Vistula

San

Sosnowiec

Wheat

Wheat

Katowice

Rzeszów

Rybnik

Wheat

Kraków

Tarnów

Wheat

Dunajec

Wisloka

Bielsko-Biała

Wheat

B E S K I D M T S.

G A L I C I A

L. Solińskie

Żilina

Ondava

C A R P A T H I A N S

Martin

Váh

Poprad

Prešov

Laborec

Trenčín

S L O V A K I A

Hron

Košice

Torysa

Wheat

Nitra

Banská Bystrica

Mangnesite

Slaná

Nitra

Hron

Mangnesite

Iron

Lučenec

Miskolc

Ipel'

Tista

Copper

Nyíregyháza

Corn

Danube

Wheat

Wheat

BUDAPEST

Debrecen

H U N G A R Y

Wheat

Wheat

esfehérvár

Veszprém

Sárviz

Szolnok

Beretyő

Corn

L. Balaton

Kecskemét

Wheat

H U N G A R I A N P L A I N

Danube

Körös

Corn

Kapos

Corn

Corn

Tisza

Corn

Szekszárd

Wheat

Szeged

Baja

Pécs

Corn

R O M A N I A

Wheat

Y U G O S L A V I A

UKRAINE

SOLIDARITY

Many Polish people work in heavy industries, like coal mining and shipbuilding. In 1980, discontent over poor working conditions led to a strike at this shipyard in Gdańsk and to the birth of Solidarity, the Soviet bloc's first independent trade union. Solidarity has significantly influenced Polish politics.

TIMBER

Beechwood toy

Apart from the lowland area around the Danube River, the landscape of the Czech Republic and Slovakia is mountainous. Both countries have relatively small populations and much of the land is still covered with forest. Both countries have large timber industries. Some timber – mainly pine – is used to make furniture. Beech is often used for the manufacture of toys. Look for ¬

RELIGION

For a thousand years, through invasions, wars, repression – and times when the country almost ceased to exist – the Polish people have found strength in their religious faith. Even during the last 40 years of communist government – which actively discouraged religion of any kind – 90 percent of the population remained devout Catholics.

Wild boar, shown on this Polish stamp, are still found in the region.

Morning mist rising over the western Carpathians.

PAPRIKA

The flat plains in Hungary are among the most fertile farming areas in Europe. Cereals, sugar beets, and fruit are among the main crops. Sweet red peppers – from which paprika is made – are also grown. Paprika is a vital ingredient in many Hungarian dishes.

BUDAPEST

Budapest, the Hungarian capital, was once two towns – Buda on the Danube's right bank, and Pest on the left. The town was very badly damaged during World War II, but many of its historic buildings have since been carefully restored. This vast domed parliament building in Pest faces across the river to Buda.

SLOVAKIA
POP: 5,381,000

Ernö Rubik, a Hungarian, invented this complex puzzle.

SPA BATHS

Hot thermal springs were used for medicinal purposes in ancient Greece and Rome. The Romans were the first to develop baths – like this one in Budapest, where bathers enjoy a game of chess. Hungary now has 154 hot-spring baths, which are open to the public. The Czech Republic and Slovakia have 900 mineral springs and 58 health spas, which are reserved for medicinal purposes only. It is hoped that more tourists will come to the region to use the thermal springs. Look for 🌿

Hungary's famous horses are bred on the Hungarian Plain.

1 2 3 4 5 6 7 8 9 10 11 12 13 14 15 16

M N O P Q R S T

ITALY AND MALTA

AT VARIOUS TIMES in the past 2,000 years Italy has influenced the development of European civilization. From this narrow, boot-shaped peninsula the Romans established a vast empire throughout Europe and North Africa; Christianity was first adopted as an official religion by a Roman emperor, and Rome later became the center of the Catholic church. In the 14th century, an extraordinary flowering of the arts and sciences, known as the Renaissance, or "rebirth," started in Italy and transformed European thought and culture. Italy at this time was divided into independent city-states and was later ruled by foreign nations, including France and Austria. But by 1870, after centuries of foreign domination, Italy became an independent and unified country. Despite a lack of natural resources and defeat in World War II, Italy has become a major industrial power. The country has long suffered from corruption and organized crime, but recent changes show promise of more political stability in the future.

PASTA

The Italian explorer Marco Polo is said to have brought the recipe for pasta to Italy when he returned from his great journey to China. Pasta is a type of dough made by adding water to wheat flour. It has become one of the world's most popular foods. It can be made into different shapes and filled with meat or vegetables.

Orecchioni (large ears)

Cappelletti (little hats)

Round tortellini (small pies)

Masks like these are worn during the February carnival in Venice, which includes plays, masked balls, and fireworks.

Pinnacles of the Dolomites in northeastern Italy.

VERONA

The ancient Romans were skillful engineers, and many of their remarkable buildings are still standing today. The foundations of much of Italy's road system was also built by the Romans. Verona is based on the Roman grid street plan. The town's ancient amphitheater seats 22,000 and is still used.

Silk scarf

Suede shoe

DESIGN

Italians place great emphasis on design and produce beautiful products. This flair for design is particularly obvious in their cars and clothes. The fashion houses of Rome, Florence, Milan, and Venice rival those of Paris, and Italian shoes and clothes are widely exported.

THE PO VALLEY

Between the Alps and the Apennines lies a huge triangular plain, drained by Italy's greatest river, the Po. The majority of the country's agriculture, population, and industry is concentrated in this region. Its major cities like Milan and Turin are important industrial and commercial centers.

Farming

Milan

Turin

The Alps

Genoa: major seaport and industrial center

Po

Alpine rivers supply water for HEP and irrigation

VENICE

This historic city is built on a number of islands in a shallow lagoon. Many buildings stand on wooden stilts driven into the mud. Venice's future is now uncertain, threatened by flooding and pollution.

Mountain passes link Italy to the rest of Europe

N

SLOVENIA

Trieste

A D R I A T I C

Gulf of Venice

Udine

Piave

Chioggia

Treviso

Mestre
Venice

Adige

SAN MARINO
POP: 23,000

Ancona

Comacchio
Lagoon

Ferrara

Padua

Vicenza

Verona

Ravenna

Cérvia

Rimini
Riccione

Pesaro

Bologna

Forlì

SAN MARINO

Potenza

Mantova

Modena

Po

A P E N N I N E S

Arezzo

L. Trasimeno

Cremona

Reggio
nell'Emilia

Parma

Prato

Pistoia

Florence

Siena

T U S C A N Y

Brescia

Piacenza

Lucca

Pisa

Arno

Livorno

Pyrite

Bergamo

Monza

Alessandria

Genoa

Viareggio

Milan

La Spezia

Gulf of Genoa

Novara

Asti

Savona

Po

Alassio

L I G U R I A N   S E A

Turin

San Remo

Cuneo

A L P S

ITALY
POP: 57,956,000

SWITZERLAND

AUSTRIA

FRANCE

A distant view of the snow-capped Apennines.

MALTA
Malta's position on the Mediterranean shipping routes explains its important role in the history of the region. The Romans, Arabs, French, Turks, Spanish, and British have all colonized or fought over the island. In 1964 it became independent. Today, its main income comes from tourism and its port facilities.

ROMAN CATHOLICS
Christianity is the world's most widespread religion. It is based on the life and teaching of Jesus Christ. Within Christianity there are different groups. Roman Catholicism, with its center in Rome, is the largest group, with over one billion members. Catholics have a special reverence for Mary, the mother of Jesus.

VATICAN CITY
This walled city in the center of Rome is the headquarters of the Roman Catholic Church and official residence of the Pope. It is the smallest independent state in the world, dominated by the great St. Peter's Basilica, seen here. The city has its own newspaper, coins, stamps, railroad, and radio stations.

VATICAN CITY
POP: 1,000

AGRICULTURE
Agriculture is very important to the Italian economy. The main crops are olives, citrus fruits, and wine. The best farming region is the Po Valley in the north. Southern Italy has always suffered from its hilly terrain and low rainfall, but thanks to irrigation and modern farming methods, agriculture has improved since the 1950s.

Italians are passionate soccer fans.

Italian national team shirt

Bottles of Chianti are often sold in a wicker casing called a fiasco.

MOTOR VEHICLES
Many Italian car manufacturers are based around the cities of Milan and Turin. Italian engineers and designers have developed some of the finest vehicles in Europe, both high-performance cars and cheaper, economical models. Look for

Model of Ferrari car

Sardinia, a large island in the Mediterranean.

MALTA
POP: 370,000

KEYBOX

Wine: Italy is the world's largest wine producer. Recently, the wine industry has brought in rules for higher quality and better control. Look for

Oil refining: Italy is more dependent on imported fuel than any European country. Crude oil has to be imported and refined. Look for

Sightseeing: Millions of tourists visit Italy each year to see its historic towns, famous buildings, and museums. Look for

Cereals	Industrial center
Rice	Vehicle manufacture
Citrus fruits	Tourism
Vegetable oil	Archaeological sites
Mining	Pollution

*Map labels:*
Otranto · Olive · Olive · Lecce · Brindisi · Gallipoli · Taranto · Gulf of Taranto · Olive · Crotone · Olive · Gulf of Squillace · Catanzaro · Olive · Bari · Olive · Olive · Olive · Altamura · Marble · Bradano · Manfredonia · L. Varano · Aluminum · Tremiti Is. · Foggia · Wheat · Olive · Campobasso · Wheat · Wheat · Oats · Benevento · Olive · Potenza · Agri · Sapri · Olive · Olive · Olive · Pescara · Oats · Olive · Sangro · Olive · Cosenza · Olive · Reggio di Calabria · Strait of Messina · Stromboli · Salerno · Pompeii · Gulf of Salerno · Sorrento · Capri · Naples · Bay of Naples · Ischia · Salina · Lipari · Vulcano · Lipari Is. · Filicudi · Alicudi · Ustica · Messina · Taormina · Catania · Augusta · Syracuse · Enna · Caltanissetta · Olive · Wheat · Potash · Gulf of Gela · Ragusa · Olive · Cefalù · SICILY · Sulfur · Olive · Salso · Agrigento · Olive · Palermo · Belice · Trapani · Egadi Is. · Pantelleria · Linosa · Pelagie Is. · Lampedusa · Lampione · VALLETTA · Gozo · MALTA · L'Aquila · Olive · Nisa · ROMA (ROME) · VATICAN CITY · Ostia · Anzio · Frosinone · Olive · Olive · Pontine Is. · Civitavecchia · L. Bracciano · Vulci · TYRRHENIAN SEA · MEDITERRANEAN SEA · IONIAN SEA · Olbia · Nuoro · Tirso · Sassari · Alghero · Olive · Oristano · SARDINIA · Mannu · Iglesias · Zinc · Lead · Cagliari · Gulf of Cagliari · Sarroch · C. Spartivento · San Pietro · Sant'Antioco · Strait of Bonifacio · Copper

KM · MILES · 150 · 125 · 100 · 75 · 50 · 25 · 0 · 75 · 50 · 25

N

THE WESTERN BALKANS

THIS TROUBLED REGION of southeastern Europe consists of a wide variety of landscapes, religions, peoples and languages. The region was invaded many times, and from the 14th to 19th centuries was under foreign occupation. After World War II, both Albania and Yugoslavia were ruled by communist governments. When the Yugoslav dictator, Marshal Tito, died in 1980 the Yugoslav government became less centralized, and former republics demanded their independence. Serbia, the largest and most powerful republic, resisted the break-up of Yugoslavia. In 1991, a bloody civil war broke out between Serbia and Croatia and, eventually, between Serbs and Muslims in Bosnia. Albania was isolated by its communist government from the rest of Europe and became economically backward. The country has now shaken off its communist rulers and held democratic elections. The economy, however, is still in chaos.

The spectacular scenery of northern Slovenia.

SLOVENIA
POP: 2,016,000

CROATIA
POP: 4,801,000

Nugget of mercury ore

BOSNIA & HERZEGOVINA
POP: 4,446,000

Slovenia is a major producer of mercury, used in thermometers.

YUGO

This car, the Yugo, is manufactured in former Yugoslavia at Kragujevac. It was designed for foreign export, but the economic disruption caused by the civil war has dealt a death blow to this industry. Slovenia has had more success; French cars are made there under licence, and are sold to the domestic market.
Look for ⊷

UNDER FIRE

The world looked on in horror as Dubrovnik, a beautiful city with an untouched center dating back 1,000 years, came under Serbian attack in 1991. Sarajevo, the Bosnian capital, was another casualty; many of its historic churches and mosques were hit by shells. Other historic towns in Bosnia and Croatia have also suffered irreparable damage during the war.

TOURISM

Many tourists used to visit former Yugoslavia, attracted by the country's beautiful scenery, warm climate and stunning coastline. By the late 1980s, an average of 9 million visitors were coming to Yugoslavia every year. However, the violent civil war has now virtually put an end to the tourist industry. Look for ⚓

KEYBOX

Mining: Albania has some of the world's largest chromium reserves. Exports are hampered by outdated mining equipment and frequent strikes. Look for ⛏

Refugee centres: The war in former Yugoslavia has forced over a million people to leave their homes and seek asylum in nearby countries. Look for ⛺

🌾	Cereals	⚒	Coal
🍲	Mixed fruits	⚡	Hydroelectric power
🍇	Wine	🏭	Industrial center
🚬	Tobacco	🚗	Vehicle manufacture
🎣	Fishing	⚓	Tourism

MARKETS

In peacetime, local markets in the region are packed with people and well stocked with a wide range of produce from nearby farms. Large quantities of fruit and vegetables are grown in the mild, warm climate of the Croatian coast and in western Bosnia. Look for 🚢

FOLKLORE

Variations in national costume reflect the many different traditions and peoples living in this region. In Slovenia, for example, costumes show a strong Alpine influence – leather trousers and gathered *dirndl* skirts. Further south, the Dubrovnik region is famous for its costume of white dresses, embroidered blouses and vests. Folk-music and dancing take place at religious festivals and on market-days, and are also performed for tourist groups.

				KM
0	50	100	150	
0	50	100	150	MILES

Walnuts flourish in the warm summers and well-drained soils of Yugoslavia.

IRON GATES

The Danube, the second-longest river in Europe, passes through Serbia on its journey from Germany to the Black Sea. As the river leaves the broad plains of Hungary, it is forced through this narrow gorge, called the Iron Gates. In 1972, Romania and Yugoslavia built a power station here to use the water to make electricity. Look for ▄▄

YUGOSLAVIA
POP: 10,931,000

CIVIL WAR

In 1990 Yugoslavia, crippled by an economic crisis, began to break up into independent countries. Serbia fiercely resisted this process, and fighting erupted in both Croatia and Bosnia. The Serbs began to force Bosnian Muslims out of their homes and settle there themselves, a policy which is called "ethnic cleansing".

LANGUAGE DIFFERENCES

The main language of the former Yugoslavia is Serbo-Croatian. It can be written in two different ways, using either the Roman or Cyrillic alphabet. Cyrillic is a Slavic alphabet created in the 9th century by two Greek brothers, who were Christians. Other languages used in this area include Slovenian and Macedonian.

Postage stamp using Roman alphabet

Postage stamp using Cyrillic alphabet

There is very little farming in the mountains of Montenegro.

ALBANIA

There is little traffic in the central square in Albania's capital, Tirana: until recently, private cars were banned. Albania is now emerging from 50 years of isolation. Under communism, free speech and religion were forbidden. Even beards were not allowed. Although democratic elections have been held, the economy is in ruins and the government is unable to control the country. The Albanians are having great difficulty adjusting to the changes, and crime and vandalism are now serious problems.

MACEDONIA
POP: 2,093,000

ALBANIA
POP: 3,429,000

Grapes

Water-melon

Tomato

Potatoes

ALBANIAN AGRICULTURE

Although its economy is based on farming, Albania still has difficulties feeding its own population, which is the fastest-growing in Europe. The main crops are potatoes, corn, wheat, sugar beet, fruits, and vegetables. Until recently, most of the land was owned and farmed by the state, but today it is farmed by individual families.

Mixed valley farming gives way to barren mountains in central Albania.

RELIGION

This beautiful church on the shores of Lake Ohrid dates back to the medieval period, when Macedonia followed the Eastern Orthodox church. Later, Bosnia, Montenegro, and Serbia were occupied by the Islamic Turks and became largely Muslim countries.

ROMANIA AND BULGARIA

ROMANIA AND BULGARIA ARE LOCATED in southeastern
Europe, on the shores of the Black Sea. The Danube River
forms the border between the two countries, and the most
fertile land in the region is found in the river's vast valley
and delta. Forests of oak, pine, and fir trees grow on the
slopes of the Carpathian and Balkan mountains.
Romania and Bulgaria were occupied by Romans, Bulgars,
Hungarians, and Turkish Ottomans, but this troubled history ended
when they became independent countries in the late 19th and early
20th centuries. After two world wars, both countries became part of
the Soviet communist bloc. Although they are no longer
communist, economic reform has been slow, and
unemployment, high prices,
and food shortages are still
constant problems.

Rose petal

ROSE OIL
Used in
perfume, rose
oil is literally
worth its weight in
gold. Central Bulgaria
produces most of the world's
supply. The world's largest rose gardens
are at Kazanlŭk. Look for ❧

THE PRESIDENTIAL PALACE
Under Romania's repressive communist
leader, President Ceaușescu, food and
energy supplies were rationed. Despite
this, the president started a series of
expensive building projects, such as this
presidential palace in Bucharest. In 1989,
the Romanian people rose up against
communism and executed their president.

TOBACCO
Bulgaria is the world's second largest
exporter of cigarettes. Tobacco is grown
in the fertile valleys of the Maritsa
River. This woman is sorting tobacco
leaves, ready for selling. Look for 🌰

YOGURT
Yogurt, made from
the milk of cows,
sheep, or goats, is an
important part of the
Bulgarian diet. Many
Bulgarians claim that eating yogurt
helps them live to a ripe old age.

Small farms in the
wooded valleys of
central Romania.

The Alexander Nevsky
church in Sofia
celebrates
liberation from
Turkish rule.

KEYBOX

Vehicle manufacture: Romanian
factories make copies of French
vehicles for export to China,
Russia, and many Western
countries. Look for 🚚

High-tech industry: Electronics
earns Bulgaria foreign currency,
although the computer industry is
suffering from international
competition. Look for 💻

Spas: Mineral springs and health
treatments are provided by many
spa resorts, which are a popular
tourist attraction. Look for 🍃

Shipping canal: The Danube-
Black Sea Canal enables ships to
avoid the slow journey through
the Danube Delta. Look for ⚓

🐂	Cattle	⛏	Mining
🌾	Cereals	⚒	Oil
🍇	Wine	🛢	Gas
🪈	Tobacco	🏭	Industrial center
🌿	Roses	✎	Tourism

Bulgaria is the
world's fourth largest
wine exporter.

RILA MONASTERY
The walls of Rila
monastery are
decorated with no
less than 1,200 superb wall paintings. The monastery
became a symbol of the Bulgarians' struggle to preserve
the Christian faith during centuries of Turkish rule. The
monastery was originally founded in 1335 and was rebuilt
after it burned to the ground in the 19th century.

Map labels: UK, Wheat, Zinc, Lead, Copp, Satu Mare, Baia Mare, Gold, Wheat, Beef, Corn, Oradea, Beef, Dairy, Iron, Aluminum, Cluj-Napoca, Cor, Transylvania, Wheat, ROM, Wheat, Corn, Arad, Corn, Wheat, Mures, Alba Iulia, Co M, Dairy, Wheat, Dairy, Deva, Iron, Timișoara, Iron, Beef, Iron, Corn, Iron, Manganese, CARPAT, Wheat, Reșița, Râmnicu V, Târgu Jiu, Copper, Băile Herculane, Chromium, Beef, Beef, YUGOSLAVIA, Drobeta-Turnu-Severin, Corn, Corn, Dairy, Craiova, Vidin, Wheat, Jiu, Danube, Wheat, Wheat, Iron, Corn, Beef, Mikhaylovgrad, Vratsa, B, Copper, Bee, Iron, BALK, SOFIA (SOFIYA), Pernik, Dair, L. Iskŭr, Beef, Struma, Rila, MACEDONIA, Zinc, Lead, Velingra, RHODOPE M, Sandanski, Bee, GR

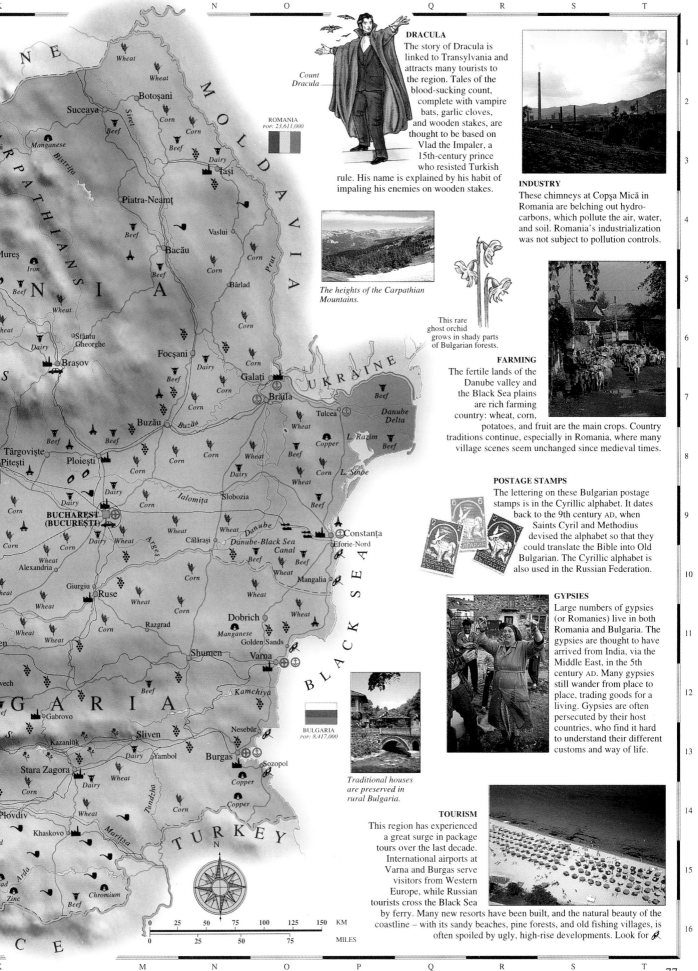

ROMANIA
POP: 23,611,000

DRACULA

The story of Dracula is linked to Transylvania and attracts many tourists to the region. Tales of the blood-sucking count, complete with vampire bats, garlic cloves, and wooden stakes, are thought to be based on Vlad the Impaler, a 15th-century prince who resisted Turkish rule. His name is explained by his habit of impaling his enemies on wooden stakes.

Count Dracula

The heights of the Carpathian Mountains.

This rare ghost orchid grows in shady parts of Bulgarian forests.

INDUSTRY

These chimneys at Copşa Mică in Romania are belching out hydro-carbons, which pollute the air, water, and soil. Romania's industrialization was not subject to pollution controls.

FARMING

The fertile lands of the Danube valley and the Black Sea plains are rich farming country: wheat, corn, potatoes, and fruit are the main crops. Country traditions continue, especially in Romania, where many village scenes seem unchanged since medieval times.

POSTAGE STAMPS

The lettering on these Bulgarian postage stamps is in the Cyrillic alphabet. It dates back to the 9th century AD, when Saints Cyril and Methodius devised the alphabet so that they could translate the Bible into Old Bulgarian. The Cyrillic alphabet is also used in the Russian Federation.

GYPSIES

Large numbers of gypsies (or Romanies) live in both Romania and Bulgaria. The gypsies are thought to have arrived from India, via the Middle East, in the 5th century AD. Many gypsies still wander from place to place, trading goods for a living. Gypsies are often persecuted by their host countries, who find it hard to understand their different customs and way of life.

BULGARIA
POP: 8,417,000

Traditional houses are preserved in rural Bulgaria.

TOURISM

This region has experienced a great surge in package tours over the last decade. International airports at Varna and Burgas serve visitors from Western Europe, while Russian tourists cross the Black Sea by ferry. Many new resorts have been built, and the natural beauty of the coastline – with its sandy beaches, pine forests, and old fishing villages, is often spoiled by ugly, high-rise developments. Look for

GREECE

FROM THE EARLIEST TIMES, the life and economy of Greece has been shaped by its geography. It is a country of rugged mountains, isolated valleys, remote peninsulas, and more than 1,400 scattered islands. The difficulty of traveling by land has turned Greece into a seafaring nation, which owns the second largest fleet of merchant ships in the world. Ninety percent of its imports and exports are carried by sea rather than by road. Most people in Greece make their living from farming, but in recent years, tourism has become an important source of income. Tourists visit Greece not only for its warm, Mediterranean climate and beautiful landscape, but also for its ancient ruins. Many of these date from the 5th century BC, when the country was the cultural center of the Western world, the birthplace of democracy, and home of great thinkers such as Socrates, Plato, and Aristotle.

THE ORTHODOX CHURCH

Greek Orthodox bishop

Most Greek Christians belong to the Orthodox Church. This was founded in Constantinople (modern Istanbul) in the 4th century AD. The Eastern Orthodox Church established there still flourishes in Greece, Eastern Europe, and Russia.

GREEK SALAD

Parsley

Many Greek farms are small, growing just enough vegetables and fruit for the farmer's family. Lettuces, cucumbers, tomatoes, olives, herbs, and cheese are the most common products.

Eggplant
Cucumber
Beef tomato

ATHENS

Athens is famous for its Acropolis ("high place"), crowned by the Parthenon temple. Smog all too often obscures the Acropolis, and cars are banned from the city on certain days to reduce pollution.

The Parthenon temple (built 432 BC) was the center of religious life in classical Athens.

KEYBOX

Archaeological sites: Remains from ancient Greece are found all over the country, attracting many visitors. Look for ⅲ

Sultanas and currants: Greece is the world's largest exporter of these fruits. Small, black currants are named after the town of Corinth. Look for ❦

The Olympic Games: The event started in Olympia in 776 BC. Sports included running, wrestling, boxing, horse racing, javelin, and discus. Look for ⚬⚬⚬

🦋 Citrus fruit		🐬 Fishing	
🍇 Wine		⚓ Mining	
🫙 Vegetable oil		⚒ Oil	
🌿 Cotton		🏭 Industrial center	
🌿 Tobacco		🎣 Tourism	

CLASSICAL MUSIC

Tuning peg
Fretted fingerboard
Neck
String
Pegbox inlaid with mother-of-pearl
Soundhole
Body
Bridge

The bouzouki is a stringed instrument, similar to a lute or a guitar, which is used in traditional Greek music. Folk dances, national costumes, and music are still very popular at religious festivals such as Easter, and on special occasions such as weddings.

THE CORINTH CANAL

Athens is separated from the Ionian Sea by a narrow neck of land called the Isthmus of Corinth. In 1893 the Greeks cut a canal through the isthmus. It is 3.9 miles (6.3 km) long, but only just wide enough for a ship to squeeze between the cliffs on either side. Look for ⇌

SACRED OIL

Olives have been grown in Greece for over 2,000 years. In ancient times, the olive was sacred to Athena, the goddess of war, and olive wreaths were worn as a symbol of victory. Today, olives and olive oil are major exports. Look for 🫒

Olives and cypresses grow throughout Greece.

BULGARIA

Serres

Drama

Kavala

Xanthi

Komotini

THRACE

TURKEY

Alexandroupoli

Marble

Thasos

Samothraki

Olives
ygyros

Singitic Gulf
of Kassandra

Limnos

AEGEAN SEA

Ayios
Evstratios

orades

Skiros

Evvoia

Kymi

Olives
ives

Chalkida

Lesvos

Olives

Olives

Magnesite

Mytilini

Chios

Chios

Olives

Marathon

ATHENS

Karystos

Piraeus

Lavrio

Andros

Samos

Samos

Tinos

Kéa

Mykonos

Ikaria

Kíthnos

Siros

Cyclades

Sérifos

Paros

Marble

Naxos

Dodecanese

Sífnos

Amorgos

Kos

Kos

Milos

Ios

Astipálaia

Thira

Rhodes

Rhodes

Monólithos

Olives

Karpathos

SEA OF CRETE

Crete

Chania

Rethymno

Irakleio

Knossos

Agios
Nikolaos

Olives

Olives

MEDITERRANEAN SEA

SEA

N

GREECE
POP: 10,200,000

0 25 50 75 100 125 KM

0 25 50 75 MILES

Greek doll wearing
a traditional
wedding dress.

Hand-painted
pottery made in
local workshops

TOURISM
Over 5 million tourists visit Greece every year, creating an enormous demand for goods and services. Hotels, restaurants, and shops employ many people, while holiday purchases boost the Greek economy. Local workshops produce handcrafted items such as pottery, leather bags, and sandals for the tourist market.

A monastery perches on a vertical rock in central Greece.

FISHING
Fishing is an important part of the Greek economy, but the eastern Mediterranean has been overfished. Only mullet, squid, sardines, and tuna are found in any quantity. Look for

The Mediterranean squid can grow to a length of 2 ft (0.6 m)

Sponges, found in the Mediterranean, are obtained by diving.

HILL FARMING
Greece, with its mountainous landscape, has the largest number of small hill-farms in Europe. The soil is poor and many people are needed to work the land: nearly a third of the Greek labor force is employed in agriculture – more than anywhere else in Europe.

ADAPTABLE GOATS
Hardy goats are ideally suited to Greece's rugged landscape. They are tough and sure-footed, and able to survive on limited food resources. Goat's milk is used for making yogurt and cheese. Goat skin is also made into leather and young goats (kids) are a great delicacy.

ΑΘΗΝΑ
Greek has its own alphabet, which dates back 2,500 years. This says "Athens."

A PLACE IN THE SUN
People have been coming to Greece for centuries to visit the remains of ancient Greek cities and temples. Today, many visitors come from northern European countries, especially Scandinavia, the UK, and Germany. Thira, seen here, is just one of many popular island resorts. Look for

Olive trees grow in rows on the high, arid mountains of central Crete.

AN ISLAND LIFE
Tourism is more profitable than traditional pursuits such as farming and fishing. Today, yachts are beginning to outnumber fishing boats in local ports.

THE BALTIC STATES AND BELARUS

THE THREE BALTIC STATES – Latvia, Lithuania, and Estonia – made history in 1990-91 when they became the first republics to declare their independence from the Soviet Union. This was the end of a long series of invasions and occupations by the Vikings, Germans, Danes, Poles, and Russians. A new era had begun, but many of the old problems – food shortages, pollution, weak economies – still remained. The region's flat landscape is well drained by lakes and rivers and is ideal for farming. The main crops are grains, sugar beets, and potatoes. In Belarus, heavy industry like machine building and metalworking is important, while the Baltic states manufacture electronics and consumer goods. Nearly half the population of the Baltic states are Russians who have moved there to work in industry. The Baltic Sea, although frozen in the winter months, gives access to the markets of northern Europe. Industrialization has left a terrible legacy. Summer resorts along the Baltic coast have been closed to visitors because of polluted seawater, and Belarus was badly hit by the nuclear accident at Chernobyl in the Ukraine in 1986, when 70 percent of the radioactive fallout landed on its territory.

ESTONIA
POP: 1,572,000

LITHUANIA
POP: 3,782,000

NEW CURRENCY
When the three Baltic states separated from the Soviet Union, they all stopped using the rouble and introduced their own currencies. Companies which had been owned and run by the communist state came under private ownership, and the Baltic States encouraged investment in these industries from abroad.

One of the many lakes of Lithuania.

Spider trapped in amber

BALTIC GOLD
Amber is the fossilized sap of ancient trees. The Baltic states produce two-thirds of the world's amber, most of it found along Lithuania's "amber coast." Amber has been collected and traded since prehistoric times. It is a precious stone but is also valued for its medical properties. Even today it is used to treat rheumatism. Look for 🔵

MINSK
Although Minsk was founded over 900 years ago, it has no historic buildings. The city was virtually destroyed by bombing during World War II, when half of Minsk's population is estimated to have been killed. After the war, the city was rebuilt and became one of the industrial centers of the former Soviet Union.

Sour cream

NATIONAL DISH
Draniki is the national dish of Belarus. It is made of grated potatoes fried in vegetable oil and served with sour cream. Potatoes are grown everywhere, and are one of Belarus's main products. Large numbers of dairy cattle are kept on its extensive pastureland.

Beetroot mixed with sour cream

Draniki

KEYBOX

Cattle: The Baltic states were the centers of beef and dairy production for the former Soviet Union. Look for 🐄	
Oil: The Baltic states used to obtain free oil by pipeline from the former Soviet Union. Now they depend on Estonia's oil shale deposits. Look for 🛢	
Peat: This region has large supplies of peat – a fuel made from carbonized plant material found in bogs. Look for ⛏	

🐖	Pigs	🚢	Fishing port
🌰	Sugar beets	⛑	Mining
🌱	Potatoes	🏭	Industrial center
⧗	Flax	🚢	Shipbuilding
🌿	Timber	💻	High-tech industry

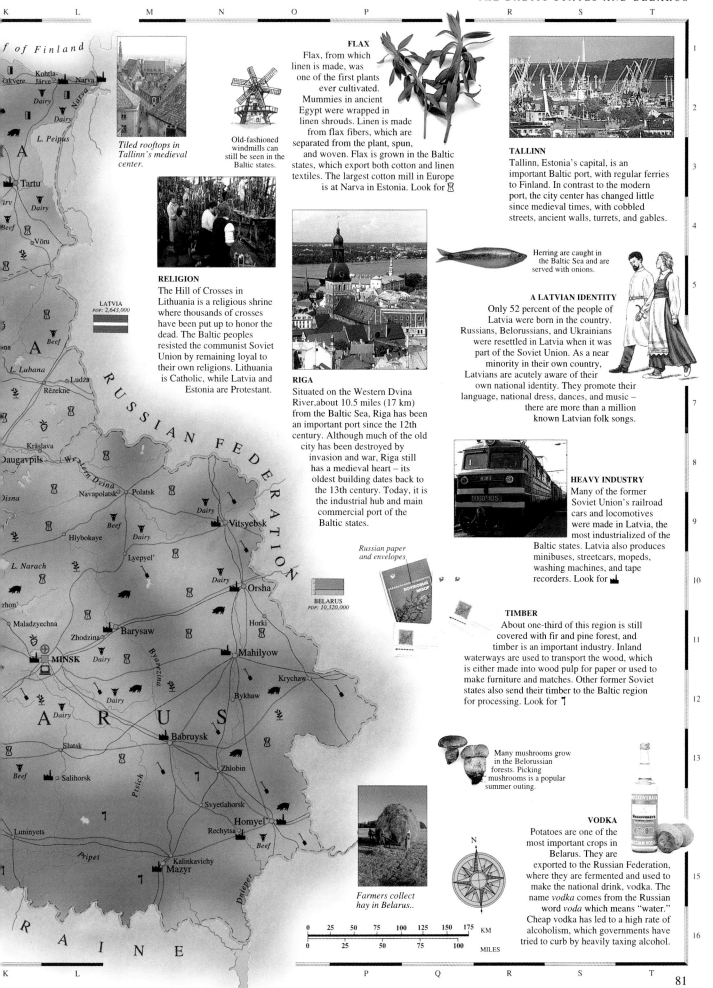

FLAX

Flax, from which linen is made, was one of the first plants ever cultivated. Mummies in ancient Egypt were wrapped in linen shrouds. Linen is made from flax fibers, which are separated from the plant, spun, and woven. Flax is grown in the Baltic states, which export both cotton and linen textiles. The largest cotton mill in Europe is at Narva in Estonia. Look for ☒

Tiled rooftops in Tallinn's medieval center.

Old-fashioned windmills can still be seen in the Baltic states.

TALLINN

Tallinn, Estonia's capital, is an important Baltic port, with regular ferries to Finland. In contrast to the modern port, the city center has changed little since medieval times, with cobbled streets, ancient walls, turrets, and gables.

RELIGION

The Hill of Crosses in Lithuania is a religious shrine where thousands of crosses have been put up to honor the dead. The Baltic peoples resisted the communist Soviet Union by remaining loyal to their own religions. Lithuania is Catholic, while Latvia and Estonia are Protestant.

LATVIA
POP: 2,643,000

RIGA

Situated on the Western Dvina River, about 10.5 miles (17 km) from the Baltic Sea, Riga has been an important port since the 12th century. Although much of the old city has been destroyed by invasion and war, Riga still has a medieval heart – its oldest building dates back to the 13th century. Today, it is the industrial hub and main commercial port of the Baltic states.

Herring are caught in the Baltic Sea and are served with onions.

A LATVIAN IDENTITY

Only 52 percent of the people of Latvia were born in the country. Russians, Belorussians, and Ukrainians were resettled in Latvia when it was part of the Soviet Union. As a near minority in their own country, Latvians are acutely aware of their own national identity. They promote their language, national dress, dances, and music – there are more than a million known Latvian folk songs.

Russian paper and envelopes

BELARUS
POP: 10,320,000

HEAVY INDUSTRY

Many of the former Soviet Union's railroad cars and locomotives were made in Latvia, the most industrialized of the Baltic states. Latvia also produces minibuses, streetcars, mopeds, washing machines, and tape recorders. Look for ⊨

TIMBER

About one-third of this region is still covered with fir and pine forest, and timber is an important industry. Inland waterways are used to transport the wood, which is either made into wood pulp for paper or used to make furniture and matches. Other former Soviet states also send their timber to the Baltic region for processing. Look for ⅂

Many mushrooms grow in the Belorussian forests. Picking mushrooms is a popular summer outing.

VODKA

Potatoes are one of the most important crops in Belarus. They are exported to the Russian Federation, where they are fermented and used to make the national drink, vodka. The name *vodka* comes from the Russian word *voda* which means "water." Cheap vodka has led to a high rate of alcoholism, which governments have tried to curb by heavily taxing alcohol.

Farmers collect hay in Belarus..

| 0 | 25 | 50 | 75 | 100 | 125 | 150 | 175 | KM |
| 0 | | 25 | | 50 | | 75 | | 100 | MILES |

EUROPEAN RUSSIA

THE RUSSIAN FEDERATION is the largest country in the world. Stretching across two continents – Europe in the west and Asia in the east – it is twice the size of the USA. The Ural Mountains form the division between the European and Asian parts of the country. The Russian Federation has fertile farmlands, vast mineral deposits, and abundant timber, oil, and other natural resources. Despite its size and natural wealth, Russia is currently in a state of political and economic turmoil. After centuries of rule by czars (emperors), the world's first communist government took power in Russia in 1917; five years later the country became the Union of Soviet Socialist Republics (USSR), which included many of the territories that were formerly parts of the Russian Empire. During 74 years of communist rule, the Soviet Union became an industrial and military superpower, but at an appalling cost to its people and environment. Economic problems led to liberal reforms beginning in the mid-1980s, but the reforms unleashed a whirlwind of change which led to the fall of the communist regime in December 1991. By then most of the non-Russian republics had declared independence. The new Russian Federation is now struggling to become a democracy.

RELIGION

Moscow is the spiritual center of the Russian Orthodox Church. For many decades, the church was persecuted in Russia; today, churches are re-opening, and many Russian people are turning back to religion. Beautiful icons (religious images painted on wood), like this one, adorn the churches and people's homes.

САНКТ-ПЕТЕРБУРГ

The name "St. Petersburg," written in Russia's Cyrillic alphabet, which was devised by Christian missionaries in the 10th century.

Northern Russia is covered with coniferous forest called taiga.

ST. PETERSBURG

St. Petersburg, the capital of Russia from 1712-1918, was founded by Czar Peter the Great in 1703. It is built on 12 islands linked by bridges and has many elegant 18th-century buildings.

Many wooden churches built in the 17th century still stand on small islands in Lake Onega.

MOSCOW

The city of Moscow was founded in the 12th century. At its center is a fortified citadel called the *Kremlin*. Its stone walls enclose the grand palace of the czars, four cathedrals, and a church. The *Kremlin* became – and remains – the country's seat of government.

St. Basil's, Moscow, built in the 16th century

RUSSIAN FEDERATION
POP: 150,638,000
(EUROPEAN RUSSIA)
POP: 108,950,000

## Map labels

KARA SEA
Baydarata Bay
Kara Strait
Vaygach I.
Vorkuta
Novaya Zemlya
BARENTS SEA
Kolguyev I.
Chesha Bay
Usa
Izhma
Uranium
Pechora
Kama
Syktyvkar
Kotlas
MOUNTAINS
Mezen'
Pinega
Arkhangel'sk
Northern Dvina
WHITE SEA
KOLA PENINSULA
Murmansk
Iron
L. Umbozero
Copper
Nickel
Iron
Phosphate
Aluminium
Kem'
L. Pyaozero
L. Topozero
L. Segozero
L. Onega
Onega
Oats
Oats
Barley
Oats
Rye
Vologda
Kostroma
Barley
Rye
Oats
Velikaya
Oats
Kirov
Cherepovets
Rybinsk
Res.
Volga
Yaroslavl'
Moscow-Volga Canal
Ivanovo
Vladimir
Gzhel'
NORWAY
FINLAND
Petrozavodsk
L. Ladoga
Aluminium
Rye
Rye
Tver'
MOSCOW (MOSKVA)
Gulf of Finland
St. Petersburg
Novgorod
Rye
Barley
Rye
ESTONIA
Pskov
Nebel'
Oats
Smolensk
Dnieper
LATVIA
BELARUS

Historic cathedrals and monasteries line the banks of the Volga at Yaroslavl'.

LACQUERED BOX

Traditional Russian crafts have never been so popular – they have found a market in the West and earn Russia foreign currency. Lacquered boxes have been made in the Moscow region for the last four centuries. The papier-mâché boxes are decorated with miniature paintings of folk stories, rural scenes, dances, forests, and fairy tales and are then lacquered.

A scene from a Russian folk tale

FAST FOOD?

With the end of communism, foreign companies are investing in Russia and many joint ventures are being encouraged. For Western countries, Russia provides a vast new market. Several Western fast-food companies have opened restaurants in Moscow. They accept payment in roubles and are popular with local people, although waiting for hours is not unknown.

BALLET

Ballet originally developed in Western Europe, but in the late 19th century it was completely changed by Russian artists. Inspired largely by one man, Diaghilev, Russian ballet became creative and exciting. The male dancer became more important, and greater attention was paid to the music and the costumes. Russia's most famous ballet companies are the Kirov and the Bolshoi. Both are a source of national pride.

A tutu, the costume worn by ballerinas

Ballet shoe

MiG fighter plane

MAKING WAVES

The manufacture and sale of weapons, such as this MiG fighter plane, has been badly hit by the end of the Cold War. At Nizhniy Novgorod, where nuclear submarines used to be built, many shipyard workers are now making a semiautomatic washing machine, called the "Wave." Large numbers of unsold machines fill the former shipyard's warehouses. Look for ✈

CHESS

Pottery from the town of Gzhel' near Moscow is collected by people all over the world. The patterns are painted by hand using brushes made from squirrel hair. Cobalt-blue patterns are then enameled on to a background of white. This chess set, made in Gzhel', reflects the popularity of the game here – Russia has produced many of the world's grand masters of chess.

Enameled chessboard

Chess piece

Model of a Lada hatchback

LADA

In 1965, the Russians signed a deal with Fiat, the Italian car company. A factory was built at Tol'yatti and is the largest car plant in the former Soviet Union. Ladas (based on the Fiat) are manufactured here, and some are exported to the West. Few Russians own a car, but the demand for imported Western cars is growing. Look for 🚗

MINERAL WEALTH

Mines are a common sight in Russia. There are large reserves of coal around Moscow. Nickel, copper, phosphates, and cobalt are found in the far north. Iron, sulfur, copper, gold, and nickel are mined in the south and southwest. Look for ⛏

Traditional handmade wooden toy, in the form of a child and dancing bear.

Fur hats with earflaps are essential in Russia's freezing winters.

KEYBOX

Reindeer: Nomads in the north herd reindeer, which are used to carry loads and for their meat, milk, and skins. Look for 🦌

Hydroelectric power: Vast dams on the Dnieper and Volga rivers power electricity generators, which supply large cities and other republics. Look for ⚡

Vehicle manufacture: Cars are manufactured along the Volga. The truck plant at Naberechnoye Chelny is the largest in the world. Look for 🚚

Pollution: Huge numbers of factories, operating without environmental controls, are polluting the region's rivers. Look for 🏭

Cereals	🌾
Sugar beets	🥬
Citrus fruits	🍊
Tobacco	🌿

Mining	⛏
Coal	⚙
Industrial center	🏭
Aerospace industry	✈

KM
MILES
0 100 200 300 400 500
0 50 100 150 200 250 300

N

UKRAINE, MOLDAVIA, AND THE CAUCASIAN REPUBLICS

THE CAUCASUS MOUNTAINS run between the Black and Caspian seas. Higher in places than the Alps, they form a natural barrier between the flat steppes of the Russian Federation to the north and the plateau of Southwest Asia. The newly independent states to the south of the Russian Federation are rich in natural resources. Ukraine, the largest country in Europe, is dominated by a flat and fertile plain where huge quantities of cereals are grown on large farms. Ukraine also possesses extensive coal and iron ore deposits and is heavily industrialized. Wine and fruit are produced in Moldavia (also known as Moldova) and Georgia, where the climate is mild and the soil is fertile. Mountainous Armenia is rich in minerals, while Azerbaijan has plentiful oil.

Cereals being harvested in the fertile fields of Ukraine.

WINE
A quarter of the former Soviet Union's wine was produced in Moldavia, which is well known for its champagne. Vines also thrive on the warm, sunny hills of eastern Georgia, where wine and brandy are produced. Look for ❦

Georgian brandy

Moldavian wine

BORSCHT
Vegetable soups are the main food for many rural people in cold countries throughout the world. Russia's famous beet soup, *borscht,* comes from Ukraine. There, the *borscht* also contains other root vegetables such as potatoes and carrots. *Borscht* is often served with savory turnovers called *piroshki.*

Borscht, beet soup

Sour cream

MOLDAVIA
POP: 4,350,000

Piroshki, savory pastries

CHERNOBYL
In 1986, a radiation leak at Chernobyl nuclear power station caused panic all over Europe. More than 100,000 people were evacuated from the area around the plant, where towns now stand desolate and empty. More than two million people still live in fear and uncertainty in the contaminated areas.

KEYBOX

Oil: *There is a large oil field under the delta of the Kura River in Azerbaijan. Offshore wells are also being dug in the Caspian Sea. Look for* ⬧

Hydroelectric power: *Dams on the Dnieper River supply water for crops and for electricity. The rivers of the Caucasus also provide electricity. Look for* ⬛

High-tech: *Electrical and electronic equipment such as TVs and computers are made in the Caucasian republics. Look for* 💻

✹ Cereals		♟ Mining
❦ Wine		⛏ Coal
❧ Tea		🏭 Industrial center
⚘ Sunflowers		✎ Tourism
🐟 Fishing		☢ Nuclear pollution

BLACK SEA TOURISM
The Crimea attracts millions of visitors who cram onto the crowded beaches to enjoy the warm sun. Many visitors come for their health, rest, and a regimen of healthy eating, massage, and exercise. Look for ✎

The barrier of the Caucasus Mountains blocks cold air from the north

Hardy crops like corn, which can withstand frosts, are grown on lowlands

Black Sea

Tbilisi

Sevastop

Yerevan

Mountains force humid air to rise. It falls as rain in Georgia

Grapes and fruits grown in valleys

Cotton production along lower Kura R.

CASPIAN SEA

Baku

N →

THE CAUCASUS MOUNTAINS
Armenia, Azerbaijan, and Georgia – the Caucasian republics – are isolated from the Russian Federation by the Caucasus Mountains. The warm subtropical climate of the region allows an exotic range of crops to be grown. Georgia has a humid climate, so tea and citrus fruits are cultivated. In the drier east, the rivers running down from the mountains are used to water the fields.

BLACK BREAD
Ukraine was known as the former Soviet Union's "breadbasket." Its broad flat steppes, with their fertile black earth, are intensively cultivated: wheat, buckwheat, potatoes, rye, and flax are grown on vast farms. Much of Ukraine's countryside consists of endless fields of cereals, the view broken only by the occasional haystack.

Matrioshka dolls are hand painted. Each is made from a single piece of wood.

The Ukraine is the world's largest producer of buckwheat. Although it is ground up to make flour, buckwheat is not a true cereal.

UKRAINE
POP: 52,498,000

KIEV
Kiev, founded in the 9th century, is the capital of Ukraine. St. Sophia's cathedral, with its gilded domes, has been Kiev's most famous landmark since 1037. Kiev is situated on the banks of the Dnieper River, the republic's main waterway. It is within easy reach of the Black Sea ports, as well as being near Ukraine's industrial center.

COAL
About one-third of the former Soviet Union's coal came from the area around Donets'k in Ukraine, where there are about 40 deep mines. Miners working here are reasonably well paid, but gas explosions and the frequent breakdown of equipment put them at risk. Death rates in these mines are 10 times higher than in mines in the USA. Look for 🐦

INDUSTRIAL HEARTLAND
Ukraine's Donbass region, with its rich reserves of coal, iron, manganese, and other minerals, is a major industrial area. Heavy industry, such as iron- and steelworks, engineering, and chemicals, still dominate the region, but today cars, aircraft, televisions, and computers are also manufactured here. Look for 🏭

CAUCASIAN CONFLICT
When the Caucasian republics were part of the Soviet Union, many different peoples were forced to live side by side. Since these countries became independent, many pent-up resentments have been unleashed. For example, fighting has erupted between Armenian Christians and Muslim Azeris over Nagorno-Karabakh, an Armenian area within Azerbaijan's borders.

TEA
Tea is a popular drink throughout the former Soviet Union, and over 90 percent of the tea consumed there is grown in Georgia. Both black and green teas are grown on large tea plantations. Tea is served black and strong, with sugar or lemon. Look for 🌿

Decorated Black Sea fiddle, from Georgia.

SUNFLOWERS
Sunflowers are an important crop in southern Ukraine. The seeds, which can be eaten, contain oil and protein. Sunflower oil is used for cooking. The seeds are also used in the manufacture of margarine and soap and are mixed with corn and peas for cattle feed. Look for ♀

The snow-capped peaks of the Caucasus Mountains.

AZERBAIJAN
POP: 7,507,000

CAVIAR
Caviar, served on toast

The Russian sturgeon is a large fish which can grow up to 23 ft (7 m) in length. Sturgeon eggs, called caviar, are an expensive delicacy. Sturgeon live in the Black and Caspian seas and swim up rivers like the Dnieper to breed in fresh water. Hydroelectric dams on these rivers have disrupted the sturgeons' routes, and polluted water is causing concern about falling numbers of fish. Look for 🐟

GEORGIA
POP: 5,478,000

TEXTILES
Georgia is famous for its silk and textiles. Brightly colored and patterned cotton fabrics are woven with gold and silver thread. Worn by women as headscarves, these fabrics are seen throughout the Caucasus.

The Swallow's Nest Castle, high on a rock near Yalta.

ARMENIA
POP: 3,816,000

White-backed vulture
Gyps bengalensis
Wingspan: 7 ft (2.2 m)

Cheetah
Acinonyx jubatus
Length: 7 ft (2.2 m)

Aye-aye
Daubentonia madagascariensis
Length: 18 in (45 cm)

AFRICA

AFRICA IS THE SECOND largest continent after Asia, and the only one through which the Equator and both tropics run. It is also home to the world's longest river, the Nile. The climate and vegetation roughly mirror each other on either side of the Equator. In the extreme south and along the Mediterranean coast in the north, hot dry summers are followed by mild wet winters. Similarly, the land around each tropic is hot and starved of rain, so great deserts have formed. Africa's immense tropical savannah grasslands are prone to drought, but around the Equator high rainfall has produced lush tropical rain forests. The volcanoes and strangely elongated lakes in the Great Rift Valley are evidence of cracks in the Earth's crust that threaten to split Africa apart eventually.

HOT SAHARA
The inhospitable Sahara desert covers one-third of Africa. Temperatures can exceed 120°F (50°C).

Burchell's zebra
Equus burchelli
Height: 4 ft (1.2 m)

Umbrella thorn acacia
Acacia tortillis
Height: 60 ft (18 m)

MISTY RAIN FOREST
Tropical rain forests only grow where temperatures are always high and rain is abundant. Here in central Africa, it rains every day – more than 7 ft (2 m) falls each year.

Malachite is a copper-rich ore found in many parts of eastern Africa.

THUNDERING WATERFALL
The Zambezi River winds slowly through dry woodlands before reaching the Victoria Falls. Here it plummets 354 ft (108 m), creating so much noise and spray that it is known as "the smoke that thunders."

GREAT RIFT VALLEY
Cracks in the Earth's crust have made a valley 3,750 miles (6,000 km) long and up to 55 miles (90 km) wide.

The South African turban shell looks like a headdress made of coiled cloth.

SERENGETI PLAIN
Savannah – grassland and open woodland – is home to huge herds of grazing animals, including wildebeest and zebra.

SAND DUNES IN THE NAMIB
The intensely hot Namib Desert forms a narrow strip down Africa's southwest coast. Rainfall is less than 6 in (15 cm) a year, but sea mists from the cold currents along the coast provide enough moisture for some plants and animals to survive.

Shells like this black miter can be found in shallow water along the west African coast.

SOUTHERN AFRICA
Rain is so low in southern Africa that for most of the year few plants show themselves above ground. As soon as the rains come, however, a barren landscape is transformed into a brilliant mass of flowers.

Gaboon viper
Bitis gabonica
Length: 7 ft (2 m)

OKAVANGO DELTA
Not all rivers run to the sea. The Okavango River ends in a huge inland swamp that attracts thousands of water loving animals, such as hippopotamuses.

CROSS-SECTION THROUGH AFRICA

L. Victoria
Great Rift Valley (western)
Serengeti Plain
Ruwenzori Mountains
Great Rift Valley (eastern)
Atlantic Ocean
Congo Basin
Indian Ocean

9,843 (3,000)
Sea level 0
-14,764 (-4,500)
Feet (meters)
A
Length: *2,8000 miles (4,500 km)*
B

African elephant
Loxodonta africana
Height: 13 ft (4 m)

Desert scorpion
Androctonus australis
Length: 3 in (8 cm)

Mountain go
Gorilla gorill
Height: 6 ft (

MEDITERRANEAN SEA

EURASIAN PLATE
AFRICAN PLATE

C. Bon

Strait of
Gibraltar

Madeira Ridge

Monaco
Basin

Madeira

▲ ATLAS MTS.

Canary Is.

Chott El Jerid

Gulf of Sirte

Nile Delta

Qattâra
Depression
-436ft

LIBYAN DESERT

Nile

L. Nasser

NUBIAN
DESERT

RED SEA

ARABIAN PLATE
AFRICAN PLATE

IRANIAN PLATE
ARABIAN PLATE

Persian Gulf

Tropic of Cancer

20°

ARABIAN

PENINSULA

S A H A R A

TASSILI N'AJJER
7,080ft ▲
▲ 9,574ft
AHAGGAR

TIBESTI

▲ 11,205ft

Blue Nile

Ras Dashen ▲
15,158ft

Gulf of Aden

Socotra

C. Caseyr

S A H E L

L. Chad

White Nile

Sudd

L. Tana

ETHIOPIAN

HIGHLANDS

Shebeli

Verde

Senegal

Niger

Massina

Black Volta

Niger

Benue

Guinea
Basin

L. Volta

Niger Delta

Fernando Pó

Príncipe I.

São Tomé I.

ADAMAWA
HIGHLANDS

▲ Mt. Cameroon
13,354ft

Gulf of Guinea

Ubangi

Zaire

Congo
Basin

Congo

L. Albert

L. Turkana

EAST
AFRICAN
PLATEAU

RUWENZORI MTS.

L. Victoria

SERENGETI
PLAIN

Ngorongoro
Crater

Rift Valley

Equator

Somali
Basin

INDIAN

B.

OCEAN

Zanzibar

A.

L. Tanganyika

L. Mweru

L. Rukwa

L. Nyasa

Comoro Is. △

Zambezi

Madagascar

Tsiafajovona 20 °
▲ 8,672ft

A T L A N T I C   O C E A N

Mid-Atlantic Ridge

AFRICAN PLATE

Mid-Atlantic Ridge

Angola
Basin

C. Fria

Okavango

NAMIB DESERT

Okavango
Delta

L. Kariba

Limpopo

KALAHARI
DESERT

Namaqualand

11,424ft ▲

Orange R.

DRAKENSBERG

Natal
Basin

Tropic of Capricorn

Madagascar
Basin

Mozambique Channel

Walvis Ridge

SOUTH AMERICAN PLATE

Cape
Basin

Cape of Good Hope

C. Agulhas

Agulhas
Basin

South West Indian Ridge

40°

Agulhas Ridge

AFRICAN PLATE
ANTARCTICA PLATE

60°

BOTTLE TREES

Plants can resist drought by reducing their leaf size and enlarging their stems to store water. Here in Madagascar's dry woodlands, huge-trunked baobabs, or "bottle trees," grow alongside spiny Dideria.

Black rhinoceros
Diceros bicornis
Length: 12 ft (3.6 m)

■ ■ !

KEY TO SYMBOLS

▲ Mountain
△ Volcano
Mangroves
Wetlands
Coral reef
Plate margins with direction of movement

KEY TO NATURAL VEGETATION

Mediterranean-type
Hot desert
Tropical grassland
Tropical rain forest

Temperate grassland
Mountain
Dry woodland

NORTHWEST AFRICA

OVER THE CENTURIES, Northwest Africa has been invaded by many peoples. The entire north coast from the Red Sea to the Atlantic was once part of the Roman Empire. Later colonization by Italy, Great Britain, Turkey, Spain, and France contributed to the culture of the countries, but it was the 7th-century Arab conquest which fundamentally changed the region. The conversion of the original peoples – the Berbers – to Islam, and the use of Arabic as a common language, gave these countries a sense of unity which remains today. In fact, the region is sometimes called the Maghreb, which means "west" in Arabic. In the northwest, the Atlas Mountains form a barrier between the wetter, cooler areas along the coast and the great Saharan Desert. This desert is the biggest on Earth and is still growing. Water shortages and lack of land for farming are problems throughout the region, especially as the population of the Maghreb is increasing rapidly. In Algeria and Libya, however, the desert has revealed hidden riches – abundant oil and natural gas.

FEZ – AN ISLAMIC CITY

This view of the city of Fez in Morocco shows the flat-roofed houses that are traditional in this region. Seen from the narrow streets, the houses look blank and windowless, but this is because they are designed to face inward onto central courtyards which are cool and private. Islamic cities may appear to be chaotic mazes of streets, but in fact they are laid out following guidelines set in the holy book of Islam, the *Koran*.

The Moroccans make a refreshing tea from the spearmint plant.

MOROCCO
POP: 28,913,000

WESTERN SAHARA
POP: 200,000

Morocco occupied the whole of Western Sahara in 1979

BERBERS

Berbers were the original people of northwest Africa. When the Arabs invaded, they were driven out of the fertile coastal areas. Many Berbers still live in remote villages or towns – such as here at Boumalne-Dadès – high in the Atlas Mountains, where their lifestyle and language have remained unchanged for centuries.

Couscous is the basic ingredient of many North African dishes. It is made of tiny pellets of flour, called semolina.

WESTERN SAHARA

Western Sahara is a sparsely populated desert area lying between Morocco and Mauritania. It was a Spanish colony until 1976 but is now fighting for independence from Morocco, which claims two-thirds of the country and the phosphates found there. This photo shows young members of the liberation movement.

The Ahaggar Mountains, Algeria, jut up in the middle of the Sahara.

KEYBOX

Mining: Huge quantities of phosphates come from the sands of Western Sahara and Morocco. They are the vital raw material for fertilizers. Look for 🪖

Gas: Algeria has vast reserves of natural gas, much of it exported to Europe – some by pipeline to Italy across the Mediterranean Sea. Look for 🔥

Archaeological sites: Early civilizations, such as the Romans, built cities in the desert and along the coast of North Africa. Look for 🏛

🐑 Sheep		⛴ Fishing port	
🐄 Citrus fruits		🛢 Oil	
🌴 Dates		🏭 Industrial center	
🍇 Wine		🏺 Tourism	
🫒 Vegetable oil		🌴 Oases	

CARPETS AND RUGS

Hand-knotted carpets and rugs, with their distinctive bold patterns and deep pile, are made throughout the region. In Morocco the most important carpet factories are in Rabat and Fez. Craftworkers often work together in cooperatives to maintain high quality and to control prices.

Painted plate

Leather bag

TOURISM

Tourism is a vital source of foreign income for Morocco and Tunisia. When oil prices fell in the 1980s, tourism took the place of oil as the main source of foreign income. Modern hotels, built in traditional styles, have sprung up along the coast. Both countries produce handicrafts for tourists, such as leather and brassware. Look for 🏺

THE TUAREG

The Tuareg are a nomadic tribe who inhabit a huge area of the Sahara. In the past they controlled the great camel caravans which crossed the desert to the Mediterranean, carrying slaves, ivory, gold, and salt. Today, some Tuareg still follow the traditional desert way of life, but many have become settled farmers.

NORTH COAST AGRICULTURE
Along the Mediterranean coast and in sheltered valleys in the Atlas Mountains, the soil is rich and the climate mild. In these areas, farmers can grow crops such as grapes, olives, cereals, and citrus fruit. Sheep, goats, and cattle are kept throughout the region, especially in Tunisia.

"BREAD OF THE DESERT"
The fruit of the date palm has been eaten for centuries. Dates are rich in protein and provide food for people and animals. They grow around desert oases, where the climate is hot and dry and there is water in the ground. Every part of a date palm has some use. Look for 🌴

KAIROUAN
For Muslims, the 9th-century Great Mosque in the desert at Kairouan, Tunisia, is the holiest place in Africa. The enormous courtyard – where the people pray – is paved in marble and surrounded by a forest of columns. The interior is decorated with beautiful glazed tiles.

Ruins of the Roman port of Leptis Magna in Libya.

A Saharan oasis – an island of green in a sea of sand.

TUNISIA
POP: 9,905,000

ALGERIA
POP: 29,350,000

LIBYA
POP: 5,587,000

#### Map labels
MEDITERRANEAN SEA
ALGIERS (ALGER)
Mostaganem, Olive, Blida, Bejaïa, Skikda, Annaba, Bizerte, TUNIS, Sousse, Monastir, Sétif, Constantine, Jendouba, Kairouan, Tiaret, Olive, Iron, Timgad, Tébessa, Sfax, Batna, Biskra, Phosphates, Gafsa, Laghouat, Chott Melrhir, Tozeur, Gabès, Jerba I., Chott El Jerid, El Oued, Medenine, Ghardaïa, Touggourt, TUNISIA, TRIPOLI (ṬARĀBULUS), Al Khums, Ouargla, Gharyān, Yafran, Leptis Magna, Mişrātah, Ghadāmis, Surt, Gulf of Sirte, Al Bayḑā, Derna, Al Marj, Cyrene, Tobruk, Benghazi, Ajdābiyā, Marsá al Burayqah, Great Manmade River Project, Al Jaghbūb, TRIPOLITANIA, CYRENAICA, Great Manmade River Project, Hūn, LIBYA, Birāk, Adīrī, Sabhā, Great Manmade River Project, Awbārī, Murzuq, FEZZAN, Illizi, Ghāt, Al Kufrah, ALGERIA, NIGER, CHAD, SUDAN, EGYPT, TASSILI N'AJJER, AHAGGAR MTS., Tamanrasset, SAHARA

WOOD SHORTAGE
The main source of energy for many African people is burning wood. But tree roots help to bind the soil together, and when large numbers of trees are cut down, the soil can be blown or worn away. This allows the desert to spread. People who live in treeless areas spend hours searching for wood to burn and must then carry it long distances to their villages. Collecting wood is traditionally women's work.

An Algerian stamp showing the traditional dress for men.

OIL IN LIBYA
Until the discovery of oil in 1958, many people in Libya were very poor. The money from oil has enabled Libya to construct roads and railways, improve education, and develop industry and agriculture. Libyan oil is in great demand because it has no sulfur in it. This means that when it is burned, it gives out very little pollution. Look for ⚓

Classical Arab lute from Morocco.

WATER PIPELINE
Deep beneath the Sahara are vast underground supplies of water. The Libyans are building a series of huge pipelines like the one shown under construction here, which will carry this water across the desert to the coastal areas. It will be used to water the farmland and increase crop production. This is known as the Great Man-made River project, and the first phase is nearly completed.

NORTHEAST AFRICA

WATERED AND FERTILIZED BY THE NILE, the longest river in the world, Egypt is a fertile strip running through the Sahara Desert. The first people settled there about 8,000 years ago, and by the time of the pharaohs, Egypt had become one of the world's first great civilizations. Today, Egypt is a relatively stable democracy, with a growing number of industries and control of the Suez Canal, one of the world's most important waterways. To the south are the highlands of Ethiopia and Eritrea. This area is fertile and well-watered in places, but recent droughts have made life precarious for the farmers and nomads who live there. The countries of Somalia, Sudan, and Ethiopia have been beset by terrible problems, including drought, famine, religious conflicts, and civil war. About half of Africa's 4.5 million refugees come from this area. In 1993, Eritrea gained independence from Ethiopia, after a civil war which lasted 30 years.

TOURIST SOUVENIRS

Large numbers of "ancient Egyptian" *scarabs* (beetles) and other fake antiques are made locally and sold to tourists. City streets are lined with market stalls and the small workshops where these goods are made. Tourism has stimulated this informal economy.

SUEZ CANAL

Opened in 1869, the Suez Canal is one of the world's largest artificial waterways and a vital source of income for Egypt. It connects the Red Sea with the Mediterranean, offering a shortcut from Europe through the Persian Gulf to India and the Far East. On average, 21,250 ships a year use the canal.

Coptic cross

THE COPTIC CHURCH

Although Ethiopia is surrounded by Islamic countries, about 40 per-cent of its population is Christian. The isolated Ethiopian church developed into a unique branch of Christianity, called the Coptic church.

COTTON

Egypt produces about a third of the world's high-quality cotton. Textile industries, such as spinning, weaving, and dyeing cotton, are also important. Cotton is the coolest fabric to wear during hot summers. Egyptian men often wear a long-sleeved cotton garment, or *jelaba*. Look for ⌂.

Cotton jelaba

The gold death mask of the Pharaoh Tutankhamun, c. 1352 BC

Tomb dwelling in Cairo's City of the Dead

CAIRO

Cairo is the largest city in the Islamic world and is also one of the fastest growing. Its current population is estimated at 9.5 million, but it is said to be increasing at a rate of 1,500 people a day. New arrivals live in squalid shantytowns on the outskirts of the city. The City of the Dead, a huge ancient cemetery outside Cairo, has now been occupied by the homeless.

AGRICULTURE

Although there is fertile land in southern Ethiopia, farming methods are inefficient. The scratch plow is widely used but, as its name implies, it is only able to turn over the surface of the soil. After a few years, the nutrients in the soil are used up, and crops will no longer grow.

TOURISM

Visitors from all over the world go to Egypt to see the pyramids and other ancient sites. Income from tourism helps to maintain these ancient sites. The Temple of Isis at Philae would have been flooded by the Aswān Dam, so it was moved, brick by brick, to another island. Look for ⌂.

The Giza pyramids were built as tombs for the pharaohs.

EGYPT
pop: 59,713,000

The ancient Egyptians used this reedlike plant, called *papyrus*, to make paper.

THE GIFT OF THE NILE

The Nile River floods in the summer, carrying rich mud from the highlands of Sudan and Ethiopia to the deserts of Egypt. This creates some of the most fertile land in the world. Nearly 99 percent of the Egyptian population lives along the banks of the Nile.

### Map labels

MEDITERRANEAN SEA
RED SEA
ISRAEL
SINAI
Gulf of Suez
Gulf of Aqaba
LIBYAN DESERT
NUBIAN DESERT
L. Nasser
LIBYA
EGYPT
Nile

Marsa Matrûh
Qattâra Depression
Alexandria
El Mansûra
Port Said
Tanta
Suez Canal
Ismâ'ilîya
CAIRO (EL QAHIRA)
Giza
Suez
Saqqara
Helwân
Bûr Safâga
Beni Suef
Ras Gharib
El Faiyûm
El Minya
Asyût
Sohâg
Abydos
Qena
Thebes
Luxor
Kom Ombo
Idfu
Valley of the Kings
Aswân
Philae
Aswân High Dam
Abu Simbel
Wadi Halfa

Djibouti is mainly arid desert, populated by nomads. Its busy port dominates the economy.

Donkeys are used throughout the region for pulling carts and as beasts of burden.

DJIBOUTI
POP: 526,000

ERITREA
POP: 3,920,000

SUDAN
POP: 27,061,000

ETHIOPIA
POP: 51,000,000

SOMALIA
POP: 9,077,000

SOMALIA

The Somalis overthrew their brutal dictator, President Barre, in 1991. A serious drought has since turned Somalia into a disaster area. Aid efforts have been blocked by a civil war between tribes, and millions of people are starving. Many Somalis have flocked to relief camps in search of food. Look for △

Coffee, grown in the Ethiopian Highlands, is a valuable crop.

Unleavened bread, enjera

Vegetables in sauce, wat

TEF

The most common food crop in Ethiopia is *tef* – a grain unique to this region. It is used to make *enjera*, a gray unleavened bread which is eaten with meat and vegetables in a spicy sauce (*wat*). This is the Ethiopian national dish.

NOMADISM

For centuries this region has been populated by nomads, such as the Dinka of Sudan, who live by grazing their goats and camels on any available pastureland. They move from place to place according to the seasons and the weather conditions.

Southeast Sudan is administered by Kenya

Dates: Egypt is the world's largest date producer. Date pits dating to 4,500 BC have been found in Egypt. Look for 🌴

Dams: Both the Aswān High Dam, opened in 1970, and Sudanese Dam projects control the Nile, providing irrigation and electricity. Look for ▥

Aromatic oils: Frankincense is exported by Somalia. It is taken from trees by making cuts in the bark. It is used in incense and perfume. Look for ⬤

Cattle	Industrial center	Oil
Sheep	Archaeological sites	
Coffee	Refugee camps	
Peanuts	Oases	
Cotton		

KM MILES
500 300
400
300 200
200 100
100
N

Places (map labels)

Boosaaso, Garoowe, Gaalkacyo, Burco, Berbera, Hargeysa, Jijiga, Harer, Beledweyne, Baydhabo, MOGADISHU (MUQDISHO), Marka, Juba, Jiib, Kismaayo, Dire Dawa, Awash, Goba, Asela, Awasa, L. Abaya, L. Rudolf, Jima, Gore, Nekemte, Debre Markos, ADDIS ABABA, Debre Birhan, L. Tana, Bahir Dar, Gonder, Dese, Adwa, Aksum, Mekele, Massawa, ASMARA, Dahlak Archipelago, Kassala, Gedaref, Khashm el Girba Dam, Khartoum North, KHARTOUM, Omdurman, Wad Medani, Sennar Dam, Ed Damazin, Er Roseires Dam, Kosti, Ed Dueim, Jebel Aulia Dam, El Obeid, Kaduqli, Malakal, Jonglei Canal, Wau, Rumbek, Juba, En Nahud, Nyala, El Fasher, Nuri, Meroë, Atbara, Ed Damer, DJIBOUTI, Assab, Blue Nile, White Nile, Shebeli, Genale, Awash, Atbara

HORN OF AFRICA, Gulf of Aden, INDIAN OCEAN, ETHIOPIAN HIGHLANDS, SOMALIA, ETHIOPIA, ERITREA, SUDAN, KENYA, UGANDA, ZAIRE, CENTRAL AFRICAN REPUBLIC, CHAD

WEST AFRICA

THE LANDSCAPE OF WEST AFRICA ranges from the sand dunes of the Sahara through the dry grasslands of the Sahel region to the tropical rain forests in the south. There is just as much variety in the peoples of the region – more than 250 different tribes live in Nigeria alone. In the north, most people are Muslim, a legacy of the Arab traders who controlled the great caravan routes across the Sahara and brought Islam with them. It was from West Africa, particularly the coastal regions, that millions of Africans were transported to North and South America as slaves. Today many people in West Africa make their living by farming or herding animals. Crops such as coffee and cocoa are grown on large plantations. Like the logging industry, which is also a major source of earnings, these plantations are often owned by foreign multinational companies who take most of the profits out of the region. Recent discoveries of oil and minerals offer the promise of economic prosperity, but this has been prevented by falling world prices, huge foreign debts, corruption, and civil wars.

Calabash (bowl) made from a decorated gourd.

DAKAR
Dakar, the capital of Senegal, is one of the main ports in West Africa. It lies on the Atlantic coast and has a fine natural harbor, large modern docks, and ship repair facilities. It is the country's main industrial center.

KEYBOX

Vegetable oil: The oil palm is widely grown throughout West Africa. Palm oil is used by people in the region and some is exported. Look for

Research center: At a center in Ibadan, Nigeria, new disease-resistant varieties of corn, cassava, and other crops have been bred. Look for

Film industry: Burkina has a large film industry, subsidized by the government, with studios in Ouagadougou and an annual film festival. Look for

Shipping registry: Many of the world's shipping countries register their ships in Liberia because of low taxes and lax employment rules. Look for

🫘	Coffee	🌲	Forest products
🥜	Cocoa	🐟	Fishing
🥜	Peanuts	⛏	Mining
🌿	Cotton	🛢	Oil
7	Timber	🏭	Industrial center

Kano mosque, built to serve the largely Islamic population in northern Nigeria.

TOURISM
Tourism in this region has expanded rapidly. In Gambia, the number of visitors has risen from 300 in 1965 to over 100,000 a year in the 1990s. Most tourists stay along the Atlantic coast, but many also go on trips into the bush.

DEFORESTATION
The population of West Africa is growing rapidly. Vast areas of forest have been cut down, for wood or to clear farmland to feed these extra people. This problem is particularly bad in the Ivory Coast, where little forest is left. Look for 7

MAURITANIA
POP: 2,399,000

WESTERN SAHARA

SENEGAL
POP: 8,610,000

GAMBIA
POP: 1,106,000

GUINEA-BISSAU
POP: 1,096,000

GUINEA
POP: 6,897,000

Cocoa pod
Cocoa beans
Pulp

SIERRA LEONE
POP: 4,863,000

COCOA
The ancient Aztec people of Mexico were the first to make a drink called *chocolatl* from the seeds of the cacao tree, brought to West Africa by European colonizers. The region now produces over half the world's supply of cocoa beans. Look for

LIBERIA
POP: 3,136,000

IVORY COAST
POP: 14,891,000

AFTER INDEPENDENCE
Since independence, some African countries have been plagued by many problems, such as unstable governments and foreign debts. Ivory Coast, however, is one of West Africa's most prosperous countries. Its last president built this cathedral when he had the capital moved to his family village at Yamoussoukro.

Zouérate
Fdérik
Iron
Nouâdhibou
Râs Nouâdhibou
Gum arabic
Atar
Gum arabic
Râs Timirist
Copper
Tidjikdja
MAURITANIA
NOUAKCHOTT
Gum arabic
L. Rkiz
Aleg
Rosso
Kiffa
Senegal
Saint-Louis
Kaédi
Néma
Louga
Phosphates
Matam
Nioro
SENEGAL
Phosphates
DAKAR
Diourbel
Copper
Kayes
Kaolack
BANJUL
GAMBIA
Tambacounda
BISSAU
Georgetown
Palm
Kolda
Ziguinchor
Bafatá
Iron
Iron
BAMAKO
Palm
GUINEA-BISSAU
Bijagós Archipelago
Palm
Labé
Aluminium
Gold
Bougouni
Aluminium
Niger
Sikasso
Kindia
Kankan
CONAKRY
Iron
Odienné
Korho
SIERRA
Diamonds
MONTS DU TOURA
FREETOWN
Diamonds
IVOR
LEONE
Voinjama
Bo
Kenema
Nzérékoré
Man
Gold
L. de K
Rubber
Iron
Daloa
Robertsport
Gbarnga
Gold
YAMOUSSOUKR
MONROVIA
Buyo Res.
Buchanan
Rubber
Palm
Tchien
Gagnoa
LIBERIA
Manganese
Rubber
Pal
Greenville
Canally
Harper

SA
MAURITANIA
S
ATLANTIC OCEAN

GROUNDNUTS

Peanuts, or ground nuts, grow on low, bushy plants and ripen in the ground. They are grown throughout West Africa. Most of the crop is then made into oil, which is used for cooking. Look for 🥜

MALI
POP: 11,124,000

A deserted village at the bottom of dramatic rocky outcrops in Mali.

BURKINA
POP: 10,628,000

MARKETS

Markets play a vital role, for both people living in towns and for farmers in the surrounding area. Here, women of the Dogon people in Mali display their wares at a market. In much of Africa women are responsible for growing crops, both for sale and as food for their families.

DESERT ON THE MARCH

The Sahara Desert is slowly spreading into the Sahel, helped by droughts, deforestation, and overuse of land for farming. In 1973, the area was devastated by a famine, in which 100,000 people died. Since then, many schemes have been introduced to prevent the desert from spreading any further.

A ceremonial figure. Many West African religious beliefs have spread to Central and South America and the Caribbean.

A lone acacia tree in the desert area of Niger.

NIGER
POP: 9,386,000

NIGERIA
POP: 88,514,501

THE WODAABE

The Wodaabe are among the last nomads in Africa. They graze their herds in the borderlands between Niger and Nigeria. Every year they hold a festival at which the men compete for the title of "most beautiful and charming man." The judges are women. The men wear makeup which emphasizes their eyes and teeth.

GHANA
POP: 17,959,000

TOGO
POP: 4,264,000

BENIN
POP: 5,560,000

OIL IN NIGERIA

Nigeria's economy has been transformed by oil. Discovered in the 1950s, oil accounts for about 95 percent of export earnings, and has paid for the development of new industries. Look for ⛏

NIGER RIVER

The Niger flows both north and south during its long journey to the Atlantic. Much of its course passes through the Sahel, where persistent droughts have reduced water levels. In this region the river often evaporates completely during the dry season. As it reaches the wetter tropics in Nigeria, the amount of water increases, and farmers use large amounts of it for crops and livestock.

N

| 0 | 100 | 200 | 300 | 400 | 500 | KM |

| 0 | 50 | 100 | 150 | 200 | 250 | 300 | MILES |

Map labels: ALGERIA, LIBYA, CHAD, MALI, NIGER, NIGERIA, BURKINA, BENIN, TOGO, GHANA, CAMEROON, SAHARA, SAHEL, PLATEAU DU MANGUENI, PLATEAU DU DJADO, TALAK, TENERE, AIR, ADRAR DES IFOGHAS, AZAOUAD, Timbuktu, Gao, L. Niangay, Mopti, Ouahigouya, Koudougou, OUAGADOUGOU, Fada-Ngourma, Dapaong, Bolgatanga, Wa, bo-Dioulasso, Tamale, Kara, Sokodé, Sunyani, Kumasi, Abengourou, Cape Coast, Sekondi-Takoradi, ACCRA, LOMÉ, PORTO-NOVO, Cotonou, Abomey, Ibadan, Abeokuta, Lagos, Benin City, Ilorin, Oshogbo, Ogbomosho, Onitsha, Owerri, Aba, Calabar, Port Harcourt, Niger Delta, Bight of Benin, NIAMEY, Dosso, Tillabéry, Birni n'Konni, Tahoua, Sokoto, Maradi, Gusau, Katsina, Zinder, Diffa, Nguru, Nguigmi, L. Chad, Hadejia, Maiduguri, Kano, Zaria, Kaduna, Bauchi, Jos, JOS PLATEAU, Minna, ABUJA, Lokoja, Makurdi, Yola, Benue, Taraba, Gongola, Agadez, Uranium, Manganese, Phosphates, Iron, Tin, Gold, Rubber, Palm, Aluminium, Gum arabic, L. Volta, Kainji Res., Red Volta, White Volta, Black Volta, Oueme, Niger, Sokoto, Natitingou, Parakou, Kandi, Atakpamé

CENTRAL AFRICA

MUCH OF THIS REGION IS COVERED in dense tropical rain forest, drained by the great Congo (Zaire) River and its tributaries. The climate is hot and humid. All the countries have small populations, and many of them have French as their official language – a legacy from the days when they were French colonies. Zaire, the third-largest country in Africa, has rich mineral deposits, but it has declined economically since independence. In 1997 Zaire adopted the name Democratic Republic of the Congo. Chad has been torn apart by civil wars, and the Central African Republic has suffered from corrupt governments. Both countries are desperately poor. Equatorial Guinea has suffered so much from bad government that some 100,000 people have emigrated. Abundant minerals and oil have made Gabon the richest country in the region. Oil is also of major importance in the Congo, and both countries have relatively large urban populations. Relatively prosperous, Cameroon is home to more than 200 different peoples.

HEALTH CLINIC

Traditional African medicine is still widely practiced in this region. Western medicine has also been successfully used to cure or control many diseases. Medicines are often dispensed at village clinics like this one. But there are still major problems – many babies do not survive and there is a great shortage of doctors. In Chad, for example, over 40,000 people have to share one doctor.

A wooden figure from Cameroon, made to honor an ancestor.

LAKE CHAD

Lake Chad lies at the point where Chad, Cameroon, Niger, and Nigeria meet. Due to a series of droughts, the rivers that feed the lake have shrunk to little more than streams and reduced it to a tenth of its former size. Fish from Lake Chad – such as this *tilapia* – are a major source of food for the people who live in the surrounding areas. But each year the fishermen must haul their boats farther to reach the lake's receding water.

CHAD
POP: 6,537,000

PYGMIES

Several groups of pygmies live scattered through the rain forests of Central Africa. They still survive mainly by hunting and gathering, but they also trade with neighboring peoples and have learned to speak their languages. Pygmies rarely reach a height of more than 4 ft (125 cms). This pygmy hut, made of banana fronds, is in a forest clearing in the Central African Republic.

Forested valleys and hills around Loubomo, Congo.

CENTRAL AFRICAN REPUBLIC
POP: 3,026,000

RELIGION

The main religion in this region is Christianity, but many Africans follow the traditional religions of their ancestors. They believe in many gods and spirits, who are often associated with natural forces or the elements, such as trees and thunder. This photo shows a ritual dance from Cameroon.

Dancer dressed as a leopard spirit

River flowing through dense rain forest in Cameroon.

CAMEROON
POP:13,651,000

TRADITIONAL HOUSING

Traditional African houses vary from area to area, according to the building materials available locally. The walls of these houses in Cameroon are made of mud and the roofs of straw. Building a house is one of the regular family tasks. As the family grows, new houses are added to the group.

LIBYA

TIBESTI

NIGER

CHAD

SUDAN

CENTRAL AFRICAN REPUBLIC

NIGERIA

CAMEROON

Faya

Biltine

Abéché

Mongo

Am Timan

Mao

Ati

Bol

L. Chad

Kousséri

N'DJAMENA

Maroua

Guider

Garoua

L. Lagdo

Bongor

Logone

Chari

Ergué

Lai

Moundou

Goré

Bossangoa

Sarh

Salamat

Ndélé

Kaga-Bandoro

Bria

Birao

Copper

Diamonds

Diamonds

Chromium

Aollo

Banyo

Alumínum

Ngaoundéré

Bouar

Bamenda

Bumenga

Gold

Tin

LIBREVILLE
Libreville, Gabon's capital, was founded in the mid-19th century as a settlement for freed French slaves; its name means "free town" in French. The city has expanded rapidly since the discovery of oil in the 1970s and is now a major port.

TIMBER
Huge quantities of valuable hardwoods are cut down in the tropical rain forests of Gabon and used for plywood and veneer. Eucalyptus trees, which require only seven years of growth before they can be cut down, are increasingly grown for conversion into wood pulp. Most of the timber companies are foreign-owned and take their profits out of the country.

Port-Gentil, Gabon's chief port, is on the Ogooué River.

EDUCATION
Since the 1960s, when many African countries achieved independence, improving education has been a major goal. Crowded classrooms and lack of books and equipment, however, are recurrent problems. Some countries, like Congo and Gabon, have compulsory education from six to sixteen, but few African children are able to continue beyond primary level. Here, children attend a village school in Cameroon.

Coconuts are one of the principal crops of São Tomé and Príncipe.

AGRICULTURE
The main foods in the region are cassava and yams, both root crops that grow in tropical and sub-tropical regions. Cassava is often grown in forest clearings, as shown here in Cameroon. It is turned into flour by pounding it to extract the sap. Yams, similar to potatoes, can be mashed or boiled.

DIAMONDS AND COBALT
Zaire is rich in a wide variety of minerals, particularly cobalt and industrial diamonds. It is the world's largest producer of both minerals. Cobalt is used in the manufacture of special steels – such as those required to withstand high temperatures – and for making magnets. Industrial diamonds are used for cutting and grinding hard surfaces. Look for ◆.

Alluvial diamond

ZAIRE'S LIFELINE
The Congo (Zaire) River sweeps in a huge arc through the region's rain forests on its route to the Atlantic Ocean. In Zaire, the road and rail networks are in disrepair, so the river acts as the country's principal lifeline. Riverboats transport people and goods and act as markets, health clinics, and bars.

KEYBOX

Cotton: Chad is said to be the world's third-poorest country. Attempts are being made to increase output of its main export, cotton. Look for ✹

Oil: Cameroon, Gabon, and Congo are all dependent on exporting oil. Zaire also has huge reserves which are, as yet, undeveloped. Look for ♣

♫	Bananas	🍌	Tobacco
☘	Coffee	🐟	Forest products
🥜	Cocoa	◐	Fishing port
🥜	Peanuts	⛏	Mining
🍶	Vegetable oil	⚒	Industrial center

EQUATORIAL GUINEA
POP: 410,000

SAO TOME AND PRINCIPE
POP: 136,000

GABON
POP: 1,115,000

CONGO
POP: 2,062,000

ZAIRE
POP: 45,142,000

SÃO TOMÉ & PRÍNCIPE

CABINDA
(Angola)

### Map labels
UGANDA, TANZANIA, RWANDA, BURUNDI, ZAIRE, ZAMBIA, ANGOLA, CONGO, GABON, EQUATORIAL GUINEA, SAO TOME, Príncipe, ATLANTIC OCEAN, Gulf of Guinea

L. Albert, L. Edward, L. Kivu, L. Tanganyika, L. Mweru, MITUMBA MTS, Boyoma Falls, L. Tumba, L. Mai-Ndombe

Bunia, Isiro, Butembo, Goma, Bukavu, Uvira, Kalemie, Kabalo, Manono, Kamina, Kongolo, Kindu, Kasongo, Kisangani, Aruwimi, Buta, Bumba, Lualaba, Lomami, Lodja, Lusambo, Mbuji-Mayi, Kananga, Mwene-Ditu, Dilolo, Kolwezi, Manganese, Likasi, Lubumbashi, Bandundu, Kikwit, Kenge, Kinshasa, Matadi, Boma, Brazzaville, Pointe-Noire, Loubomo, Libreville, Lambaréné, Mouila, Tchibanga, Oyem, Makokou, Port-Gentil, Kribi, Bata, Ebolowa, Bitam, Ouesso, Impfondo, Owando, Djambala, Mbandaka, Boende, Ilebo, Tshikapa, Tshuapa, Kasai, Kwilu, Kwango, Kwa, Kwa, Lulua, Sangha, Ubangi, Congo (Zaire), Ogooué, Dja, Djoué

Gold, Rubber, Tin, Palm, Iron, Zinc, Cobalt, Copper, Lead, Diamonds, Uranium, Manganese

N

KM / MILES
0 100 200 300 400 500
0 100 200 300

95

CENTRAL EAST AFRICA

EAST AFRICA'S WEALTH lies in its land. Most people make their living from farming or cattle herding. Large areas covered with long grass, scrub, and scattered trees, called savannah, provide grazing for domestic and wild animals alike. But some land, especially in Uganda and Zambia, cannot be used because of tsetse fly, which is dangerous to both animals and humans. Tea, coffee, and tobacco are grown as cash crops throughout the area, especially in Kenya and Malawi. Uganda has great potential for farming, but for the last 20 years it has been crippled by civil wars. Zambia, Rwanda, Burundi, and Uganda all suffer from having no seaports. Industry is poorly developed in the region, except in Kenya, and only Zambia is rich in minerals. Burundi and Rwanda are densely populated, and Kenya now has the world's fastest-growing population. After economic decline in the 1980s, Tanzania is slowly recovering.

THE SAMBURU
In Kenya's northern plateau region, tribes like the Samburu continue to follow the traditional way of life of their ancestors. They live by grazing their herds of cattle, sheep, and goats on the savannah. This *moran*, or warrior, wears numerous strings of beads, distinctive ivory earrings, and always carries two spears and a knife.

TRAINS
Countries with no coastline are very dependent on road and rail transport to link them to industrial centers and main ports. Although the African rail network is expanding, tracks are often poorly maintained. Here, people board a train at Kampala in Uganda.

PREDATORY FISH
Thirty years ago the Nile perch was introduced into Lake Victoria to increase fish production. Although the lake is vast, this fish now occupies every corner and is killing off the original fish population. Look for ➤

AIDS
AIDS is a worldwide problem, but it is particularly widespread in Africa. Many people on the continent already suffer from diseases and malnutrition, which makes them more vulnerable to the illnesses associated with AIDS.

WILDLIFE RESERVES
Africa's great plains contain some of the world's most spectacular species of wildlife. All the countries in the region have set aside huge areas as national parks where animals are protected. Wildlife safaris attract thousands of tourists and provide countries with much needed foreign income. Look for ⊞

POACHING
Africa's wildlife parks have helped preserve the animals, but poaching remains a major problem. Recently, in an attempt to save the elephants, a worldwide ban on the sale of ivory was imposed. But policing the parks is very costly; poachers are armed and dangerous. Here, in Tanzania, wardens are burning a poacher's hut.

Tsetse fly carries a disease that can kill cattle and humans.

COPPER
There are huge deposits of copper in central Africa, centered around Ndola in Zambia. This region is often called the Copperbelt. Copper accounts for 90 percent of Zambia's export earnings, but low prices in recent years and the discovery of cheaper substitutes have badly affected the industry. Supplies of copper are nearly used up, which could mean disaster for the Zambian economy. The Copperbelt now has improved transport links, such as the Tanzam Railway, which take the refined copper to various destinations. Look for ◑

Copper bracelets

Vultures cluster in a lone tree on the Tanzanian grasslands.

KEYBOX

Coffee: A valuable cash crop, coffee is grown in Uganda, Kenya, Tanzania, and Rwanda. Kenya plans to triple production by the year 2000. Look for ❧	
Market gardening: Kenya has ideal conditions for growing vegetables and fruit, which are exported in large quantities, mainly to Europe. Look for ✈	
Hydroelectric power: The Kariba Dam on the Zambezi River, built by Zambia and Zimbabwe, supplies both nations with electricity. Look for ▤	
Refugee camps: Warfare in neighboring countries has caused thousands of refugees to flee to temporary camps in the region. Look for ⌂	

⬇	Sugarcane	🌲	Forest products
🥥	Coconuts	🐟	Fishing
🌱	Tea	⛏	Mining
☕	Cotton	🏭	Industrial center
🌿	Tobacco	⊞	Wildlife reserves

AFRICAN VILLAGE
East African villages usually consist of a series of huts enclosed by thorn fences. This aerial photo shows a village belonging to the Masai tribe. A Masai man may have several wives. Each wife has her own huts, enclosed by a fence. The livestock is taken out to graze by day and driven into the fenced enclosure at night.

0	100	200	300	400	500	KM
0	50	100	150	200	250	300	MILES

N

Z

Solwez

West Lunga

Zambezi

Z   A   M

A
N
G
O
L
A

Liuwa Plain

Kafue

K A
F L

Mongu

Zambezi

Sioma

Victoria Falls

NAMIBIA

Livin

BOTSWANA

Z

A   B   C   D   E   F   G

The Ruwenzori Mountains between Zaire and Uganda.

Southeast Sudan is administered by Kenya

UGANDA
POP: 19,278,000

RWANDA
POP: 7,500,000

BURUNDI
POP: 5,800,000

KENYA
POP: 28,794,000

TANZANIA
POP: 31,698,000

MALAWI
POP: 11,552,000

ZAMBIA
POP: 9,623,000

Traditional East African bags, made from sisal, an important Kenyan and Tanzanian crop.

TEA CULTIVATION

East Africa's highlands are ideal for growing tea, especially in Kenya and Malawi. Most tea is grown on large plantations, often owned by foreign companies. In Kenya many Africans now grow tea on small farms. It is processed at factories which are co-operatively owned. Look for ⚘

African dhows sailing off the coast of the island of Zanzibar.

Cloves are one of Zanzibar's chief exports.

NAIROBI

Kenya's capital city now has more sky-scrapers than many European cities. But so many people have come from the countryside to Nairobi to find work that the city's services, such as the water supply and drainage, have been strained to their limit.

RIFT VALLEY

The Great Rift Valley stretches for over 6,000 miles (9,600 km) from Turkey to Mozambique, splitting into two arms in East Africa. In this region it contains lakes, swamps, ravines, and volcanoes, which in some cases reach heights of over 3,280 ft (1,000 m). On the well-watered, fertile slopes of the valley, crops like coffee and tea are grown. In the warm, damp coastlands, tropical crops such as sugar are cultivated.

Uganda: cattle grazed in dry lowlands

Semidesert used by nomads for grazing cattle

Kampala

Nairobi

R. Nile

Poor soils, low rainfall, prone to tsetse fly

Mombasa

Kilimanjaro

Dar esSalaam

INDIAN OCEAN

Coastal lowlands: tropical crops

Highland areas: coffee and tea grown on fertile soils, with reliable rainfall

SOUTHERN AFRICA

THE WEALTHIEST and most dominant country in this region is South Africa. Black African lands were gradually settled in the 19th century by Dutch colonists, their descendants – the Afrikaners – and the British. When vast deposits of gold and diamonds were discovered in the late 19th century, the country became rich. In 1948 the government introduced a system of "separate development," called *apartheid*, which separated people according to their color and gave political power to whites only. This policy led to isolation and sanctions from the rest of the world's nations, which only ended after the abolition of apartheid. The first democratic elections were held in 1994. After years of conflict, South Africa has now become a more integrated society. Most of the countries around South Africa rely on its industries for trade and work. After 30 years of unrest, Namibia has won independence from South Africa. Mozambique and Angola are both struggling for survival after years of civil war. Zimbabwe has a relatively diverse economy, based on agriculture and its rich mineral resources.

INDUSTRY
South Africa is the region's industrial leader. Johannesburg, the country's largest city, is seen here behind the huge mounds of earth excavated from the gold mines. Look for ⛏

URANIUM
Namibia is rich in copper, diamonds, tin, and other minerals. The mining industry accounts for 90 percent of its export earnings. At Rössing, in the Namib Desert, uranium is extracted from a huge open-pit mine and exported abroad. Look for ☢

KEYBOX

Fishing: Overfishing by both foreign and local fleets is a major threat to Namibia's once-rich fishing grounds. Controls are in operation. Look for ➤

Oil: Civil war in Angola has disrupted industry, but its oil reserves – the only major ones in the region – so far have been little affected. Look for ♠

Wildlife reserves: Most of the region's countries have set aside large areas as wildlife parks, which are popular tourist attractions. Look for ⊞

🐂	Cattle	🌿	Tea
🌾	Cereals	🌿	Tobacco
🍋	Citrus fruits	☢	Mining
🍇	Wine	⛏	Coal
☕	Coffee	🏭	Industrial center

BUSHMEN
Bushmen – or *San* – are one of the few groups of hunter-gatherers left in Africa. These people can be traced far back into African history. Today, some 1,000 bushmen still live in the harsh environment of the Kalahari Desert.

The Ndebele people of the Transvaal often paint their houses in bright colors.

ANGOLA
POP: 11,440,000

The *ilimba* drum from Zimbabwe is made from the hard shell of a gourd.

NAMIBIA
POP: 1,739,000

A lone thorn tree in the hot, sandy Namib Desert.

CAPE TOWN
Sprawled along the lower slopes of Table Mountain, and overlooking Table Bay, Cape Town has a spectacular setting. It is a busy port and the city where South Africa's parliament meets. Until the Suez Canal was opened, Cape Town lay on the main shipping route between Europe and Asia. Its harbor was often used by ships sheltering from the gales and stormy seas off the Cape of Good Hope.

THE SANGOMA
In most African tribal societies there is a traditional healer called a *sangoma*, who cares for the sick, predicts the future, and generally looks after the well-being of the people.

Fresh corn

CORN
Corn is one of the main crops grown in this region. In the 1980s, the introduction of new kinds of seed and wider use of fertilizer greatly increased corn production. Because most men work in industry, women cultivate the crops required to feed the family. Look for ✿

DIAMONDS
Botswana was one of the world's poorest nations when it became independent. Its economy has now been transformed by the discovery of diamonds in the Kalahari Desert, and diamonds make up 80 percent of its exports. Look for ◉

Acacia trees are a common sight on the savannah.

SUN CITY
The tourist resort of Sun City lies to the west of Johannesburg. Visitors from the region, and the rest of the world, are drawn to its luxury hotels, casino, game park, and other attractions.

Poster for one of the political groups in Mozambique

MOZAMBIQUE
When Mozambique was given independence by Portugal in 1975, the country was unprepared for self-government. Continuous civil war for the last 20 years has left thousands dead, the economy in ruins, and many starving.

Lake Kariba is a huge artificial lake.

OSTRICH FARMS
Ostrich feathers were once in great demand as fashion accessories. Ostrich farmers grew rich and became known as Feather Barons. Feathers are no longer fashionable, but ostriches are still raised for their meat around Oudtshoorn, in South Africa.

Platinum is mined in northwestern South Africa.

"TOWNSHIPS"
The apartheid system meant that many black people were forced to live in "townships", often some distance from their work. The largest and best known is Soweto. People from Soweto – which means "South-Western Townships" – travel daily to work in Johannesburg.

Platinum crystal

GOLD
Southern Africa has the richest deposits of valuable minerals in Africa. These miners are drilling for gold near Johannesburg, the area where gold was first discovered in 1886. This work is usually done by black Africans, but a mixed labor force will be more common in future. Gold from South Africa is often sold abroad in the form of coins called Krugerrands. Look for ◉

LESOTHO'S WATER PROJECT
In contrast with surrounding areas, Lesotho's Maluti Mountains have plenty of water. Dams and tunnels are being constructed to transfer water and electricity to neighboring South Africa.

Lengthy tunnels transfer water between dams

Matsoku Dam
Maluti Mts.
Mashai Dam
Katse Dam
Mohale Dam
Tsoelike Dam
Ntoahae Dam
Orange R.
LESOTHO
SOUTH AFRICA

**Map labels:**
TANZANIA
ZAMBIA
MALAWI
L. Nyasa
Rovuma
Lugenda
Mocimboa da Praia
Pemba
Nacala
Nampula
Moçambique
MOZAMBIQUE POP: 15,300,000
Mozambique Channel
ZIMBABWE POP: 11,845,000
BOTSWANA POP: 1,532,000
Zambezi
Cabora Bassa L.
Tete
L. Kariba
Mana Pools
Chinhoyi
Chromium
Bindura
HARARE
Chitungwiza
Victoria Falls
Hwange
Tin
Iron
Gold
Quelimane
ZIMBABWE
Gorongosa
Gweru
Gold
Corn
Mutare
Chimoio
Beira
Bulawayo
Chromium
Masvingo
Chromium
Save
Zinave
Beef
Corn
Francistown
Selebi-Phikwe
Nickel
Banhine
Serowe
Beef
Thohoyandou
Mahalapye
Limpopo
Kruger
Beef
Pietersburg
Inhambane
Wheat
Platinum
GABORONE
TRANSVAAL
Sun City
Platinum
Diamonds
Xai-Xai
Soweto
PRETORIA
Uranium
MBABANE
Johannesburg
MAPUTO
Manzini
Vereeniging
SWAZILAND
Klerksdorp
SWAZILAND POP: 882,000
Vaal
Gold
NATAL
Kimberley
Wheat
LESOTHO
Tugela
MASERU
Pietermaritzburg
LESOTHO POP: 2,025,000
Mafeteng
Beef
Durban
Orange R.
Corn
Umtata
Bisho
Beef
East London
Grahamstown
Port Elizabeth
SOUTH AFRICA POP: 43,715,000
INDIAN OCEAN
Hwange
ai Pan
Makgadikgadi Pans
Shashe
Limpopo
Beef
Corn

Scale:
0 100 200 300 400 500 600 KM
0 100 200 300 MILES

N

THE INDIAN OCEAN

THE INDIAN OCEAN is the smallest of the world's oceans, but some 5,000 islands – many of them surrounded by coral reefs – are scattered across its area. Beneath its surface, three great mountain ranges converge toward the ocean's center – an area of strong seismic and volcanic activity. The ocean reaches its greatest depth – 24,400 ft (7,440 m) – in the Java Trench. More than one billion people – about a fifth of the world's population – live in the countries around the Indian Ocean, representing an immense range of cultures and religions. Heavy monsoon rain and tropical storms cause flooding along the ocean's northern coasts. The world's largest oil fields are located around the Persian Gulf.

KARACHI

In the mid-19th century a railroad was built along the Indus River valley to Karachi, which developed into a large port and industrial city. When Pakistan became an independent nation in 1947, Karachi became the country's capital. It has now been replaced by the new city of Islamabad in the north.

ISLANDS

The islands of the Indian Ocean include enormous ones like Madagascar, coral atolls like the Maldives, and volcanic islands like Réunion. All are threatened by rising sea levels, which reduce the area of land available. Coral reefs are being eroded, leaving islands increasingly exposed to ocean tides and flooding.

MONSOON

Farmers in the lands around the Indian Ocean are wholly dependent on the coming of the monsoon rains. In May or June, the western arm of the monsoon sweeps in from the Arabian Sea, bringing torrential downpours which move north through India. At the same time, the monsoon's eastern arm curves out of the Bay of Bengal, driving north as far as the Himalayan foothills. About 85 percent of India's annual rainfall occurs during the monsoon periods.

Mangroves grow along many of the Indian Ocean's coasts.

FISHING

Large-scale fishing is far less developed in the Indian Ocean than in either the Atlantic or Pacific. Fishing is difficult because there are relatively few areas of shallow sea. Small-scale fishing, however, provides a valuable source of food. Many fishermen, like these Sri Lankans, use basic and often inefficient methods. Tuna is the most important catch in the area. Look for

The loggerhead turtle is one of the Indian Ocean's many endangered species.

SUGAR

Sugar was first brought to Mauritius by the Dutch in the 1600s. Ninety percent of the island's arable farmland is covered by sugar plantations. But today sugar has been replaced in importance by textiles, which now account for nearly half the island's exports. Look for

Sugar cane

TOURISM

The Indian Ocean islands are great tourist attractions. The islands welcome the money this brings, but the sheer number of visitors threatens to destroy the islands' environment. Look for

Hotel complex on an island in Mauritius

Once thought extinct, the coelacanth has been found, alive and well, off southeast

### Map labels

Port Said
Suez Canal
Suez
Nile
RED SEA
Djibouti
Aden
Gulf of Aden
Tigris
Euphrates
Basra
Kuwait City
Persian Gulf
Manama
Bahrain
ARABIA
Safalah
Masirah
Ra's al Hadd
Gulf of Oman
Chah Bahar
Indus
Karachi
ARABIAN SEA
Bombay
Vishakhapatnam
Madras
Cochin
C. Comorin
Laccadive Is. (India)
MALDIVES
MALE
MALDIVES POP. 255,000
Socotra (Yemen)
C. Xaafuun
Mombasa
Dar es Salaam
MORONI
COMOROS
Grande Comore
Aldabra Is. (Seychelles)
Amirante Is. (Seychelles)
SEYCHELLES
VICTORIA
Mahé
C. Bobaomby
Antsiranana
Antananarivo
MAHAJANGA
Mascarene Plat.
Masirah
Somali Basin
Carlsberg Ridge
Maldive Ridge
BRITISH INDIAN OCEAN TERRITORY (UK)
Diego Garcia
INDIAN
Calcutta
Ganges
Bay of Bengal
Andaman Is. (India)
Nicobar Is. (India)
Trincomalee
Sri Lanka
Colombo
Dondra Head
Irrawaddy
Rangoon
ANDAMAN SEA
Mekong
Gulf of Thailand
George Town
Strait of Malacca
Melaka
Singapore
Tin
SOUTH CHINA SEA
JAVA SEA
Borneo
Sumatra
Java
Java Trench
COCOS IS. (Australia)
CHRISTMAS IS. (Australia)
ASHMORE & CARTIER IS. (Australia)
AFRICA
ASIA

STRAIT OF MALACCA

Since ancient times, ships trading between the Indian and Pacific oceans have passed through the shallow waters of the Strait of Malacca. This is the main route through the Indonesian archipelago. Ports like Melaka – seen here – have prospered from this trade.

N

2000KM   MILES
1500   1000
1000   750
          500
500   250
0   0

Huge ice floes drift north from Antarctica, becoming a major hazard to shipping.

DHOW

The Arab dhow has been one of the principal sailing boats in the Indian Ocean for over 4,000 years. Arabs used these sturdy craft on the trade routes from the Persian Gulf to China. Their cargoes included spices, cowrie shells, dates, and slaves. Their large lateen, or triangular, sails make them easy to maneuver.

Mizzen-mast

Furled lateen sail

Mainmast

POLLUTION

The Indian Ocean is particularly at risk from oil pollution from tankers carrying Persian Gulf oil. The Persian Gulf itself is severely polluted by oil spills from ships, rigs, and refineries. During the Gulf War of 1991, huge quantities of oil were released into the Gulf waters, causing appalling damage. Look for ●

MAURITIUS
POP: 1,140,000

MADAGASCAR
POP: 13,309,000

ANTARCTICA

SANCTUARY

Many species of whales breed in the Indian Ocean. In 1979, most of the ocean was designated a whale sanctuary to protect them. The dugong – a marine mammal – is also threatened with extinction. Although it lives for up to 70 years, it matures late and produces few young in its lifetime. It is vegetarian, feeding exclusively on sea grasses.

Dugong

MADAGASCAR

This huge island off Africa's east coast is desperately poor. Most Madagascans make their living from farming, cattle herding, or logging. In the last 25 years the population has doubled, and the constant need for land and fuel has massively reduced the once-extensive forests. The staple food is rice. The main exports are coffee and vanilla.

Vanilla pod

Vanilla seed

SEYCHELLES
POP: 75,000

NAVAL BASES

The Indian Ocean is important to the major world powers as a link between the Atlantic and Pacific oceans, and as the main route for tankers bringing oil from the Persian Gulf. The USA has a base on Diego García. The French have a naval base on the island of Réunion. Look for ▮▮▮

Huge baobab trees on the island of Madagascar.

KEYBOX

Shellfishing: An area near Karachi has been developed as a major shrimp nursery. It employs thousands of local workers. Look for ➤

Industrial center: Due to low labor costs and tax incentives, new industries, including textiles, have been developed in Mauritius. Look for ▮

Mining: Tin is dredged off the west coast of Thailand and east coast of Sumatra. Dredging can damage the seabed and mangroves. Look for ●

Sugarcane	Gas
Coconuts	Tourism
Fishing	Underwater wrecks
Fishing port	Whales
Oil	Military bases

Cape Town
Durban
Simon's Town
Cape of Good Hope
Limpopo
Fremantle
Cockburn Sound
AUSTRALIA

O C E A N

Southeast Indian Ridge
South Indian Basin
Australia Basin
Broken Ridge
Mid-Indian Ridge
Amsterdam I. (France)
St-Paul I. (France)
Kerguelen Plateau
Kerguelen (France)
Heard I. Macdonald Is. (Australia)
Crozer Basin
Crozet Is. (France)
Prince Edward Is. (South Africa)
Madagascar Basin
Madagascar Ridge
Atlantic-Indian Basin
Fatafangana
Toliara
C. Volimena

Cedar of Lebanon
Cedrus libani
Height: 130 ft (40 m)

Common hamster
Cricetus cricetus
Length: 12 in (30 cm)

Waxwing
Bombycilla garrulus
Length: 8 in (18 cm)

NORTH AND WEST ASIA

NORTH AND WEST ASIA contains some of the world's most inhospitable environments. In the south, the Arabian Peninsula is almost entirely a baking hot desert where no plants can grow. To the north, a belt of rugged, snow-capped mountains and high plateaus cross the continent. The climate becomes drier and more extreme toward the center of the continent. Dry hot summers contrast with bitterly cold winters. Cold deserts give way to treeless plains known as steppe, then to huge marshes, and to the world's largest needleleaf forest. In the extreme north, both land and sea are frozen for most of the year. Only in summer do the top layers of soil thaw briefly allowing plants of the tundra, such as moss and lichen, to cover the land.

Arabian oryx
Oryx leucoryx
Height: 4 ft (1.2 m)

Baikal seal
Phoca sibirica
Length: 5 ft (1.5 m)
Found only in Lake Baikal

Darkling beetle
Sternodes species
Length: 1 in (2 cm)

HOT BATHS
These strange white terraces formed in southwestern Asia in much the same way that a kettle develops scale. Underground water heated by volcanic activity dissolves minerals in rocks. These are deposited when the water reaches the surface and cools.

Blue turquoise, a semiprecious stone mainly found in cold areas of north Asia.

DROUGHT-TOLERANT TREES
Plants growing near the Black Sea minimize water loss during the long hot summers. Most have wax-covered leaves through which little water can escape.

The fossilized head of *Gallimimus*, an ostrichlike dinosaur that once lived in Asia.

SINAI'S ROCK "MUSHROOMS"
In deserts, sand particles whipped along by high-speed winds create natural sculptures. Rock at the base of the "mushroom" has been more heavily eroded than rock above, leading to these unusual landforms.

▲ VOLCANO
There are more than 30 active volcanoes on the Kamchatka peninsula, part of the Pacific Ocean's "Ring of Fire." Volcanic activity is due to the deep underground movements of the Eurasian plate.

COLD FOREST
Strong but flexible trunks and a tentlike shape help needleleaf trees withstand the great weight of snow that covers them throughout the long winter.

REGENERATING FOREST
Unlike many plants, juniper trees are able to withstand the acid soils of needleleaf forests. Here junipers cover the floor of a dense pine forest.

FROZEN RIVER
The Lena River rises near Lake Baikal, the world's deepest and oldest freshwater lake. Like other Siberian rivers, it flows into the Arctic Ocean and is frozen over for eight or nine months of the year.

HOT DESERTS
The Arabian Desert is one of the hottest and driest places in the world. Temperatures frequently reach 120°F (45°C) and very little rain falls.

CROSS-SECTION THROUGH NORTH AND WEST ASIA

Ural Mts
Kirghiz Steppe
Arctic Ocean
Kara Sea
Aral Sea
Kara Kum
Iranian Plateau
Arabian Sea

-4,921 (-1,500)
0 Sea level
-9,843 (-3,000)
Feet (meters)

A   *Length: 4,000 miles (6,400 km)*   B

COLD WINTER DESERT
Large parts of Central Asia are covered in deserts that are hot in summer but very cold in winter. A river has been naturally dammed to form this lake, which is unusual in this dry region.

Reindeer
Rangifer tarandus
Body length: 7 ft (2.2 m)

Pallas's cat
Felis manul
Length: 26 in (65 cm)

Gray wolf
Canis lupus
Length: 5 ft (1.4 m)

Siberian iris
Iris sibirica
Height: 4 ft (1.2 m)

BROADLEAF DECIDUOUS FOREST
Broadleaf trees, such as oaks, have
larger, wider leaves than needleleaf
trees, such as pines. Broadleaf (or
deciduous) trees shed all their leaves
at once in the autumn; needleleaf (or
coniferous) trees shed and
replace their leaves all
through the year.

The head of a
fossilized
Benthosuchus,
which lived in
Asia over 200
million years ago.

ARCTIC OCEAN

North Pole

Lomonsov Ridge

Canada Basin

New
Siberian Is.

LAPTEV SEA

BERING SEA

Aleutian Is.

VERKHOYANSK
RANGE

SEA OF
OKHOTSK

▲ 9,708ft

NORTH AMERICAN PLATE
EURASIAN PLATE

STANOVOY RANGE

▲ 9,840ft

Amur

Nansen Basin

Severnaya
Zemlya

TAIMYR
PENINSULA

Lena
Delta

Arctic Circle

Franz Josef
Land

Svalbard

Novaya
Zemlya

KARA SEA

5,581ft

C E N T R A L
S I B E R I A N
P L A T E A U

S I B E R I A

Lena

Kerulen

Limit of Permanent Ice Sheet

Greenland

GREENLAND SEA

NORWEGIAN SEA

BARENTS
SEA

WEST
SIBERIAN
PLAIN

Ob'

Yenisey

Angara

L. Baikal

Iceland

6,214ft

Irtysh

E U R O P E

U R A L   M O U N T A I N S

▲13,784ft

ALTAI MTS.

DZUNGARIA

ATLANTIC OCEAN

NORTH
SEA

BALTIC
SEA

L. Zaysan

L. Alakol'

Ili

TIEN SHAN

▲ Pobeda Peak
24,407ft

A S I A

KIRGHIZ
STEPPE

L. Balkhash

BLACK SEA

CAUCASUS

CASPIAN SEA

ARAL
SEA

Syr Darya

KYZYL KUM

Lenin Peak
23,407ft

Commanism
Peak
24,591ft
25,231ft

H I M A L A Y A S

EURASIAN PLATE
INDO-AUSTRALIAN PLATE

Karagiya
Depression
433ft

KARA KUM

Amu Darya

HINDU KUSH

ANATOLIA

▲12,251ft

TAURUS MTS.

EURASIAN PLATE
IRANIAN PLATE

Ganges

Tropic of Cancer

IRANIAN PLATE
AFRICAN PLATE

Cyprus

Euphrates

Tigris

ZAGROS MOUNTAINS

DASHT-E-KAVIR

▲14,922ft

IRANIAN
PLATEAU

DASHT-E-LUT

IRANIAN PLATE
ARABIAN PLATE

IRANIAN PLATE
INDO-AUSTRALIAN PLATE

Indus

INDIAN
SUBCONTINENT

MEDITERRANEAN SEA

SYRIAN
DESERT

Dead
Sea

SINAI
DESERT

AN NAFUD

Persian Gulf

Gulf of
Oman

• B

Bay of
Bengal

RED SEA

ARABIAN
PLATE

AFRICAN PLATE

A R A B I A N

P E N I N S U L A

RUB' AL KHALI

ARABIAN
SEA

Arabian
Basin

Chagos or Laccadive
Plateau

Sri Lanka

A F R I C A

Gulf of Aden

Socotra

Ceylon Plain

Equator

INDIAN OCEAN

TURKEY AND CYPRUS

SITUATED PARTLY IN EUROPE and partly in Asia, Turkey is also balanced between modern Europe and its Islamic past. For 600 years, the Ottoman Turks ruled over a great empire covering a quarter of Europe, but by the early 20th century their empire had disappeared. In the 1920s, Mustapha Kemal Atatürk forcibly modernized Turkish society. Today, Turkey is becoming increasingly industrialized; textile and food-processing industries dominate the economy. In the central plateau, however, farmers and herders live as they have done for centuries, adapting their lives to the harsh environment. To the north, the Black Sea is rich in fish, and the fertile areas around its shores are well suited to farming. The beautiful western and southern coasts are strewn with the remains of ancient Greek settlements, attracting 1.5 million tourists to Turkey every year.

ISTANBUL
Istanbul is divided in two by a strait of water called the Bosporus. One part of the city is in Europe, the other in Asia. Its buildings are also a mix of East and West: grand mosques, graceful minarets, and exotic bazaars rub shoulders with modern shops, offices, and restaurants.

TURKEY
POP: 63,204,000

The harbor and castle of St. Peter at Bodrum.

STREET TRADERS
Large numbers of people from the countryside go to Turkey's cities to try to make a living. Many of them sell goods, food, or drink on the streets or from makeshift market stalls. Others work as shoeshiners, carrying their equipment in highly decorated brass cases.

A CLASSICAL LEGACY
The temple of Athena in Priene is one of Turkey's many ancient treasures. The Aegean coast was colonized by the ancient Greeks as early as 700 BC. Many people go to Turkey to visit the dramatic remains of Greek cities and temples. Look for ▥

Blue Mosque, Istanbul

MOSQUE
Modern Turkey does not have a state religion. It was once an Islamic country, but earlier this century reforms limited the powers of the clerics and introduced civil law. Recently, however, there has been an Islamic revival, and modern Turks are going back to many customs from their rich Islamic past.

Dried apricot

Almond

Hazelnut

Peach

Fig

This strange landscape is in Cappadocia, central Turkey.

AGRICULTURE
Turkey has a varied landscape and climate. This means that many different types of crop can be grown there, and the Turks are able to produce all their own food. Cereals, sugar beet, grapes, nuts, cotton, and tobacco are all major exports. Hazelnuts are grown along the shores of the Black Sea. Figs, peaches, olives, and grapes are grown along the Mediterranean coast and in the coastal lowlands. Cereals are cultivated on the central plateau. Farms are still relatively small and only gradually being modernized, but despite this productivity is high.

KEYBOX

Tobacco: *Turkey is a major producer. Dark Turkish tobacco is grown around the Black Sea and Aegean coasts. Look for* ↘

Tourism: *Coastal resorts are developing rapidly. Airports cater for growing numbers of visitors from northern Europe. Look for* ⚓

Dams: *Ambitious dam-building programs, especially in the southeast, are being used for hydroelectric power and for watering farmland. Look for* ▦

🌾	Cereals	⚓	Cotton
🍓	Sugar beet	🐟	Fishing
🍋	Citrus fruit		Carpet weaving
🍇	Wine	🏭	Industrial center
🫒	Vegetable oil	▥	Archaeological site

ANKARA
Ankara has been the capital of Turkey since 1923. It is a planned modern city with boulevards, parks, and many high-rise apartments. Until recently, the city suffered from terrible pollution, caused by people burning brown coal, or lignite, for heating. Now, clean natural gas is piped into the city from the Russian Federation.

BULGARIA

GREECE

Edirne   Kirklareli

Wheat   Wheat

Tekirdağ   Sariyer   Bosporus   Beykoz

Istanbul   Izmit

Gallipoli   Dardanelles   Sea of Marmara   Adapazari

Çanakkale   Bandirma   Gemlik   Iznik

Troy   Bilecik   Sakarya

Olives   Bursa   Eskişehir

Olives   Balikesir   Wheat   Bar

Pergamon   Ayvalik   Olives   Kütahya

Olives   Wheat

Akhisar   Uşak   Afyon   Bolv

Manisa   Demirköprü Barrage

Izmir   Olives

Ephesus   Nazilli   Pamukkale   L. Eğridir

Kuşadasi   Aydin   L. Beys

Priene   Aphrodisias   Denizli   Isparta

Miletus   Burdur   Bey

Didyma   Milâs   Olives

Halicarnassus   Mugla

Bodrum   Olives   Perge

Marmaris   Antalya   Side

Dalaman   Fethiye   Oludeniz

MEDITERRANEAN

TURKISH FOOD

Typical Turkish food consists of fresh fruit, vegetables, meat and fish, flavored with spices such as cinnamon and cumin. Lamb is the most common meat. It is often grilled on a skewer to make a kebab, or minced and made into spiced meatballs, served with rice or cracked wheat (*bulgur*). Yogurt is eaten everywhere, often mixed with cucumber, garlic, or mint to make a refreshing side dish.

Bulgur wheat
Tomato
Olive
Bay leaf
Yogurt with cucumber
Lamb shish kebab

KILIMS

Knotted-pile carpets, called *kilims*, were first made many centuries ago by the Turks' nomadic ancestors. Each region of Turkey produces carpets with slightly different patterns and colors, although today chemical dyes are often used instead of the traditional vegetable colorings. Look for

Anchovies are caught in the Black Sea.

Veined rapa whelk

A 10th-century church on Lake Van in eastern Turkey.

RURAL LIFE

Life in the high plateaus of central Turkey is very hard. The winters are severe and the landscape is desolate. Most people live as nomadic herders or small-scale farmers. Many people leave these areas to live in the overcrowded cities or go to the rich countries of northern Europe as "guest workers."

Mohair comes from the Angora goat, native to central Turkey.

Glazed tiles made in Iznik decorate many Turkish mosques.

Turkish delight
Turkish coffee pot

In 1983 the north of the island proclaimed itself the Turkish Republic of Northern Cyprus. It is recognized only by Turkey.

CYPRUS
POP: 742,000

CYPRUS

Cyprus is the largest island in the east Mediterranean. Cypriots are a mixture of Greek and Turkish speakers. After independence in 1959, conflict between the two communities resulted in the United Nations sending a peacekeeping force, which still remains. Despite their presence, there was a Turkish invasion in 1974. Since then, the island has been split into two parts.

WOMEN WORKERS

Although Turkish women are equal by law, traditions of male authority still persist, especially in the countryside. It is common to see old women doing backbreaking work in the fields, while their husbands look on. On the other hand, some Turkish women have succeeded in powerful jobs as politicians, judges, or bank directors.

COFFEE

Turkey, like other Middle Eastern countries, has a long tradition of coffee drinking. Turkish coffee is made by pounding the beans to a powder and then boiling this with sugar to make a strong, dark brew. Coffee houses are favorite meeting places, where people also smoke pipes, play cards, and chat.

THE NEAR EAST

CAUGHT BETWEEN the continents of Europe and Asia, the Near East is bordered on the west by the fertile coasts of the Mediterranean Sea, and on the east by the arid deserts of Arabia. Some of the world's earliest civilizations were born here, while the history of three of the world's greatest religions – Judaism, Christianity, and Islam – is closely bound up with the region. Imperial conquerors, crusaders, and Muslim warriors battled fiercely over this territory, and by the 17th century much of the region was part of the Turkish Ottoman Empire. In 1918, the region came under the control of Britain and France; a dangerous mixture of religions and passionate nationalism plunged the area into conflict. Today, Lebanon is just beginning to emerge from a fierce civil war between Christians and Muslims. Israel, which became a Jewish state in 1948, has been involved in numerous wars with its neighbors, and there is considerable unrest among its Palestinian population. Many Palestinian refugees, who have left Israel, are living in camps in Jordan and Lebanon. Despite these problems, the Near East continues to survive economically. Israel is highly industrialized and a world leader in advanced farming techniques. Syria has its own reserves of oil and is gradually becoming more industrialized.

Carnation
Rose
Grapefruit
Orange
Lemon
Lime

FARMING

Although about half of Israel is desert, it is self-sufficient in most food, and actually exports agricultural produce, especially citrus fruits and flowers. Israeli farming uses advanced irrigation techniques and is highly mechanized. Many farms are run as *kibbutzim*; the land is owned by members, who share work and profits. Look for

JERUSALEM THE GOLDEN

The historic city of Jerusalem is held sacred by three major religions: Judaism, Christianity, and Islam. Throughout its history, it has been the object of pilgrimage and religious crusades. For Jews, the Wailing Wall, seen here, is the holiest site, while the Dome of the Rock is sacred to Muslims.

Skullcap, yarmulke

JUDAISM

Judaism is one of the oldest religions in the world. Jews believe in one God and follow codes of behavior based on the Torah, the first part of the Old Testament, which is written in Hebrew, plus other scriptures. Modern Hebrew is the language of Israel.

The Torah

Prayer shawl

UZI GUNS

Israel is a major arms producer, developing weapons for its own army, such as this Uzi gun, as well as medium-range missiles to deter Arab enemies. Military service in the Israel Defence Force (IDF) is compulsory for all Israeli citizens. Men must serve three years, unmarried women two years.

Lake Tiberias, known in the Bible as the Sea of Galilee.

WATER WARS

Water is in very short supply throughout this region. Where water resources are shared (for example, Israel and Jordan share the Jordan River), disputes can occur. Israel leads the way in irrigation techniques. Fields are watered by drip irrigation – holes in pipes dispense exactly the right amount of water required, avoiding wastage.

DEAD SEA MUD

The Dead Sea, 1,300 ft (400 m) below sea level, is an enclosed salt lake. Salt levels are six times higher than in other seas, so no fish live in these waters. The Dead Sea is rich in minerals, some of which have medical properties.

Dead Sea mud is used as a skin conditioner and cure for arthritis

Soap made from Dead Sea mud

KEYBOX

Cotton: Syria's most profitable cash crop is cotton. The area of land devoted to cotton has been expanded in recent years. Look for 🌿

Tourism: People come to this region from all over the world to visit archaeological sites, ancient cities, and holy places. Look for 📷

Refugee camps: Palestinian refugees have fled from Israel to Jordan and Lebanon. Many fled to Jordan from Kuwait after the 1991 Gulf War. Look for ⛺

🌾	Cereals	⛏	Mining
🌱	Sugar beets	⚒	Oil
🍃	Citrus fruits	🏭	Industrial center
🫒	Vegetable oil	⚒	Tourism
🚬	Tobacco	🌿	Irrigated agriculture

LEBANON
West Bank: site of extensive Jewish settlement
SYRIA
Golan Heights: site of extensive Jewish settlement
Jerusalem
Jericho
Tel Aviv-Yafo
Gaza Strip: self-rule agreed 1993
ISRAEL
JORDAN
EGYPT
N

Sinai, captured by Israel in 1967, returned to Egypt in 1982

A TROUBLED HISTORY

After 1917, many Jews emigrated from Europe to Palestine, their ancient homeland. The State of Israel was created in 1948, driving out the Palestinian Arabs who had also lived there for centuries. Decades of conflict between Israel and its Arab neighbors followed. In 1967 the Israelis seized Sinai, the Gaza Strip, the West Bank, and the Golan Heights. Home rule of the Gaza Strip and Jericho was given to the Palestinians in 1994.

N

S I
Gulf of Suez

0	50	100	150	KM
0	25	50	75	100	MILES

Krak des Chevaliers is a
12th-century crusader
castle in Syria.

TURKEY

Tigris

Wheat   Barley

Al Hasakah

A L   J A Z I R A H

Barley

Wheat

L. Assad

Barley   Wheat

Ar Raqqah   Barley

Wheat

Olive

Ḥalab

Olive

Barley

Wheat

Wheat

Dayr az Zawr

Euphrates

Al Lādhiqīyah

Barley

Ḥamāh

Olive

S Y R I A

Barley

I R A Q

Tartūs

Krak des
Chevaliers

Ḥimṣ

Tudmur

Phosphates

Wheat

Tripoli

S H A M I Y A H

Olive

Wheat

D E S E R T

Barley

Ba'abda   Baalbek

BEIRUT
(BEYROUTH)

Zahlé

Wheat

Wheat

Saïda

DAMASCUS
(DIMASHQ)

Soûr

Al Qunayṭirah   Barley

GOLAN HEIGHTS

Wheat

Haifa   Wheat

S Y R I A N

L. Tiberias

Nazareth   As Suwaydā'

ISRAEL

Irbid

D E S E R T

Dar'ā   Barley

WEST BANK

Olive

Tel Aviv-Yafo   Al Mafraq

olon   Petah
Tiqwa

Az Zarqā'

Ramla   Aṣ Salṭ   **AMMAN**

Jericho   Al Azraq

JERUSALEM
(YERUSHALAYIM)

AZA STRIP

Gaza   Dead Sea

Olive

n Yūnis
Rafah

Beersheba   Masada

J O R D A N

Brôníne   Al Karak

Enash

Wheat

Aṭ Ṭafīlah

Phosphates

Phosphates

N E G E V

E

D E S E R T

G

Petra

Y

Ma'ān

P

Copper

T

S A U D I   A R A B I A

Elat   Al 'Aqabah

olan Heights:
ccupied by Israel

Wadi Rum

est Bank and
aza Strip:
ccupied by
rael under
alestinian
dministration

Gulf of Aqaba

WAR-TORN LEBANON

Lebanon became independent in 1944. Christians, about 40 percent of the population, held most of the wealth and power. The Muslim majority felt discriminated against. This grievance exploded into a bitter civil war in 1975. Agreements have now created a fragile peace.

The pomegranate fruit is grown in Israel.

LEBANON
POP: 3,082,000

ISRAEL
POP: 5,971,000

SYRIA
POP: 14,171,000

Hubble-bubble
tobacco pipe

HUBBLE-BUBBLE

Throughout the Arab world, men enjoy spending their leisure hours in cafés, drinking tea or coffee, playing cards or backgammon, and smoking. Often they smoke pipes called hubble-bubbles which draw the smoke into the mouth through water and a long tube. Tobacco is grown in Syria and exported to other countries in the region. Look for ⤏

DAMASCUS SOUK

Damascus, the capital of Syria, is one of the oldest cities in the world – its history goes back 4,000 years. At its center, next to the main mosque, is a typical Middle Eastern *souk* (marketplace). Small, winding covered streets are lined with stalls selling a wide range of produce. Behind the stalls are the workshops where craftsmen make their wares.

The Arabian *tibia*, one of the rich variety of shells found in the Red Sea.

The hills and plateaus of Israel's Negev Desert.

JORDAN
POP: 4,234,000

ROSE-RED CITY

Petra, founded about 400 BC, was the capital city of the Nabateans, a people from the Arabian peninsula who grew wealthy on the profits of the Arabian incense and spice trade. The city is located deep in a canyon, and its buildings are carved out of the soft pink limestone of the canyon walls. Large numbers of visitors come to Jordan to see ancient sites such as Petra, and to enjoy the resorts and scuba diving in the Red Sea.

Wadi Rum in Jordan, where the desert meets sandstone hills.

BEDOUIN

The Bedouin are nomadic herders who live in dry regions of the Near East and Africa. They keep cattle, sheep, and goats, which provide them with milk and meat and can be sold for food such as wheat, dates, and coffee. The Bedouin move from place to place, following the wet and dry seasons, in search of grazing land for their animals.

THE MIDDLE EAST

THE WORLD'S FIRST cities developed about 5,500 years ago in the area between the Tigris and Euphrates rivers. The land in this region is dry, but these early people created ingenious irrigation techniques to direct the river water onto their fields of crops. In AD 570, the Prophet Mohammed, founder of the Islamic religion, was born in Mecca in modern-day Saudi Arabia. Islam soon spread throughout the Middle East, where it is now the dominant religion, and then to the rest of the world. In recent years, the discovery of oil has brought great wealth to the region, and with it, rapid industrial and social change. Both Iran and Iraq earn huge revenues from oil, but they have been troubled by dictatorship and political unrest, as well as by a ten-year war. In 1991, the region was devastated by the Gulf War, which brought UN troops to the Middle East to fight against Iraq.

For centuries, Marsh Arabs have lived in the swampy delta of the Tigris and Euphrates.

MIDDLE EASTERN FOOD
Farming in the Arabian peninsula has been transformed by new irrigation methods. Saudi Arabia now exports wheat; the United Arab Emirates exports vegetables. Elsewhere, lentils and chickpeas are the main food crops.

Pistachio nuts
Aduki beans
Green lentils
Red lentils
Dates
Chickpeas

BAGHDAD
Baghdad, Iraq's capital since 1918, has grown dramatically over the last 20 years but was badly damaged during the Gulf War. The city has been rebuilt. Massive monuments to President Hussein once again adorn its streets.

ARAB DRESS
In summer, when temperatures in the Gulf reach 122° F (50° C), layers of loose robes and a headdress are worn to make the heat bearable.

Kufiyah, *male headdress*
Khimar, *veil worn by women*
Hirz, *amulet charm case*
Aqaal, *used to secure headdress*

ISLAM
Mecca is Islam's holiest place; according to Islamic teaching, every Muslim should make a pilgrimage to the city. Believers should also pray five times a day, give alms to the poor, and fast during the month-long period of *Ramadan*.

Camels, known as "ships of the desert," can go for days without water. They are used to carry loads.

MAKING THE DESERT BLOOM
Water, scarce all over this region, is carefully managed. More than 60 percent of the world's desalination plants are on the Arabian peninsula. They are used to extract the salt from seawater to make it drinkable. Look for ()

YEMEN
Unlike the rest of the Arabian peninsula, Yemen has enough rainfall to water its crops. Most crops are grown on mountain terraces in the highlands. The country is self-sufficient in barley, lentils, sorghum, corn, and coffee. Look for ♦

The minaret of the Great Mosque at Sāmarrā, Iraq.

Yemen's capital, San'ā, dates back to the 7th century.

KEYBOX

Archaeological sites: The ancient cities of the Middle East, such as Ur, date back to 3,500 BC. They are the oldest cities in the world. Look for ≜

Dams: A series of dams and barrages have been built along the Tigris and Euphrates to provide water for the dry plains of southern Iraq. Look for ⊞

Industrial center: Saudi Arabia's economy has been dominated by oil. It is seeking to widen its range of industries. Look for ⚒

Cereals		Oil	
Dates		Gas	
Rice		Carpet weaving	
Fishing		Desalination plants	

IRAQ
POP: 21,882,000

SYR

JORDAN
EGYPT

SYRIAN DESERT

An Nabk
Wādī al
Wādī
'Ar 'ar
Sakākah
Al Jawf
Ha'il
AN NAFUD

Gulf of Aqaba
Tabūk
Wheat
Wheat

SAUDI ARABIA
POP: 18,171,000

NEJD
Burayd

HEJAZ
Wheat
Wheat
Yanbu al Bahr
Medina
Wheat

RED SEA
Mecca
Jedda
Tā' if
Wheat

S A
A R A

ASIR
Al Bāhah
Wheat
Khaybar
Barley
Abhā
Khamīs Mushayt
R

Jīzān
Najrān
Sa'dah

Kamarān I.
Barley
Barley
RAMLAT
Hajjah
Al Mahwīt
Ma'rib
SAN'A
Y
Hodeida
Millet
Dhamār
Millet
Ibb
Ta'izz
Al Bayda'
Ataq
Hab
H A

YEMEN
POP: 14,361,000

Al Mukhā
Lahij
Zinjibar
Bab el Mandeb
Aden

KURDS
There are 25 million Kurds. They are one of the largest groups of stateless people in the world. Their homeland, Kurdistan, straddles three countries: Turkey, Iraq, and Iran. Many Kurds were forced to leave this area during the Gulf War and now live in refugee camps on the Iranian and Iraqi borders with Turkey.

Shahyad Monument

TEHRAN
The last shah (king) of Iran used his great wealth to modernize the country by building dams, power stations, factories, and roads. He ruled as a dictator, and the cities of Iran were filled with monuments in his name. Islamic fundamentalists overthrew the shah in 1979.

TEXTILES
Iran is famous for its superb handmade carpets. They are produced by a combination of weaving and knotting the wool, often using patterns which are several hundred years old. They are colored with vegetable dyes. Look for

Finely embroidered textiles like this saddlebag are typically Kurdish.

The Zagros Mountains lie in southwestern Iran.

OIL
The discovery of oil in the Persian Gulf region has brought enormous wealth to the Middle East. The region now supplies 30 percent of the world's oil; Saudi Arabia is the world's largest single exporter. Pipelines cross the desert, and huge tankers pick up oil from the coastal terminals, making the gulf one of the world's busiest seaways. Look for

An oil pipeline snakes across the Arabian desert.

KUWAIT
POP: 1,626,000

BAHRAIN
POP: 592,000

QATAR
POP: 500,000

UNITED ARAB EMIRATES
POP: 1,820,000

IRAN
POP: 64,073,000

OMAN
POP: 2,239,000

CENTRAL ASIA

THE CENTRAL ASIAN REPUBLICS lie on the ancient Silk Road between Asia and Europe, and their historic cities grew up along this route. Afghanistan controlled the trade route south into Pakistan and India, through the Khyber Pass in the Hindu Kush mountains. The hot, dry deserts of Central Asia and high, rugged mountain ranges of the Pamirs and Tien Shan were not suited to agriculture. For centuries people lived as nomads, herding sheep across the empty plains, or settled as merchants and traders in the Silk Road cities. When Central Asia became part of the Soviet Union everything changed: local languages and the Islamic religion (which had come to the region from the Middle East in the 8th century) were restricted; irrigation schemes made farming the arid land possible; oil, gas, and other minerals were exploited; industry was developed. Today, these newly independent republics are returning to the languages, religion, and traditions of their past. Afghanistan, independent since 1750, has recently suffered terrible conflict and economic collapse.

Akhal-Teke racehorse

HORSEMEN OF THE STEPPES
The nomadic peoples of the steppes travel great distances on horseback, and horse fairs and races are important events in their calendar. Ashgabat in Turkmenistan is the main breeding center for the Akhal-Teke, a much prized racehorse, which is able to maintain its speed in desert conditions.

UZBEKISTAN
POP: 23,308,000

TURKMENISTAN
POP: 4,260,000

USTYURT PLATEAU

ARAL SEA

Muynak

L. Sarykamysh

Khodzheyli · Nukus

Dashkhovuz

Urgench

Sulfur

Zaliv Kara-Bogaz-Gol

Sulfur

CASPIAN SEA

Krasnovodsk

Cheleken

Nebitdag

Kizyl-Arbat

TURKMENISTA

Bezmein

ASHGABAT (ASHKHABAD)

Kizyl-Atrek

Tedzhe

IRAN

Kowl-e-Namaksār

Hāmūn-e-

Gowd-e-Z

AGRICULTURE
Farming in this dry region depends on irrigation. The Karakum Canal is 683 miles (1,100 km) long – the longest canal in the world. It carries water from the Amu Darya toward the Caspian Sea and waters vast areas of land. Draining the river, however, has reduced the size of the Aral Sea.

Opium poppies are grown all over the region. They provide illegal money for many farmers, who supply the international drug trade.

SULFUR
Turkmenistan's sulfur deposits are among the largest in the world. Sulfur is used in the manufacture of gunpowder, medicine, ointment, and drugs. Turkmenistan also has large reserves of oil and gas, but has yet to make money from its substantial resources.

MARKETS
Towns such as Samarkand have changed little since the days of the Silk Road, and are still full of merchants and traders. Bazaars and streetside stalls sell local fruit and vegetables, herbs, spices, silk, and cotton.

KEYBOX

Alternative energy: Sunlight is used to generate power in Central Asia, providing a clean alternative to nuclear power. Look for ⚡

Rail route: The planned Trans-Asian Railway will connect Beijing and Istanbul via Central Asia and the Caspian Sea. Look for 🚂

🐂	Cattle	👤	Mining
🐑	Sheep	⚒	Oil
🍱	Fruit	💧	Natural gas
🚬	Tobacco	〰	Carpet weaving
⚓	Cotton	🏭	Industrial center

Carrots were first grown for food in Afghanistan.

CARPETS
Carpets from Uzbekistan, Turkmenistan, northern Afghanistan, and other parts of this region are world-famous. They are made by hand-knotting and are woven from fine Karakul wool in a range of red, brown, and maroon colors. They follow distinctive geometric patterns. Carpets are used as saddle blankets, tent hangings, and prayer mats. Look for 〰

KARAKUL SHEEP
Karakul sheep are bred for their distinctive curly fleece. They are especially important in Afghanistan. Nomadic people have herded sheep in this region for many centuries. Each summer they take their flocks up to the lush mountain pastures, and in winter they are herded down onto the plains. Look for 🐑

ARAL TRAGEDY

Water from the Amu Darya is being diverted to irrigate cotton fields. Since reduced amounts of water are now flowing into the Aral Sea, it is shrinking, and is now only 60 percent of its former size. Fishing villages that once stood on the seacoast are now stranded far inland, depriving villagers of their livelihood.

The fishing village of Muynak is now over 30 miles (48 km) from the sea

Estimated sea level in year 2000

Sea level in 1989

Kokaral

Sea level in 1960

Exposed seabed becomes desert, 1960-89

Amu Darya

N

SAMARKAND

The Islamic religion reached this region in the 8th century AD. Today, after decades of suppression by the communists, Islam is once again widely followed. Most of the former Soviet Union's 60 million Muslims live in the Central Asian republics. New mosques are opened daily, and ancient religious buildings are being restored. The famous Registan Square at Samarkand is a magnificent monument to Islam, dating back to the 14th century.

The Tien Shan range of Central Asia reaches 24,460 ft (7,439 m).

WHITE GOLD

The annual cotton crop of Uzbekistan matches the entire output of the USA, but is of low quality. Cotton is so important that few other crops are grown. Look for ⚘

FRUITS OF THE DESERT

Apricot

Watermelon

Peach

Many rivers rising in the high Pamirs and Tien Shan range flow across the desert. In spring, the rivers are swollen by melted snow from the mountains, which is rich in fertile mud. Their waters are channeled onto the fields to water crops of watermelons, apricots, and peaches, creating oases of green in the arid landscape. Look for 🚤

A road through the Khyber Pass links Afghanistan and Pakistan.

Velvet hats are worn in Uzbekistan.

KABUL

The capital of Afghanistan occupies a strategic position, controlling the mountain passes to Pakistan. Large areas of Kabul were destroyed in the Afghan civil war between the communist regime (defended by the Soviet Union), and Muslim tribes (*mojahedin*), which lasted from 1979 to 1989. The city's problems did not end with the withdrawal of Soviet troops: battles still rage on the outskirts of the city between various *mojahedin* groups, and everyday life continues to be completely disrupted by the fighting.

KYRGYZSTAN
POP: 4,754,000

TAJIKISTAN
POP: 6,155,000

AFGHANISTAN
POP: 19,494,000

0 50 100 150 200 250 300 350 400 KM
0 50 100 150 200 MILES

*Map labels:*
KAZAKHSTAN
KIKISTAN
Uchkuduk
Zarafshan
Beef
Gold
Navoi
Zeravshan
Bukhara
dzhev
Beef
Karshi
Beef
Amu Darya
Karakum Canal
Ali
TORKESTAN MTS.
Meymaneh
Merghāb
Harīrūd
GHANISTAN
Helmand
Arghandāb
Qandahār
PAKISTAN
Ghaznī
Qondūz
HINDU KUSH
KABUL
Jalālābād
Khyber Pass
Pol-e Khomrī
Baghlān
Qondūz
Mazār-e Sharīf
Termez
Panj
Khorog
Pamir
PAMIRS
Kulyab
Kurgan-Tyube
Koramikhon
DUSHANBE
Tursunzade
TAJIKISTAN
Surkhob
Bartang
Ura-Tyube
Solar
Khudzhand
Samarkand
Beef
Dzhizak
L. Aydarkul'
Almalyk
Lead
Copper
Uranium
Angren
TASHKENT (TOSHKENT)
Chirchik
Solar
Fergana
Kokand
Mercury
Lead
Uranium
Mercury
Kyzyl-Kiya
Andizhan
Namangan
Uzgen
Osh
Dzhalal-Abad
Uranium
Beef
Gold
Zinc
Lead
Beef
Naryn
Naryn
KYRGYZSTAN
KIRGHIZ RANGE
Talas
Kara-Balta
Tokmak
Issyk-kul'
L. Issyk-kul'
Przheval'sk
Beef
BISHKEK (FRUNZE)
TIEN SHAN
KOKSHAAL TAU MTS.
CHINA

RUSSIA AND KAZAKHSTAN

THE URAL MOUNTAINS FORM a natural barrier between the European and the Asian parts of Russia. Although over 77 per cent of the country lies in Asia, only 27 per cent of the population live here. Siberia dominates Russia east of the Urals, stretching to the Pacific Ocean and northwards into the Arctic. The climate is severe, parts of Siberia are colder in winter than the North Pole.

Siberia has huge deposits of gold, coal, diamonds, gas, and oil, but workers had to be offered high wages and housing to work there. Today, both Russia and Kazakhstan have great economic potential, but are still coping with a legacy of severe industrial pollution.

0 200 400 600 800 1000 KM
0 100 200 300 400 500 600 MILES

HYDROELECTRIC POWER
Siberia's rivers provide 80 per cent of Russia's hydroelectric power, fuelling industry throughout eastern Russia. Massive dams, such as this one on the River Angara, provide the power for the aluminium industry. Look for

Ear of wheat

VIRGIN LANDS
In the 1950s, the Soviet Union tried to increase grain production. The empty steppes of Kazakhstan, known as the "Virgin Lands", were ploughed up to grow crops. Today, much of this farmland is reverting to steppe. Look for

KEYBOX

Industrial center: This region produces one-third of the former USSR's iron and steel. Timber processing is also very important. Look for

Pollution: Nearly 500 Soviet nuclear devices were detonated in Kazakhstan from 1949-1989. Many children in this area are malformed at birth. Look for

Military bases: Russia's far East is a highly militarized area. The Russian Pacific fleet is based at Vladivostok. ICBM bases line the southeast border. Look for

Cereals		Coal	
Timber		Oil	
Fishing		Gas	
Mining		Hydro-electric power	

KAZAKHSTAN
POP: 17,575,000

KAZAKH HORSEMEN
The first inhabitants of the steppe were a nomadic people who travelled on horseback, herding their sheep with them. They slept in felt tents like these, called *yurts*. Their descendants, the Kazakhs, still place great value on horses and riding skills, and horse racing is a popular sport. The Kazakh national drink is *kumiss* – fermented mare's milk. The traditional nomadic lifestyle of the steppe has gradually been replaced by large-scale agriculture and industry.

SPACE CENTER
The Russian space programme is based at Baykonur in Kazakhstan, where this Buran unmanned shuttle was launched in 1988. Russia's achievements in space technology started with the launch of the Sputnik satellite in 1957. Since then, Russia has been responsible for the first man in space, the first woman cosmonaut, and the first space walk. The Mir orbital station has now been in space for over five years.

FINLAND
ESTONIA
LATVIA
BELORUSSIA
UKRAINE
GEORGIA
TURKMENISTAN
UZBEKISTAN
KIRGHIZSTAN
CHINA

Murmansk
BARENTS SEA
Novaya Zemlya
KARA SEA
KOLA PENINSULA
WHITE SEA
Kolguyev I.
Baydarata Bay
YAMAL PENINSULA
L. Pyaozero
Kem'
Arkhangel'sk
Mezen'
Pechora
Vorkuta
Salekhard
Gulf of Ob
St. Petersburg
Pskov
Novgorod
Petrozavodsk
L. Onega
Onega
Cherepovets
Vologda
Kotlas
Syktyvkar
WEST SIBERIAN PLAIN
Nevel'
Rye
Smolensk
Tver'
Aluminium
MOSCOW
Yaroslavl'
Ivanovo
Vladimir
Chromium
Kaluga
Tula
Orël
Ryazan'
Nizhniy Novgorod
Cheboksary
Kirov
Kama
Coal
Ob'
Bryansk
Kursk
Lipetsk
Voronezh
Tambov
Saransk
Kazan'
Izhevsk
Perm'
Manganese
Platinum
Nizhniy Tagil
Irtysh
Nizhnevartovsk
Penza
Ul'yanovsk
Saratov
Tol'yatti
Naberezhnyye Chelny
Serov
Yekaterinburg
Vakh
SEA OF AZOV
Maize
Wheat
Balakovo
Samara
Ufa
Gold
Copper
Tyumen'
Oats
Rostov-na-Donu
Krasnodar
Volgograd
Sulphur
Ural'sk
Orenburg
Wheat
Magnitogorsk
Chelyabinsk
Kurgan
Sochi
Stavropol'
Elista
Wheat
Copper
Iron
BLACK SEA
Cherkessk
Astrakhan
Vladikavkaz
Groznyy
Iron
Wheat
Copper
Atyrau
Aktyubinsk
Kustanai
Petropavlovsk
Oats
Omsk
Itatka ICBM Base
Makhachkala
Emba
Chromium
Iron
Kokchetav
Novosibirsk
CASPIAN SEA
Fort Shevchenko
Aktau
KIRGHIZ STEPPE
Barley
Wheat
Akmola
Wheat
Novokuznetsk
KAZAKHSTAN
Aluminium
L. Tengiz
Copper
KAZAKH UPLANDS
Pavlodar
Wheat
Barnaul
ARAL SEA
Manganese
Arkalyk
Karaganda
Gold
Aleysk
Air Base
Biy
Baykonur
Zhezkazgan
Semipalatinsk
Ust' Kamenogorsk
Kzyl-Orda
Copper
Wheat
Balkhash
L. Balkhash
L. Zaysan
Chu
Syr Darya
Ili
Shymkent
Zhambyl
Kapchagay
Taldy-Kurgan
ALMA-ATA (ALMATY)

112

SIBERIAN GOLD

The discovery of gold on the upper part of the Lena River in the 1840s led to a gold-rush. But conditions for 19th-century prospectors were terrible – they slept in flimsy huts in freezing temperatures, and many died. Today, the region has four major gold- fields as well as 800 diamond mines. Look for 🐚

A herd of reindeer graze on the tundra in northern Siberia.

A COLD CLIMATE

Siberian towns are built to withstand the region's harsh climate. Many houses are built on stilts, as frost damages normal foundations. Winters in the far north are extremely long – some towns do not see daylight for up to 47 days a year. Fruit and vegetables are grown locally in heated greenhouses.

Siberian huskies are used for pulling sledges and hunting.

The Kamchatka peninsula is a remote wilderness.

A child's toy wooden sledge from Siberia.

TRIBESPEOPLE

The Chukchi people who live on the Kamchatka peninsula traditionally survive by hunting, reindeer herding, and fishing. But the animals' natural habitats are slowly disappearing as forests are cut down for timber, and lakes and rivers are polluted by industrial waste. This is depriving the Chukchi hunters of their livelihood.

Fur hat

FUR

Hunters, trappers, and fur-traders have been making a profitable living from Russia's animals since the 17th century. Siberia in particular has rich animal resources. The far East of the country has tigers and leopards, while the forests are home to the brown bear (often used as a symbol for Russia), sable, ermine, mink, lynx and foxes. Overhunting has reduced the numbers of these animals in the wild, so most fur now comes from animals bred specially on fur farms.

INDUSTRIAL POLLUTION

Uncontrolled industrial growth has led to severe pollution problems in this region. The level of carbon emissions – caused by burning coal and oil – would not be acceptable in the West. Many children's illnesses in Russia are caused by contaminated air.

Lake Baikal contains 20 per cent of the world's fresh water.

Russians heat water for tea in urns called samovars.

RUSSIAN FEDERATION
POP: 150,638,000
(SIBERIA)
POP: 40,250,000

Map labels:
C. Dezhneva · ALASKA (USA) · Wrangel I. · Provideniya Air Base · CHUKCHI SEA · C. Navarin · Anadyr' Air Base · Tin · Pevek · Gold · Ayon I. · Ust' Chaun Air Base · Ambarchik · Bear Is. · Kolyma · OLOY RANGE · KORYAK RANGE · Cape Olyutorskiy · Ossora · Karaginskiy Is. · C. Sivuchiy · Ust'-Kamchatsk · KAMCHATKA · Petropavlovsk-Kamchatskiy · C. Lopatka · Paramushir Is. · Magadan · Okhotsk · Korkodon · KOLYMA RANGE · Oktyabr'skiy

The Kurile Islands are administered by the Russian Federation, but claimed by Japan.

EAST SIBERIAN SEA · Pioner I. · Severnaya Zemlya · October Revolution I. · Bolshevik I. · C. Chelyuskin · TAYMYR PENINSULA · LAPTEV SEA · L. Taymyr · Olenek Bay · Tiksi · Olenek · Gold · CENTRAL SIBERIAN PLATEAU · Khatanga · PUTORANA MTS. · Copper · Nickel · Olenek Air Base · Anabat · Diamonds · Yana · Indigirka · Adycha · Tin · Sartang · VERKHOYANSK RANGE · Lena · Vilyuy · Diamonds · Yakutsk · Suntar · Anga · Aldan · Maja · DZHUGDZHUR RANGE · C. Yelizavety · Vostochnyy · SEA OF OKHOTSK · Sakhalin · Poronaysk · Yuzhno-Sakhalinsk · Kurile Islands · SEA OF JAPAN · PACIFIC OCEAN · Lower Tunguska · RUSSIAN FEDERATION · SIBERIA · Stony Tunguska · Diamonds · Gold · Olekma · Gold · Angara · Krasnoyarsk · Iron · Uranium · Bratsk · Ust'-Ilimsk · STANOVOY RANGE · Zeya Reservoir · Skovorodno · Komsomol'sk-na-Amure · Sovetskaya Gavan · L. Baikal · Gold · Molybdenum · Svobodnyy ICBM Base · Blagoveshchensk · Oats · Khabarovsk · Romanovka · Shilka · Gold · Amur · Ussuri · Wheat · Gold · Tin · Angarsk · Irkutsk · Chita ICBM Base · Ulan-Ude · Olovyannaya ICBM Base · Gold · Tin · Vladivostok · CHINA · MONGOLIA · NORTH KOREA · Kyzyl

Komodo dragon
Varanus komodoensis
Length: 10 ft (3 m)

Golden pheasant
Chrysolophus pictus
Length: 3ft (1 m)

King cobra
Ophiophagus hannah
Length: 18 ft (5.5 m)

SOUTH AND EAST ASIA

THE WORLD'S 10 HIGHEST PEAKS, including Mount Everest, are all found in the Himalayas and other mountain ranges in the center of this region. At these altitudes, monsoon rains fall as snow on mountain tops. The melted snow from the mountains feeds some of the largest rivers in the world, such as the Ganges and Irrawaddy, which have created huge deltas where they enter the sea. Fingers of land stretch into tropical seas, and volcanic island chains border the continent. In tropical areas high rainfall and temperatures support vast areas of forest. Inland, a climate of extremes prevails, with baking hot summers and long harsh winters. Cold desert and grassy plains cover much of the interior.

▲ VOLCANIC ROCK
This huge granite rock on Sri Lanka was formed in the mouth of a volcano. It is surrounded by forest.

Gingko
Gingko biloba
Height: 100 ft (30 m)

The tiger cowrie is found on coral reefs.

▲ YOUNG MOUNTAINS
Himalaya is the Nepalese word for "home of the snows." The range began to form about 40 million years ago – recent in the Earth's history.

△ ISLAND VOLCANOES
Plants are growing again on the scorched slopes of Bromo in Java, one of a chain of active volcanoes around the southeast Pacific.

TROPICAL RAIN FOREST
Rain forests grow in layers: an understory with creepers and the main canopy through which tallest trees protrude.

Giant panda
Ailuropoda melanoleuca
Length: 5 ft (1.5 m)

HIDDEN CAVES
This maze of limestone caves along the Gulf of Thailand has been carved by rainwater.

△ SACRED MOUNTAIN
Mount Fuji, Japan's highest peak, is surrounded by temperate broadleaf trees. Once an active volcano, Mount Fuji has not erupted for 300 years. The snow-capped summit is the rim of a volcanic crater.

The royal cloak scallop shell is found in the waters of the Pacific Ocean.

⬇ MANGROVES IN SILHOUETTE
Mangroves grow along many coastlines, giving some protection during tropical storms.

Rafflesia
Rafflesia pricei
Width: 3 ft (1 m)

TROPICAL ISLAND
There are thousands of tiny coral islands in this region. Many are volcanic in origin, like this one in the South China Sea.

CROSS-SECTION THROUGH SOUTH AND EAST ASIA

Plateau of Tibet
Great Plain of China
Yellow Sea
Korea
Himalayas
Daxue Shan
Red Basin
Sea of Japan
Thar Desert
Honshū
24,607 (7,000)
Sea level 0
-14,764 (-4,500)
Feet (meters)
A
B
Length: 5,000 miles (8,000 km)

COLD HIGH NEPAL
No trees are to be found above 10,000 ft (3,000 m) in the Himalayas, although dwarf shrubs and grasses can withstand the harsher conditions up to 15,000 ft (4,500 m). Higher still, the rock is bare or covered in snow.

Wild yak
Bos grunniens
Length: 9 ft (3 m)

Chinese river dolphin
Lipotes vexillifer
Length: 8 ft (2.4 m)

Siberian tiger
Panthera tigris
Length: 8 ft (2.4 m)

Orangutan
Pongo pygmaeus
Height: 5 ft (1.5 m)
■ !

KEY TO SYMBOLS

▲ Mountain

△ Volcano

❉ Mangroves

▦ Wetlands

Coral reef

■ Plate margins with
direction of movement

KEY TO NATURAL VEGETATION

□ Cold desert

□ Mountain

□ Hot desert

□ Tropical rain forest

Coniferous forest ■

Temperate grassland ■

Broadleaf forest ■

Temperate rain forest ■

Dry woodland ■

■ **AUTUMN ON HOKKAIDO**
Hokkaidō is the most northerly
of Japan's four islands. Its
mountainous landscape is
covered with broadleaf forests.
The climate is moderated by the
sea: winters are milder and
rainfall is heavier than at
the same latitude on
the mainland.

Arctic Circle

60

S I B E R I A

Probable
plate
margin

SEA OF OKHOTSK

NORTH AMERICAN PLATE

EURASIAN PLATE

Sakhalin

Kurile Is.

▲5,617ft

GREATER KHINGAN RANGE

Amur

Kurile Trench

14,784ft ▲

ALTAI MTS.

Kerulen

**G O B I
D E S E R T**

MANCHURIAN
PLAIN

L. Khanka

Hokkaidō

40°

▼ Turpan Depression
-505ft

L. Bosten

Lop Nur

Yellow R.

T I E N   S H A N

▲ 24,407ft

Tarim

**TAKLA MAKAN
DESERT**

Qinghai Hu

SEA OF JAPAN

Kegon Falls
331ft

Korea

Honshū

Japan Trench

HINDU KUSH

▲25,253ft

Indus

▲K2
28,253ft

▲ 25,339ft

KUNLUN MTS.

**QAIDAM
BASIN**

Jinsha

DAXUE SHAN

Wei He
12,360ft ▲

Yellow R.

Huai He

**GREAT PLAIN
OF CHINA**

Korea Strait

YELLOW
SEA

Unzen △
4,459ft

Shikoku

Kyūshū

▲ Fuji
12,389ft

PACIFIC PLATE

 late

ATE

ble plate
margin

**P L A T E A U
O F   T I B E T**

Q I N   L I N G

24,790ft ▲

**Red
Basin**

Dongting Hu

Yangtze

Poyang Hu

Gan He

EAST CHINA SEA

Ryukyu Is.

EURASIAN PLATE

PHILIPPINE PLATE

32,088ft ▼

PACIFIC PLATE

H I M A L A Y A S

Manaslu
26,760ft ▲

Mt. Everest
29,030ft ▲

N A N   L I N G

Yuan

7100ft ▲

Tropic of Cancer

INDIAN PLATE

INDO-AUSTRALIAN PLATE

Indus

Dhaulagiri
26,812ft ▲

▲ Kangchenjunga
28,210ft

GANGES PLAIN

Mali Hka

Brahmaputra

Taiwan Strait

Taiwan

20°

**THAR
DESERT**

Ganges

Narmada

Rann
of Kutch

DECCAN PLATEAU

Godavari

Ganges
Delta

Irrawaddy

Salween

Mekong

Gulf of Tongking

Hainan

Mt. Pinatubo △
57,712ft

Philippines

*Philippine
Basin*

**P A C I F I C

O C E A N**

Krishna

**Bay of
Bengal**

Irrawaddy
Delta

Isthmus of Kra

Tônlé Sap

Mekong
Delta

S O U T H   C H I N A   S E A

South China Basin

Philippine Trench

32,997ft ▼

rsoppa
Falls
830ft

Cauvery Falls
331ft

Andaman
Is.

Gulf
of
Thailand

Palk Strait

Nicobar Is.

Strait of Malacca

ANDAMAN SEA

MALAY PENINSULA

Yap Trench

-27,977ft ▼

Comorin

Sri Lanka

INDO-AUSTRALIAN PLATE

Ceylon Plain

CELEBES
SEA

Probable
plate margin

Halmahera

Equator

Mid-Indian Ridge

Chagos Trench

Ninety East Ridge

INDO-AUSTRALIAN PLATE

**Wharton
Basin**

Sumatra

Sunda
Shelf

Borneo

Celebes

Seram

Moluccas

16,503ft ▲

MAOKE MTS.

New
Guinea

*Mid-Indian
Basin*

A N   O C E A N

Java Trench

J A V A   S E A

E A S T   I N D I E S

Flores

Timor

ARAFURA SEA

△ Krakatau
2,667ft

Papandayan △
8,547ft

Kelud△
5,679ft

Bromo
8,468ft

△ Tambora
9,256ft

Bali

Java

80°

100°

120°

PACIFIC PLATE

INDO-AUSTRALIAN PLATE

B

THE INDIAN SUBCONTINENT

SOUTH OF THE HIMALAYAS, the world's highest mountains, lies the Indian subcontinent. In the north of the region, the Buddhist kingdoms of Nepal and Bhutan cling to the slopes of the Himalayas. In the south, the island state of Sri Lanka hangs like a teardrop from the tip of India. The subcontinent has been invaded many times: the first invaders were Aryan tribes from the north, whose beliefs and customs form the basis of the Hindu religion. During the 16th century India was united and ruled by the Islamic Mogul emperors. Two centuries later it became a British colony. In 1947 India gained independence, but religious differences led to the creation of two countries – Hindu India and Muslim Pakistan. Eastern Pakistan became Bangladesh in 1971. Today India is an industrial power, but most of the people still live in villages and make their living from tiny farms. In spite of terrible poverty and a population of about 850 million people, India remains a relatively stable democracy.

The Thar Desert, a vast, arid region in India and Pakistan.

MOOD MUSIC

Sitar

Most traditional Indian music is improvised. Its aim is to create a mood, such as joy or sorrow. One of the main instruments is the *sitar*, which is played by plucking seven of its strings. Other strings, which are not plucked, vibrate to give the distinctive sound of Indian music.

PAKISTAN

This bus illustrates a big problem in Pakistan: overpopulation. 95 percent of the people are Muslim, and traditional Islam rejects contraception, so the birthrate is high. 3 million refugees, displaced by the war in Afghanistan, have stretched resources further.

A MARBLE MEMORIAL

The Taj Mahal at Agra in northern India was built in the 17th century by the Mogul emperor, Shah Jahan, as a tomb for his beloved wife. She was the mother of 14 children. Built of the finest white marble, the Taj Mahal is a supreme example of Islamic architecture and one of the world's most beautiful buildings.

KEYBOX

Aquaculture: This is a recent and highly successful industry in Bangladesh. Frog legs and shrimp are among the main products. Look for ➴

Hiking: Every year some 250,000 hikers visit Nepal, boosting its economy. But the extra visitors are damaging the environment. Look for 👟

Dams: Irrigation on a vast scale in the Indus Valley in Pakistan has sustained and increased the country's food production. Look for ⊞

🌾 Cereals		⚓ Cotton	
🌾 Rice		👤 Mining	
🌾 Sugarcane		⛏ Coal	
🌿 Tea		🏭 Industrial center	

INDUSTRY

After independence, India started to modernize. It is now one of the most industrialized countries in Asia. Factories make a wide range of goods, from cement to cars. Recently, the manufacture of products like machine tools and electronic equipment has increased. Local cotton is processed in mills like these in Ahmadabad. Look for ⭑

INDIAN FILMS

More films are produced in India than anywhere else in the world – including Hollywood. Bombay is the center of the Indian film industry.

Jewelry, especially silver, is one of India's main exports.

Traditional fishing boats on the coast of Sri Lanka.

PAKISTAN
POP: 138,672,000

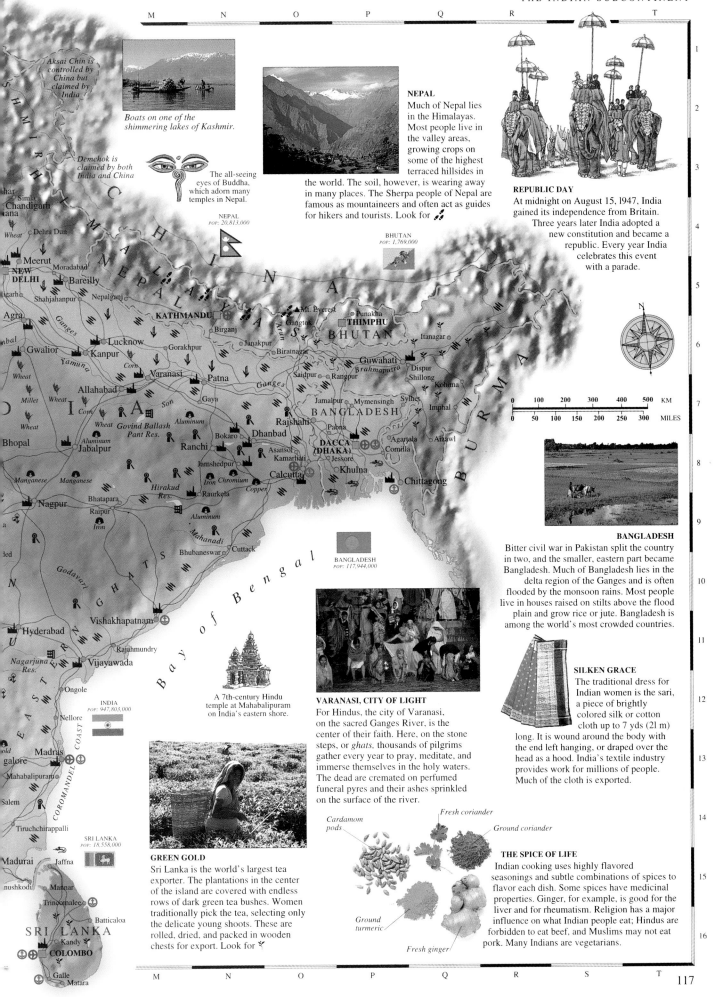

Aksai Chin is controlled by China but claimed by India

Boats on one of the shimmering lakes of Kashmir.

Demchok is claimed by both India and China

The all-seeing eyes of Buddha, which adorn many temples in Nepal.

NEPAL
Much of Nepal lies in the Himalayas. Most people live in the valley areas, growing crops on some of the highest terraced hillsides in the world. The soil, however, is wearing away in many places. The Sherpa people of Nepal are famous as mountaineers and often act as guides for hikers and tourists. Look for

NEPAL
POP: 20,813,000

BHUTAN
POP: 1,769,000

REPUBLIC DAY
At midnight on August 15, 1947, India gained its independence from Britain. Three years later India adopted a new constitution and became a republic. Every year India celebrates this event with a parade.

KATHMANDU

Mt. Everest

THIMPHU

BHUTAN

BANGLADESH

DACCA (DHAKA)

Calcutta

Chittagong

BANGLADESH
Bitter civil war in Pakistan split the country in two, and the smaller, eastern part became Bangladesh. Much of Bangladesh lies in the delta region of the Ganges and is often flooded by the monsoon rains. Most people live in houses raised on stilts above the flood plain and grow rice or jute. Bangladesh is among the world's most crowded countries.

BANGLADESH
POP: 117,944,000

SILKEN GRACE
The traditional dress for Indian women is the sari, a piece of brightly colored silk or cotton cloth up to 7 yds (21 m) long. It is wound around the body with the end left hanging, or draped over the head as a hood. India's textile industry provides work for millions of people. Much of the cloth is exported.

A 7th-century Hindu temple at Mahabalipuram on India's eastern shore.

VARANASI, CITY OF LIGHT
For Hindus, the city of Varanasi, on the sacred Ganges River, is the center of their faith. Here, on the stone steps, or *ghats*, thousands of pilgrims gather every year to pray, meditate, and immerse themselves in the holy waters. The dead are cremated on perfumed funeral pyres and their ashes sprinkled on the surface of the river.

INDIA
POP: 947,803,000

Bay of Bengal

SRI LANKA
POP: 18,558,000

Cardamom pods

Fresh coriander

Ground coriander

Ground turmeric

Fresh ginger

GREEN GOLD
Sri Lanka is the world's largest tea exporter. The plantations in the center of the island are covered with endless rows of dark green tea bushes. Women traditionally pick the tea, selecting only the delicate young shoots. These are rolled, dried, and packed in wooden chests for export. Look for

THE SPICE OF LIFE
Indian cooking uses highly flavored seasonings and subtle combinations of spices to flavor each dish. Some spices have medicinal properties. Ginger, for example, is good for the liver and for rheumatism. Religion has a major influence on what Indian people eat; Hindus are forbidden to eat beef, and Muslims may not eat pork. Many Indians are vegetarians.

SRI LANKA

COLOMBO

CHINA AND MONGOLIA

THE REMOTE MOUNTAINS, deserts, and steppes of Mongolia and the northwestern part of China are harsh landscapes; temperatures are extreme, the terrain is rugged, and distances between places are vast. Three large autonomous regions of China lie here – Inner Mongolia, Xinjiang, and Tibet. Remote Tibet, situated on a high plateau and ringed by mountains, was invaded by China in 1950. The Chinese have systematically destroyed Tibet's traditional agricultural society and Buddhist monasteries. Most of China's ethnic minorities and Muslims (a legacy of Silk Road trade with the Middle East) are located in Inner Mongolia and Xinjiang. Roads and railroads are being built to make these secluded areas accessible, and rich resources of coal are being exploited. Mongolia is a vast, isolated country. It became a communist republic in 1924 but has now reestablished democracy. Most people still live by herding animals, although new industries have begun to develop.

MONGOLIAN STEPPES
About half the Mongolian population still live in the countryside, many as nomadic herders. Nomads live in *gers* – circular tents made of felt and canvas stretched over a wooden frame. They herd yaks, sheep, goats, cattle, and camels and travel great distances on horseback.

Cylinder containing written prayer

In Tibet, written prayers are placed in prayer wheels. These small cylinders are rotated by hand.

The Tien Shan range in central Xinjiang.

KASHI MARKET
The city of Kashi is located in the far west of China. With its Muslim mosques, minarets, and lively bazaar, it is more like a city in the Middle East than China. Its Sunday market, the biggest in Asia, attracts up to 60,000 visitors. A vast array of goods are sold there: horses, camels, livestock, grains, spices, and cloth.

ADAPTABLE YAKS
Herders in Mongolia and Tibet keep yaks. They thrive at high altitudes, surviving extreme cold and even burrowing under snow for grass. Yaks provide milk, butter, meat, wool, and leather. In Tibet, yak butter is served with tea. Look for ¥

KEYBOX

Timber: Forests in eastern Tibet have been cut down by the Chinese. Bare hillsides encourage flooding, landslides, and soil erosion. Look for ⑂

Coal: Mongolia is a major exporter of coal to the Russian Federation. There are also open-pit mines in Xinjiang and Inner Mongolia. Look for ⌒

Pollution: Nuclear tests in Xinjiang have caused radiation fallout, pollution, and many birth defects. Look for ☢

Cattle and yaks		Mining
Sheep		Oil
Cereals		Industrial center
Mixed fruit		Oases

Oases: winter and spring wheat, corn, rice, and cotton are grown

Takla Makan Desert

Tarim R.

Lop Nur: saline lake

→ N

Passes through Tien Shan range

Turpan oasis: fruit and cotton are grown on irrigated land

SILK ROAD OASES
The oases of Xinjiang lie on the edge of the Takla Makan Desert in the foothills of the Tien Shan range. They are watered by melted snow from the mountains and sheltered by warm winds coming down the mountain slopes. Towns grew up next to the oases, which lie along the ancient Silk Road.

The high plateau of Tibet, known as "the roof of the world."

KAZAKHSTAN

L. Uvs
Ulaangom
L. Hyar
Ölgiy
Altay
Hovd
Har Us L.
Beef
Irtysh
Wheat
Yaks
Beef

ALTAI MTS.

Karamay
Beef

XINJIANG UIGHUR

Yining
Kuytun
Shihezi
Ürümqi
Beef
Wheat
Wheat
Turpan
Corn
Han
Iron

AUTONOMOUS

TIEN SHAN
Aksu
Wheat
Korla
L. Bosten
Wheat
Corn

KYRGYZSTAN

Wheat
Kashi
Wheat

TAJIKISTAN

AFGHANISTAN

Shache
Wheat

PAKISTAN

KARAKORUM MTS.

Beef
Hotan
Wheat
Wheat

Tarim

REGION

Tarim Basin

TAKLA MAKAN DESERT

Lop Nur

C H

Lenghu
Da C

ALTUN MTS.

KUNLUN MTS.
Beef
Yaks
Go

Aksai Chin is controlled by China but claimed by India

INDIA

Demchok is claimed by both China and India

Gar

Yaks

Yaks

Yaks

TIBETAN

TANGGULA MT

AUTONOMOUS

Tangra Yumco
Siling Co
Nam Co
Nagqu
Yaks

REGION

GANGDISE RANGE
Brahmaputra (Yarlung Zangbo)
Xigazê
Wheat
Wheat
Lhasa
Yaks
Nyingchi

HIMALAYAS

NEPAL
Nyalam
Gyangze
Yamzho Yumco
Beef
Mt. Everest
Yaks

BHUTAN
IND

NATIONAL GAMES
Horse racing, archery, and wrestling competitions are held all over Mongolia every July 11, the day of the national Nadam festival. Mongols are among the most accomplished riders in the world. They learn to ride as children, and some of the jockeys are only three years old.

MONGOLIA
POP: 2,560,000

STEEL CITY
Railroads were built in the 1950s to transport coal and iron from the north of the country. Baotou is the center of iron and steel production in Inner Mongolia. Look for ⚒

CHINA
POP: 1,252,188,000
(NORTHWEST CHINA)
POP: 43,099,600

THIS MAP SHOWS THE NORTH-WESTERN PART OF CHINA ONLY. THE REST OF CHINA IS SHOWN ON PAGES 120-121.

A camel caravan crosses the Gobi Desert.

THE GREAT WALL
The Great Wall of China is 1,500 miles (2,400 km) long and runs from the Chinese coast to Central Asia. Much of the present Great Wall was built in the early 15th century. It was intended to protect the Chinese against invasions by the nomadic Mongols to the north.

Bactrian camels, with two humps, are used as pack animals in this region.

TRADITIONAL MEDICINE
Traditional Chinese medicine restores harmony between the body, mind, and environment. Xining is a major export center for traditional medicines such as caterpillar fungus, antlers, musk, and rhubarb.

Dried fungus, Sliced deer antler, Gardenia fruit, Lycium fruit, Dried rhubarb

CHINA'S SORROW
The shallow, slow-moving Yellow River rises in the high mountains of Tibet and brings fertile mud to the arid plains of northern China. However, buildup of muddy deposits on the river's bed has lifted the river level above its banks, periodically causing terrible floods and famines.

POTALA PALACE
The spectacular Potala Palace in Lhasa, capital of Tibet, was built in the 17th century. It was the residence of the Dalai Lama, the head of the Buddhist faith in Tibet. When Tibet was invaded by China in 1950, Buddhism was brutally repressed by the Chinese. In 1959, there were more than 6,000 monasteries in Tibet; by 1979 only five remained.

Loose tea leaves are compressed into hard blocks, easily carried by Tibetan nomads.

STAPLE FOODS
In contrast to the rest of China, rice is not the main food crop in the northern regions. Cereals, such as wheat, millet, oats, buckwheat, and barley are grown on irrigated land or oases. Noodles and steamed buns (mantou) are the main bulk food of the north, served with spicy barbecued meat. Look for 🌾

Wheat, Millet, Barley

CHINA AND KOREA

THE LANDSCAPE OF SOUTHEASTERN CHINA ranges from mountains and plateaus to wide river valleys and plains. One-fifth of all the people on Earth live in China, and most Chinese live in the eastern part of the country. For centuries, China was isolated from the rest of the world, ruled by powerful emperors and known only to a handful of traders. In the 19th century, the European powers and Japan forced China to open its borders to trade, starting a period of rapid change. In 1949, after a long struggle between nationalists and communists, the People's Republic of China was established as a communist state. Taiwan became a separate country. The communist government has encouraged foreign investment, technological innovation, and private enterprise, although calls for democracy have been suppressed. Korea was dominated by its powerful Chinese and Japanese neighbors for many years. After World War II, Korea was divided in two. North Korea became one of the most isolated and repressive communist regimes in the world. South Korea transformed itself into a highly industrialized nation.

PEKING OPERA
Traditional Chinese opera dates back 2,000 years and combines many different elements – songs, dance, mime, and acrobatics. The stories are based on folktales. Makeup shows the characters' personalities – kind, loyal, or wicked, for example.

Sesame oil   Dried mushroom

FOOD
Chinese food varies widely from region to region. Its most famous cuisine comes from the area around Canton and uses a huge range of ingredients – it is said that people from this region will "eat anything with wings except airplanes and anything with legs except the table". Chinese food has become popular all over the world.

Soy sauce
Dried prawn

INDUSTRY
Although China has extensive reserves of coal, iron ore, and oil, its heavy industry is state-run, old-fashioned, and inefficient. 70 percent of China's energy is provided by coal. About half of China's coal comes from large, well-equipped mines; the rest is extracted from small local pits. These mines are notorious for their high accident rates. Look for 🅡

THIS MAP SHOWS THE SOUTH-EASTERN PART OF CHINA ONLY. THE REST OF CHINA IS SHOWN ON PP. 118-119.

The Great Wild Goose pagoda at Xi'an was built in the 7th century AD. It formed part of a Buddhist monastery.

BABY BOOM
China's population is now over a billion, stretching resources such as land, food, and education to the limit. Couples with only one child receive various benefits. If a second child is born, these benefits are withdrawn.

Tea, China's national drink, is grown on terraced hillsides in the south of the country.

KEYBOX

Hydroelectric power: China's rivers have great potential; dams, lakes, and canals provide flood control and irrigation as well as electricity. Look for 🔛

Economic zones: The Chinese government has set up special industrial zones, encouraging foreign investment through tax incentives. Look for 🏭

Refugees: Vietnamese refugees come to Hong Kong by boat. In 1991, there were over 61,000 Vietnamese in Hong Kong's detention camps. Look for 🛖

Borders: The most militarized border in the world divides Korea into communist North and democratic South. Look for ⚔

	Cereals		Mining
	Rice		Coal
	Tea		Oil
	Timber		Industrial center
	Fishing		Shipbuilding

AGRICULTURE
China feeds its vast population from only 7 percent of the world's farmland. In the fertile southern part of the country, the fields can yield three harvests every year – two crops of rice and a third crop of vegetables or cereals. Look for 🌾

MONGOLIA

Yumen

Great Wall

WESTERN CHINA

Wuwei

Yine

NINGXIA AUTONOMOUS REGION

Lanzh

Wheat

Whe

Yalong

Dadu He

Jinsha

Mianyang

Litang

Chengo

Leshan   Chongqi
Zigong

Xichang

Aluminum
Copper
Panzhihua   Dongchuan   Guiya

Dali

Kunming   Corn
Hongshui H

Gejiu   Corn
Tin   Cor

MYANMAR (BURMA)

Salween

Mekong

LAOS

VIETNAM

Pingxia

N

RACIAL MINORITIES
This woman comes from the Hani people, one of the many different ethnic minorities who live in southwest China. Most minority groups live in remote, sparsely inhabited regions. Many still follow traditional lifestyles based on herding, hunting, or growing food for their families.

0	100	200	300	400	500	600	KM

0	100	200	300	MILES

THE DRAGON THRONE
The Hall of Supreme Harmony houses the Dragon Throne, seat of the former emperors of China. It is the largest building in Beijing's Forbidden City and dates back to the 15th century. Ordinary citizens were banned from this area, which was reserved for the emperor and his courtiers. Today, the Forbidden City has been restored and opened to the public; it attracts millions of tourists every year.

北京
The word *Beijing*, written in Chinese. Each symbol stands for a word or an idea.

A jade vase. Jade is China's most precious stone.

COMMUNISM
In the 1960s, China suffered a campaign of terror against artists, politicians, and intellectuals. Although the regime is now more liberal, political messages displayed on walls are often the only way of challenging the government.

GINSENG
Korea exports this precious root, which is widely used in traditional Asian medicine. It is also popular in the West where it is thought to improve health and promote long life and vigor.

Ginseng roots are grown for 4-6 years, then steamed and dried

Rice fields in South Korea. Rice thrives in the mild south.

LAND OF MIRACLES
The Korean economy was devastated by World War II, but during the last 40 years South Korea has undergone an economic miracle. Today, it has a major shipbuilding industry and modern steelworks; cars, computers, televisions, and VCRs pour off production lines. A quarter of all South Koreans live in the capital, Seoul, which has become one of the world's largest cities.

SHANGHAI
The port of Shanghai is the largest city in China. In the 19th century, foreign countries who were involved in trade with China claimed sections of the city. They established commercial buildings and warehouses, giving central Shanghai the appearance of a European city. Today, Shanghai has become important as a center of heavy industry.

The roofs of Wen-wu Temple, on Taiwan's Sun Moon Lake.

Playing Ping-Pong is a national passion in China.

THE LITTLE DRAGON
Taiwan has one of Asia's wealthiest economies. The country produces about 10 percent of the world's computers and also specializes in textiles and shoe manufacturing. The Taiwanese refer to their country as the Republic of China, but China does not recognize the country under this name.

HONG KONG
The rocky island of Hong Kong became a British Crown Colony in the 19th century. In 1997 it will be returned to China, when it will become a "special administrative region." Hong Kong has the busiest container port in the world and is a center of trade, finance, manufacturing, and tourism.

JAPAN

THE LAND OF THE RISING SUN, as Japan is sometimes called, was ruled for centuries by powerful warlords called *shōguns*, who discouraged any contact with the outside world. When traders from America and Europe arrived, Japan's isolation suddenly ended, the *shōgun* was overthrown, and an emperor ruled the country. Over the next century, Japan transformed itself into one of the world's richest nations, a change in fortune all the more remarkable considering the country's geography. Japan consists of four main islands and 4,000 smaller islands. The majority of its 123 million people live closely packed together around the coast, since two-thirds of the land is mountainous and thickly forested. Japan has few natural resources and has to import most of its fuel and raw materials. The Japanese have concentrated on improving and adapting technology imported from abroad. Today, Japanese companies are world leaders in many areas of research and development, a success partly due to their management techniques, which ensure a well paid and loyal workforce.

The Kurile Islands are administered by the Russian Federation, but claimed by Japan.

The Japanese are skilled at *bonsai* – the art of producing miniature trees and shrubs.

The Hidaka Mountains on the large island of Hokkaido.

FOOD
The Japanese eat a lot of fish because there is not enough farmland to keep cattle for meat or dairy produce.

Rice

Seaweed

Lacquer dish

Marinated raw fish

SHIPBUILDING
A large number of the ships sailing the world today were made in Japan. Countries such as South Korea can now build ships more cheaply, however, and Japan's industry is declining. To remain competitive, Japanese shipbuilders are building specialized ships such as cruise liners and developing new products like oil-drilling platforms. Look for

JAPAN
POP. 126,320,000

RICE CULTIVATION
Rice is Japan's main food. Although only about 11 percent of the land is suitable for farming, Japan produces enough rice for its own needs. The crop is intensively cultivated on small plots of land using fertilizers and sophisticated machinery, like this rice planter. The warm, wet summers in southern Japan are ideal for growing rice. Look for

Silk kimono

FISHING
Fish is a very popular food in Japan. Huge quantities are caught each year by the country's fishing fleet – the world's largest. One million tons of fish and shellfish are also bred every year on fish farms. These tuna are on sale in Tokyo's fish market. Look for

KABUKI THEATER
There are two forms of traditional Japanese theater: Noh and Kabuki. Noh is very old: the plays are based on myths of the gods and contain music and symbolic dancing. Kabuki theaters have plays based on stories of great heroes of the past. This photo shows a scene from a Kabuki play.

A miniature television produced in Japan.

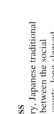

TRADITIONAL DRESS
Until the 19th century, Japanese traditional dress varied greatly between the social classes. In the royal courts, long-sleeved robes called *kimonos* were worn. Made of silk, these were wound around the body and tied with a sash. *Kimonos* are still worn on special occasions.

SEA OF OKHOTSK

Iturup

Shikotan

Kunashir

Habomai Is

Yekaterina Strait

Nemuro

Kushiro

Abashiri

Kitami

Obihiro

Asahikawa

Ishikari

ISHIKARI MTS.

HIDAKA MTS.

Sapporo

Hokkaidō

Otaru

Ishikari B.

Tomakomai

Uchiura Bay

Hakodate

Tsugaru Strait

Seikan Tunnel

Fukushima

Okushiri-tō

Rebun-tō

Reshiri-tō

Wakkanai

La Pérouse Strait

OU MTS.

Aomori

Hachinohe

Morioka

Akita

Yamagata

Sendai

Fukushima

Niigata

Sado

Toyama Bay

Toyama

Nagano

Utsunomiya

Koriyama

Mito

Hitachi

Iwaki

SEA OF JAPAN

Honshū

JAPAN'S CAPITAL CITY

During the 500 years of its existence, Tokyo has survived fire, flood, earthquakes, and destruction by war. Each disaster has required massive rebuilding. Earthquake-resistant materials and construction techniques, which enable a building to sway rather than fall, have allowed new skyscrapers to replace older buildings. But the danger of earthquakes remains, and there are plans to move the capital to a safer site farther north.

Japanese motorbike

VEHICLE INDUSTRY

Japanese vehicle manufacturers became world leaders in the 1980s thanks to their stylish designs, new technology, and efficient production methods. Today, motor vehicles are the country's biggest export. Japanese vehicle manufacturers have also opened a number of factories overseas – in Europe, the USA, and elsewhere. Countries in areas like Eastern Europe can supply cheaper labor than in Japan. Look for ⊞

KEYBOX

Financial center: Japan is a leading member of the world financial community. Its stock exchange ranks second in the world. Look for 🖾

Skiing: The Japanese Alps in Honshū are excellent for skiing. In 1998, the Winter Olympics will be held near Nagano.

Rail routes: The Shinkansen, or bullet train, runs from Tokyo to Fukuoka at an average speed of 122 miles (195 km) per hour. Look for ⚑

⚓ Fishing ports	〰 Rice
⚒ Industrial center	🍇 Mixed fruits
⊞ Vehicle manufacture	◁ Citrus fruits
⛴ Shipbuilding	🌿 Tea
▭ High-tech industry	☙ Tobacco

Mount Fuji is Japan's sacred mountain.

RELIGION

There are two main religions in Japan – Buddhism and Shinto. People often follow both: it is common to be married with Shinto rituals, but buried with Buddhist ones. There are numerous Buddhist and Shinto shrines and temples in Japan. They are usually built of wood – and therefore vulnerable to fire – and temples like Ginkakuji in Kyōto have been rebuilt several times.

To relieve overcrowding, developers build upward and into the sea on reclaimed land

Intensively cultivated lowlands due to shortage of farmland

Rice and other crops grown in fertile volcanic soils and ideal climate

Mt. Fuji

Tokyo Bay

Industrial and urban areas

SAGAMI SEA

Yokohama

Tokyo City

SITE OF TOKYO

Built around Tokyo Bay, and hemmed in by mountains, Tokyo is unable to spread further inland or along the coast. The sprawling built-up region around Tokyo and Yokohama is the world's largest urban area and is sometimes called a megalopolis. It has a population of over 27 million people and accounts for 25 percent of Japan's industrial production.

COMMUTING

Most Japanese people live in the cities, but few can afford to live in the city centers, so most have to commute to work. Trains are fast and efficient, but so overcrowded that special guards are employed to push commuters into the cars.

A bottle of rice wine, or sake, Japan's national drink.

COMPUTERS

The Japanese excel at producing miniature electronic goods, such as computers and televisions. They have set such high standards that few countries can match them. A silicon chip able to hold 1,000 pages of newsprint in its memory is being developed.

The beautiful rocky coast of the Oki Islands, which lie in the Sea of Japan.

PACIFIC OCEAN

JAPAN

Sagami Sea

Izu Is.

Yokosuka

Yokohama

Mt. Fuji

Shizuoka

Hamamatsu

Okazaki

Nagoya

Gifu

L. Biwa

Kyōto

Ōsaka

Kōbe

Wakayama

Shingū

Wakasa B.

Tottori

Matsue

Okayama

Kurashiki

Takamatsu

Tokushima

Kōchi

Nakamura

CHUGOKU MTS.

Hiroshima

Yamaguchi

Matsuyama

Inland Sea

Shikoku

Uwajima

Hamada

Hagi

Shimonoseki

Ōita

Beppu

Kitakyūshū

Fukuoka

Saga

Kyūshū

Kumamoto

Miyazaki

Nobeoka

Saseho

Nagasaki

Amakusa Is.

Kagoshima

AMAKUSA SEA

Ōsumi Strait

Ōsumi Is.

Tanega-shima

Yaku-shima

Gotō Is.

Iki

Tsushima

Korea Strait

EAST CHINA SEA

Tokara Is.

Ryūkyū Is.

Amami-ōshima

Amami Is.

Tokuno-shima

Okinoerabu-jima

Okinawa Is.

Okinawa

Naha

Oki Is.

Dōzen

KM	0	50	100	150	200	250
MILES	0	50	100	150		

MAINLAND SOUTHEAST ASIA

MUCH OF THIS REGION is mountainous and covered with forest. Most of the people live in the great river valleys, plateaus, or fertile plains. Farming is the main occupation, with rice the principal crop. Of the seven countries, only Thailand was not a British or French colony. Thais are deeply devoted to their royal family and the Buddhist faith. The Federation of Malaysia includes 11 states on the mainland, joined in 1963 by Sabah and Sarawak in Borneo. This union of east and west has produced one of the world's most successful developing countries. Singapore, at first part of Malaysia, became a republic in 1965. The island controls the busy shipping routes between the Indian and Pacific oceans. Cambodia, Laos, and Vietnam have all suffered from many years of warfare. Cambodia's future is still uncertain, but the other two countries show signs of economic recovery. Myanmar (Burma) has become increasingly isolated from the world by its repressive government.

BUDDHISM
Except for Malaysia, the main religion in this region is Buddhism. In Thailand and Burma, where almost all the people are Buddhists, every young man puts on the saffron robe, shaves his head, and enters a monastery for several months.

TIMBER
Thailand was once a major producer of teak, but so much of the country's forests have been cut down that commercial logging was banned in 1989 – until forests recover. Myanmar is now the world's principal teak exporter. Here, huge logs float down the Irrawaddy River. Look for ⌐

Lacquer tray

Making lacquer ware is a traditional craft in Thailand.

Boats on the Irrawaddy, the great river of Burma.

OPIUM
For the poor hill tribes of the "Golden Triangle" – the remote area where Burma, Laos, and Thailand meet – growing opium poppies is one of the few sources of income. Useful painkillers can be made from the poppies, but so too are dangerous drugs such as heroin. Governments are encouraging people in this area to grow other crops, including flowers and tobacco.

Poppy seeds

Dried opium poppy

MYANMAR (BURMA)
POP: 47,502,000

LAOS
POP: 5,015,000

VIETNAM
Rice is the principal crop in this country. As Vietnam is so mountainous, most people live in the two main river deltas. Two-thirds of the farmed land is devoted to growing rice. The wet field, or *paddy*, is planted by women. Look for ⌐

Durian fruit is grown throughout the region.

RUBIES
Several types of precious stones are mined in northeastern Myanmar. The glowing red rubies from this region are considered the finest in the world. Many people in Asia believe that wearing a ruby protects you from harm. Today Myanmar has a virtual monopoly over the ruby trade. Look for ◈

Ruby   *Calcite*

FISHING
Fish is one of the main foods in this area. Thailand has a thriving fish canning industry. Fish farming on the inland lake of T'ônlé Sap, Cambodia, is also successful. Here, in Myanmar, fish are caught from small huts built over the water. Look for ⌐

### Map labels

Gulf of Tongking
Hong Gai
Thai Nguyen
HANOI
Hai Phong
Nam Dinh
Thanh Hoa
Vinh
Lang Son
Tangsten
Tin
Ha Giang
L. Thac Ba
Iron
Viet Tri
Red R.
Black R.
Son La
Xam Nua
Chromium
Muang Pakxan
VIENTIANE
Phongsali
Nam Ou
Louang Namtha
XiangKhoang
Muang Xaignabouri
Nam Ngum Dam
Ban Houayxay
Chiang Rai
Muang Nan
Mekong
SiriKit Res.
Chiang Mai
Muang Lampang
Tungsten
Manganese
Iron
LAOS
C H I N A
L A O S
MYANMAR (BURMA)
B U R M A
Rubies
Myitkyina
KUMON RANGE
Bhamo
Katha
Lashio
Lead
Zinc
Irrawaddy
Mandalay
Amarapura
Shwebo
Sagaing
Myingyan
Monywa
Pakokku
Pagan
Chauk
Minbu
Thayetmyo
Prome
Sandoway
Henzada
Pegu
Sittang
Toungoo
Pyinmana
Tin
Taunggyi
L. Inle
Salween
Chindwin
CHIN HILLS
Sittwe
Ramree I.
Bay of Bengal
BANGLADESH
I N D I A
Iron
Iron

124

VIETNAM
POP: 70,900,000

VIET NAM

Quang Ngai
Nha Trang
Da Nang
Hue
Saravan
Qui Nhon
Attapu
Pakxé
Champasak
Buon Me Thuot
Da Lat
Lumphat
Krâchéh
Muang Không
Kâmpóng Cham
Bien Hoa
Ho Chi Minh City
Kâmpóng Chhnang
Tay Ninh
Svay Riêng
Can Tho
Stoeng Trêng
PHNOM PENH
Takéo
Long Xuyen
Rach Gia
Phumi Sâmraông
Angkor Wat
Bătdâmbâng
Poŭthĭsăt
Kâmpóng Thum
Kâmpôt
Krông Kaôh Kông
Kâmpóng Saôm
Muang Yasothon
Ubon Ratchathani
Nakhon Ratchasima
Chanthaburi
Sisakét
Chon Buri
Pattaya
Rayong
Phet Buri
Phnum Sâmraông
Kâmpóng Cham

THAILAND
POP: 58,836,000

CAMBODIA
POP: 9,660,000

C A M B O D I A
T H A I L A N D

Mekong
Mae Nam Mun
Mae Nam Ping
Mae Klong
Srinagarind Res.

Muang Khong
Sen
San

Nakhon Sawan
Ayutthaya
BANGKOK (KRUNG THEP)
Sari Buri
Prachin Buri
Kanchanaburi
Rat Buri
Phet Buri
Prachuap Khiri Khan
Chumphon
Surat Thani
Nakhon Si Thammarat
Trang
Hat Yai
Songkhla
Pattani
Narathiwat
Yala
Kota Baharu

Gulf of Thailand

Phangan I.
Samui I.
Luang Lagoon

ISTHMUS OF KRA

Phuket I.

SOUTH CHINA SEA

Angkor Wat

The ancient temple (wat) of Angkor in Cambodia.

SINGAPORE
Singapore's modern container port and skyscrapers reflect its status as the financial and industrial center of Southeast Asia. Over 25,000 vessels dock at Singapore each year; tourists pour into the island's airports; products and people are carried into Malaysia and beyond by efficient transport systems. Shipbuilding and oil refining are among the main industries.

SINGAPORE
POP: 2,705,100

Orchids are grown in northern Thailand as an alternative to opium, and are widely exported.

WEST MALAYSIA
POP: 15,840,000

M A L A Y S I A

Kuala Terengganu
Kuantan
Dungun
Kuala Lumpur
Seremban
Melaka
Johor Baharu
SINGAPORE
Port Dickson
Kelang
Ipoh
Telok Intan
Taiping
Butterworth
George Town
Alor Setar
Langkawi

CAMERON HIGHLANDS
Pahang

Strait of Malacca
Strait of Singapore

KM MILES
400
350 250
300 200
250 150
200
150 100
100
50   50
0   0

The Cameron High-lands, Malaysia.

ELECTRONICS
Thailand and Malaysia are both industrializing rapidly. They have many factories where electronic products like this pocket calculator are assembled. Both countries now export a large number of manufactured goods. Malaysia makes its own car, the Proton; Thailand is a leading manufacturer of integrated circuits.

ANDAMAN SEA

Gulf of Martaban

Amherst
Ye
Tavoy
Mergui
Tungsten
Rubber
Tin

Mergui Archipelago

PALM OIL
The oil palm comes from West Africa, but it has been successfully introduced into Malaysia and Indonesia. Palm oil and palm kernel oil (used in soap and as edible oils) are made from the fruit. Malaysia started production to lessen its dependence on the rubber crop, which is increasingly being replaced by synthetic alternatives. Look for 🌴

ELEPHANTS
Compared to a tractor, a working elephant needs little fuel, does not rust, and needs no spare parts. A tractor lasts for 30 and is six years. An elephant lasts for 30 and is less harmful to the environment. Elephants are used to move timber and to take tourists for rides in the forest.

PINEAPPLES
Thailand has become the world's biggest exporter of canned pineapple; 50 percent of the product goes to the USA. The pineapples are processed in factories where the skin is removed, the stem cut out, and the fruit sliced into rings or chunks. Some of the largest factories in Thailand are owned by Japanese companies.

Pineapple ring
Pineapple fruit

Siamese cats originally came from Thailand, once called Siam.

FLOATING MARKET
Bangkok, Thailand's capital, is a noisy, hectic city, full of Buddhist temples – *wats* – and congested with traffic. The city was built on an island in the river, and the canals – or *klongs* – were once the city's streets. The few canals that remain are still used by flatboats – called *sampans* – to transport fresh fruit and vegetables from the country-side to the floating markets, where the *sampans* act as shops.

KEYBOX

Mining: Malaysia is the world's biggest producer of tin, but its resources are becoming depleted. Look for ⛏

Dam: A series of dams is planned on the Mekong River to provide HEP and irrigation. All six countries involved must first reach agreement. Look for 🏛

Tourism: More than 3 million tourists visit Thailand each year, and tourism has become a major source of foreign currency. Look for 🏖

〰 Rice	⛏ Fishing
Coconuts	⚒ Coal
Vegetable oil	⬮ Gas
Timber	▮ Industrial center
Forest products	ff Archaeological site

MARITIME SOUTHEAST ASIA

SCATTERED between the Indian and Pacific oceans lies a huge crescent of mountainous tropical islands – the East Indies. The largest country in this region is Indonesia, which was ruled by the Dutch for nearly 350 years. Over half its 13,677 islands are still uninhabited. The island of Borneo is shared between Indonesia, the Malaysian enclaves of Sabah and Sarawak, and the Sultanate of Brunei. Indonesia's national motto, "Unity in diversity," ideally suits a country made up of 362 different peoples speaking over 250 dialects and languages. Indonesia's seizure of East Timor in 1975 has resulted in a long and bloody resistance by the islanders. Java, the main island, is so crowded that thousands of people have been moved to less populated islands. The Philippines, ruled for three centuries by Spain, then for about 50 years by the USA, consists of over 7,000 islands. It is the only mainly Christian country in Asia. Much of the region is covered by forests, which contain some of the finest timber in the world.

COCONUTS

Indonesia and the Philippines are the world's major coconut growers. Every part of the tree has its uses, even the leaves. The kernel is dried to make copra, from which a valuable oil is obtained. Look for 🥥

Kernel

Helicopter

STILT VILLAGES

Many of the villages in th region are built over wate The houses are made of local materials like wood and bamboo and built on stilts to protect them from vermin and flooding. For houses built on land, rais floors also provide shelte for the owner's animals which live underneath.

BRUNEI

The Sultanate of Brunei became ri when oil was discovered in 1929. This golden-domed mosque, built the country's newfound wealth, to above the capital, Bandar Seri Begawan. The small, predominant Muslim population pays no taxes enjoys free education and health c

AIRCRAFT INDUSTRY

Indonesia has developed a thriving aircraft industry. About 12,000 workers assemble helicopters and aircraft at Bandung in Java. The factories are jointly owned by five international aircraft manufacturers. The first solely Indonesian-designed aircraft will soon be completed.

RELIGION

Although about 90 percent of Indonesians are Muslim, many of their religious ceremonies contain elements of other religions – like Hinduism and Buddhism – which blend with local traditions and beliefs. Recently, Islam has become more dominant. More girls now wear the Islamic headdress, like these pupils at a school in Sumatra.

Borobudur, the great 8th-century Buddhist temple on Java.

MALAYSIA
POP: 17,567,000
(EAST MALAYSIA: SABAH AND SARAWAK)
POP: 3,360,000

BRUNEI
POP: 288,000

Dense rain forest on Sumatra is home to elephants and tigers.

KEYBOX

🫙	**Vegetable oil:** Indonesia is now one of the world's major producers of palm oil. It has many uses, from hydraulic brake fluids to cooking oil. Look for 🫙
🔬	**Research center:** Near Manila in the Philippines, the Rice Research Institute has developed many of the world's modern high-yield types of rice. Look for ⬤
🏴‍☠️	**Pirates:** Pirate attacks on vessels in the area are increasing, especially at night and in the busy shipping lanes of the Strait of Singapore. Look for ☠️
〰️ Rice	🐟 Fishing
🥥 Coconuts	⛏️ Mining
🌴 Timber	⛽ Oil
🌲 Forest products	🏭 Industrial center

JAKARTA

Situated on the island of Java, Indonesia's capital, Jakarta, has the largest population of any city in Southeast Asia – and it is still growing rapidly. It was once the center of the region's Dutch trading empire, and many typical Dutch buildings still stand in the old part of the city. At night, skyscrapers glitter above the city's modern center.

*Map labels:*

SOUTH CHINA SEA
Kota Kin
BANDAR SERI BEGAWAN
Natuna
Miri Kuala
Natuna Is.
MALAYSIA (EAST)
BRUN
Sibu
Sarikei
Kuching
SARAWAK
Borneo
Pontianak
Kapuas
SCHWANER MTS.
MULLER MTS.
Barito
Mendawai
TAMABO
Rubber
Rubber
Rubber
Palm
Kualakapuas
Banjarmasin

Banda Aceh
Rubber
Belawan
Medan
Pematangsiantar
Simeulue
L. Toba
Palm
Sibolga
Nias
Anambas Is.
Strait of Singapore
Bintan
Sumatra
Tanjungpinang
Pini
Pakambaru
Batu Is.
Lingga
Padang
Singkep
Siberut
Batanghari
Jambi
Bangka
Sipura
Karimata
Pangkalpinang
North Pagai
Rubber
Tin
South Pagai
BARISAN MTS.
Rubber
Palembang
Belitung
Bengkulu
Rubber
Tin
Palm
JAVA SEA
Enggano
Bawean
Tanjungkarang
INDONESIA
JAKARTA
Bogor
Cirebon
Semarang
Madura
Sukabumi
Bandung
Surabaya
Borobudur
Kediri
Yogyakarta
Malang
Jember
Denpa
Java
Banyu
INDIAN OCEAN

PHILIPPINES
POP: 70,559,000

Gong chimes

A *bonang*, one of the
instruments in a
gamelan orchestra.

Batik cloth

SHADOW PUPPETS
The shadow puppet
shows of Indonesia,
wayang, are centuries old.
The puppets are made from
buffalo hide. Their faces are
intricately carved to express
their characters; the hero has
a beautiful nose, the
demon a short, ugly one.
The puppet show is often
accompanied by an orchestra,
called a *gamelan*, which can
contain up to 40 players.

THE PHILIPPINES
Although the Philippines gained
independence in 1946, the country
has maintained close political and
economic ties with its previous
colonizer, the USA. English is
widely spoken, especially in
schools, and American products
and customs are widespread –
particularly around the
huge U.S. military bases
near Manila, which
were closed down
in 1992.

BATIK
For over 1,000
years the art of
batik has been
practiced in Indonesia, particularly
in Java. Wax and dyes are used in
a complex process to print colors
and designs onto a variety of
fabrics. Batik fabrics are often
made into a garment called a
sarong, which can be worn by
both men and women.

*Cinnamon
stick*

Peppercorns

Nutmeg

Cloves

Spices
from the
Moluccas – known
as the Spice Islands.

RICE TERRACES
Rice can be grown on
lowland paddy fields
or on terraces cut into the mountainous slopes.
Some of the terraces in the region are said to be
more than 2,000 years old. These remarkable
structures help prevent soil erosion; an ancient
and complex system of sluices and canals
waters the rice. Look for ⧚

TIMBER
Fine hardwoods such as teak grow
in Indonesia's tropical rain forests.
Now one of the world's major
exporters of wood, especially
plywood, Indonesia has built large-
scale pulp and paper mills.
Deforestation, especially here in
Borneo, remains a major problem
throughout the region. Look for ⫭

*Cowrie shell
necklace*

IRIAN JAYA
Irian Jaya – the
western portion of New Guinea –
is Indonesia's biggest province. Its
densely forested and mountainous
terrain has helped isolate it from
Western influences. Many peoples
in this region continue their local
traditions, including the use of
cowrie shells as a form of currency.

*Planting rice at dusk in a rice
paddy on Bali.*

INDONESIA
POP: 208,660,000

KM							
0	100	200	300	400	500	600	KM
0	50	100	150	200	250	300	350	MILES

THE PACIFIC OCEAN

THE PACIFIC IS THE LARGEST and deepest of the world's oceans. It covers a greater area of the Earth's surface than all the land areas combined. At its deepest point – 36,197 ft (11,033 m) down in the Mariana Trench – it is deep enough to cover Mount Everest. More than half the world's population lives around the shores of the Pacific. The ocean's northern and western edges, known as the outer Pacific, are fringed with chains of islands, such as the Aleutians. The inner Pacific islands fall into three main groups: Melanesia, Micronesia and Polynesia. With the development of modern communications, trade and co-operation between countries surrounding the ocean – sometimes referred to as the "Pacific Rim" – is increasing. Countries such as Japan, Australia, and New Zealand want the South Pacific made into a nuclear-free zone, which would prevent all testing of nuclear weapons.

The Aleutians, a chain of volcanic islands in the Pacific.

A coral atoll in French Polynesia.

CONTAINER PORTS
Today, fruit, meat, and many other goods are moved round the world in huge metal containers. Here, a ship waits to be unloaded at Kōbe, one of Japan's main container ports.

COCONUTS
The coconut palm is called "tree of life" by Pacific Islanders because it provides so many of their daily needs, such as food and building materials. Here, the white "meat" of the coconut is dried to make copra, which yields oil. Look for

FISHING
Pacific Islanders fish mainly for food, although any surplus catch may be sold. Many fish are caught in the North Pacific by commercial fleets operating far from their home bases. The biggest catches are made by Japan, Korea, Taiwan, and the USA. The main fish caught is tuna. Look for

Skipjack tuna

FIJI
Fiji is a group of volcanic islands surrounded by coral reefs. Although one of the few South Pacific islands to develop tourism, Fiji's economy is still dominated by the sugarcane crop – shown here being harvested. Recently, a number of tax-free factories have been set up which export a variety of products overseas; clothing, in particular, has proved very successful. Look for

Tropical growth on an island in the Tonga group.

ISLANDS
The Pacific islands are scattered over a huge area, far from any industrial center and from each other. Some of the islands are high and volcanic, others are low coral atolls. They are home to over five million people whose one great shared resource is the sea. A huge variety of fish and shellfish are caught from small boats and by diving. In general, the soil of the islands is poor.

KEYBOX
Fishing: Since the first salmon farms were set up in 1982 around Chiloé Island, Chile, salmon farming has become a major industry. Look for

Mining: The South Pacific island of Nauru has become prosperous through the export of phosphates, which are used to make fertilizers. Look for

Pollution: Nuclear testing carried out by the USA and France has polluted certain islands in the South Pacific. Look for

Sugarcane		Fishing ports	
Coconuts		Tourism	
Timber		Whales	
Shellfish		Military bases	

128

K L M N O P Q R S T

Outrigger float
Wooden dugout hull
An outrigger canoe, the traditional craft of the Pacific Islanders.

NATURAL HAZARDS

The Pacific region is plagued by tropical storms, called typhoons. The area is also prone to tidal waves, or *tsunamis*, which are caused by a volcanic eruption or earthquake taking place underwater. A *tsunami* travels at great speed across the ocean, increasing to a huge size when it reaches shallow waters around the coast.

MILITARY BASES

Powerful nations like the USA are able to control and monitor vast expanses of ocean with their large navies. Fleets are stationed at strategic points, such as the USA's base at Guam. Its naval headquarters in the western Pacific is at Pearl Harbor on Hawaii, shown here. Look for ▦

Giant clam

FARMING THE SEA

Aquaculture – farming the sea for food – has gone on for centuries. China and Korea produce large quantities of seaweed each year; all kinds of shellfish are cultivated. The once plentiful giant clam, recently endangered due to overfishing, can now be bred on farms. It is cultivated in the coastal waters of the South Pacific. Look for 🦪

MARSHALL ISLANDS
POP: 48,000

UNITED STATES
POP: 263,563,000
HAWAII
POP: 1,160,000

KIRIBATI
POP: 66,000

SURFING

Riding waves on a surfboard is a popular sport. The world's major surf sites are on coasts facing great expanses of ocean, where waves can grow and gather speed before they break on the seashore. The Pacific has many superb surfing areas, such as Hawaii.

GALAPAGOS ISLANDS

The British naturalist Charles Darwin used his observations of the plants and animals on the Galápagos Islands as evidence for his theory of evolution. The islands are still inhabited by species found nowhere else in the world, such as this giant tortoise.

Over 600 of these massive stone figures stand on Easter Island.

TOURISM

Despite improved air and sea links, tourism in the South Pacific islands is still relatively undeveloped. Islands lack modern facilities such as roads and hotels, and many suffer from a shortage of fresh water. Here a cruise ship anchors off Fiji. Look for 🏊

TONGA
POP: 101,000

WESTERN SAMOA
POP: 162,000

**Map labels:**

NORTH AMERICA
Yukon
Gulf of Alaska
Prince Rupert
Vancouver
Seattle
Columbia
Mendocino Fracture Zone
San Francisco
Monterey
Long Beach
San Diego
Colorado
Murray Fracture Zone
PACIFIC OCEAN
Harbor
HONOLULU
HAWAII (USA)
Clarion Fracture Zone
JOHNSTON ATOLL
ROWMAN REEF (USA)
PALMYRA ATOLL (USA)
Line Islands
Kiritimati (Christmas I.)
AMERICAN SAMOA
Islas Revillagigedo (Mexico)
Albatross Plateau
Clipperton I. (France)
Clipperton Fracture Zone
CENTRAL AMERICA
Panama City
Cocos Ridge
Buenaventura
Galápagos Is. (Ecuador)
Guayaquil
Chimbote
Callao
SOUTH AMERICA
Peru Basin
Peru-Chile Trench
Ilo
Antofagasta
Marquesas Is.
FRENCH POLYNESIA
COOK ISLANDS (New Zealand)
Tuamotu Archipelago
Papeete
Tahiti
SOCIETY IS. (France)
Muroroa
Gambier Is.
PITCAIRN IS. (UK)
Tubuai Is.
Austral Ridge
East Pacific Rise
Easter I. (Chile)
Isla San Félix (Chile)
Isla San Ambrosio (Chile)
Islas Juan Fernández (Chile)
Chile
Valparaíso
Concepción
Chiloé I.
Southwest Pacific Basin
Pacific Antarctic Ridge
South East Pacific Basin
SOUTHERN OCEAN
ANTARCTICA
C. Horn

N

0 500 1000 1500 2000 2500 3000 KM
0 500 1000 1500 MILES

TONGA
POP: 101,000

VANUATU
POP: 143,000

Koala
Phascolarctos cinereus
Length: 31 in (80 cm)

Funnel-web spider
Atrax robustus
Length: 1 in (3 cm)

Raggiana's bird of paradise
Paradisaea raggiana
Length: 4 ft (1.4 m)

OCEANIA

OCEANIA INCLUDES AUSTRALIA, New Zealand, and numerous island groups in the Pacific. Australia – the smallest, flattest, and driest continent – has been worn down by 3,000 million years of exposure to wind and rain. Away from Australia, along the edges of the continental plates, volcanic activity is common because the plates are still moving. These plate movements greatly affect New Guinea, the Pacific Islands, and New Zealand. Elsewhere in the Pacific Ocean, thousands of tiny coral islands have grown on the tops of undersea volcanic mountains. Climates vary greatly across the region, from the wet tropical climates of the islands in the outer Pacific to the hot, dry deserts of central Australia. Tropical rain forest can be found in northern Australia and on New Guinea.

Cider gum tree
Eucalyptus gunnii
Height: 76 ft (25 m)

SURF AND SAND
Powerful waves from the Tasman Sea wash the southeast coast of Australia, creating long, sandy beaches.

AUSTRALIA'S RAIN FOREST
Over 600 different types of trees grow in the tropical rain forest on the Cape York Peninsula. Mists often hang over the forest.

DESERT MOUNTAINS
For millions of years, erosion has scoured the center of Australia. Mountains like Mount Olga have been reduced to stumps of sandstone.

Taipan
Oxyuranus scutellatus
Length: 12 ft (3.6 m)

TROPICAL GRASSLAND
Three great deserts dominate the center of Australia. On the desert margins, some rain falls, enabling scattered trees and grasses to grow.

DRY WOODLAND
Gum trees – otherwise known as eucalyptus – abound in Australia. Many species are adapted to dry conditions, with leaves that hang straight down to avoid the full heat of the sun.

TEMPERATE RAIN FOREST
Far from other land and surrounded by ocean, much of New Zealand has high rainfall and is warm all year round. These conditions encourage the unique plants of the temperate rain forest.

HOT NEW ZEALAND
Steam rises from pools of sulfurous boiling water and mud, signs of volcanic activity along the plate margins. The heat comes from deep within the earth.

Black opal, a precious stone found in Australia.

Giant white buttercup
Ranunculus lyalii
Size: 3 ft (1 m)

THE PINNACLES
Western Australia's weird limestone pinnacles stand out in the sandy desert. Rain and plant roots have shaped the pillars over the last 25,000 years.

NEW ZEALAND'S ALPS
Rising steeply from the coast, the Southern Alps cover 80 percent of South Island. Glaciers moving down the mountains carved deep inlets – fjords – along the southwest coast.

CROSS-SECTION THROUGH AUSTRALIA AND OCEANIA

Exmouth Plateau
Indian Ocean
Mt. Bruce
Great Victoria Desert
Flinders Ranges
Australian Alps
Pacific Ocean
New Zealand
Tasman Sea

9,843 (3,000)
Sea level 0
-14,764 (-4,500)
Feet (meters)

A
Length: 4,500 miles (7,250 km)
B

Red kangaroo
Macropus rufus
Height: 6 ft (2 m)

Brown kiwi
Apteryx australis
Height: 14 in (35 cm)

Giant clam
Tridacna gigas
Shell: 5 ft (1.5 m)

Butterfly fish
Chaetodon auriga
Length: 8 in (20 cm)

PACIFIC OCEAN

Philippine
Basin

Caroline Ridge

Melanesian
Basin

Gilbert Ridge

Equator

CELEBES SEA

Celebes
Basin

Probable plate
margin

BISMARCK SEA

New Ireland

Solomon Islands

New
Guinea

Manam△ 6004ft
BISMARCK
RANGE
▲Mt. Wilhelm
14,784ft

Mt. Ulawun△ 7,661ft
New Britain

△Mt. Bagana
6,559ft

INDO-AUSTRALIAN PLATE

ARAFURA SEA

Torres Strait

OWEN STANLEY
RANGE
13,242ft

SOLOMON SEA

New Britain Trench

Coral Sea Basin

CORAL
SEA

Vanuatu

West Fiji
Basin

Fiji

New Hebrides Trench
30,103ft

Probable plate
margin

20°

TIMOR
SEA

ARNHEM
LAND

CAPE YORK
PENINSULA

Great Barrier Reef

New
Caledonia

Tropic of Capricorn

South Fiji
Basin

North
Australian
Basin

Gulf of
Carpentaria

Victoria

KIMBERLEY
PLATEAU
▲2999ft

Finders

GREAT DIVIDING RANGE

Lord Howe
Seamounts

New Caledonia
Basin

Exmouth
Plateau

TANAMI
DESERT

Great
Artesian
Basin

North
Island

GREAT SANDY
DESERT

MACDONNELL RANGES
4,954ft

SIMPSON
DESERT

Lord Howe Rise

L. Mackay

▲Mt. Bruce
4,023ft

GIBSON DESERT

Mt. Olga▲
3,507ft

▲Uluru
2,848ft

AUSTRALIA

L. Eyre
-52ft ▽

▲5,399ft

L. Taupo
Ruapehu△
9,176ft

40°

Perth
Basin

•Pinnacles
Desert

GREAT VICTORIA
DESERT

NULLARBOR PLAIN

L. Torrens

FLINDERS
RANGES

Darling

Murray

New
Zealand

Cook Strait

South
Island

Great Australian
Bight

Mt. Kosciusko
7,317ft
AUSTRALIAN ALPS

TASMAN
SEA

Probable plate
margin
Sutherland Falls
1,903ft

▲Mt. Cook
5ft

SOUTHERN ALPS

[B]

South Australian
Basin

Bass Strait

Tasmania

South Tasman
Rise

Macquarie Ridge

Campbell
Plateau

60°

SOUTHERN OCEAN

INDO-AUSTRALIAN PLATE
ANTARCTIC PLATE

PACIFIC PLATE

PACIFIC PLATE
ANTARCTIC PLATE

Antarctic Circle

South Indian Basin

Probable plate
margin

ROSS SEA

ANTARCTICA

CORAL ISLAND
Coral grows in warm shallow seas.
Coral reefs surround many Pacific
islands, like this one in Fiji, and
form Australia's Great Barrier Reef.

The southern triton
is common in
Australian waters.

Frilled lizard
Chlamydosaurus kingii
Length: 3 ft (1 m)

KEY TO SYMBOLS

▲ Mountain

△ Volcano

Mangroves

Wetlands

Coral reef

▲ Plate margins with
direction of movement

KEY TO NATURAL VEGETATION

Dry woodland

Tropical grassland

Hot desert

Temperate grassland

Tropical rain forest

Mediterranean-type

Temperate rain forest

AUSTRALIA AND PAPUA NEW GUINEA

AUSTRALIA IS A LAND OF EXTREMES. It is the world's smallest, flattest continent, with the lowest rainfall. The landscape ranges from rain forest along the north coast, to arid desert, called the Outback, in the center, to snowfields in the southeast. It is also one of the most urbanized countries; 70 percent of the population lives in towns and cities in the coastal regions, while much of the interior remains sparsely inhabited. Until two centuries ago this vast land was solely occupied by Aboriginal peoples, but in 1788 convict settlers from Britain established a colony on the southeast coast. Since then immigration, especially from Europe, has played a vital part in Australia's development. Australia is a wealthy and politically stable country with rich natural resources, steady population growth, and increasingly strong trade links in the Pacific area, especially with Japan and the USA. Papua New Guinea, the eastern half of the mountainous island of New Guinea, was once an Australian colony, but became independent in 1975.

FLYING DOCTOR

In the Australian Outback, the nearest neighbor can live vast distances away. For a doctor to cover such huge areas by road would be impossible. About 60 years ago, the Royal Flying Doctor Service was established. In an emergency, a caller can contact the service by radio, 24 hours a day, and receive medical treatment within hours.

Quartz — *Gold*

MINING

Australia has large deposits of minerals such as gold, uranium, coal, and diamonds. The mining of these minerals played an important part in the early development of the continent. Improved mining techniques have led to a resurgence in gold mining in Western Australia. Look for 🅐

Yam
Cassava

Cassava and yam are staple foods in Papua New Guinea.

THE GREAT OUTDOORS

Australia's climate is ideal for water-sports and other outdoor activities. But Australians are increasingly aware of the danger of skin cancer because of the hole in the ozone layer above the Antarctic, and are learning to take precautions when in the sun.

KEYBOX

Cattle: Australia has about 24 million cattle and exports beef and veal to over 100 countries, especially Japan and the USA. Look for 🐂

Mining: Papua New Guinea has recently become a major producer of gold, which is mined on the mainland and on one of the outlying islands. Look for 🅐

Pearls: Large South Sea pearls are cultivated in oysters in the waters along Australia's northwest coast. These are called "cultured" pearls. Look for 🐚

🐑	Sheep	⛴	Fishing ports
🌾	Cereals	♜	Coal
🌿	Sugarcane	🏭	Industrial center
🌲	Timber	✈	Major airstrips
🍇	Wine	✈	Tourism

FIRST INHABITANTS

Aboriginal peoples believe they have occupied Australia since "before time began." Early Aboriginal societies survived by hunting and gathering. They had their own traditions of storytelling, ceremonies, and art. Today, 66 percent of Aboriginal peoples live in towns. Here, 200 years after the first European settlement, activists march through Sydney demanding land rights. The government has introduced programs to improve Aboriginal standards of living, education, and employment.

TIMOR SEA

INDIAN OCEAN

Melville I.
Bathurst I.
Clarence Strait
DARWIN
C. Londonderry
Joseph Bonaparte Gulf
Beef
C. Leveque
Collier Bay
Wyndham
Diamonds
KIMBERLEY PLATEAU
Beef
Iron
KING LEOPOLD RANGES
Victoria
Beef
Beef
Broome
Fitzroy
Halls Creek
Beef
Beef
NO
Monte Bello Is.
Barrow I.
North West C.
Dampier
Port Hedland
GREAT SANDY DESERT
Iron
TE
HAMERSLEY RANGE
Iron Ashburton
Iron
Manganese
L. Mackay
L. Disappointment
MACDON
L. Macleod
WESTERN
Gold
GIBSON DESERT
Carnarvon
Murchison
Gold
Meekatharra
L. Carnegie
L. Wells
Gold
AUSTRALIA
GREAT VICTORIA DESERT
Shark Bay
Dirk Hartog I.
Gold
Mount Magnet
Nickel
A
Geraldton
Gold
Nickel
Zinc
L. Barlee
Gold
Nickel
Oats
L. Moore
Kalgoorlie
Dairy
Wheat
Gold
Nickel
NULLARBOR PLAIN
PERTH
Fremantle
Rockingham
Dairy
Gold
Gold
C. Naturaliste
Bunbury
Augusta
Dairy
Barley
Esperance
C. Pasley
Great Australian Bigh
C. Leeuwin
Albany

The world's finest opals come from northern New South Wales.

WINE PRODUCTION

When Europeans began to settle in Australia, they brought with them skills including winemaking. The British first began to grow grapes in South Australia, which now produces over half the country's wines and brandies. With the continued arrival of Europeans, other grapes were added, including the famous French and German varieties. Grapes are now grown throughout the country, most notably in Western Australia in recent years. Australia is now producing vintages of international quality. Look for 🍇

MOUNTAIN BARRIERS

In highland areas of Papua New Guinea, the mountain ranges have formed natural barriers between the different groups of people, helping to preserve a remarkable variety of cultures and languages. Over 700 different languages are still spoken there today.

PAPUA NEW GUINEA
POP: 4,100,000

PAPUA NEW GUINEA

Papua New Guinea's mountainous terrain and fast-flowing rivers make much of the country inaccessible by road. An extensive network of airstrips have been built, and today almost every town and village has its airstrip. Look for ⌐⊏

TOURISM

Two million tourists visit Australia each year, making tourism the country's fastest growing industry. The Great Barrier Reef is a major attraction, but the reef's fragile ecosystem is vulnerable to damage caused by divers and pollution. Look for 🐠

Uluru (Ayers Rock) is a sacred site for some Aboriginal peoples.

Merino sheep are famous for their wool

SHEEP FARMING

Australia has about a sixth of the world's sheep – some 175 million of them. These produce a third of the world's wool, especially the fine-quality wool used to make clothes. About 97 percent of Australia's wool is exported, much of it to Japan, Western Europe, and China. Look for 🐑

SYDNEY

The concrete "sails" of the Sydney Opera House are a fitting emblem for one of the world's greatest sea-ports. Australia's largest city grew from the first European settlement on the continent, established by the British in 1788. Sydney will host the Olympic Games in the year 2000.

CULTURAL DIVERSITY

Immigration has been very important for the development of Australia. People from many different countries now live there, such as these Vietnamese schoolchildren, who live in a Sydney suburb.

Lush, tropical rain forest in Queensland.

The Aboriginal peoples are skilled artists. This bark painting shows a crocodile.

AUSTRALIA
POP: 18,300,000

The red granite shoreline of eastern Tasmania.

KM
0 100 200 300 400 500 600
0 100 200 300
MILES

NEW ZEALAND

NEW ZEALAND LIES deep in the southern Pacific, about halfway between the Equator and the South Pole, 932 miles (1,500 km) from Australia, its nearest large neighbor. New Zealand was one of the last places on Earth to be inhabited by people. The first settlers were Maoris from the Polynesian islands in the Pacific. They were followed by Europeans, who now make up about 86 per cent of the population. From 1840 to 1907 New Zealand was a British colony. Sheep farming was the main source of wealth. But since the 1970s – when Britain joined the EU and cut its imports from New Zealand dramatically – new markets have had to be found in Southeast Asia.

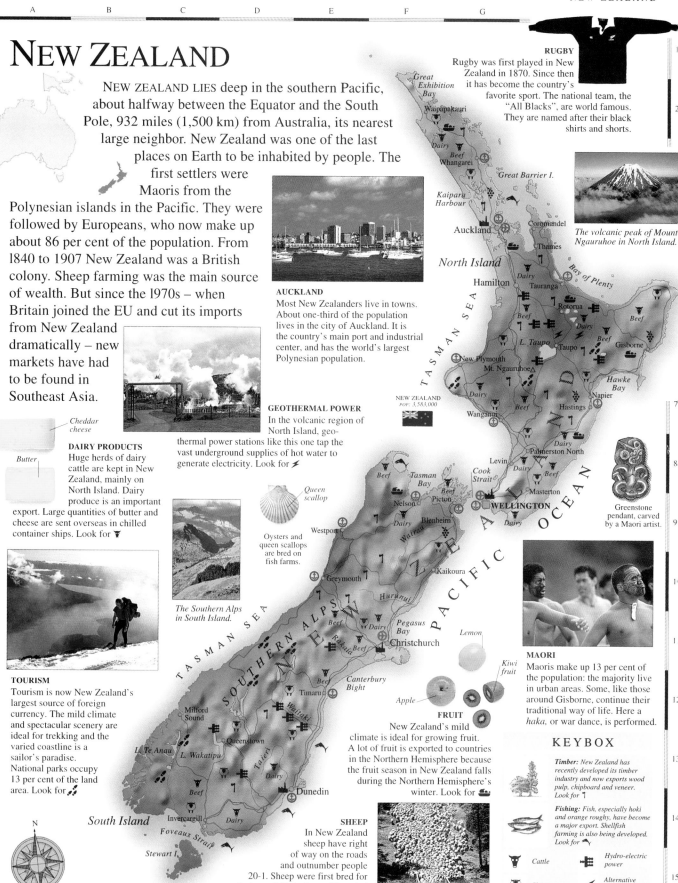

RUGBY
Rugby was first played in New Zealand in 1870. Since then it has become the country's favorite sport. The national team, the "All Blacks", are world famous. They are named after their black shirts and shorts.

The volcanic peak of Mount Ngauruhoe in North Island.

AUCKLAND
Most New Zealanders live in towns. About one-third of the population lives in the city of Auckland. It is the country's main port and industrial center, and has the world's largest Polynesian population.

GEOTHERMAL POWER
In the volcanic region of North Island, geo-thermal power stations like this one tap the vast underground supplies of hot water to generate electricity. Look for ⚡

Cheddar cheese

Butter

DAIRY PRODUCTS
Huge herds of dairy cattle are kept in New Zealand, mainly on North Island. Dairy produce is an important export. Large quantities of butter and cheese are sent overseas in chilled container ships. Look for ▼

Queen scallop

Oysters and queen scallops are bred on fish farms.

The Southern Alps in South Island.

TOURISM
Tourism is now New Zealand's largest source of foreign currency. The mild climate and spectacular scenery are ideal for trekking and the varied coastline is a sailor's paradise. National parks occupy 13 per cent of the land area. Look for

FRUIT
New Zealand's mild climate is ideal for growing fruit. A lot of fruit is exported to countries in the Northern Hemisphere because the fruit season in New Zealand falls during the Northern Hemisphere's winter. Look for

Lemon

Kiwi fruit

Apple

MAORI
Maoris make up 13 per cent of the population: the majority live in urban areas. Some, like those around Gisborne, continue their traditional way of life. Here a haka, or war dance, is performed.

Greenstone pendant, carved by a Maori artist.

SHEEP
In New Zealand sheep have right of way on the roads and outnumber people 20-1. Sheep were first bred for their wool. But when refrigerated ships were developed, frozen lamb could be exported to Europe. Now exports go to the Middle East, Asia and the USA. Look for ▼

KEYBOX

Timber: New Zealand has recently developed its timber industry and now exports wood pulp, chipboard and veneer. Look for ⌐

Fishing: Fish, especially hoki and orange roughy, have become a major export. Shellfish farming is also being developed. Look for

🐂 Cattle		Hydro-electric power
🐑 Sheep	⚡	Alternative power
Mixed fruit	🏭	Industrial center
Wine		Trekking

NEW ZEALAND
POP: 3,583,000

North Island

Great Exhibition Bay
Waipapakauri
Whangarei
Great Barrier I.
Kaipara Harbour
Auckland
Coromandel
Thames
Hamilton
Tauranga
Rotorua
Bay of Plenty
L. Taupo
New Plymouth
Mt. Ngauruhoe
Taupo
Gisborne
Hawke Bay
Napier
Hastings
Wanganui
Palmerston North
Levin
Masterton
WELLINGTON
Cook Strait

South Island

Tasman Bay
Nelson
Picton
Blenheim
Westport
Greymouth
Kaikoura
Hurunui
Pegasus Bay
Christchurch
Canterbury Bight
Timaru
Milford Sound
Queenstown
L. Te Anau
L. Wakatipu
Dunedin
Invercargill
Foveaux Strait
Stewart I.

TASMAN SEA
PACIFIC OCEAN
SOUTHERN ALPS
NEW ZEALAND

N

0	50	100	150	200	250	300	KM
0	50	100	150				MILES

A B C D E F G H I

GLOSSARY

This list provides clear and simple meanings for certain geographical and technical terms used in this atlas.

Acid rain Rain which has been made poisonous by industrial pollution.

AIDS (Acquired Immune Deficiency Syndrome). A fatal condition spread by infected blood and certain body fluids.

Alliance A union of nations, which has been agreed by treaty for economic, political, or military purposes.

Alluvium Loose material, such as **silt**, sand, and gravel, carried by rivers.

Alternative energy Sources of energy which can be renewed – including solar or wind power. These forms of energy, unlike fossil fuel energy from coal and oil, do not produce pollution.

Apartheid The policy, developed in South Africa, of separating peoples by race. Non-whites did not have the same democratic rights, and many public institutions were restricted to one race only.

Aquaculture Cultivation of fish and shellfish in lakes, **estuaries**, rivers, or the sea.

Archipelago A group of islands.

Atoll A circular or horseshoe-shaped coral reef enclosing a shallow area of water.

Bilingual Speaking two languages.

Biotechnology The use of living organisms in the manufacture of food, drugs, and other products. Yeast, for example, is used to make beer and bread.

Buddhism A religion that began in India in about 500 BC. It is based on the teachings of Buddha, who believed that good or evil deeds can be rewarded or punished in this life, or in other lives that will follow. Buddhists aim to achieve inner peace by living their lives according to the example set by Buddha.

Cash crop Agricultural produce grown for sale, often for foreign export, rather than to be consumed by the country or locality where it was grown.

Christianity A religion that began in the 1st century BC. Christians believe in one God and follow the teachings of Jesus Christ, whom they believe was the Son of God.

Civil war A war between rival groups of people who live in the same country.

Classical Art, architecture, or literature which originated in the time of the ancient Greeks and Romans.

Colony A territory which belongs to another country. Also a group of people living separately within a country.

Communism An economic and political system of the 19th and 20th centuries in which farms, factories, and the goods they produce, are owned by the state.

Coniferous Trees or shrubs, like pines and firs, which have needles instead of leaves. Most are evergreen.

Conquistador The word is Spanish for "conqueror," and was applied to the Spanish explorers and invaders of Mexico and parts of South America in the 16th century.

Consumer goods Objects such as food, clothing, furniture, cars, and televisions which are purchased by people for their personal and private use.

Continental plates The huge interlocking plates which make up the Earth's surface. A plate margin is an area where two plates meet, and is the point at which **earthquakes** occur most frequently.

Continental shelf The edge of a landmass which forms a shallow, raised shelf in the sea.

Cosmopolitan Influenced by foreign cultures.

Cottage industry The manufacture of products – often traditional ones like textiles or pottery – by people in their own homes.

Crude oil Oil in its original state, before chemicals and other products have been removed by various processes in a refinery.

Crusades A series of wars from the 11th to 13th centuries when Christian European armies fought against non Christian, often Islamic, armies for possession of the Holy Land, or Palestine.

Cultural heritage Anything handed down from a country's past, such as its traditions, art, and architecture.

Currency The money of a particular country.

Deforestation The cutting of trees for timber or clearing of forest for farmland. The land is often left bare, leading to soil erosion and increasing the risk of flooding and landslides.

Democracy A political system in which everyone above a certain age has the right to vote for the election of his or her representatives in the national and local governments.

Desertification The creation of deserts either by changes in climate or by overgrazing, over-population, **deforestation,** or overcultivation.

Developing world Parts of the world which are still undergoing the process of industrialization.

Dictator A political leader who assumes absolute rule of a nation.

Earthquake A trembling or more violent movement of the ground caused by **seismic activity.** Earthquakes occur most frequently along **continental plate** margins.

Economy The organization of a country's finances, exports, imports, industry, agriculture, and services.

Ecosystem A community of plants and animals dependent on each other and on the habitat in which they live.

Electronics The use of electricity to produce signals that carry information and control devices such as telephones or computers.

Emigrant A person who has moved from one country or region to settle in another country or region.

Empire A large group of countries ruled by one person – an emperor.

Equator An imaginary East-West line that circles the middle of the Earth at equal distance from the **Poles**. The Equator also marks the nearest point on the Earth's surface to the Sun, so it has a consistently hot climate.

Estuary The mouth of a river, where the tide's salt water meets the fresh water of the river.

Ethnic diversity People of several different cultures living in the same region.

Ethnic minority A group of people who share a culture and are outnumbered by others living in the same region.

European Union (EU) (or European Community, EC) A group of European countries linked together by treaty to promote trade, industry, and agriculture within a **free-market economy.**

Exports Goods produced in a country but sold abroad.

Fauna Animals of a region.

Flora Plants of a region.

Foreign debt The money owed by one country to the government, banks, or institutions of one or more other countries.

Foreign exchange Money brought into a country from abroad, usually by the sale of **exports**, by **service industries,** or by tourism.

Free-market economy An economy which is regulated by the price of goods bought and sold freely in national and international markets.

Geothermal energy Electricity produced from hot rocks under the Earth's surface. These heat water and produce steam, which can then be used to generate electricity.

Geyser A fountain of hot water or steam that erupts periodically as a result of underground streams coming into contact with hot rocks.

Greenhouse effect A rise in the global temperature caused as heat, reflected and radiated from the Earth's surface, is trapped in the atmosphere by a build up of "greenhouse" gases, such as carbon dioxide. Also called "global warming."

Habitat A place or region where a certain animal or plant usually lives.

Heavy industry Industry that uses large amounts of energy and raw materials to produce heavy goods, such as machinery, ships, or locomotives.

Hunter-gatherers People who do not grow their food, but obtain it by hunting it and gathering it from their environment. There are few hunter-gatherer groups left in the world today.

Hydroelectric power (HEP) Electricity produced by harnessing the force of falling water.

ICBM (Intercontinental Ballistic Missile) A missile, usually with a nuclear warhead, that can be fired from one continent to land in another.

Immigrant A person who has come to live in a country from another country or region.

Incentives Something that arouses or encourages people to greater efforts.

Inflation The rate at which a country's prices increase.

Informal economy An economy in which people buy and sell from each other, not through shops or markets.

Infrastructure The buildings, transportation, and communication links that enable goods to be produced and then moved around within a country.

Irrigation A system of watering dry areas. Water is carried or pumped to the area through pipes or ditches.

Islam A religion founded in the Middle East in the 7th century AD by the prophet Mohammed. Its followers, called Muslims (or Moslems), believe in one God – called Allah. The rules and beliefs of Islam are contained in its holy book, the *Koran.*

Islamic fundamentalist A person who strictly follows the rules and beliefs of Islam contained in the holy book, the Koran. See **Islam.**

Isthmus A narrow piece of land connecting two larger bodies of land, surrounded on two sides by water.

Labor intensive An activity which requires large amounts of work or large numbers of workers to accomplish it.

Lent A period of time lasting 40 days observed by Christians during which they fast and prepare for the festival of Easter.

Lignite Woody or brown coal.

Living standards The quality of life in a country, usually measured by income, material possessions, and levels of education and health care.

Malnutrition A prolonged lack of adequate food.

Market gardening Farms and **smallholdings** growing fruit and vegetables for sale.

Megalopolis A very large or continuous urban area in which several large towns or cities have joined as their urban areas have spread.

Metropolis A major city, often the capital.

Militarized zone An area occupied by armed military forces

Multinational company A company which has branches, or factories, in several countries.

Nationalists Groups of people united in their wish for independence from a government or from foreign rule.

Neutral country A country which refrains from taking part in international conflicts.

Nomad A person who does not settle in one place for any length of time, but moves in search of hunting or grazing land.

Oil shale Flaky rock containing oil.

Pastoralist A person who makes a living from grazing livestock.

Peat Decomposed vegetation found in bogs. It can be dried and used as fuel.

Peninsula A strip of land surrounded on three sides by water.

Permafrost Permanently frozen ground. The surface thaws in summer, but water cannot drain away through the frozen subsurface. Typical of **subarctic** areas.

Pharmaceuticals The manufacture of medicinal drugs.

Plantation A large farm on which only one crop is usually grown.

Plate margin See **Continental plates.**

Polar regions The regions around the North and South Poles which are permanently frozen, and where the temperature only rises above the freezing point for a few months of the year.

Poles, the The term applied to the North and South Poles, the northernmost and southernmost points of the Earth's axis or rotation.

Prairie A Spanish/American term for a large area of grassland.

Privatization When state-owned activities and companies are taken over by private firms.

Protestant A member of one of the main Christian religions founded in the 16th century by those who did not agree with all aspects of the Roman Catholic Church. Protestantism became one of the main branches of **Christianity**.

Quota A maximum quantity imposed on the number of goods produced, imported, or exported by a country.

Rain forest Dense forest found in hot and humid equatorial regions; often called tropical rain forest.

Raw materials Substances in a natural or unrefined state used in the manufacture of goods, like cotton for textiles and bauxite for aluminum.

Refugees People who flee their own country or region because of political, religious, or racial persecution.

Republic The form of government in a country that has no monarch. The head of state is usually a president, like the President of the USA.

Reservation An area of land set aside for occupation by specific people, plants, or animals.

Revenue Money paid to a government, like taxes.

Roman Catholic A Christian who accepts the Pope as his or her spiritual leader.

Rural In, or belonging to, the countryside.

Savannah Tropical grasslands where an annual dry season prevents the growth of most trees.

Seismic activity Tremors and shocks in the Earth's crust usually caused by the movement of plates along a fault.

Service industry An industry that supplies services, such as banking, rather than producing manufactured goods.

Shantytown An area in or around a city where people live in temporary shacks, usually without basic facilities such as running water.

Silt Small particles, finer than sand, often carried by water and deposited on riverbanks, at river mouths and harbors. See also **alluvium.**

Smallholding A plot of agricultural land smaller than a farm.

Socialism Political system in which the economy is owned and controlled by the state and not by private companies or individuals.

Soviet bloc All those countries which were ruled directly or indirectly by the communist government of the former USSR.

Staple crop The main crop grown in a region.

Staple food The basic part of a diet, such as rice or bread.

Steppes An extensive, grass-covered and virtually treeless plain, such as those found in Siberia.

Stock Exchange A place where people buy and sell government bonds, **currency,** stocks, and financial shares in large private companies.

Strategic Carefully planned or well placed from a military point of view.

Subarctic The climate in **polar** regions, characterized by extremely cold temperatures and long winters.

Technological The application of science through the use of machines.

Temperate The mild, variable climate found in areas between the **tropics** and cold **polar** regions.

Tropic of Cancer, Capricorn Two imaginary lines of latitude drawn on the Earth's surface above and below the Equator. The hottest parts of the world are between these two lines.

Tropics, the An area between the **Equator** and the **tropics of Cancer and Capricorn** that has heavy rainfall, high temperatures, and lacks any clear seasonal variation.

Tundra Vegetation found in areas within the Arctic Circle, such as dwarf bushes, very short grasses, mosses, and lichens.

United Nations (UN) An association of countries established to work together to prevent wars and to supply aid, advice, and research on an international basis.

Urban area Town, city or extensive built-up area.

West, the Those countries in Europe and North America with **free-market economies** and **democratic** governments.

Western The economic, cultural, and political values shared by countries belonging to **the West.**

Dorling Kindersley would like to thank the following for their help supplying objects for photography: Catherine Lucas, Clare Carolin, Dina Adkins, Clive Webster; Russian Connections for supplying the *draniki* on p.5 and p.80; Mexicolore, London, for skeleton and *sarape* on p.38; Fiat Auto SpA for Fiat Tempra on p.47; Uruguayan Embassy for scarf on p.49; Rosenthal Studio Haus Ltd., London, for glass fruit on p.57; Heal's, London, for child's chair on p.57; Minans Restaurant, London, for *rijstaffel* on p.64; Philips Consumer Electronics, London, for television on p.65; BMW (GB) Ltd., Bracknell, for car on p.66; Leica UK, London, for camera on p.67; Watches of Switzerland Ltd., London, for watch on p.69; Hannah Kodicek for puppet on p.70; Henry Marchant Ltd., London, for Bohemian glass on p.70 and ballet costume on p.83; Exico Ltd., London, for wooden duck on p.71; The Greek Shop, London, for doll on p.79; Soccer Scene, London for football shirt on p.73 and rugby shirt on p.134; Gucci, London, for shoes and scarf on p. 72; Embassy of Latvia for currency on p.80; Embassy of Lithuania for currency on p.80; The Russian Shop, London, for chess set, child's toy, lacquered box on p.83; Georgian scarf and Russian dolls on cover and p.85, *samovar* and doll on p.112 and mink hat on p.113; Liberty's, London, for rug on p.88; African Centre, London, for African sculptures on p.93, cover and p.94; Sofra Restaurant, London, for coffee pot and dish on cover and p.123; Covent Garden Oriental Carpets for carpet and saddle cloth on p.110; Ranger Arms Co. Ltd. for gun on p.106; Sandra Schneider for *yarmulke*, prayer book, shawl, etc. on p.106; Saree Emporium, London, for saris on p.117; East West Herb Shop, London, for herbal medicines on p.119; Chuntex (UK) Ltd. for computer monitor on p.121; Tourism Authority of Thailand for lacquer work on p.124.

Map symbols designed by: Kenny Laurenson

Other help supplied by: Crispian Martin St. Valery, Alastair Owens, Janet Oswald, Rosemary Cowan, Jane Lewis, Judy Chamberlain, Michael Capon and George Heritage.

Antarctic terrain supplied by Mullard Space Science Laboratory, University College London, using data from the radar altimeter aboard the European Space Agency's ERS-1 satellite

PICTURE CREDITS:
Heather Angel: 86cl. **B. and C. Alexander:** 25tl, 25tr, 51cl. **Max Alexander:** 63ccr. **P. and G. Bowater:** 69cb. **Chris Branfield:** front cover cl. **Duncan Brown:** 117bl. **J Allan Cash:** front cover bl. 31tr, 36tc, 38cr, 42cl, 42bc, 44bc, 49tcr, 56cr, 57bd, 70bl, 57br, 57br, 58tr, 60bl, 61c, 61bl, 61b, 62cl, 71c, 74ct, 76c, 76bc, 78br, 92 c, 93br, 94bl, 100br, 104ct, 104cl, 105bc, 108bl, 108br, 109tr, 110br, 114rt, 117cr, 120cbr, 123c, 127tc. **Cephas:** 49ctr. **Mark Chapman:** 93tcl. **J.R.Chapman:** 88cr, 88br, 96tr, 111c, 117tl. **Oliver Crimmon:** 96ctr. **Ann Clarke:** 40bc. **John Cleare/Mountain Camera:** 40bcl. **Stephanie Colasanti:** 106cr. **Bruce Coleman:** 65br, 118br; Gene Ahrens 26ch, 27tl, 27cr; Alain Compost 126cr, 126bl; Gerald Cubitt 13bl, 98cl, 99bc, 99cb, 114ct, 114ctr, 114cbl, 116bl; Francisco J.Erize 50cl; M. P. L Fogden 35c; Jeff Foott Productions 20ct; Christer Fredriksson 86ctr; Dr. Charles Henneghien 93tc; Hans Gerd Heyer 121cbr; Udo Hirsch 129cbr; David Houston 89tl; Johnny Johnson 50cc;

Herbert Kranawetter 75br; O. Langrand 95tl; Wayne Lankinen 30bcl; Thor Larsen 51bc; Leonard Lee Rue 21cbr; Luiz C. Marigo 13cbl, 40ctr; Larry Mulvehill/Black Star 120ct; John Murray 114cl, 128cbl; Orion Press 122cr; Charlie Ott 20tl; Dieter and Mary Plage 40ctl; Dr. Eckhart Pott 38c; Dr. Sandro Prato 73cl, 128cb; Fritz Prenzel 128cb, 128br; Hans Reinhard 50bl, 71bc; N.Tomalin 35tr; Konrad Wothe 101tl; Jonathan T. Wright 32c, 83tl; J. Zwanepoel 65cl. **Colorific** Linda Bartlett 75c; Steve Benbow 75bc; Marcus Brooke 102ctl; David Burnett/Contact Press 33ctr; Paul Conklin 32cl; John Dominis 74cl; Enrico Ferorelli 33ct; Frank Hermann 94tr; Anthony Joyce 31tl; Sarah Meltzoff/Black Star 133tr; Christopher Morris/Blackstar 75tr; Peter Nacke/Picture Group 84clb; Lehtikuva Ov 14cb; Reza/Black Star 15tl; Malcolm Sanders 133tl; Michael St. Maur Sheil 99c; Peter Turnley/Blackstar 84tr. **Comstock:** 72ct. **Steven J. Cooling:** 99ct, 134cbl. **Lupe Cuhna:** 48tc. **James Davis/Worldwide:** 24bc, 46br, 52bl, 53cr, 69bl, 89ct, 107bl. WVF/Maarten Udema 112cl. **Ecoscene:** Peter Hulme back cover tc, 55tl. **Lynn Edelman:** 45tc. **Chris Fairclough:** 90c, 106c, 116cl, 117c; P. George 117tc. **Sydney Freelance:** 132bl. **Ronald Grant Archive:** 116bl. **Sonia Halliday:** Jane Taylor 107br. **R. Hanbury Tennison:** 77cbr. **Robert Harding:** front cover cr, 11tr, 13tr, 14cr, 15tc, 23cb, 26cr, 27bcl, 35cr, 39cb, 39bl, 45cl, 46tcr, 46tr, 49cr, 49br, 52cl, 56ccr, 56cl, 56c, 61tc, 63cbr, 65tl, 65bl, 68tr, 68cl, 68br, 76cl, 78cl, 79tr, 80cr, 89tr, 89tcr, 90br, 91bl, 93bc, 98cbl, 116bc, 116br, 117bcr, 125tcl, 125cr, 125bcl, 125cb, 125br, 127tcr; Mohamed Amin 108cl; Bildagentur Schuster/Eckhardt 66cl, 66tr, 67cl, 78cbr; Bildagentur Schuster/Scholz 85tr; Graham Birch 126tr; C.E.Clark 99cr; C.Dela 95ctl; F.Dubes 63bc; Alan L.Durand 85cbr; Explorer/J. P. Nacivet 62c; Robert Fereck 45tc; Fournie 124cr; Robert Francis 13c, 39bcr; Lee Frost 78c; James Green 79bcr; Ian Griffiths 94cr, 133tcr; Gavin Heller 43bl, 115tl; Michael Jenner 104cb, 107cr; Paolo Koch 126ncr; David Lomax 42cr, 43tc; Claude Martine 63cb; Photri 10tr, 10br, 27c; Chris Rennie 39cr, 77tc, 131tr; David Rolf Richardson 77bc; Sassoon 77bd; M. Short 79cb, 105cb, 105bl; Julia Thorne 51br; David Tokeley 116ct; Adina Tovy 29bl; Vadaz 68cr; A. C.Waltham 34c, 34br; Elizabeth Weiland 119tl; G. M.Wilkins 99tl; Adam Woolfitt 53cl, 64tr, 64c, 75tc, 102ct, 104br. **Paul Harris:** 24ct, 24cb, 25br, 82cl, 83br, 113tr, 113ctr, 113cbr, 118tcr, 119cl, 122c. **J. Henderson:** 76cb. **John Heseltine:** 59tr. **Leila Hilland:** 131br. **Jimmy Holmes /Himalayan Images:** 118c, 118cl, 119c, 122cl, 123tl. **Pippa Hurst:** 88cl. **Hutchison Library:** 24cl, 43br, 94bl, 117cr, 124cl; Robert Aberman 104bl; John Egan 79cr; Sarah Errington 100cr, 112bc; J.G.Fuller 129tc; John Hatt 102br; Richard House 47ctl; Victoria Ivleva 81c; Joan Klatchko 52cbr; Bernard Regent 130ctl; Kirsten Rodgers 44tc; Prue Rankin Smith 42tr; Andrei Solomonov 85ct; Tony Souter 73bl. **A. Hyman:** 110c. **ICCE** S. M. Andrews 86ctl, 89br. **Image Bank:** 9ccl; Peter Hendrie, 85bc; H.J.Adkers 50ct; Gio Barto 88tr; Vladimir Birgus 81tcl; Ira Block 22c; David Brownell 35tcr; P. and G. Bowater 23tr; Edward W. Bower 28cl; Luis Castaneda 29bc; Gerard Champlong 34cl; Gary S. Champan 42bcr; S. Costa 47bc; Melchior Di Giacomo 15bl, 43c; Wendy Dison 119bl; Tom Owen Edwards 51cbl, 75cr; Grant V. Faint 69tc; Francisco Onatanon 61br; John R. Ramey 35bl; Guido Alberto Rossi front cover bl, 43tr, 43cr, 100bcl; Steve Satushek 23tl, 56cbl, 112cb; Erik Leigh Simmons 118tc; John Lewis Stage 47tl; Peter Turner 28cb; Frank Wing 120tr; Hans Wolf 67bcr. **Images** 61cr, 130cl; Andris Apse 130cbr; Horizon 127tr. **Impact:** B. Babanov/Vika 113tcl; A. Bradshaw/Visons 113tcr; Steve Piers Cavendish 96ct, 97ctr; Rupert Conant 71tr; Anita Corbin 126c; John Denhan 66tl; Colin Jones 28bl; Mike McQueen 114bcr; M. Milivojevic 70bl; Paul O'Driscoll 99tcr. **Ann Jousiffe:** 89br.

Kaleidoscope: Victor Englebert 93cbr. **Frank Lane:** D.Hoadley 12 tr; W. Wisniewski 53bl, 102cbr. **Anthony Lambert:** 77cr. **Nicki Liddiard:** 58cr. **Life File:** 48bl; Sue Davies 29c, 44tr; Juliet Highet 79br; Eddy Tan 60tr; Sergei Verein 113bl. **Catherine Lucas:** 96c. **Magnum:** Abbas 45tcr, 95bc; Eve Arnold 90bl; Bruno Barbey 92cl, 109tr, 109cr, 123cl, 124bl; Rene Burri 34bl; M. Franck 91tr; S. Franklin 90ctr, 108tr; Thomas Hoepker 66cr, 67cr; David Hurn/J.Hillelson 89cr; Hiroji Kubota 119cbr; Fred Mayer 102cr; Gideon Mendel 92bc; Eli Reed 107tl; Marc Riboud 102bl, 109bc; Dennis Stock 26c, 28br; Kryn Taconis/John Hillelson 22br; Chris Steele-Perkins 91br, 98c; Dennis Stock 53tr. **Military and Research Services/**Todd Shipyards: 101tcl. **Tim Motion:** 60c, 62cr. **National Maritime Museum:** 101br. **Natural History Photographic Agency:** ANT 133ct; Anthony Bannister 86bcl; Stephen Krasemann 128tr; Dr. Ivan Polunin 114cbr; John Shaw 134cl. **Nature Photographers:** Peter Craig Cooper 98cbr; Mark Pidgeon 87bl; Roger Tidman 97tl. **New Zealand Tourist Office:** 134cr. **Nissan:** 58br. **Oxford Scientific Films:** J.Nettis 76cbr. **Panos:** 46cbr; Heidi Bradner 70ct; Matthew Boysons 52cr; Alain le Garsmeur 119tr. **Philips CED Publicity:** 65tcr. **Pictor:** back cover tl, 12ctr, 13cr, 14c, 22bl, 23cl, 28c, 31br, 32br, 33cbl, 47cr, 48tr, 55ctr, 59cl, 86cb, 86bcr, 90tr, 98bc, 101bc, 102cbl, 124c, 129ctr, 130bl. **John Pilkington:** 111cr. **Pirelli Cables:** 53br. **Planet Earth Pictures:** 20cl; Yuri Shibnev 102tr, 103tr; John Eastcott/Yva Momatiuk 13tc; William M. Smithey Jr. 21cbl. **Philip Powell:** front cover cbl. **Quadrant:** 45tr. **Donna Rispoli** 127c. **Science Photo Library:** Martin Bond 9ccr; David Parker 9 cr; Ray Ellis 13br; Simon Frazer 55cr; John Heseltine 55cbl; Michael Martin 55tcl; Novosti Press Agency 112ct. **South American Pictures:** 44cr, 45bl, 49tcr. **Spectrum:** 55ctl, 55cb; Jean Paul Nacivet 55tr. **Frank Spooner:** Tordai 88c. **John Massey Stewart:** 81tl. **Still Pictures:** 25tc; Doug Armand 100tr; Mark Edwards 38bc, 93tr, 95c, 95bl; Edward Parker 94cl; Hjalte Tin 113tl. **Tony Stone:** 105tr, 37bl, 55cbr, 58c, 67bcl, 79rt, 84ccr, 114cl, 114cb, 123tc, 123cl, 130cb, 130br; Glen Allison 32tr; Doug Armand 69bc, 73c; John Beatty 53bc, 101bcr; Oliver Benn 40tr; Ken Biggs 12tcr; Allan Bramley 130ct; Doug Boult 24c; Michael Busselle 59bc; Julian Calder 111c, 121tl; Mike Caldwell 74bl; John Callahan 121bc; Hubert Camille 62bc; Bryn Campbell 52tc; Paul Chesley 121cr, 130ctr, 134br; Paul Damien 33tl; Nicholas De Vore 40cb; Doris De Witt 28tr; Sepp Dietrich 71cb; Richard Elliot 134cb; John Garrett 132 cl; Margaret Gowan 120bl; David Hanson 36bl, 37ctl, 71br; David Hiser 21cb, 51cl, 128bl; Ernst Hohne 67bl; Gary Irving 30bc, 30bcr; Geoff Johnson 111tr; H. Richard Johnson 11ctr; Chris Kaploka 130cr; Oldrich Karasek 70c; Mitch Kezan 96cl; John Lamb 130ctr; Peter Lamberti 11cbr; John Lawlor 37tl; Alan Levenson 125bc; Lukasseck 34cb; Angus Mackillop 15ctl; Doug Mazell 122ctr; Roger Mear 50br; Lawrence Migdale 59cr; Ian Murphy 59br, 64bl; Donald Nausbaum 41bl; Nicholas Parfitt 86cbr,96br; Tom Raymond 29cr; Mitch Reardon 2c,113cb; Steven Rothfeld 14br; David Schultz 33tr; Mark Segal 30c; Hugh Sitton 96cl, 100cr, 14cbr; Adam Smith 47cl; P. and K. Smith 36cr; Robin Smith 131bl; Bill Staley 21ctr; Alena Vikova 72tr; Charlie Waite 59bl, 73tr; Ken Wilson 133bc. **Ina Strading:** 81ct. **Survival Anglia** 3Cr; Ross Bray 107bc; John Newby 93cr; Mauri Rautkari 94bcl. **Zefa:** 20ctl, 29cbr, 51ctl, 66bl, 70tc, 73br, 80c, 81tr, 94br, 106ctr; P. W. Bading 22tr; Jim Brandenburg 131cl; Damm front cover br, 97cr; P. Fera 57tr, 109br; K. Goebel 27bcr, 108cr; Jens Herrman 91cb; Hunter 22cl; Janicek 105cr; Minden 96bl; Sonak 84bl; Steenmans 83tr.

INDEX

Throughout the Atlas, population figures have been taken from the latest official estimates.

HOW TO USE THE GRID

Grid references in the Index help you to find places on the map. For example, if you look up Nairobi in the Index, you will see the reference 97 O5. The first number, 97, is the page number of the map on which Nairobi appears. Find the letters and numbers which border the page, and trace a line across from the letter and down from the number. This directs you to the exact grid square in which Nairobi is located.
The numbers that appear after the names are the page numbers, followed by the grid references.

There are two sorts of factbox in the index. Countries that are more important economically or politically in their area have a larger factbox.

In the factboxes, many statistics are not yet available for the new states of the world. When we have been unable to find the correct figure, N/A is given, which stands for not available.

Population density
This is the total population divided by the land area of a country.

Average life expectancy
This is the average life expectancy at birth, barring war or natural disasters.

Literacy
This is the percentage of people over the age of 15 years who can read and write a simple sentence. Where figures for male (m) and female (f) have not been available, we have used an average (av.).

Death penalty
The countries with Yes use the death penalty regularly. Some of the states with No still have a law permitting the death penalty but do not use it.

Percentage of urban population
This is the percentage of the total population who live in towns or cities.

Calories consumed daily
The recommended daily number for a healthy life is about 2500 calories; the inhabitants of some countries consume far more than others.

The following abbreviations have been used in the index:

anc. = ancient name
Arch. = Archipelago
C. = Cape
E. = East
Ft. = Fort
I. = Island
Is. = Islands
L. = Lake
Mt. = Mountain
Mts. = Mountains
N. = North
N.P. = National Park
Pen. = Peninsula
prev. = previously
Pt. = Point
Res. = Reservoir
R. = River
S. = South
St. = Saint
var. = variant name
W. = West

A

A Coruña (var. La Coruña) Spain 52 J8, 60 G3
Aachen Germany 67 C11
Aalst Belgium 65 F14
Aarau Switzerland 68 F9
Aare *River* Switzerland 68 E9
Aba Nigeria 93 O13
Ābādān Iran 109 L7
Abajo Mountains *Mountain range* Utah, USA 35 K5
Abakan Russian Federation 112 J11
Abashiri Japan 122 M3
Abaya, L. *Lake* Ethiopia 91 J16
Abéché Chad 94 K7
Abengourou Ivory Coast 93 K12
Åbenrå Denmark 56 H16
Abeokuta Nigeria 93 N12
Aberdare Range *Mountain range* Kenya 97 O5
Aberdeen Scotland, UK 52 K7, 58 J8
Aberdeen South Dakota, USA 33 N6
Aberdeen Washington, USA 36 G7
Aberystwyth Wales, UK 59 G14
Abhā Saudi Arabia 108 H13
Abidjan Ivory Coast 93 K13
Abilene Texas, USA 35 P10
Abitibi, L. *Lake* Ontario/Quebec, Canada 25 K11
Abomey Benin 93 M12
Abu Dhabi (var. Abū Zabī) United Arab Emirates 109 N11
Abu Simbel *Archaeological site* Egypt 90 F9
Abū Zabī *see* Abu Dhabi
Abuja Nigeria 93 O11
Abydos *Archaeological site* Egypt 90 G8
Abyssinia *see* Ethiopia
Acapulco Mexico 39 M14
Accra Ghana 93 L13
Acheloos *River* Greece 78 H7
Achinsk Russian Federation 112 J10
Acklins I. *Island* Bahamas 43 M5
Aconcagua *Mountain* Argentina 41
Ad Dafrah *Desert region* United Arab Emirates 109 N12
Ad Dahna *Desert region* Saudi Arabia 109 L10
Ad Dammām Saudi Arabia 109 M9
Ad Dawḥah *see* Doha
Ad-Diwaniyah Iraq 109 K5
Adak I. *Island* Aleutian Is. Alaska, USA 22 A6
Adamawa Highlands *Physical region* Cameroon 87
Adana Turkey 105 M10
Adapazari Turkey 104 I5
Adare, C. *Cape* Victoria Land, Antarctica 50 E12
Addis Ababa Ethiopia 91 J15
Adelaide South Australia, Australia 133 L13
Aden Yemen 100 E7, 108 I16
Aden, Gulf of *Sea feature* Arabia/E Africa 87, 91 N14, 100 E7, 103, 114
Adige *River* Italy 72 H7
Adīrī Libya 89 O8
Adirondack Mts. *Mountain range* New York, USA 27 L7
Adiyaman Turkey 105 O9
Admiralty Is. *Island group* Papua New Guinea 133 N1
Adrar Algeria 88 J8
Adrar des Ifôghas *Mountain range* Mali 93 M6
Adrian Michigan, USA 31 O10
Adriatic Sea S Europe 54, 72 K10, 74 I9
Adwa Ethiopia 91 J13
Adycha *River* Russian Federation 113 N6
Aegean Sea Greece/Turkey 54, 79 M7, 104 F7
Ağri (var. Karaköse) Turkey 105 R6
Afghanistan *Country* C Asia 110-111

Afghanistan 110-111

a Dari, Pashto · 🕮 Afghani · ● 66 · ♥ 42 · ◒ £7.03 · ◗ (m) 44% (f) 14% · ⬚ 8 · ✚ 5148 · ✿ Yes · 🏛 18% · ⫯ 2022

Africa *Continent* 8, 11, 12, 13, 15, 87, 103
African Plate *Physical feature* 8, 20, 41, 54, 87, 103, 115
'Afrīn *River* Syria/Turkey 107 N2
Afyon Turkey 104 J8
Agadez Niger 93 P7
Agadir Morocco 88 G6
Agartala India 117 P8
Agattu I. *Island* Aleutian Is. Alaska, USA 22 A4
Agen France 62 J13
Agios Nikolaos Crete, Greece 79 N16
Agra India 117 K5
Agri *River* Italy 73 M14
Agrigento Sicily 73 J18
Aguarico *River* Ecuador 44 D8
Aguascalientes Mexico 39 L10
Agulhas Basin *Sea feature* Atlantic/Indian Ocean 87
Agulhas, C. *Cape* South Africa 87, 98 J16
Agulhas current *Ocean current* Indian Ocean 12
Agulhas Ridge *Sea feature* Atlantic Ocean 87
Ahaggar *Mountain range* Algeria 87, 89 L11
Ahmadabad India 116 I8
Ahvāz Iran 109 M6
Aïr *Mountain range* Niger 93 P7
Aix-en-Provence France 63 O13
Aizawl India 117 Q8
Ajaccio Corsica 63 S16
Ajdābiyā Libya 89 Q7
Ajmer India 116 J6
Akanthou Cyprus 105 L12
Akhisar Turkey 104 H7
Akimiski I. *Island* Canada 24 J8
Akita Japan 122 K7
Akmola (var. Akmolinsk, Tselinograd) Kazakhstan 122 G11
Akmolinsk *see* Akmola
Akola India 117 K9
Akpatok I. *Island* Canada 25 N3
Akron Ohio, USA 31 Q10
Aksai Chin *Disputed region* China/India 16, 117 L1, 118 F10
Aksaray Turkey 105 L8
Akseki Turkey 104 J10
Aksu China 118 F7
Aksum Ethiopia 91 J13
Aktau (var. Shevchenko) Kazakhstan 112 D10
Aktyubinsk (var. Aqtöbe) Kazakhstan 112 E10
Akyab *see* Sittwe
Al 'Amārah Iraq 109 L6
Al 'Aqabah (var. Aqaba) Jordan 107 L14
Al Azraq Jordan 107 N10
Al Bāḥah Saudi Arabia 108 H12
Al Baṣrah Iraq 109 L7
Al Bayḍā Libya 89 R6
Al Bayḍā' Yemen 108 I16
Al Buraymī Oman 109 O11
Al Ghaydah Yemen 109 L16
Al Hoceima Morocco 88 J4
Al Hudaydah *see* Hodeida
Al Hufūf Saudi Arabia 109 L10
Al Ḥadīthah Iraq 108 J4
Al Ḥasakah Syria 107 R2
Al Hillah Iraq 109 K5
Al Jaghbūb Libya 89 S7
Al Jawf Saudi Arabia 109 N10
Al Jubayl Saudi Arabia 109 L9
Al-Juf *see* El Djouf
Al Karak Jordan 107 M11
Al Khābūrah Oman 109 O11
Al Khums Libya 89 O6
Al Kufrah Libya 89 S10
Al Kūt Iraq 109 L5
Al Kuwayt *see* Kuwait City
Al Lādhiqīyah (var. Latakia) Syria 107 M4
Al Madinah *see* Medina
Al Mafraq Jordan 107 M9
Al Maḥwīt Yemen 108 I15
Al Manāmah *see* Manama
Al Marj Libya 89 Q6
Al Mukallā Yemen 109 K16
Al Mukhā (var. Mocha) Yemen 108 H16
Al Qunayṭirah Syria 107 M8
Al Qurnah Iraq 109 L6
Alabama *River* Alabama, USA 29 K8
Alabama *State* USA 29
Alajuela Costa Rica 42 E13
Alakol', L. *Lake* Kazakhstan 103
Alamogordo New Mexico, USA 35 M10
Åland Is. *Island group* Finland 57 M11
Alanya Turkey 105 K10
Alapaha *River* Georgia, USA 29 N9
Alaska *State* USA 22, 51
Alaska, Gulf of *Sea feature* Alaska, USA 10, 20, 22 G9, 129 L3
Alaska Peninsula *Physical feature* 20
Alaska Range *Mountain range* Alaska, USA 10, 20, 22 G7
Alassio Italy 72 C9
Alazani *River* Azerbaijan/Georgia 85 Q12
Alba Iulia Romania 76 I6
Albacete Spain 61 M10
Albania *Country* SE Europe 75

Albania 75

a Albanian · 🕮 Lek · ● 312 · ♥ 73 · ◒ £0.22 · ◗ (av.) 15% · 🏛 35%

Albany Georgia, USA 29 M9
Albany New York, USA 26-27
Albany Oregon, USA 36 G9
Albany Western Australia, Australia 132 G14
Albany *River* Ontario, Canada 24 J9
Albatross Plateau *Sea feature* Pacific Ocean 129 O7
Albert Canal *Waterway* Belgium 65 I14
Albert, L. *Lake* Uganda/Zaire 87, 97 L3, 95 P12
Albert Lea Minnesota, USA 30 H8
Albert Nile *River* Uganda 97 M2
Alberta *Province* Canada 23
Albertville *see* Kalemie
Albi France 63 L13
Albina Suriname 44 O6
Ålborg Denmark 56 I14
Albuquerque New Mexico, USA 35 L8
Albury New South Wales, Australia 133 N14
Alcántara Res. *Reservoir* Spain 60 H9
Aldabra Is. *Island group* Seychelles, Indian Ocean 100 E9
Aldan *River* Russian Federation 113 N9
Aleg Mauritania 92 G7
Aleksinac Serbia, Yugoslavia 75 O8
Alençon France 62 J6
Aleppo *see* Ḥalab
Alert *Research center* Canada 51 O11
Alessandria Italy 72 D7
Ålesund Norway 52 L7, 56 H8
Aleutian Basin *Sea feature* Bering Sea 103
Aleutian Is. *Island group* Alaska, USA 22 B6, 128 J4
Aleutian Trench *Sea feature* Pacific Ocean 20, 128 J4

Alexander Arch. *Island group* Alaska, USA 22 H11
Alexandretta *see* Iskenderun
Alexandria (var. El Iskandarīya) Egypt 90 F6
Alexandria Louisiana, USA 28 H8
Alexandria Romania 77 L10
Alexandria Virginia, USA 29 R3
Alexandroupoli Greece 79 N2
Aleysk Air Base *Military center* Russian Federation 112 I11
Algeciras Spain 60 I15
Alger *see* Algiers
Algeria *Country* N Africa 88-89

Algeria 88-89

a Arabic · 🕮 Dinai · ● 28 · ♥ 66 · ◒ £0.64 · ◗ (m) 70% (f) 45% · ⬚ 74 · ✚ 43 · ✿ Yes · 🏛 52% · ⫯ 2866

Alghero Sardinia 73 G13
Algiers (var. Alger; anc. Icosium) Algeria 52 K9, 89 L4
Aliakmon *River* Greece 78 I4
Alicante Spain 61 N11
Alice Springs Northern Territory, Australia 133 K9
Alicudi *Island* Lipari Is., Sicily 73 K16
Aligarh India 117 K5
Alkmaar Netherlands 64 H8
Allahabad India 117 M7
Allegheny Mts. *Mountain range* West Virginia, USA 29 Q3
Allentown Pennsylvania, USA 27 K12
Allier *River* France 63 M11
Alma-Ata (var. Almaty) Kazakhstan 112 G13
Almalyk Uzbekistan 111 N6
Almaty *see* Alma-Ata
Almelo Netherlands 64 M9
Almería Spain 61 M13
Alor *Island* Indonesia 127 N15
Alor Setar Malaysia 125 I17
Alotau Papua New Guinea 133 O4
Alpena Michigan, USA 31 O6
Alphen aan den Rijn Netherlands 64 H10
Alps *Mountain range* C Europe 8, 11, 54, 63 P11, 68 G11, 72 D6
Altai Mts. *Mountain range* Asia 103, 105, 118 I5
Altamura Italy 73 N13
Altay Mongolia 118 J5
Altdorf Switzerland 68 G10
Altiplano *Physical region* Bolivia 41
Alton Illinois, USA 31 J13
Altoona Pennsylvania, USA 26 I12
Altun Ha *Archaeological site* Belize 42 C6
Altun Mts. *Mountain range* China 118 H9
Alturas California, USA 37 I12
Alytus Lithuania 80 I10
Am Timan Chad 94 K8
Amakusa Is. *Island group* Japan 123 C15
Amakusa Sea Japan 123 B15
Amami Is. *Island group* Japan 123 B19
Amami-ōshima *Island* Amami Is., Japan 123 B18
Amarapura Burma 124 G7
Amarillo Texas, USA 35 O8
Amasya Turkey 105 M5
Amazon *River* S America 41, 44 G9, 46 H7, 53 F12
Amazon Basin *Physical region* Brazil 11, 41
Amazonia *Physical region* S America 44 G8, 46 C8
Ambarchik Russian Federation 51 R5, 113 O4
Ambato Ecuador 44 C9
Amblève *River* Belgium 65 K16
Ambon Ambon, Indonesia 127 O13
Amboseli *National park* Kenya 97 P6
Ambre, Cap d' *see* Bobaomby, C.
Ambriz Angola 98 C14
Ameland *Island* West Frisian Is. Netherlands 64 K6
American Samoa *Dependent territory* Polynesia, Pacific Ocean 129 K9
Amersfoort Netherlands 64 J10
Amery Ice Shelf *Coastal feature* Indian Ocean Coast, Antarctica 50 G8
Ames Iowa, USA 33 Q9
Amfissa Greece 78 I8
Amga *River* Russian Federation 113 N9
Amherst Burma 125 G11
Amiens France 63 L3
Amirante Is. *Island group* Seychelles 100 F9
Amistad Res. *Reservoir* Mexico/Texas, USA 35 O13
Amlia I. *Island* Aleutian Is., Alaska, USA 22 B7
Amman (var. Rabbah Ammon; anc. Philadelphia) Jordan 107 M10
Ammassalik Greenland 51 N15
Ammersee *Lake* Germany 67 I16
Amol Iran 109 O4
Amorgos *Island* Cyclades, Greece 79 O12
Amritsar India 116 J3
Amstelveen Netherlands 64 I10
Amsterdam Netherlands 64 I9
Amsterdam New York, USA 27 L9
Amsterdam I. *Island* Indian Ocean 101 I13
Amstetten Austria 69 P5
Amu Darya *River* C Asia 103, 111 L8
Amundsen Gulf *Sea feature* Northwest Territories, Canada 23 K6
Amundsen-Scott *Research center* Antarctica 50 E9
Amundsen Sea Pacific Ocean, Antarctica 50 C10

---

a Language (official or most commonly spoken) · 🕮 Currency · ● Population density per square mile · ♥ Average life expectancy · ◒ Price of 1 dozen hen's eggs · ◗ Literacy · ⬚ Number of TVs per 1,000 people · ✚ Number of people per doctor · ✿ Death penalty · 🏛 Percentage of urban-based population · ⫯ Average number of calories consumed daily per person

Ballarat Victoria, Australia 133 M14
Balleny Is. *Island group* Pacific Ocean, Antarctica 50 F12
Balsas *River* Mexico 39 M12
Baltic Sea N Europe 52 M7, 54-55, 57 M13, 70 J1, 80 G4, 103
Baltimore Maryland, USA 29 S3
Baltimore Virginia, USA 52 D9
Baltiysk Russian Federation 80 E9
Bălți Moldavia 84 G7
Bamako Mali 92 I9
Bambari Central African Republic 94 K10
Bamenda Cameroon 94 E10
Ban Houayxay Laos 124 J9
Banda Is. *Island group* Indonesia 127 P13
Banda Sea SE Asia 127 N13, 128 F9
Bandar-e Abbās Iran 109 O9
Bandar-e Būshehr Iran 109 M8
Bandar Seri Begawan (var. Brunei Town) Brunei 126 J9
Bandirma Turkey 104 H6
Bandon Oregon, USA 36 F10
Bandundu (prev. Banningville) Zaire 95 I14
Bandung Java, Indonesia 126 G15
Bangalore India 117 K13
Bangassou Central African Republic 94 L10
Banggai Is. *Island group* Indonesia 127 N12
Banggi *Island* Malaysia 127 K8
Bangka *Island* Indonesia 126 D11
Bangkok (var. Krung Thep) Thailand 125 J12
Bangladesh (prev. East Pakistan) *Country* S Asia 117

Bangladesh 117

a Bengali • 🍽 Taka • ♦ 2103 • ♥ 52 • 🥚 £0.68 • ♥ (m) 47% (f) 22% • 🖵 5 • ✚ 6219 • 🐍 Yes • 🏙 16% • 🍴 2021

Bangor Maine, USA 27 Q6
Bangor Northern Ireland, UK 59 F11
Bangui Central African Republic 94 J10
Bangweulu, L. *Lake* Zambia 97 L12
Banhine N.P. *National park* Mozambique 99 N10
Bani *River* Mali 92 I9
Banja Luka Bosnia and Herzegovina 74 J5
Banjarmasin Borneo, Indonesia 126 J13
Banjul (prev. Bathurst) Gambia 92 F9
Banks I. *Island* Northwest Territories, Canada 20, 23 L5, 51 N8
Banks L. *Lake* Washington, USA 36 J6
Banningville *see* Bandundu
Banská Bystrica Slovakia 71 L11
Bantry Bay *Bay* Ireland 59 A14
Banyo Cameroon 94 F10
Banyuwangi Java, Indonesia 126 J15
Baoji China 121 K9
Baotou China 119 N8
Bar Montenegro, Yugoslavia 75 L10
Bar-le-Duc France 63 N5
Baranavichy (var. Baranovichi) Belarus 80 J13
Baranovichi *see* Baranavichy
Barbados *Country* West Indies 43 T14

Barbados 43

a English • 🍽 Dollar • ♦ 1554 • ♥ 75 • 🥚 £1.65 • ♥ (m) 99% (f) 99% • 🏙 45%

Barbados *Island* West Indies 41
Barbuda *Island* Antigua & Barbuda 43 T10
Barcelona Spain 61 Q6
Barcelona Venezuela 44 J4
Bareilly India 117 L5
Barents Sea Arctic Ocean 51 R12, 54, 82 L5, 103
Bari Italy 73 N13
Barinas Venezuela 44 G5
Barisan Mts. *Mountain range* Sumatra, Indonesia 126 E12
Barito *River* Borneo, Indonesia 126 J11
Bârlad Romania 77 N5
Barlee, L. *Lake* Western Australia, Australia 132 G12
Barnaul Russian Federation 112 I11
Barnstaple England, UK 59 G16
Baroda *see* Vadodara
Barquisimeto Venezuela 44 H4
Barra *Island* Scotland, UK 58 E8
Barranquilla Colombia 44 E4
Barreiras Brazil 47 K11
Barreiro Portugal 60 F10
Barrie Ontario, Canada 25 K14
Barrow Alaska, USA 22 H4
Barrow Ireland 59 D13
Barrow I. *Island* Western Australia, Australia 132 E8
Barstow California, USA 37 M18
Bartang *River* Tajikistan 111 P8
Bartica Guyana 44 M6
Barysaw (var. Borisov) Belarus 81 M11
Basel *see* Basle
Basilan *Island* Philippines 127 M8
Basle (var. Basel) Switzerland 68 F8
Basque Provinces *Region* Spain 61 L4
Basra Iraq 100 E4
Bass Strait *Channel* Australia 131, 133 N15
Basse-Terre Guadeloupe 43 S12
Basse Terre *Island* Guadeloupe 43 S12
Bassein Burma 124 E10
Basseterre St Kitts & Nevis 43 S10
Bastia Corsica 63 S14
Bastogne Belgium 65 K18

Basutoland *see* Lesotho
Bata Equatorial Guinea 95 E11
Batangas Luzon, Philippines 127 L4
Batanghari *River* Sumatra, Indonesia 126 E12
Batavia New York, USA 26 I8
Batavia *see* Jakarta
Bătdâmbâng Cambodia 125 K13
Bath England, UK 59 I16
Bathurst New Brunswick, Canada 25 P11
Bathurst *see* Banjul
Batman Turkey 105 Q8
Batna Algeria 89 M4
Baton Rouge Louisiana, USA 28 I9
Batticaloa Sri Lanka 117 L16
Battle Creek Michigan, USA 31 N9
Batu Is. *Island group* Indonesia 126 D11
Bat'umi Georgia 85 O13
Bauchi Nigeria 93 P11
Bautzen Germany 67 N11
Bavaria *Region* Germany 67 J14
Bavarian Alps *Mountain range* Austria/Germany 67 J17
Bawean *Island* Indonesia 126 I14
Bay City Michigan, USA 31 O8
Bayamo Cuba 43 K6
Bayan Har Mts. (var. Bayan Har Shan) *Mountain range* China 119 K11
Bayan Har Shan *see* Bayan Har Mts.
Baydarata Bay *Sea feature* Russian Federation 82 O6, 112 I6
Baydhabo (var. Baidoa) Somalia 91 M17
Baykonur Kazakhstan 112 F11
Bayonne France 62 H14
Bayram-Ali Turkmenistan 111 K9
Bayreuth Germany 67 J13
Beagle Channel *Channel* Argentina 49 L20
Bear Is. *Island group* Russian Federation 113 O4
Bear L. *Lake* Idaho/Utah, USA 34 J2
Beaufort Sea Arctic Ocean 10, 20, 22 J6, 51 N7
Beaufort West South Africa 98 J15
Beaumont Texas, USA 35 T12
Beauvais France 63 L4
Beaver I. *Island* Michigan, USA 31 M5
Bečej Serbia, Yugoslavia 75 M4
Béchar Algeria 88 J6
Bedford Indiana, USA 31 M13
Be'er Sheva' *see* Beersheba
Beersheba (var. Be'er Sheva') Israel 107 L11
Bei'an China 121 P3
Beijing *see* Peking
Beira Mozambique 99 O9, 101 D11
Beirut (var. Beyrouth; anc. Berytus) Lebanon 107 M7
Beja Portugal 60 G12
Bejaïa Algeria 89 L4
Belarus (var. Belorussia) *Country* NE Europe 80-81

Belarus 80-81

a Belorussian • 🍽 Ruble • ♦ 129 • ♥ 73 • 🥚 £2.31 • ♥ (m) 99% (f) 99% • 🖵 268 • ✚ 246 • 🐍 Yes • 🏙 66% • 🍴 N/A

Belawan Sumatra, Indonesia 126 D9
Belaya Tserkov *see* Bila Tserkva
Belcher Islands *Island group* Canada 25 K5
Beledweyne Somalia 91 M16
Belém Brazil 46 J7
Belfast Northern Ireland UK 59 F11
Belfort France 63 P6
Belgaum India 116 I11
Belgian Congo *see* Zaire
Belgium *Country* W Europe 65

Belgium 65

a Dutch, French • 🍽 Franc • ♦ 787 • ♥ 76 • 🥚 £1.25 • ♥ (m) 99% (f) 99% • 🖵 452 • ✚ 309 • 🐍 No • 🏙 97% • 🍴 3902

Belgorod Russian Federation 83 E12
Belgorod-Dnestrovskiy *see* Bilhorod-Dnistrovs'kyy
Belgrade (var. Beograd) Serbia, Yugoslavia 75 N5
Belgrano II *Research center* Antarctica 50 D7
Beli Drim *River* Serbia, Yugoslavia 75 N9
Beli Timok *River* Serbia, Yugoslavia 75 P8
Belice *River* Sicily 73 I18
Belitung *Island* Indonesia 126 G13
Belize *Country* C America 42

Belize 42

a English • 🍽 Dollar • ♦ 22 • ♥ 68 • 🥚 £0.92 • ♥ (m) 93% (f) 93% • 🏙 50%

Belize *River* Belize 42 C6
Belize City Belize 42 C6
Belle Fourche *River* Wyoming, USA 33 K7
Belle Île France 62 G8
Belle Isle *Island* Newfoundland, Canada 25 R7
Belle Isle, Strait of *Channel* Newfoundland, Canada 25 R8
Bellevue Washington, USA 36 H6
Bellingham Washington, USA 36 H5
Bellingshausen Plain *Sea feature* Pacific Ocean 41

Bellingshausen Sea Pacific Ocean, Antarctica 50 B9
Bellinzona Switzerland 68 H12
Bello Colombia 44 E6
Belmopan Belize 42 C6
Belo Horizonte Brazil 47 L13
Beloit Wisconsin, USA 31 K9
Belorussia *see* Belarus
Belyy Is. *Island group* Russian Federation 112 I5
Bemidji Minnesota, USA 30 G3
Benares *see* Varanasi
Bend Oregon, USA 36 I9
Bendery *see* Tighina
Bendigo Victoria, Australia 133 M14
Bengal, Bay of *Sea feature* India/SE Asia 103, 100 J6, 115, 117 P9, 124 D9
Benghazi Libya 89 Q6
Bengkulu Sumatra, Indonesia 126 E13
Benguela Angola 98 G6
Benguela current *Ocean current* S Atlantic Ocean 12
Beni *River* Bolivia 45 H13
Beni Mellal Morocco 88 I6
Beni Suef Egypt 90 F7
Benidorm Spain 61 O11
Benin (prev. Dahomey) *Country* W Africa 93

Benin 93

a French • 🍽 Franc • ♦ 114 • ♥ 51 • 🥚 £0.86 • ♥ (m) 32% (f) 16% • 🏙 38%

Benin, Bight of *Sea feature* W Africa 93 N13
Benin City Nigeria 93 O12
Bennington Vermont, USA 27 M9
Benton Harbor Michigan, USA 31 M10
Benue *River* Cameroon/Nigeria 87, 93 P12
Beograd *see* Belgrade
Beppu Japan 123 D14
Berat Albania 75 M13
Berau, Gulf of *Sea feature* Irian Jaya, Indonesia 126 Q12
Berbera Somalia 91 M14
Berbérati Central African Republic 95 H11
Berbice *River* Guyana 44 M7
Berdyans'k Ukraine 85 L8
Berettyő *River* Hungary/Romania 71 N14
Bereza *see* Byaroza
Bergama *see* Pergamon
Bergamo Italy 72 E6
Bergen Norway 52 K7, 56 H10
Bergen *see* Mons
Bergen op Zoom Netherlands 65 G12
Bergisch Gladbach Germany 67 E11
Bering Sea Pacific Ocean 10, 20, 22 C7, 103, 113 R5, 128 J3
Bering Strait *Channel* Arctic Ocean/Pacific Ocean 20, 22 E4, 103, 128 J2
Berlin Germany 66 L9
Bermejo *River* Argentina/Bolivia 48 K5
Bermuda *Dependent territory* Atlantic Ocean 52 F9
Bermuda *Island* Atlantic Ocean 20
Bermuda Rise *Sea feature* Atlantic Ocean 20
Bern Switzerland 68 E10
Bernese Alps *Mountain range* Switzerland 68 F12
Beroea *see* Ḥalab
Berry Is. *Island group* Bahamas 43 K2
Bertoua Cameroon 94 G10
Beruni Uzbekistan 110 J5
Berytus *see* Beirut
Besançon France 63 O7
Beskid Mts. *Mountain range* C Europe 71 L9
Bethel Alaska, USA 22 H7
Bethlehem West Bank 107 L10
Beykoz Turkey 104 I5
Beyrouth *see* Beirut
Beyşehir Turkey 104 J9
Beyşehir, L. *Lake* Turkey 104 J9
Bezmein Turkmenistan 110 H8
Bhamo Burma 124 H6
Bhatapara India 117 M9
Bhavnagar India 116 I8
Bhopal India 117 K8
Bhubaneswar India 117 N9
Bhumiphol Res. *Reservoir* Thailand 124 H10
Bhutan *Country* S Asia 117

Bhutan 117

a Dzongkha • 🍽 Ngultrum • ♦ 80 • ♥ 49 • 🥚 £0.56 • ♥ (m) 51% (f) 25% • 🏙 5%

Biak *Island* Indonesia 127 R11
Białystok Poland 71 O4
Biddeford Maine, USA 27 O8
Biel Switzerland 68 E9
Biel, L. *Lake* Switzerland 68 E10
Bielefeld Germany 66 F10
Bielsko-Biała Poland 71 L9
Bien Hoa Vietnam 125 N14
Big Spring Texas, USA 35 O11
Bighorn *River* Montana/Wyoming, USA 32 J6
Bighorn Mts. *Mountain range* Wyoming, USA 32 J7
Bihać Bosnia and Herzegovina 74 I5
Bijagós Archipelago *Island group* Guinea-Bissau 92 F10
Bijelo Polje Montenegro, Yugoslavia 75 M9

Bikini *Island* Marshall Islands, Pacific Ocean 128 I7
Bila Tserkva (var. Belaya Tserkov) Ukraine 84 I5
Bilbao Spain 61 L3
Bilecik Turkey 104 I6
Bilhorod-Dnistrovs'kyy (var. Belgorod-Dnestrovskiy) Ukraine 84 I8
Billings Montana, USA 32 I6
Biloxi Mississippi, USA 28 J9
Biltine Chad 94 K7
Bindura Zimbabwe 99 M8
Binghamton New York, USA 27 K10
Bingöl Turkey 105 Q7
Bintan *Island* Indonesia 126 F11
Bío-Bío *River* Chile 49 H12
Birāk *Oasis* Libya 89 O8
Birao Central African Republic 94 L8
Biratnagar Nepal 117 O6
Birganj Nepal 117 N6
Birkenhead England, UK 59 H13
Birmingham Alabama, USA 29 L7
Birmingham England, UK 59 I14
Birni n'Konni Niger 93 O9
Biscay, Bay of *Sea feature* Spain 54, 61 L3
Biscay Plain *Sea feature* Atlantic Ocean 54
Bishkek (prev. Frunze) Kyrgyzstan 111 Q4
Bisho South Africa 99 L15
Bishop California, USA 37 K15
Biskra Algeria 89 L5
Bislig Mindanao, Philippines 127 N7
Bismarck North Dakota, USA 33 M5
Bismarck Arch. *Island group* Papua New Guinea 133 O1
Bismarck Range *Mountain range* Papua New Guinea 131, 133 N2
Bismarck Sea Papua New Guinea 131, 132 O1
Bissau Guinea-Bissau 92 F10
Bistriţa Romania 76 J3
Bitlis Turkey 105 R8
Bitola Macedonia 75 O13
Bitterroot Range *Mountain range* Idaho/Montana, USA 32 G6
Biysk Russian Federation 112 I11
Bjelovar Croatia 74 J3
Black Forest (var. Schwarzwald) *Physical region* Germany 67 F15
Black Hills *Mountain range* South Dakota/Wyoming, USA 33 L7
Black R. (var. Song Da) *River* China/Vietnam 124 L8
Black R. *River* Arkansas/Missouri USA 28 J4
Black Rock Desert *Desert region* Nevada, USA 20, 34 F1
Black Sea (var. Chernoye More, Kara Deniz) Asia/Europe 52 N8, 54, 77 P11, 85 M11, 103, 105 N4
Black Volta *River* West Africa 87, 93 K10
Blackpool England, UK 59 H13
Blackwater *River* Ireland 59 C14
Blagoveshchensk Russian Federation 113 O11
Blanca, Bahía *Sea feature* Argentina 49 L12
Blanca, Costa *Coastal region* Spain 61 O11
Blanco, Cape *see* Nouadhibou, Râs
Blanice *River* Czech Republic 70 H10
Blantyre Malawi 97 O15
Blenheim New Zealand 134 G9
Blida Algeria 89 L4
Bloemfontein South Africa 99 K13
Blois France 63 K7
Bloomington Illinois, USA 31 K12
Bloomington Indiana, USA 31 M13
Bloomington Minnesota, USA 30 H6
Blue Mesa Dam *Dam* Colorado, USA 35 L5
Blue Mountains *Mountain range* Oregon/Washington, USA 36 K9
Blue Nile (var. Bahr el Azraq) *River* Ethiopia/Sudan 87, 91 H13
Blue Nile *River* 87
Bluefields Nicaragua 42 E11
Bo Sierra Leone 92 H12
Bo Hai *Sea feature* China 121 N7
Boa Vista Brazil 46 F6
Boaco Nicaragua 42 D10
Bobaomby, C. (var. Cap d' Ambre) *Cape* Madagascar 100 E10
Bobo-Dioulasso Burkina 93 K10
Bóbr *River* Poland 70 I6
Bobruysk *see* Zaire
Bocas del Toro Panama 42 F14
Bochum Germany 66 E10
Bodensee *see* Constance, L.
Bodø Norway 57 L4
Bodrum Turkey 104 G9
Boende Zaire 95 K12
Bogor Java, Indonesia 126 G14
Bogotá (prev. Santa Fe) Colombia 44 E6
Bohemian Forest (var. Böhmerwald) *Physical region* Czech Republic/Germany 67 L14
Böhmerwald *see* Bohemian Forest
Bohol *Island* Philippines 127 M6
Boise Idaho, USA 32 F8
Bokaro India 117 N8
Bokna Fjord *Coastal feature* Norway 56 H11
Bol Chad 94 H7
Bolgatanga Ghana 93 L10
Bolivia *Country* S America 45

Bolivia 45

a Aymara, Quechua, Spanish • 🍽 Boliviano • ♦ 18 • ♥ 60 • 🥚 £0.52 • ♥ (m) 85% (f) 70% • 🖵 163 • ✚ 2100 • 🐍 No • 🏙 51% • 🍴 1916

Bologna Italy 72 G8

---

a Language (official or most commonly spoken) • 🍽 Currency • ♦ Population density per square mile • ♥ Average life expectancy • 🥚 Price of 1 dozen hen's eggs • ♥ Literacy • 🖵 Number of TVs per 1,000 people • ✚ Number of people per doctor • 🐍 Death penalty • 🏙 Percentage of urban-based population • 🍴 Average number of calories consumed daily per person

139

Carlyle L. *Lake* Illinois, USA 31 K14
Carmen I. *Island* Mexico 38 H7
Carnarvon Western Australia, Australia 132 E10
Carnegie, L. *Lake* Western Australia, Australia 132 H10
Carolina Brazil 46 K9
Caroline Is. *Island group* Federated States of Micronesia, Pacific Ocean 128 H8
Caroline Ridge *Sea feature* Pacific Ocean 131
Carpathians *Mountain range* E Europe 54, 71 L10, 77 L4, 84 E6
Carpentaria, Gulf of *Sea feature* Northern Territory/Queensland, Australia 131, 133 L6
Carson City Nevada, USA 34 E3
Cartagena Colombia 44 E4, 53 D11
Cartagena Spain 61 N12
Cartago Costa Rica 42 E13
Cartwright Newfoundland, Canada 25 R6
Casa Grande Arizona, USA 34 H8
Casablanca Morocco 52 K9, 88 H5
Cascade Range *Mountain range* USA 20, 36 I8
Caseyr, C. *Cape* Somalia 87
Casper Wyoming, USA 33 K9
Caspian Sea *Lake* Asia/Europe 54-55, 83 G16, 85 T13, 103, 109 N2, 110 F7, 112 C10
Castellón de la Plana Spain 61 O8
Castelo Branco Portugal 60 G9
Castries St Lucia 43 T13
Castro Chile 49 G15
Cat I. *Island* Bahamas 42 I5
Catalonia *Region* Spain 61 P6
Catamarca Argentina 48 I8
Catanduanes *Island* Philippines 127 M4
Catania Sicily 73 L18
Catanzaro Italy 73 N16
Catskill Mts. *Mountain range* New York, USA 27 L10
Cauca *River* Colombia 44 E5
Caucasus Mts. *Mountain range* Europe/Asia 54, 83 E16, 85 P11, 103
Cauquenes Chile 48 G12
Cauvery Falls *Waterfall* India 115
Cavally *River* Ivory Coast 92 I13
Caxito Angola 98 G4
Cayenne French Guiana 44 P7, 53 F11
Cayman Brac *Island* Cayman Islands 42 I6
Cayman Islands *Dependent territory* Caribbean Sea 42 H6
Ceará Plain *Sea feature* Atlantic Ocean 41
Cebu Cebu, Philippines 127 M6
Cebu *Island* Philippines 127 M6
Cedar *River* Iowa, USA 33 Q8
Cedar Rapids Iowa, USA 33 R9
Cedros I. *Island* Mexico 38 F5
Cefalù Sicily 73 K17
Celaya Mexico 39 M11
Celebes (var. Sulawesi) *Island* Indonesia 115, 127 L12, 131
Celebes Basin *Sea feature* SE Asia 131
Celebes Sea SE Asia 115, 127 M9, 128 F8, 131
Celje Slovenia 74 H2
Celle Germany 66 H9
Celtic Shelf *Sea Feature* Atlantic Ocean 54
Central African Republic *Country* C Africa 94-95

Central African Republic (C.A.R.) 94-95

ⓐ French · 🏦 Franc · ♦ 13 · ♥ 49 · ◖ £4.30 · ♥ (m) 52% (f) 25% · 🏠 47%

Central America *Region* 20, 41
Central Arizona Project *Irrigation project* Arizona, USA 34 I9
Central Siberian Plateau *Physical region* Russian Federation 103, 113 L6
Centralia Illinois, USA 31 K14
Cerralvo I. *Island* Mexico 38 I8
Cerro Bonete *Mountain* Chile 41
Cerro de Pasco Peru 44 D12
Cēsis Latvia 80 J5
České Budějovice Czech Republic 70 H10
Cesma *River* Croatia 74 I3
Cetatea *see* Bucharest
Ceuta *Spanish enclave* NW Africa 88 I4
Cévennes *Mountain range* France 63 M13
Ceyhan *River* Turkey 105 N9
Ceylon *see* Sri Lanka
Ceylon Plain *Sea feature* Indian Ocean 103, 115
Chad *Country* C Africa 94

Chad 94

ⓐ Arabic, French · 🏦 Franc · ♦ 12 · ♥ 48 · ◖ £2.15 · ♥ (m) 42% (f) 18% · 🏠 30%

Chad, L. *Lake* C Africa 87, 93 R9, 94 H7
Chagai Hills *Mountain range* Pakistan 116 F4
Chagos-Laccadive Plateau *Sea feature* Indian Ocean 103, 115
Chagos Trench *Sea feature* Indian Ocean 115
Chāh Bahār Iran 100 G5, 109 Q11
Chaitén Chile 49 H15
Chalbi Desert *Desert region* Kenya 97 P2
Chalcis *see* Chalkida
Chalkida (var. Chalcis) Greece 79 K8
Châlons-sur-Marne France 63 N5
Chambal *River* India 117 K6
Chambéry France 63 O10
Chambord France 63 K7
Champaign Illinois, USA 31 L12
Champasak Laos 125 M12

Champlain, L. *Lake* New York/Vermont, USA 27 M6
Chañaral Chile 48 G7
Chandigarh India 117 K4
Changchun China 121 P5
Changsha China 121 L12
Changzhi China 121 L8
Chania Crete, Greece 79 L15
Channel Islands *Island group* UK 59 H18, 62 G4
Channel-Port-aux-Basques Newfoundland, Canada 25 R10
Chanthaburi Thailand 125 K13
Chapala, L. *Lake* Mexico 39 L11
Chardzhev (prev. Chardzhou) Turkmenistan 111 K8
Chardzhou *see* Chardzhev
Charente *River* France 62 I10
Chari *River* Chad 94 H8
Chariton *River* Iowa/Missouri, USA 33 R10
Charleroi Belgium 65 G16
Charles, Cape *Cape* Virginia, USA 29 S5
Charleston South Carolina, USA 29 P8
Charleston West Virginia, USA 29 P3
Charleville Queensland, Australia 133 N10
Charlotte North Carolina, USA 29 P6
Charlotte Amalie Virgin Islands (US) 43 R9
Charlottesville Virginia, USA 29 Q4
Charlottetown Prince Edward Island, Canada 25 Q11
Chartres France 63 K5
Chashma Barrage *Dam* Pakistan 116 I2
Châteauroux France 63 K8
Chatham Is. *Island group* New Zealand, Pacific Ocean 128 J12
Chattahoochee *River* Alabama/Georgia, USA 29 M7
Chattanooga Tennessee, USA 29 M6
Chauk Burma 124 F8
Chaumont France 63 N6
Cheboksary Russian Federation 83 I11
Cheboygan Michigan, USA 31 N5
Cheju South Korea 121 P9
Chelan, L. *Lake* Washington, USA 36 I6
Cheleken Turkmenistan 110 F6
Chelm Poland 71 P7
Chelyabinsk Russian Federation 112 G9
Chelyuskin, C. *Cape* Russian Federation 113 L4
Chemnitz Germany 67 L11
Chenab *River* India/Pakistan 116 J3
Chengdu China 120 J10
Chequamegon Bay *Physical feature* Wisconsin, USA 30 J4
Cherbourg France 62 H4
Cherepovets Russian Federation 82 H9
Cherkasy Ukraine 84 J5
Cherkessk Russian Federation 83 E15
Chernigov *see* Chernihiv
Chernihiv Ukraine 84 I3
Chernivtsi (var. Chernivtsi) Ukraine 84 F6
Chernobyl Ukraine 84 I4
Chernovtsy *see* Chernivtsi
Chernoye More *see* Black Sea
Chernyakhovsk Russian Federation 80 G10
Chesapeake Bay Maryland/Virginia, USA 29 S4
Chesha Bay *Sea feature* Russian Federation 82 L6
Chester England, UK 59 H13
Chesterfield Inlet *Sea feature* Northwest Territories, Canada 23 N6
Chesuncook L. *Lake* Maine, USA 27 P4
Chetumal Mexico 39 T12
Cheyenne Wyoming, USA 33 K10
Cheyenne *River* South Dakota/Wyoming, USA 33 M7
Chi-lung Taiwan 121 O13
Chiang Jiang *see* Yangtze
Chiang Mai Thailand 124 I9
Chiang Rai Thailand 124 I9
Chiba Japan 123 L11
Chibougamau Quebec, Canada 25 L10
Chicago Illinois, USA 31 L10
Chichén Itzá *Archaeological site* Mexico 39 T11
Chiclayo Peru 45 C11
Chico California, USA 37 H13
Chicoutimi Quebec, Canada 25 N11
Chidley, C. *Cape* Quebec, Canada 25 O2
Chiemsee *Lake* Germany 67 K16
Chifeng (var. Ulanhad) China 119 Q6
Chihuahua Mexico 39 K5
Chile *Country* S America 48-49

Chile 48-49

ⓐ Spanish · 🏦 Peso · ♦ 46 · ♥ 72 · ◖ £0.67 · ♥ (m) 94% (f) 93% · 📺 205 · ✚ 2383 · ❁ Yes · 🏠 86% · ↟ 2581

Chile Basin *Sea feature* Pacific Ocean 41, 129 Q12
Chile Chico Chile 49 I16
Chile Rise *Sea feature* Pacific Ocean 41
Chillán Chile 49 G12
Chillicothe Ohio, USA 31 P13
Chiloé I. *Island* Chile 41, 49 G15, 129 Q13
Chilpancingo Mexico 39 N13
Chimbote Peru 45 C12, 129 Q9
Chimkent *see* Shymkent
Chimoio Mozambique 99 N9
Chin Hills *Mountain range* Burma/India 124 E7

China *Country* E Asia 9, 118-119, 120-121

China 118-121

ⓐ Mandarin · 🏦 Yuan · ♦ 319 · ♥ 70 · ◖ £0.37 · ♥ (m) 84% (f) 62% · 📺 31 · ✚ 1077 · ❁ Yes · 🏠 33% · ↟ 2639

China Lake Naval Weapons Center *Military center* California, USA 37 L17
Chinandega Nicaragua 42 C10
Chindwin *River* Burma/India 124 F6
Chingola Zambia 97 K13
Chinhoyi (var. Sinoia) Zimbabwe 99 M8
Chioggia Italy 72 H7
Chios Chios, Greece 79 O8
Chios *Island* Greece 79 O8
Chipata Zambia 97 M13
Chippewa, L. *Lake* Wisconsin, USA 30 J5
Chirchik Uzbekistan 111 N6
Chiriquí, Gulf of *Sea feature* Panama 42 E15
Chişinău (var. Kishinev) Moldavia 84 H8
Chita ICBM Base *Military center* Russian Federation 113 M11
Chitré Panama 42 G15
Chittagong Bangladesh 117 P8
Chitungwiza Zimbabwe 99 M8
Chobe *River* Botswana/Namibia 99 K8
Chobe N.P. *National park* Botswana 99 K8
Chojnice Poland 71 K3
Cholula *Archaeological site* Mexico 39 N12
Choluteca Honduras 42 C9
Choma Zambia 96 J16
Chon Buri Thailand 125 J13
Ch'ŏngjin North Korea 121 Q5
Chongqing China 120 J11
Chott El Jerid *Physical region* Algeria 87 M6
Choybalsan Mongolia 119 O4
Christchurch New Zealand 134 F11
Christiania *see* Oslo
Christiansted Virgin Islands 43 R10
Christmas I. *Dependent territory* Indian Ocean 100 M10
Chu *River* Kazakhstan/Kyrgyzstan 112 F12
Chubut *River* Argentina 49 I15
Chūgoku Mountains *Mountain range* Japan 123 E12
Chukchi Sea Arctic Ocean 51 P5, 113 P2
Chumphon Thailand 125 H14
Chuquicamata Chile 48 G5
Chur Switzerland 68 I10
Churchill Manitoba, Canada 23 O11
Churchill *River* Manitoba, Canada 23 O11
Churchill Falls Newfoundland, Canada 25 P7
Cienfuegos Cuba 42 I4
Cincinnati Ohio, USA 31 O13
Cirebon Java, Indonesia 126 H15
Citlaltépetl, Mt. *Mountain* Mexico 20
Ciudad Bolívar Venezuela 44 J5
Ciudad del Este Paraguay 48 O6
Ciudad Guayana Venezuela 44 K5
Ciudad Juárez Mexico 39 K3
Ciudad Madero Mexico 39 O10
Ciudad Obregón Mexico 38 I5
Ciudad Real Spain 61 K10
Ciudad Victoria Mexico 39 N9
Čiovo *Island* Croatia 74 I8
Civitavecchia Italy 73 H11
Clair Eagle L. *Lake* California, USA 37 H12
Claremont New Hampshire, USA 27 N8
Clarence Strait *Channel* Northern Territory, Australia 132 I5
Clarenville Newfoundland, Canada 25 T9
Clarion Facture Zone *Sea feature* Pacific Ocean 129 M7
Clarksville Tennessee, USA 29 L4
Clearwater Florida, USA 29 N13
Clermont Queensland, Australia 133 O9
Clermont-Ferrand France 63 M10
Cleveland Ohio, USA 31 P10
Clipperton Fracture Zone *Sea feature* Pacific Ocean 129 M7
Clipperton I. *Dependent territory* C. America, Pacific Ocean 129 O7
Cloncurry Queensland, Australia 133 M8
Clovis New Mexico, USA 35 N9
Cluj-Napoca Romania 76 I4
Clyde *River* Scotland, UK 58 H10
Coast Ranges *Mountain range* N America 10, 20, 37 G13
Coatzacoalcos Mexico 39 Q13
Cobán Guatemala 42 B7
Cobija Bolivia 45 H13
Cochabamba Bolivia 45 I15
Cochin India 100 I7, 116 J15
Cochrane Chile 49 I17
Cochrane Ontario, Canada 24 J11
Cockburn Sound Australia 101 M12
Coco *River* Honduras 42 E9
Cocos Is. *Dependent territory* Indian Ocean 100 L10
Cocos Plate *Physical feature* 8, 20, 41
Cocos Ridge *Sea feature* Pacific Ocean 41, 129 P8
Cody Wyoming, USA 32 I7
Coeur d'Alene Idaho, USA 32 F4
Coiba I. *Island* Panama 42 F15
Coihaique Chile 49 H16
Coimbatore India 116 J14
Coimbra Portugal 60 F8
Colbeck, C. *Cape* Pacific Ocean Coast, Antarctica 50 D11
Colchester England, UK 59 L15
Colditz *Castle* Germany 67 L11
Colhué Huapí, L *Lake* Argentina 49 I16
Colima Mexico 39 K12
Colima *Volcano* Mexico 20

Coll *Island* Scotland, UK 58 F8
Collier Bay *Sea feature* Western Australia, Australia 132 H6
Colmar France 63 P6
Cologne (var. Köln) Germany 67 E11
Colombia *Country* S America 44

Colombia 44

ⓐ Spanish · 🏦 Peso · ♦ 82 · ♥ 69 · ◖ £0.54 · ♥ (m) 88% (f) 86% · 📺 115 · ✚ 1102 · ❁ No · 🏠 70% · ↟ 2598

Colombian Basin *Sea feature* Caribbean Sea 41
Colombo Sri Lanka 100 I7, 117 K16
Colombus Nebraska, USA 33 O10
Colón Argentina 48 M9
Colón Panama 42 G14
Colonia Uruguay 48 N9
Colorado *River* Mexico/USA 20, 35 K5, 37 O18, 38 G1, 41, 129 N5
Colorado *State* USA 35
Colorado Plateau *Physical region* Arizona, USA 34 I7
Colorado Project *Irrigation project* Colorado, USA 34 H10
Colorado Springs Colorado, USA 35 M5
Columbia Missouri, USA 33 R11
Columbia South Carolina, USA 29 P7
Columbia *River* Canada/USA 20, 23 K14, 36 K5, 129 N4
Columbine, C. *Cape* South Africa 98 I15
Columbus Georgia, USA 29 M8
Columbus Indiana, USA 31 N13
Columbus Mississippi, USA 29 K7
Columbus Ohio, USA 31 P12
Colville *River* Alaska, USA 22 H5
Comacchio Lagoon *Lake* Italy 72 H8
Comayagua Honduras 42 C8
Comilla Bangladesh 117 P8
Communism Peak (var. Pik Kommunizma, prev. Mt. Stalin) *Peak* Tajikistan 103
Como, L. *Lake* Italy 72 E6
Comodoro Rivadavia Argentina 49 K16
Comorin, C. *Cape* India 100 I7, 115
Comoros *Country* Indian Ocean 100 E10

Comoros 100

ⓐ Arabic, French · 🏦 Franc · ♦ 571 · ♥ 56 · ◖ £1.19 · ♥ (m) 56% (f) 40% · 🏠 28%

Comoros Is. *Island group* Indian Ocean 87
Conakry Guinea 92 G11
Concepción Chile 49 G12, 129 Q12
Concepción Paraguay 48 M5
Conchas L. *Lake* New Mexico, USA 35 M10
Conchos *River* Mexico 38 J5
Concord California, USA 37 H15
Concord New Hampshire, USA 27 N8
Concordia Argentina 48 M9
Congo *Country* C Africa 95

Congo 95

ⓐ French · 🏦 Franc · ♦ 18 · ♥ 53 · ◖ £1.43 · ♥ (m) 70% (f) 44% · 🏠 41%

Congo (var. Zaire) *River* C Africa 11, 53 M12, 87, 95, J12, 98 G2, 95 I13
Congo Basin *Physical region* Congo/Zaire 11, 87
Connecticut *River* USA 27 N7
Connecticut *State* USA 27 N8
Constance, L. (var. Bodensee) *Lake* C Europe 54, 67 G17, 68 H8
Constantine Algeria 89 M4
Constantinople *see* Istanbul
Constanţa Romania 77 P9
Contwoyto L. *Lake* Northwest Territories, Canada 23 M9
Coober Pedy South Australia, Australia 133 K11
Cook Islands *Dependent territory* Polynesia, Pacific Ocean 129 K10
Cook, Mt. *Mountain* New Zealand 131
Cook Strait *Channel* New Zealand 128 I12, 131, 134 G8
Cooktown Queensland, Australia 133 N6
Cooper Creek *River* Queensland/South Australia, Australia 133 L11
Coos Bay Oregon, USA 36 F10
Copán *Archaeological site* Honduras 42 C8
Copenhagen Denmark 56 J15
Copiapó Chile 48 G7
Coppermine Northwest Territories, Canada 23 L8
Coppermine *River* Northwest Territories, Canada 23 L8
Copşa Mică Romania 76 J6
Coquilhatville *see* Mbandaka
Coquimbo Chile 48 F9
Corabia Romania 76 J10
Coral Sea Pacific Ocean 128 H10, 131, 133 O4
Coral Sea Basin *Sea feature* Pacific Ocean 131
Coral Sea Is. *Dependent territory* Pacific Ocean 128 H10
Cordillera Cantábrica *Mountain range* Spain 54, 60 I4
Córdoba Argentina 48 J9
Córdoba Spain 60 J12
Cordova Alaska, USA 22 G9
Corfu Corfu, Greece 78 F5

ⓐ Language (official or most commonly spoken) · 🏦 Currency · ♦ Population density per square mile · ♥ Average life expectancy · ◖ Price of 1 dozen hen's eggs · ♥ Literacy · 📺 Number of TVs per 1,000 people · ✚ Number of people per doctor · ❁ Death penalty · 🏠 Percentage of urban-based population · ↟ Average number of calories consumed daily per person

141

Corfu *Island* Ionian Is. Greece 78 E5
Corinth Greece 78 J9
Corinth Canal *Waterway* Greece 78 J9
Corinth, Gulf of *Sea feature* Greece 78 I9
Corinto Nicaragua 42 C10
Cork Ireland 59 C14
Corner Brook Newfoundland, Canada 25 R9
Corning New York, USA 26 J10
Cornwall *Region* England, UK 59 F17
Cornwallis I. *Island* Northwest Territories, Canada 23 N4
Coro Venezuela 44 H4
Coromandel New Zealand 134 H4
Coromandel Coast *Coastal region* India 117 L13
Coronel Chile 49 G12
Corpus Christi Texas, USA 35 R15
Corrib, Lough *Lake* Ireland 59 B12
Corrientes Argentina 48 M7
Corse *see* Corsica
Corsica (var. Corse) *Island* France 54, 63 S15
Cortellazzo Italy 72 I7
Cortland New York, USA 27 K9
Çorum Turkey 105 M6
Corumbá Brazil 47 G13
Corvallis Oregon, USA 36 G9
Cosenza Italy 73 N13
Costa Rica *Country* C America 42

Costa Rica 42

a Spanish • 💷 Colon • ◆ 146 • ♥ 75 • ○ £0.48 •
♥ (m) 93% (f) 93% • 🏛 47%

Côte d'Azur *Coastal region* France 63 Q13
Côte d'Ivoire *see* Ivory Coast
Cotonou Benin 93 M12
Cotopaxi *Volcano* Ecuador 41
Cottbus Germany 66 M10
Council Bluffs Iowa, USA 33 P10
Courantyne *River* Guyana/Suriname 44 N7
Courland Lagoon *Coastal feature* Lithuania/Russian Federation 80 F9
Courtrai *see* Kortrijk
Coventry England, UK 59 J14
Covilhã Portugal 60 G8
Covington Kentucky, USA 29 N2
Cozumel I.. *Island* Mexico 39 T11
Cracow *see* Kraków
Craiova Romania 76 J9
Cranbook British Columbia, Canada 23 K15
Crawley England, UK 59 K16
Cree L. *Lake* Saskatchewan, Canada 23 M12
Cremona Italy 72 F7
Cres *Island* Croatia 74 G5
Crescent City California, USA 37 F11
Crete *Island* Greece 54, 79 L15
Crete, Sea of Greece 79 M15
Crimea (var. Krym) *Peninsula* Ukraine 54, 85 K9
Crna *River* Macedonia 75 O12
Croatia (var. Hrvatska) *Country* SE Europe 74-75

Croatia 74-75

a Serbo-Croat • 💷 Dinar • ◆ 211 • ♥ 72 • ○ £1.20 •
♥ (m) 96% (f) 84% • 🖵 N/A • ✚ 523 • 🐍 No •
🏛 51% • 🍴 N/A

Croker I. *Island* Northern Territory, Australia 132 J4
Crooked I. *Island* Bahamas 43 L5
Crotone Italy 73 O16
Crozet Basin *Sea feature* Indian Ocean 101 G13
Crozet Is. *Island group* Indian Ocean 50 I5, 101 F14
Cruzeiro do Sul Brazil 46 A9
Cuango *River* Southern Africa 98 H3
Cuanza *River* Angola 98 G4
Cuba *Country* Caribbean Sea 42-43

Cuba 42-43

a Spanish • 💷 Peso • ◆ 250 • ♥ 76 • ○ £1.04 •
♥ (m) 95% (f) 93% • 🖵 207 • ✚ 333 • 🐍 Yes •
🏛 75% • 🍴 3141

Cuba *Island* Caribbean Sea 20, 41
Cubango *see* Okavango *River*
Cúcuta Colombia 44 F5
Cuenca Ecuador 44 C9
Cuernavaca Mexico 39 N12
Cuiabá Brazil 47 G12
Cuito *River* Southern Africa 98 I8
Cuito Cuanavale Angola 98 I7
Cuitzeo, L. *Lake* Mexico 39 M11
Culiacán Mexico 39 J8
Cumaná Venezuela 44 J4
Cumberland *River* Kentucky/Tennessee, USA 29 M4
Cumberland Plateau *Physical feature* USA 29 M5
Cumberland Sound *Sea feature* Baffin I. Northwest Territories, Canada 23 R6
Cunene *River* Angola/Namibia 98 G8
Cuneo Italy 72 B8
Cunnamulla Queensland, Australia 133 N11
Curaçao *Island* Netherlands Antilles 43 N14
Curicó Chile 49 G11
Curitiba Brazil 47 J15
Cusco Peru 45 F13
Cuttack India 117 N9
Cuxhaven Germany 66 G7
Cyclades *Island group* Greece 79 M11

Cyprus *Country* Mediterranean Sea 105

Cyprus 105

a Greek, Turkish • 💷 Pound and Lira • ◆ 198 •
♥ 77 • ○ £0.61 • ♥ (m) 98% (f) 91% • 🏛 53%

Cyprus *Island* Mediterranean Sea 54, 103
Cyrenaica *Region* Libya 89 R7
Cyrene *Archaeological site* Libya 89 R6
Czech Republic *Country* C Europe 70-71

Czech Republic 70-71

a Czech • 💷 Koruna • ◆ 340 • ♥ 74 • ○ £0.47 •
♥ (m) 99% (f) 99% • 🖵 412 • ✚ 43 • 🐍 No •
🏛 77% • 🍴 3632

Czechoslovakia *see* Czech Republic and Slovakia
Częstochowa Poland 71 L8

D

Da Lat Vietnam 125 O14
Da Nang Vietnam 125 O11
Da Qaidam China 118 J9
Da Yunhe *see* Grand Canal
Dacca (var. Dhaka) Bangladesh 117 P8
Dadu He *River* China 120 I10
Dagupan Luzon, Philippines 127 L3
Dahlak Archipelago *Island group* Eritrea 91 K12
Dahomey *see* Benin
Dahûk Iraq 109 K2
Dakar Senegal 92 F8
Dakhla Western Sahara 88 E9
Đakovo Croatia 75 K4
Dalaman Turkey 104 H10
Dali China 120 H13
Dalian China 121 O7
Dallas Texas, USA 35 R10
Dalles, The Oregon, USA 36 I8
Dalmatia *Region* Croatia 74 I7
Daloa Ivory Coast 92 J12
Daman India 116 I9
Damar *Island* Indonesia 127 O14
Damascus (var. Dimashq) Syria 107 M7
Dambovița *see* Bucharest
Dampier Western Australia, Australia 132 F8
Danbury Connecticut, USA 27 M11
Danmark *see* Denmark
Danube (var. Donau, Dunaj) *River* C Europe 16, 54, 67 L14, 69 Q4, 71 L14, 75 L4, 76 I10
Danube Delta *Delta* Romania 77 D7
Danube-Black Sea Canal *Waterway* Romania 77 O9
Danville Illinois, USA 31 L12
Danville Virginia, USA 29 Q5
Danzig *see* Gdańsk
Danzig, Gulf of *Sea feature* Poland/Russian Federation 71 L1
Dapaong Togo 93 M10
Dar es Salaam Tanzania 97 Q9, 100 D9
Dar'ā Syria 107 M9
Dardanelles *Channel* Turkey 104 G5
Darhan Mongolia 119 M4
Darién, Gulf of *Sea feature* Panama/Colombia 41, 42 I15, 44 D5
Darling *River* New South Wales, Australia 131, 133 N12
Darmstadt Germany 67 F13
Darnley, C. *Physical region* Antarctic Ocean, Antarctica 50 G8
Dartmoor *Physical region* England, UK 59 G17
Daru Papua New Guinea 133 M3
Darwin Northern Territory, Australia 132 J5
Dashhovuz (prev. Tashauz) Turkmenistan 110 J3
Dasht-e Kavir (var. Great Salt Desert) *Desert region* Iran 103, 109 O5
Dasht-e Lut *Desert region* Iran 103, 109 P7
Datong China 121 L6
Daugava *see* Dvina, Western
Daugavpils Latvia 81 K8
Davangere India 116 J12
Davao Mindanao, Philippines 127 N7
Davenport Iowa, USA 33 S9
David Panama 42 E14
Davis Dam *Dam* Arizona, USA 34 H7
Davis Mts. *Mountain range* Texas, USA 35 N12
Davis Sea Indian Ocean, Antarctica 50 H9
Davis Strait *Channel* Greenland/Canada 20, 23 R5, 51 M13, 52 F7
Dawson Yukon Territory, Canada 22 I8
Dawson Creek British Columbia, Canada 23 K12
Daxue Shan *Mountain range* China 115
Dayr az Zawr Syria 107 Q4
Dayton Ohio, USA 31 O12
Daytona Beach Florida, USA 29 O12
De Aar South Africa 99 K14
De Kalb Illinois,,USA 31 K10
Dead Sea (var. Bahrat Lut) *Salt Lake* Israel/Jordan 103, 107 M10
Death Valley *Physical feature* California, USA 10, 20, 37 M16
Debre Birhan Ethiopia 91 J14
Debre Markos Ethiopia 91 I14
Debrecen Hungary 71 N13
Decatur Illinois, USA 31 K12
Deccan Plateau *Physical region* India 115, 116 J10
Dee *River* Scotland, UK 58 J8

Dehra Dun India 117 K4
Del Rio Texas, USA 35 O13
Delaware *River* USA 27 L11
Delaware *State* USA 27
Delémont Switzerland 68 E9
Delft Netherlands 65 G11
Delfzijl Netherlands 64 N6
Delicias Mexico 39 K5
Delingha China 119 K9
Delphi *Archaeological site* Greece 78 I8
Demchok *Disputed region* China/India 117 L3, 118 F11
Demerara Plain *Sea feature* Atlantic Ocean 41
Demirköprü Barrage *Dam* Turkey 104 H8
Den Helder Netherlands 64 H7
Denali (prev. Mt. McKinley) *Mountain* Alaska, USA 10, 20
Denizli Turkey 104 H9
Denmark (var. Danmark) *Country* Scandinavia 56-57

Denmark 56-57

a Danish • 💷 Krone • ◆ 314 • ♥ 75 • ○ £1.81 •
♥ (m) 99% (f) 99% • 🖵 535 • ✚ 375 • 🐍 No •
🏛 65% • 🍴 3628

Denmark Strait *Channel* Greenland/Iceland 20, 51 O15, 52 I7
Denpasar Bali, Indonesia 126 J15
Denver Colorado, USA 35 M4
Dera Ghazi Khan Pakistan 116 H4
Dera Ismail Khan Pakistan 116 I3
Derby England, UK 59 J14
Derg, Lough *Lake* Ireland 59 C13
Derna Libya 89 R6
Des Moines Iowa, USA 33 Q8
Des Moines *River* Iowa/Minnesota, USA 33 Q9
Dese Ethiopia 91 J14
Deseado *River* Argentina 49 J16
Desna *River* Russian Federation/Ukraine 84 J3
Dessau Germany 66 K10
Detroit Michigan, USA 31 O9
Deva Romania 76 I6
Deventer Netherlands 64 L10
Devoll *River* Albania 75 M13
Devon I. *Island* Northwest Territories, Canada 20, 23 O4, 51 N11
Dezful Iran 109 M6
Dezhneva *Cape* Russian Federation 113 Q2
Dhahran (var. Az Zahran) Saudi Arabia 109 M9
Dhaka *see* Dacca
Dhamār Yemen 108 I16
Dhanbad India 117 N8
Dhanushkodi India 117 K15
Dharwad India 116 J12
Dhaulagiri *Mountain* Tibet 115
Dhule India 116 J9
Diamantina *River* Queensland/South Australia, Australia 133 M9
Dickinson North Dakota, USA 33 L5
Didim *see* Didyma
Didyma (var. Didim) *Archaeological site* Turkey 104 G9
Diego Garcia *Island* British Indian Ocean Territory, Indian Ocean 100 H9
Diégo-Suarez *see* Antsiranana
Diekirch Luxembourg 65 L18
Dieppe France 63 K3
Diffa Niger 93 Q9
Digne France 63 P12
Digul *River* Indonesia 127 T14
Dijlah *see* Tigris
Dijon France 63 N7
Dikson *Research center* Russian Federation 51 T10
Dili Timor, Indonesia 127 N15
Dillon Montana, USA 32 H6
Dilolo Zaire 95 L17
Dimashq *see* Damascus
Dimbokro Ivory Coast 93 K12
Dinant Belgium 65 H17
Dinaric Alps *Mountain range* Bosnia and Herzegovina/Croatia 54, 74 I7
Dingle Bay *Sea feature* Ireland 59 A14
Diourbel Senegal 92 F8
Dipolog Mindanao, Philippines 127 M7
Dire Dawa Ethiopia 91 L14
Dirk Hartog I. *Island* Western Australia, Australia 132 E10
Disappointment, L. *Lake* Western Australia, Australia 132 H9
Disna, L. *Lake* Lithuania 81 K9
Disney World Florida, USA 29 N12
Dispur India 117 Q6
Divriği Turkey 105 O7
Diyālá *River* Iraq 109 L4
Diyarbakir Turkey 105 Q8
Dja *River* Cameroon 95 G11
Djado, Plateau du *Physical region* Niger 93 R5
Djambala Congo 95 H13
Djebal Toubkal *Mountain* Morocco 87
Djelfa Djibouti 91 L14, 100 D7
Djibouti *Country* E Africa 91

Djibouti 91

a Arabic, French • 💷 Franc • ◆ 49 • ♥ 49 •
○ £1.13 • ♥ (m) 63% (f) 36% • 🏛 81%

Dnepropetrovsk *see* Dnipropetrovs'k
Dnieper (var. Dnipro) *River* E Europe 54, 81 M15, 82 E10, 84 I5

Dniester *River* Ukraine 84 F5
Dnipro *see* Dnieper
Dnipropetrovs'k Ukraine 85 K6
Dobele Latvia 80 H6
Doboj Bosnia and Herzegovina 75 K5
Dobrich Bulgaria 77 O11
Dr Pedro P. Peña Paraguay 48 K5
Dodecanese *Island group* Greece 79 P13
Dodge City Kansas, USA 33 N13
Dodoma Tanzania 97 O8
Dōgo *Island* Oki Is. Japan 123 E11
Doha (var. Ad Dawḥah) Qatar 109 M10
Dolak *Island* Indonesia 126 S14
Dolomites *Mountain range* Alps Italy 72 H6
Dolores Argentina 49 N11
Dom *Mountain* Switzerland 54
Dominica *Country* Caribbean Sea 43 T12

Dominica 43

a English • 💷 Dollar • ◆ 249 • ♥ 75 • ○ £1.45 •
♥ (av.) 94% • 🏛 41%

Dominican Republic *Country* Caribbean Sea 43

Dominican Republic 43

a Spanish • 💷 Peso • ◆ 385 • ♥ 67 • ○ £0.42 •
♥ (m) 85% (f) 82% • 🏛 60%

Don *River* Russian Federation 54, 83 F13
Donau *see* Danube
Donawitz Austria 69 Q7
Donbass *Physical region* Ukraine 85 M6
Dondra Head *Cape* Sri Lanka 100 I7
Donegal Bay *Sea feature* Ireland 59 C11
Donets *River* Russian Federation/Ukraine 83 E13, 85 L5
Donets'k Ukraine 85 M7
Dong Hoi Vietnam 124 N10
Dongchuan China 120 I12
Dongguang China 121 M14
Dongsheng China 119 N8
Dongting Hu *Lake* China 115, 121 L11
Dønna *Island* Norway 57 K5
Donostia *see* San Sebastián
Doornik *see* Tournai
Dordogne *River* France 62 J12
Dordrecht Netherlands 65 H11
Dornbirn Austria 69 I8
Dortmund Germany 66 E10
Dortmund-Ems Canal *Waterway* Germany 66 E9
Dosso Niger 93 N9
Dothan Alabama, USA 29 L9
Douala Cameroon 95 E11
Doubs *River* France 63 O8
Douglas Arizona, USA 34 J11
Douglas Isle of Man, UK 59 G12
Douro (var. Duero) *River* Portugal 54, 60 H6
Dover Delaware, USA 27 L4
Dover England, UK 59 L16
Dover New Hampshire, USA 27 O8
Dover, Strait of *Channel* France/UK 59 M17, 63 K1
Dōzen *Island* Oki Is. Japan 123 E11
Drachten Netherlands 64 L7
Drake Passage *Channel* Atlantic Ocean/Pacific Ocean 41, 50 A7
Drakensberg *Mountain range* Lesotho/South Africa 11, 87, 99 L14
Drama Greece 79 L2
Drammen Norway 56 I11
Drau (var. Drava) *River* SE Europe 69 Q9
Drava (var. Drau) *River* SE Europe 75 K3
Drawa *River* Poland 70 I4
Dresden Germany 67 M11
Drin *River* Albania/Macedonia 75 M10
Drin Gulf *Sea feature* Albania 75 L11
Drobeta-Turnu-Severin Romania 76 H9
Drumheller Alberta, Canada 23 L14
Drummondville Quebec, Canada 25 M12
Druskininkai Lithuania 80 I11
Dubai United Arab Emirates 109 O11
Dubásari (var. Dubossary) Moldavia 84 H7
Dubawnt L. *Lake* Northwest Territories, Canada 23 N9
Dubbo New South Wales, Australia 133 O12
Dublin (var. Baile Atha Cliath; anc. Eblana) Ireland 59 E13
Dubossary *see* Dubásari
Dubrovnik Croatia 75 K9
Dubuque Iowa, USA 33 R8
Duero (var. Douro) *River* Spain 61 K6
Dugi Otok *Island* Croatia 74 G7
Duisburg Germany 66 D10
Dukhan Qatar 109 M10
Duluth Minnesota, USA 30 I4
Dumaguete Negros, Philippines 127 M6
Dumfries Scotland, UK 59 H11
Dumont d'Urville *Research center* Antarctica 50 F12
Dun Laoghaire Ireland 59 E13
Dunaj *see* Danube
Dunajec *River* Poland/Slovakia 71 M9
Dundalk Ireland 59 E12
Dundas (var. Ummannaq) Greenland 51 N11
Dundee Scotland, UK 58 I9
Dunedin New Zealand 134 I8
Dungun Malaysia 125 K18
Dunkerque *see* Dunkirk, France
Dunkirk (var. Dunkerque) France 63 L1
Dunkirk New York, USA 26 H9
Durance *River* France 63 P13
Durango Colorado, USA 35 L6

Durango Mexico 39 K8
Durazno Uruguay 48 N10
Durban South Africa 99 M14, 101 C12
Durham North Carolina, USA 29 Q5
Durrës Albania 75 L12
Dushanbe (prev. Stalinabad) Tajikistan 111 N8
Düsseldorf Germany 67 D11
Dutch East Indies see Indonesia
Dutch Guiana see Suriname
Dutch Harbor Unalaska I. Aleutian Is. Alaska, USA 22 C8
Dvina see Dvina, Northern or Dvina, Western
Dvina, Northern River Russian Federation 54, 82 J8
Dvina, Western (var. Daugava) River NE Europe 54, 80 I6, 81 M8
Dzhalal-Abad Kyrgyzstan 111 P6
Dzhambul see Zhambyl
Dzhezkazgan see Zhezkazgan
Dzhizak Uzbekistan 111 M7
Dzhugdzhur Range Mountain range Russian Federation 113 O9
Dzungaria Mountain range China/Kazakhstan 103

E

Eagle L. Lake California, USA 37 I12
Eagle L. Lake Maine, USA 27 P3
Eagle Mountain L. Lake Texas, USA 35 Q10
Eagle Pass Texas, USA 35 P14
East African Plateau Physical feature Kenya/Uganda 87
East C. Cape Papua New Guinea 133 P4
East China Sea China 115, 121 O12, 123 B17, 128 F6
East Frisian Is. Island group Germany 66 E7
East Greenland current Ocean current Atlantic Ocean 12
East Indies (var. Indonesia) Island group SE Asia 115, 131
East Liverpool Ohio, USA 31 Q11
East London South Africa 99 L15
East Pacific Ridge Sea feature Pacific Ocean 41
East Pacific Rise Sea feature Pacific Ocean 129 O9
East Pakistan see Bangladesh
East St. Louis Illinois, USA 30 J14
East Siberian Sea Arctic Ocean 51 R6, 103, 113 O3
Easter I. Island Polynesia, Pacific Ocean 129 O10
Eastern Ghats Mountain range India 117 L11
Eastmain River Quebec, Canada 25 M8
Eastport Maine, USA 27 R5
Eau Claire Wisconsin, USA 30 I6
Eblana see Dublin
Ebolowa Cameroon 95 F11
Ebro River Spain 54, 61 M5
Ecuador Country S America 44

Ecuador 44

a Spanish • 🕭 Sucre • ♦ 98 • ♥ 66 • ◒ £0.31 •
🕮 (m) 88% (f) 84% • 🏚 56%

Ed Damazin Sudan 91 H14
Ed Damer Sudan 91 H11
Ed Dueim Sudan 91 G13
Ede Netherlands 64 K10
Edéa Cameroon 95 F11
Eder River Germany 67 G11
Edessa Greece 78 I3
Edinburgh Scotland, UK 58 I10
Edirne Turkey 104 G4
Edmonds Washington, USA 36 H6
Edmonton Alberta, Canada 23 L13
Edward, L. Lake Uganda/Zaire 95 O12, 97 K4
Edwards Air Base Military center California, USA 37 L18
Edwards Plateau Physical region Texas, USA 35 P12
Eforie-Nord Romania 77 P9
Egadi Is. Island Group Sicily 73 H17
Egiyn River Mongolia/Russian Federation 119 L4
Egypt Country NE Africa 90

Egypt 90

a Arabic • 🕭 Pound • ♦ 138 • ♥ 61 • ◒ £0.52 •
🕮 (m) 63% (f) 34% • 🖵 109 • ✦ 5092 • ⚥ Yes •
🏚 47% • ⫼ 3336

Eiger, Mt. Mountain Switzerland 68 F11
Eigg Island Scotland, UK 58 F8
Eindhoven Netherlands 65 J13
Eire see Ireland
Eisenstadt Austria 69 S5
El Aaiún (var. Laâyoune) Western Sahara 88 F7
El Faiyûm Egypt 90 F7
El Fasher Sudan 91 D13
El Ferrol Spain 60 G3
El Iskandarîya see Alexandria
El Jerid, Chott Salt lake Tunisia 89 M5
El Juf see El Djouf
El Khartûm see Khartoum
El Mansûra Egypt 90 F6

El Minya Egypt 90 F7
El Obeid Sudan 91 F13
El Oued Algeria 89 M6
El Paso Texas, USA 35 L11
El Qâhira see Cairo
El Salvador Country C America 42

El Salvador 42

a Spanish • 🕭 Colon • ♦ 663 • ♥ 64 • ◒ £0.59 •
🕮 (m) 76% (f) 70% • 🏚 44%

El Suweis see Suez
Elat Israel 107 L14
Elâziğ Turkey 105 P8
Elba Island Italy 72 F10
Elbasan Albania 75 M12
Elbe River Germany 54, 66 I8
Elbe see Laba
Elbert, Mt. Mountain Colorado, USA 20
Elblag Poland 71 L2
El'brus Mountain Russian Federation 54
Elburz Mts. Mountain range Iran 109 N4
Elche Spain 61 N11
Eldoret Kenya 97 O4
Elephant Butte Res. Reservoir New Mexico, USA 35 L10
Elephant I. Island South Shetland Is. Antarctica 50 B6
Eleuthera Island Bahamas 43 L2
Elgin Scotland, UK 58 I7
Elisabethville see Lubumbashi
Elista Russian Federation 83 F14
Elk Poland 71 N3
Elko Nevada, USA 34 H2
Ellensburg Washington, USA 36 I7
Ellesmere I. Island Northwest Territories, Canada 20, 23 N1, 51 O11
Elmira New York, USA 26 J10
Eltz Castle Germany 67 E12
Elwell, L. Lake Montana, USA 32 I4
Ely Nevada, USA 34 H4
Elyria Ohio, USA 31 P10
Emba River Kazakhstan 112 E10
Emden Germany 66 E7
Emerson (Trimmu) Barrage Dam Pakistan 116 I3
Emmen Netherlands 64 N8
Emona see Ljubljana
Emperor Seamounts Sea feature Pacific Ocean 128 I5
Emporia Kansas, USA 33 P12
Empty Quarter see Rub 'al Khali
Ems River Germany 66 E9
En Nahud Sudan 91 E13
Encarnación Paraguay 48 N7
Ende Flores, Indonesia 127 M15
Enderby Land Region Antarctica 50 G7
Enewetak Island Marshall Islands, Pacific Ocean 128 H7
Enggano Island Indonesia 126 E14
England Country UK 59
English Channel France/UK 54, 59 J17, 62 I3
Enguri River Azerbaijan/Georgia 85 O11
Enid Oklahoma, USA 33 O14
Enna Sicily 73 K18
Enns River Austria 69 P7
Enriquillo, L. Lake Dominican Republic 43 N8
Enschede Netherlands 64 N10
Ensenada Mexico 38 F2
Entebbe Uganda 97 M4
Enugu Nigeria 93 O12
Ephesus Archaeological site Turkey 104 G8
Epidaurus Archaeological site Greece 78 J10
Épinal France 63 P6
Equatorial Current Ocean current Pacific Ocean 12
Equatorial Guinea Country C Africa 95

Equatorial Guinea 95

a Spanish • 🕭 Franc • ♦ 39 • ♥ 47 • ◒ £2.15 •
🕮 (m) 64% (f) 37% • 🏚 27%

Er Rachidia Morocco 88 I6
Er Roseires Dam Dam Sudan 91 H14
Erdenet Mongolia 119 L4
Ereğli Turkey 105 L9
Erenhot China 119 O6
Erfurt Germany 67 I11
Erg Chech Desert region Algeria/Mali 93 K4
Erguig River Chad 94 I8
Erie Pennsylvania, USA 26 G10
Erie, L. Lake Canada/USA 20, 24 J15, 26 G9, 31 P9
Erie Canal Waterway New York, USA 26 I8
Eritrea Country E Africa 91

Eritrea 91

a Amharic • 🕭 Birr • ♦ 97 • ♥ 48 • ◒ N/A •
🕮 (av.) 71% • 🏚 N/A

Erivan see Yerevan
Erlangen Germany 67 I13
Ernakulam India 116 J14
Erne, Lough Lake Northern Ireland, UK 59 D11
Ertix He see Irtysh
Erzincan Turkey 105 P6
Erzurum Turkey 105 Q6
Es Semara see Smara
Esbjerg Denmark 52 L7, 56 H15

Escanaba Michigan, USA 31 L5
Esch-sur-Alzette Luxembourg 65 L19
Escuintla Guatemala 42 A8
Eşfahān Iran 109 N6
Eskimo Pt. Northwest Territories, Canada 23 O10
Eskişehir Turkey 104 J6
Esla Res. Reservoir Spain 60 I6
Esmeraldas Ecuador 44 C8
Esperance Western Australia, Australia 132 H13
Espinho Portugal 60 F7
Espíritu Santo I. Island Mexico 38 H8
Esquel Argentina 49 H15
Essaouira Morocco 88 G6
Essen Germany 66 E10
Essequibo River Guyana 44 M7
Estelí Nicaragua 42 D10
Estevan Saskatchewan, Canada 23 N15
Estonia (var. Estonskaya SSR) Country NE Europe 80-81

Estonia 80-81

a Estonian • 🕭 Kroon • ♦ 91 • ♥ 48 • ◒ £0.38 •
🕮 (m) 99% (f) 99% • 🏚 71%

Estonskaya SSR see Estonia
Ethiopia (var. Abyssinia) Country E Africa 91

Ethiopia 91

a Amharic • 🕭 Birr • ♦ 124 • ♥ 48 • ◒ £0.50 •
🕮 (av.) 29% • 🖵 2 • ✦ 38359 • ⚥ Yes • 🏚 13% •
⫼ 1667

Ethiopian Highlands Mountain range Ethiopia 87, 91 J15
Etna Volcano Sicily
Etosha N.P. National park Namibia 98 H9
Etosha Pan Salt basin Namibia 98 H8
Euboea see Evvoia
Eugene Oregon, USA 36 G9
Eupen Belgium 65 L15
Euphrates River SW Asia 100 E4, 103, 105 O10, 107 R5, 109 K6
Eurasian Plate Physical feature 8, 20, 54, 87, 103, 115, 131
Eureka California, USA 37 F12
Europe Continent 8, 10, 11, 12, 13, 15, 20, 103
Europoort Netherlands 65 G11
Evanston Illinois, USA 31 L10
Evansville Indiana, USA 31 L14
Everard, L. Lake South Australia, Australia 133 K12
Everest, Mt. (var. Qomolangma Feng) Mountain China/Nepal 115, 117 O5
Everett Washington, USA 35 H6
Everglades, The Swamp region Florida, USA 20, 29 O14
Évora Portugal 60 G11
Évreux France 63 K5
Evvoia (var. Euboea) Island Greece 79 K7
Exeter England, UK 59 G16
Exmoor Physical region England, UK 59 G16
Exmouth Plateau Sea feature Indian Ocean 131
Eyasi, L. Lake Tanzania 97 N7
Eyre, L. Lake South Australia, Australia 131, 133 L11

F

Fada-Ngourma Burkina 93 M10
Faeroe Islands Dependent territory Atlantic Ocean 52 J7
Faeroe Islands Island group Atlantic Ocean 54
Faeroe Shelf Sea feature Atlantic Ocean 54
Faguibine, L. Lake Mali 93 K7
Fairbanks Alaska, USA 22 H7
Fairmont Minnesota, USA 30 G8
Faisalabad Pakistan 116 I3
Falkland Escarpment Sea feature Atlantic Ocean 41
Falkland Is. Dependent territory Atlantic Ocean 53 F15
Falkland Is. Island group Atlantic Ocean 41
Fall River Massachusetts, USA 27 O11
Falmouth England, UK 59 E17
Falun Sweden 57 L11
Famagusta Cyprus 105 L12
Faradje Zaire 95 O11
Farafangana Madagascar 101 E11
Farewell, Cape Greenland 52 H7
Fargo North Dakota, USA 33 O5
Faribault Minnesota, USA 30 H7
Farmington New Mexico, USA 35 K6
Faro Portugal 60 G13
Faro Yukon Territory, Canada 22 I9
Fårö Island Sweden 57 M13
Farvel, Cape (var. Kap Farvel) Cape Greenland 51 M16
Fax River Sweden 57 K8
Faya (var. Faya Largeau) Chad 94 J5
Faya Largeau see Faya
Fayetteville Arkansas, USA 28 H3
Fayetteville North Carolina, USA 29 Q6
Fdérik Mauritania 92 H4
Fear, Cape Cape North Carolina, USA 29 Q8
Federal Capital Territory see Australian Capital Territory
Fehmarn Island Germany 66 J6
Feira de Santana Brazil 47 N11
Felbertauern Tunnel Tunnel Austria 69 M8

Feldkirch Austria 68 I9
Felixstowe England, UK 59 M15
Femund, L. Lake Norway 56 J9
Fens, The Physical region England, UK 59 K14
Feodosiya Ukraine 85 K10
Fergana Uzbekistan 111 P6
Fergus Falls Minnesota, USA 30 F5
Fernando de Noronha I. Island Atlantic Ocean 53 I12
Fernando Póo Island Equatorial Guinea 87
Ferrara Italy 72 H8
Fethiye Turkey 105 H10
Feuilles, Rivière aux River Quebec, Canada 25 M4
Fez Morocco 88 I5
Fezzan Physical region Libya 89 O9
Fianarantsoa Madagascar 101 E11
Fier Albania 75 L13
Figueira de Foz Portugal 60 F8
Figuig Morocco 88 J6
Fiji Country Melanesia, Pacific Ocean 128 J10

Fiji 128

a English • 🕭 Dollar • ♦ 106 • ♥ 65 • ◒ £1.17 •
🕮 (m) 90% (f) 84% • 🏚 39%

Fiji Island group Melanesia, Pacific Ocean 131
Filadelfia Paraguay 48 L4
Filchner Ice Shelf Coastal feature Atlantic Ocean Coast, Antarctica 50 D8
Filicudi Island Lipari Is. Sicily 73 K16
Fimbul Ice Shelf Coastal feature Atlantic Ocean Coast, Antarctica 50 E6
Findlay Ohio, USA 31 O11
Finger Lakes Physical region New York, USA 26 J9
Finisterre, C. Coastal feature Spain 54
Finland Country N Europe 57

Finland 57

a Finnish, Swedish • 🕭 Markka • ♦ 43 • ♥ 76 •
◒ £1.54 • 🕮 (m) 99% (f) 99% • 🖵 497 • ✦ 515 •
⚥ No • 🏚 60% • ⫼ 3253

Finland, Gulf of Sea feature Baltic Sea 54, 57 O12, 81 K1, 82 E7
Firenze see Florence, Italy
Firth of Clyde Sea feature Scotland, UK 58 G10
Firth of Forth Sea feature Scotland, UK 58 I9
Fish River Namibia 98 I13
Fishguard Wales, UK 59 F15
Fitzroy River Western Australia, Australia 132 H7
Flagstaff Arizona, USA 34 I7
Flaming Gorge Dam Dam Utah, USA 35 K3
Flaming Gorge Res. Reservoir Utah/Wyoming, USA 32 I10
Flathead L. Lake Montana, USA 32 G4
Flin Flon Manitoba, Canada 23 N13
Flinders River Queensland, Australia 131, 133 M7
Flinders I. Island Tasmania, Australia 133 N15
Flinders Ranges Mountain range South Australia, Australia 131, 133 L12
Flint Michigan, USA 31 O8
Flint River Florida/Georgia 29 M9
Florence (var. Firenze) Italy 72 G9
Florence Alabama, USA 29 K5
Florence South Carolina, USA 29 P7
Florencia Colombia 44 E8
Flores Guatemala 42 B6
Flores Island Indonesia 115, 131, 127 M15
Flores Sea Indonesia 127 K15
Florianópolis Brazil 47 J15
Florida Uruguay 48 N10
Florida State USA 29 N11
Florida Keys Island group Florida, USA 29 O16
Florida, Straits of Channel Cuba/USA 29 P15
Florina Greece 78 H3
Flushing (var. Vlissingen) Netherlands 65 E13
Fly River Papua New Guinea 133 M3
Foča Bosnia and Herzegovina 75 L8
Focşani Romania 77 N6
Foggia Italy 73 M12
Foix France 63 L15
Fond du Lac Wisconsin, USA 31 K8
Fongafale Tuvalu, Pacific Ocean 128 J9
Forlì Italy 72 H8
Formentera Island Balearic Islands 61 P11
Formosa Argentina 48 M6
Fort Bliss Military Reservation Military center New Mexico, USA 35 L11
Fort Collins Colorado, USA 35 M3
Fort-de-France Martinique 43 T13
Fort Dodge Iowa, USA 33 Q8
Fort-Foureau see Kousseri
Fort Lamy see N'Djamena
Fort Lauderdale Florida, USA 29 O15
Fort McMurray Alberta, Canada 23 L12
Fort McPherson Northwest Territories, Canada 22 J7
Fort Myers Florida, USA 29 N14
Fort Nelson British Columbia, Canada 23 J11
Fort Peck L. Lake Montana, USA 32 J4
Fort Portal Uganda 97 L4
Fort Resolution Northwest Territories, Canada 23 L10
Fort Shevchenko Kazakhstan 112 D10
Fort Simpson Northwest Territories, Canada 23 K10
Fort Smith Arkansas, USA 28 H4
Fort Smith Northwest Territories, Canada 23 L11

a Language (official or most commonly spoken) • 🕭 Currency • ♦ Population density per square mile • ♥ Average life expectancy • ◒ Price of 1 dozen hen's eggs • 🕮 Literacy • 🖵 Number of TVs per 1,000 people • ✦
Number of people per doctor • ⚥ Death penalty • 🏚 Percentage of urban-based population • ⫼ Average number of calories consumed daily per person
143

Fort Smith *Region* Northwest Territories, Canada 23 L9
Fort St John British Columbia, Canada 23 K12
Fort Vermilion Alberta, Canada 23 L11
Fort Victoria *see* Masvingo
Fort Wayne Indiana, USA 31 N11
Fort Wellington Guyana 44 M6
Fort William Scotland, UK 58 G8
Fort Worth Texas, USA 35 R10
Fortaleza Brazil 46 N8, 53 H12
Forth *River* Scotland, UK 58 H9
Foveaux Strait *Channel* New Zealand 134 C14
Foxe Basin *Sea feature* Northwest Territories, Canada 23 P7
Foyle, Lough *Lake* Northern Ireland/Ireland 58 E10
France *Country* W Europe 62-63

France 62-63

ⓐ French • 🏛 Franc • ♦ 267 • ⬤ 77 • ◔ £1.61 •
♛ (m) 99% (f) 99% • 🖥 406 • ✚ 381 • ✿ No •
🏠 74% • ¶ 3465

Franceville *see* Massoukou
Francis Case, L. *Lake* South Dakota, USA 33 N8
Francistown Botswana 99 L10
Franconian Jura *Mountain range* Germany 67 J14
Frankfort Indiana, USA 31 M12
Frankfort Kentucky, USA 29 N3
Frankfurt am Main Germany 67 F12
Frankfurt an der Oder Germany 66 N9
Franz Josef Land *Island group* Russian Federation 51 R11, 54, 103
Fraser *River* British Columbia, Canada 20, 22 J13
Fraserburgh Scotland, UK 58 J7
Frauenfeld Switzerland 68 H8
Fray Bentos Uruguay 48 N9
Fredericton New Brunswick, Canada 25 P12
Frederikshåb (var. Paamiut) Greenland 51 M15
Frederikshavn Denmark 56 I13
Fredrikstad Norway 56 J12
Freeport Bahamas 43 K1
Freeport Illinois, USA 31 K9
Freeport Texas, USA 35 S13
Freetown Sierra Leone 92 G11
Freiburg im Breisgau Germany 67 E16
Freistadt Austria 69 P4
Fremantle Western Australia, Australia 101 M12, 132 F12
French Guiana *Dependent territory* S America 44
French Polynesia *Dependent territory* Polynesia, Pacific Ocean 129 M9
French Sudan *see* Mali
French Togo *see* Togo
Fresno California, USA 37 J16
Fria, C. *Cape* Namibia 87, 98 F9
Fribourg Switzerland 68 E10
Friedrichshafen Germany 67 G16
Frobisher Bay Baffin I. Northwest Territories, Canada 23 S7
Frobisher Bay *see* Iqaluit
Frobisher L. *Lake* Saskatchewan, Canada 23 M12
Frome, L. *Lake* South Australia, Australia 133 L12
Frontera Mexico 39 Q13
Frosinone Italy 73 J12
Frunze *see* Bishkek
Fuenlabrada Spain 61 K8
Fuerte Olimpo Paraguay 48 M4
Fujairah United Arab Emirates 109 O11
Fuji, Mt. *Mountain* Japan 115, 123 J11
Fukui Japan 123 H11
Fukuoka Japan 123 C13
Fukushima Japan 122 K5
Fukushima Japan 122 K9
Fulda Germany 67 H12
Fulda *River* Germany 67 H11
Fundy, Bay of *Sea feature* Canada 25 P13, 52 F8
Funen *see* Fyn
Furnas Res. *Reservoir* Brazil 47 K13
Fushun China 121 O6
Fuzhou China 121 N13
Fyn (var. Funen) *Island* Denmark 56 I16

G

Gaalkacyo Somalia 91 N16
Gabčíkovo Slovakia 71 K12
Gabès Tunisia 89 N5
Gabon *Country* C Africa 95

Gabon 95

ⓐ French • 🏛 Franc • ♦ 12 • ⬤ 54 • ◔ £2.57 •
♛ (m) 74% (f) 49% • 🏠 46%

Gaborone Botswana 99 K11
Gabrovo Bulgaria 77 L12
Gadsden Alabama, USA 29 L6
Gafsa Tunisia 89 N5
Gagnoa Ivory Coast 92 J13
Gagra Georgia 85 N11

Gainesville Florida, USA 29 N11
Gairdner, L.144 *Lake* South Australia, Australia 133 K12
Galana *River* Kenya 97 Q6
Galapagos Is. *Island group* Pacific Ocean 41, 129 P8
Galaţi Romania 77 O7
Galesburg Illinois, USA 30 J11
Galicia *Region* Poland 71 N9
Galicia *Region* Spain 60 G3
Galilee, Sea of *see* Tiberias, L.
Galle Sri Lanka 117 L16
Gallego Rise *Sea feature* Pacific Ocean 41
Gallia *see* Paris
Gallipoli Italy 73 P14
Gallipoli (var. Gelibolu; anc. Callipolis) Turkey 104 G5
Gällivare Sweden 57 N5
Gallup New Mexico, USA 35 K7
Galveston Texas, USA 35 S13
Galway Ireland 59 B12
Galway Bay *Sea feature* Ireland 59 B12
Gambia *Country* W Africa 92

Gambia 92

ⓐ English • 🏛 Dalasi • ♦ 233 • ⬤ 45 • ◔ £1.81 •
♛ (m) 39% (f) 16% • 🏠 23%

Gambier Is. *Island group* French Polynesia, Pacific Ocean 129 M10
Gan He *River* 115
Gäncä (var. Gyandzha; prev. Kirovabad) Azerbaijan 85 R13
Gander Newfoundland, Canada 25 S9
Gandi Res. *Reservoir* India 116 J7
Ganga *see* Ganges
Gangdise Range *Mountain range* China 118 G12
Ganges (var. Ganga) *River* India 100 J5, 115, 117 O7
Ganges *River basin* India 11
Ganges Delta *Delta* Bangladesh 115
Ganges Plain *Physical region* India 115
Gangtok India 117 O6
Ganzhou China 121 M13
Gao Mali 93 L8
Gap France 63 T12
Gar China 118 F11
Garda, L. *Lake* Italy 72 F6
Garden City Kansas, USA 33 M13
Garissa Kenya 97 Q5
Garmisch-Partenkirchen Germany 67 I17
Garonne *River* France 54, 62 J12
Garoowe Somalia 91 O15
Garoua Cameroon 94 G9
Garry L. *Lake* Northwest Territories, Canada 23 N8
Gary Indiana, USA 31 L10
Gaspé Quebec, Canada 25 P10
Gastonia North Carolina, USA 29 P6
Gatineau Quebec, Canada 25 L13
Gävle Sweden 57 L11
Gaya India 117 N7
Gaza Gaza Strip 107 K10
Gaza Strip *Occupied by Israel* SW Asia 107 K10
Gaziantep Turkey 105 O9
Gbarnga Liberia 92 H12
Gdańsk (prev. Danzig) Poland 71 L2
Gdynia Poland 71 K2
Gedaref Sudan 91 H13
Geelong Victoria, Australia 133 M14
Gejiu China 120 I14
Gela, Gulf of *Sea feature* Sicily 73 K19
Gelibolu *see* Gallipoli
Gelsenkirchen Germany 66 E10
Gemena Zaire 95 J11
Gemlik Turkey 104 I6
Gemsbok N.P. *National park* Botswana 98 J11
Genale *River* Ethiopia 91 K16
General Eugenio A. Garay Paraguay 41 K4
General Santos Mindanao, Philippines 127 N8
Genesee *River* New York/Pennsylvania, USA 26 I9
Geneva (var. Genève) Switzerland 68 C12
Geneva New York, USA 26 J9
Geneva, L. *Lake* France/Switzerland 54, 63 P9, 68 D12
Genève *see* Geneva, Switzerland
Genk Belgium 65 J14
Genoa (var. Genova) Italy 72 D8
Genoa, Gulf of *Sea feature* Italy 72 D8
Genova *see* Genoa
Gent *see* Ghent
Georg van Neumayer *Research center* Antarctica 50 D6
Georgetown Delaware, USA 27 K15
Georgetown Gambia 92 G9
Georgetown Grand Cayman, Cayman Islands 42 H6
Georgetown Guyana 44 M6, 53 F11
George Town (var. Pinang)Malaysia 100 L7, 125 I17
Georgia *Country* SW Asia 85

Georgia 85

ⓐ Georgian • 🏛 Ruble • ♦ 204 • ⬤ 73 • ◔ N/A •
♛ N/A • 🏠 56%

Georgia *State* USA 29
Gera Germany 67 K11
Geraldton Western Australia, Australia 132 E11

Germany *Country* C Europe 66-67

Germany 66-67

ⓐ German • 🏛 Mark • ♦ 590 • ⬤ 77 • ◔ £1.33 •
♛ (m) 99% (f) 99% • 🖥 570 • ✚ 345 • ✿ No •
🏠 86% • ¶ 3665

Gerona *see* Girona
Gersoppa Falls *Waterfall* India 115
Getafe Spain 61 K8
Gettysburg Pennsylvania, USA 26 I13
Getz Ice Shelf *Coastal feature* Pacific Ocean Coast, Antarctica 50 C10
Ghadaf, Wādī al *Seasonal watercourse* Iraq 108 J5
Ghadāmis Libya 89 N7
Ghana (prev. Gold Coast) *Country* W Africa 93

Ghana 93

ⓐ English • 🏛 Cedi • ♦ 173 • ⬤ 55 • ◔ £0.76 •
♛ (m) 70% (f) 51% • 🏠 33%

Ghanzi Botswana 98 J10
Ghardaïa Algeria 89 L6
Gharyān Libya 89 O6
Ghāt *Oasis* Libya 89 N10
Ghaznī Afghanistan 111 N12
Ghent (var. Gent) Belgium 65 E14
Ghulam Muhammad Barrage *Dam* Pakistan 116 G6
Gibraltar Gibraltar 60 I15
Gibraltar *Dependent territory* Mediterranean Sea 52 K9, 60 I15
Gibraltar, Strait of *Channel* Morocco/Spain 54, 87, 88 I4, 60 I15
Gibson Desert *Desert region* Western Australia, Australia 131, 132 H10
Giessen Germany 67 F12
Gifu Japan 123 I11
Giganta, Sierra de la *Mountain range* Mexico 39 H7
Gijón Spain 60 I3
Gila *River* Arizona/New Mexico, USA 35 K10
Gilbert Is. *Island group* Kiribati, Pacific Ocean 128 J9
Gilbert Ridge *Sea feature* Pacific Ocean 131
Gillette Wyoming, USA 33 K7
Girona (var. Gerona) Spain 61 Q5
Giresun Turkey 105 O5
Gisborne New Zealand 134 I6
Giurgiu Romania 77 L10
Giza Egypt 90 F6
Gjøvik Norway 56 J10
Gladstone Queensland, Australia 133 O9
Glåma *River* Norway 56 J9
Glarus Switzerland 68 H9
Glasgow Montana, USA 33 K4
Glasgow Scotland, UK 58 H10
Glen Canyon Dam *Dam* Utah, USA 34 J6
Glendale Arizona, USA 34 I9
Glendale California, USA 37 K18
Glendive Montana, USA 33 K5
Glens Falls New York, USA 27 M8
Gliwice Poland 71 L8
Gloucester England, UK 59 I15
Gloucester Massachusetts, USA 27 O9, 52 E8
Glubokoye *see* Hlybokaye
Gmünd Austria 69 P3
Gmunden Austria 69 O6
Gnjilane Serbia, Yugoslavia 75 O10
Goba Ethiopia 91 I15
Gobabis Namibia 98 I10
Gobi Desert *Desert region* C Asia 11, 115, 119 L7
Godavari *River* India 115, 117 L10
Godhavn Greenland 51 N13
Godoy Cruz Argentina 48 H10
Godthåb (var. Nuuk) Greenland 51 M14
Goiânia Brazil 47 J12
Golan Heights *Physical region occupied by Israel* Syria 107 M8
Gold Coast Queensland, Australia 133 P11
Gold Coast *see* Ghana
Golden Sands Bulgaria 77 O11
Golmud China 118 J10
Goma Zaire 95 O13
Gomel' *see* Homyel'
Gómez Palacio Mexico 39 L7
Gonaïves Haiti 43 M7
Gonâve, Île de la *Island* Haiti 43 M8
Gonder Ethiopia 91 I13
Gonghe China 119 L10
Gongola *River* Nigeria 93 Q10
Good Hope, Cape of *Cape* South Africa 53 M14, 87, 98 I16, 101 B12
Goondiwindi Queensland, Australia 133 O11
Goose Bay Newfoundland, Canada 25 Q7
Goose L. *Lake* California/Oregon, USA 37 I11
Gorakhpur India 117 M6
Goré Chad 94 I9
Gore Ethiopia 91 H15
Göreme Turkey 105 M8
Gorgān Iran 109 O4
Gorki *see* Horki
Görlitz Germany 67 N11
Gorlovka *see* Horlivka
Gorodets Russian Federation 82 H10
Goroka Papua New Guinea 133 N2
Gorongosa N.P. *National park* Mozambique 99 N8
Gorontalo Celebes, Indonesia 127 M11
Gorzów Wielkopolski Poland 70 I4
Gosford New South Wales, Australia 133 O13
Gospić Croatia 74 H5

Gosselies Belgium 65 G16
Gostivar Macedonia 75 N11
Göteborg Sweden 56 J13
Gotha Germany 67 I11
Gotland *Island* Sweden 57 L14
Gotō Is. *Island group* Japan 123 B14
Göttingen Germany 66 H10
Gouda Netherlands 65 H11
Gough Island *Island* Atlantic Ocean 53 K14
Gouin Res. *Reservoir* Quebec, Canada 25 L11
Goulburn New South Wales, Australia 133 O13
Govind Ballash Pant Res. *Reservoir* India 117 M7
Gowd-e-Zereh *Salt pan* Afghanistan 110 J15
Gozo *Island* Malta 73 K20
Gračanica Bosnia and Herzegovina 75 K5
Grafton New South Wales, Australia 133 P11
Grahamstown South Africa 99 L15
Grampian Mts. *Mountain range* Scotland, UK 54, 58 H8
Gran Chaco *Physical region* Argentina 41, 48 K6
Granada Nicaragua 42 D11
Granada Spain 61 K13
Grand Bahama *Island* Bahamas 43 K1
Grand Banks *Sea feature* Newfoundland, Canada 25 T10, 52 G8
Grand Canal (var. Da Yunhe) *Waterway* China 121 N9
Grand Canyon *Physical feature* Arizona, USA 20, 34 I6
Grand Cayman *Island* Cayman Islands 42 H6
Grand Falls New Brunswick, Canada 25 O11
Grand Falls Newfoundland, Canada 25 S9
Grand Forks North Dakota, USA 33 O4
Grand Island Nebraska, USA 33 O10
Grand Junction Colorado, USA 35 K4
Grand Rapids Michigan, USA 31 M8
Grand Teton Mts. *Mountain range* Wyoming, USA 32 I8
Grand Turk Turks & Caicos Islands 43 N6
Grande, Bahía *Sea feature* Argentina 49 K18
Grande, Serra *Mountain range* Brazil 46 M8
Grande Comore *Island* Comoros 100 E10
Grande Prairie Alberta, Canada 23 K13
Grande Rivière de la Baleine *River* Quebec, Canada 25 L6
Grande Terre *Island* Guadeloupe 43 T11
Grangemouth Scotland, UK 58 H9
Grants Pass Oregon, USA 37 G11
Grasse France 63 Q13
Graz Austria 69 R8
Great Abaco *Island* Bahamas 43 K1
Great Artesian Basin *Physical feature* Australia 131
Great Australian Bight *Sea feature* Australia 131, 132 J13
Great Bahama Bank *Sea feature* West Indies 42 J2
Great Barrier I. *Island* New Zealand 134 H3
Great Barrier Reef *Coral reef* Queensland, Australia 128 H10, 131, 133 O7
Great Basin *Physical region* SW USA 10, 11, 20, 34 G2
Great Bear L. *Lake* Northwest Territories, Canada 20, 23 K8
Great Bend Kansas, USA 33 O12
Great Dividing Range *Mountain range* Queensland, Australia 131, 133 O9
Great Exhibition Bay *Sea feature* New Zealand 134 F2
Great Exuma *Island* Bahamas 43 L4
Great Falls Montana, USA 32 H5
Great Inagua *Island* Bahamas 43 M6
Great Plain of China *Physical region* China 115
Great Plains *Physical region* USA 20, 33 L7
Great Rift Valley *Physical feature* SE Africa/SW Asia 8, 87, 97 O6
Great Ruaha *River* Tanzania 97 O9
Great St. Bernard Tunnel *Tunnel* Switzerland 68 E13
Great Salt Desert *see* Dasht-e-Kavir
Great Salt L. *Salt lake* Utah, USA 20, 34 I2
Great Salt Lake Desert *Desert region* Utah, USA 34 I3
Great Sandy Desert *Desert region* Western Australia, Australia 131, 132 H8
Great Slave L. *Lake* Northwest Territories, Canada 20, 23 L10
Great Victoria Desert *Desert region* Western Australia, Australia 131, 132 I11
Great Yarmouth England, UK 59 M14
Greater Antilles *Island group* Caribbean Sea 20, 41, 43 N9
Greater Khingan Range *Mountain range* China 115, 119 Q4
Gredos, Sierra de *Mountain range* Spain 60 J8
Greece *Country* S Europe 78-79

Greece 78-79

ⓐ Greek • 🏛 Drachma • ♦ 200 • ⬤ 77 • ◔ £1.11 •
♛ (m) 98% (f) 89% • 🖥 196 • ✚ 300 • ✿ No •
🏠 62% • ¶ 3825

Greeley Colorado, USA 35 N3
Green Bay Wisconsin, USA 31 L7
Green R. *River* Kentucky, USA 29 M3
Green R. *River* W USA 32, 35 K3
Greenfield Massachusetts, USA 27 N9
Greenland *Dependent territory* Arctic Ocean 10, 51, 52 H6
Greenland *Island* Arctic Ocean 20, 103
Greenland Sea *Sea feature* Arctic Ocean 51 P14, 52 J6, 103 O13
Greenock Scotland, UK 58 G9
Greensboro North Carolina, USA 29 P5

Greenville Liberia 92 I13
Greenville Mississippi, USA 28 I6
Greenville South Carolina, USA 29 O6
Greifswald Germany 66 L6
Grenada Country Caribbean Sea 43 S15

Grenada 43

a English · **≋** Dollar · **♦** 693 · **♥** 70 · **●** £3.10 · **✚** (av.) 90% · **⌂** 34%

Grenadines, The Island group St Vincent & The Grenadines 43 S14
Grenoble France 63 O11
Grevena Greece 78 H4
Greymouth New Zealand 134 E10
Grim, C. Cape Tasmania, Australia 133 M15
Grimsby England, UK 52 K8, 59 K13
Grodno see Hrodna
Groningen Netherlands 64 M6
Groote Eylandt Island Northern Territory, Australia 133 L5
Grootfontein Namibia 98 I9
Grosseto Italy 72 G10
Groznyy Russian Federation 83 F16
Grudziądz Poland 71 L3
Gstaad Switzerland 68 E11
Guacanayabo, Gulf of Sea feature Cuba 42 J6
Guadalajara Mexico 39 L11
Guadalajara Spain 61 L8
Guadalcanal Island Solomon Islands, Pacific Ocean 128 I9
Guadalquivir River Spain 54, 60 I12
Guadalupe Mexico 39 L9
Guadarrama, Sierra de Mountain range Spain 61 K7
Guadeloupe Dependent territory Caribbean Sea 43 S11
Guadiana River Portugal/Spain 60 G11
Gualeguaychu Argentina 48 M9
Guallatiri Volcano Chile 41
Guam Dependent territory Micronesia, Pacific Ocean 128 G7
Guanare Venezuela 44 H5
Guangxi Zhuang Autonomous Region China 121 K14
Guangzhou see Canton
Guantánamo Cuba 43 L6
Guantánamo Bay Sea feature Cuba 43 L7
Guarda Portugal 60 H8
Guatemala Country C America 42

Guatemala 42

a Spanish · **≋** Quetzal · **♦** 226 · **♥** 64 · **●** £0.51 · **✚** (m) 63% (f) 47% · **⌂** 39%

Guatemala Basin Sea feature Pacific Ocean 41
Guatemala City Guatemala 42 B8
Guaviare River Colombia/Venezuela 44 F7
Guayaquil Ecuador 44 C9, 129 Q8
Guayaquil, Gulf of Sea feature Ecuador/Peru 44 B9
Guaymas Mexico 38 H5
Guddu Barrage Dam Pakistan 116 H4
Guernsey Dependent territory W Europe 59 H18
Guiana Highlands Mountain range South America 41
Guider Cameroon 94 G8
Guilin China 121 K13
Guinea Country W Africa 92

Guinea 92

a French · **≋** Franc · **♦** 62 · **♥** 44 · **●** £1.21 · **✚** (m) 35% (f) 13% · **⌨** 7 · **✚** 10300 · **❀** Yes · **⌂** 26% · **⌿** 2132

Guinea, Gulf of Sea feature C Africa 53 L11, 87, 95 E11
Guinea Basin Sea feature Gulf of Guinea, Atlantic Ocean 53 K12, 87
Guinea-Bissau (prev. Portuguese Guinea) Country W Africa 92

Guinea-Bissau 92

a Portuguese · **≋** Peso · **♦** 92 · **♥** 41 · **●** £1.53 · **✚** (m) 50% (f) 24% · **⌂** 20%

Guiyang China 120 J12
Gujranwala Pakistan 116 J3
Gujrat Pakistan 116 J3
Gulf Stream current Ocean current Atlantic Ocean 12
Gulf, The see Persian Gulf
Gulfport Mississippi, USA 28 J9
Gulja see Yining
Gulu Uganda 97 M2
Gümüşhane Turkey 105 P5
Gur'yev see Atyrau
Gusau Nigeria 93 O10
Gusev Russian Federation 80 G10
Guwahati India 117 P6
Guyana (prev. British Guiana) Country S America 44

Guyana 44

a English · **≋** Dollar · **♦** 11 · **♥** 65 · **●** £2.11 · **✚** (m) 97% (f) 95% · **⌂** 35%

Guyana Basin Sea feature Atlantic Ocean 53 G11
Gwalior India 117 K6
Gwelo see Gweru
Gweru (prev. Gwelo) Zimbabwe 99 M9
Gyandzha see Gäncä
Gyangzê China 118 I13
Gyda Peninsula Physical feature Russian Federation 112 I6
Győr Hungary 71 K13
Gytheio Greece 78 I12
Gyumri (var. Kumayri; var. Leninakan) Armenia 85 P13
Gzhel' Russian Federation 82 G10

H

Ha Giang Vietnam 124 M7
Haapsalu Estonia 80 I2
Haarlem Netherlands 64 H9
Ḥabbān Yemen 108 J16
Habomai Is. Island group Japan 122 O2
Hachinohe Japan 122 L6
Hachiōji Japan 123 K11
Hadejia River Nigeria 93 Q9
Hadhramaut Region Yemen 109 K16
Haeju North Korea 121 P7
Hagen Germany 67 E11
Hagi Japan 123 D13
Hague, The Netherlands 64 G10
Hai Phong Vietnam 124 N8
Haifa (var. Hefa) Israel 107 L8
Haikou China 121 K15
Ḥā'il Saudi Arabia 108 J8
Hailar China 119 P3
Hainan Island China 115, 121 K16
Hainburg Austria 69 T4
Haines Alaska, USA 22 I10
Haines Junction Yukon Territory, Canada 22 H9
Haiti Country Caribbean Sea 43

Haiti 43

a French, Creole · **≋** Gourde · **♦** 621 · **♥** 54 · **●** £0.55 · **✚** (m) 59% (f) 47% · **⌂** 28%

Ḥajjah Yemen 108 H15
Hakkâri Turkey 105 S8
Hakodate Japan 122 K5, 128 G5
Halab (var. Aleppo; anc. Beroea) Syria 107 N3
Halden Norway 56 J12
Halicarnassus Turkey 104 G9
Halifax Nova Scotia, Canada 25 Q13, 52 F8
Halle Germany 66 K10
Hallein Austria 69 N7
Halley Research center Antarctica 50 D7
Halls Creek Western Australia, Australia 132 I7
Halmahera Island Indonesia 115, 131, 127 P10
Halmstad Sweden 56 J14
Hälsingborg Sweden 56 J15
Hamada Japan 123 D12
Hamadān Iran 109 M4
Ḥamāh Syria 107 N5
Hamamatsu Japan 123 J12
Hamar Norway 56 J10
Hamburg Germany 66 H7
Hameenlinna Finland 57 O10
Hamersley Range Mountain range Western Australia, Australia 132 F9
Hamhŭng North Korea 121 P6
Hami (var. Kumul) China 118 J7
Hamilton New Zealand 134 G5
Hamilton Ontario, Canada 25 K14
Hamm Germany 66 F10
Ḥammār, L. al Lake Iraq 109 L6
Hammerfest Norway 57 O1
Hāmūn-e-Şāberī Salt pan Afghanistan/Iran 110 J14
Handan China 121 M8
Hangayn Nuruu Mountain range Mongolia 119 K4
Hangzhou China 121 O11
Hannover see Hanover
Hanoi Vietnam 124 M8
Hanover (var. Hannover) Germany 66 H9
Har Us L. Lake Mongolia 118 J5
Ḥaraḍ Saudi Arabia 109 L10
Harare (prev. Salisbury) Zimbabwe 99 M8
Harbin China 121 P4
Hardanger Fjord Sea feature Norway 56 H10
Harderwijk Netherlands 64 J10
Harer Ethiopia 91 L15
Hargeysa Somalia 91 M14
Harīrūd River C Asia 111 L11
Harlan County L. Lake Nebraska, USA 33 N11
Harlingen Netherlands 64 J7
Harney L. Lake Oregon, USA 36 K10
Härnösand Sweden 57 M9
Harper Liberia 92 I13
Harris Island Scotland, UK 58 F7
Harrisburg Pennsylvania, USA 26 J13
Harry S. Truman Res. Reservoir Missouri, USA 33 Q12
Harstad Norway 57 M3
Hartford Connecticut, USA 27 M11
Hasselt Belgium 65 J14
Hässleholm Sweden 56 J15
Hastings England, UK 59 L17
Hastings Nebraska, USA 33 O10
Hastings New Zealand 134 H7
Hat Yai Thailand 125 I16
Hatteras, Cape Cape North Carolina, USA 20, 29 S6

Hatteras Plain Sea feature Atlantic Ocean 20
Hattiesburg Mississippi, USA 28 J8
Haugesund Norway 52 K7, 56 H11
Havana (var. La Habana) Cuba 42 H3
Havre Montana, USA 32 I4
Havre-Saint-Pierre Quebec, Canada 25 P9
Hawaii Island Pacific Ocean 12
Hawaii State USA, Pacific Ocean 129 L6
Hawaiian Is. Island group Polynesia, Pacific Ocean 8, 129 K7
Hawke Bay Sea feature New Zealand 134 I7
Ḥawrān, Wādī Seasonal watercourse Iraq 108 J4
Hay River Northwest Territories, Canada 23 L10
Hayes River Manitoba, Canada 23 P12
Hays Kansas, USA 33 N13
Hazleton Pennsylvania, USA 27 K12
Heads, The Cape Oregon, USA 36 F10
Heard and MacDonald Islands Dependent territory see Heard I, MacDonald Is
Heard I. Island Indian Ocean 50 I7, 101 H15
Heathrow Airport England, UK 59 K16
Heerenveen Netherlands 64 K7
Heerlen Netherlands 65 K15
Hefa see Haifa
Hefei China 121 N10
Heidelberg Germany 67 F14
Heilbronn Germany 67 G14
Heilong Jiang see Amur
Hejaz Region Saudi Arabia 108 H9
Helena Montana, USA 32 H5
Helgoland Bay (var. Helgoländer Bucht) Sea feature Germany 66 G6
Helgoländer Bucht see Helgoland Bay
Helmand River Afghanistan/Iran 111 L12
Helmond Netherlands 65 K12
Helsingør Denmark 56 J15
Helsinki Finland 57 O11
Helwân Egypt 90 F7
Henderson Nevada, USA 34 H7
Hengelo Netherlands 64 N10
Henrietta Maria, C. Cape Canada 24 J6
Henzada Burma 124 F10
Herāt Afghanistan 110 J12
Herisau Switzerland 68 H8
Herlen Gol see Kerulen
Hermansverk Norway 56 I9
Hermit Is. Island group Papua New Guinea 133 N1
Hermosillo Mexico 38 H4
Herrenchiemsee Castle Germany 67 K16
Herstal Belgium 65 K15
Hialeah Florida, USA 29 O15
Hibbing Minnesota, USA 30 H3
Hidaka Mts. Mountain range Japan 122 L4
Hidalgo del Parral Mexico 39 K6
Hierosolyma see Jerusalem
Hiiumaa Island Estonia 80 H2
Hildesheim Germany 66 H9
Hillsboro Oregon, USA 36 H8
Hilversum Netherlands 64 J10
Himalayas Mountain range S Asia 8, 11, 103, 115, 117 M5, 118 H14
Ḥimş Syria 107 N5
Hindu Kush Mountain range 103, 111 O10, 115
Hinnøya Island Norway 57 L3
Hirakud Res. Reservoir India 117 M9
Hirfanli Barrage Dam Turkey 105 L7
Hiroshima Japan 123 E13
Hispania see Spain
Hispaniola Island Caribbean Sea 20, 41
Hit Iraq 108 J4
Hitachi Japan 122 L10
Hitra Island Norway 56 I7
Hjørring Denmark 56 I13
Hjort Trench Sea feature 131
Hlybokaye (var. Glubokoye) Belarus 81 L9
Ho Chi Minh City (prev. Saigon) Vietnam 125 N14
Hobart Tasmania, Australia 133 N16
Hobbs New Mexico, USA 35 N10
Hodeida (var. Al Hudaydah) Yemen 108 H15
Hoek van Holland Netherlands 65 G11
Hof Germany 67 J12
Hohe Tauern Mountain range Austria 69 N8
Hohenschwangau Castle Germany 67 I17
Hohhot China 119 O7
Hokkaidō Island Japan 115, 122 L3
Holguín Cuba 43 K6
Holland Michigan, USA 31 M9
Hollywood California, USA 37 K18
Hollywood Florida, USA 29 O15
Holon Israel 107 L10
Holstebro Denmark 56 H14
Holy I. Island Wales, UK 59 G13
Holyhead Wales, UK 59 G13
Home Counties Region England, UK 59 K16
Homer Alaska, USA 22 F8
Homyel' (var. Gomel') Belarus 81 O14
Honduras Country C America 42

Honduras 42

a Spanish · **≋** Lempira · **♦** 122 · **♥** 65 · **●** £0.56 · **✚** (m) 75% (f) 70% · **⌂** 44%

Honduras, Gulf of Sea feature C America 42 C7
Hønefoss Norway 56 I11
Hong Gai Vietnam 124 N8
Hong Kong Dependent territory SE China 121 M14 128 J7
Hongshui He River China 120 J13
Hongze Hu Lake China 121 N9
Honiara Guadalcanal Solomon Islands, Pacific Ocean 128 I9

Honolulu Oahu Hawaiian Islands, Pacific Ocean 129 K6
Honshū Island Japan 115, 122 J9
Hoogeveen Netherlands 64 M8
Hoorn Netherlands 64 I8
Hoover Dam Arizona/Nevada, USA 34 H7
Hopa Turkey 105·Q4
Hopedale Newfoundland, Canada 25 P5
Hopkinsville Kentucky, USA 29 L3
Horki (var. Gorki) Belarus 81 O11
Horlivka (var. Gorlovka) Ukraine 85 M6
Hormuz, Strait of Channel Iran/Oman 109 O10
Horn of Africa Physical region Somalia 91 O14
Horn, Cape Cape Chile 49 L20, 56 F16, 129 Q14
Horsens Denmark 56 I15
Hot Springs Arkansas, USA 28 H5
Hotan China 118 F9
Houlton Maine, USA 27 Q3
Houston Texas, USA 35 S13
Hovd Mongolia 118 I5
Hövsgöl, L. Lake Mongolia 119 L3
Howland I. Dependent territory Polynesia, Pacific Ocean 128 J8
Hradec Králové Czech Republic 70 I8
Hrodna (var. Grodno) Belarus 80 I12
Hron River Slovakia 71 L11
Hrvatska see Croatia
Huai He River China 115
Huainan China 121 N10
Huambo (var. Nova Lisboa) Angola 98 H6
Huancayo Peru 45 E13
Huang He see Yellow R.
Huánuco Peru 45 D12
Huascarán Mountain Peru 41
Huddersfield England, UK 59 J13
Huddinge Sweden 57 L12
Hudiksvall Sweden 57 L10
Hudson River New York, USA 27 M10
Hudson Bay Sea feature Canada 10, 20, 23 P10, 24 I5, 52 D7
Hudson-Mohawk Gap Physical feature New York/Vermont, USA 27 M9
Hudson Strait Channel Canada 20, 23 R8, 25 M2
Hue Vietnam 125 N11
Huehuetenango Guatemala 42 A7
Huelva Spain 60 H13
Huesca Spain 61 N5
Hughenden Queensland, Australia 133 N8
Hulun Nur Lake China 119 P4
Humber River England, UK 59 K13
Humboldt River Nevada, USA 34 H2
Hūn Libya 89 P7
Hungarian Plain Physical region Hungary 54, 71 L14
Hungary Country C Europe 70-71

Hungary 70-71

a Hungarian · **≋** Forint · **♦** 295 · **♥** 71 · **●** £0.44 · **✚** (m) 99% (f) 99% · **⌨** 410 · **✚** 330 · **❀** No · **⌂** 61% · **⌿** 3644

Huntington West Virginia, USA 29 O3
Huntington Beach California, USA 37 L19
Huntsville Alabama, USA 29 L6
Huron Ohio, USA 31 P10
Huron, Lake Lake Canada/USA 20, 24 J13, 31 O6
Hurunui River New Zealand 134 F10
Husum Germany 66 G6
Hutchinson Kansas, USA 33 O12
Huy Belgium 65 J14
Hvar Island Croatia 74 I8
Hwange (prev. Wankie) Zimbabwe 99 L8
Hwange N.P. National park Zimbabwe 99 L9
Hyargas, L. Lake Mongolia 118 J4
Hyderabad India 117 K11
Hyderabad Pakistan 116 H6
Hyères, Îles d' Island France 63 P14
Hyparis see Southern Bug
Hyvinkää Finland 57 O11

I

Ialomiţa River Romania 77 N9
Iaşi Romania 77 N3
Ibadan Nigeria 93 N12
Ibagué Colombia 44 E7
Ibar River Serbia, Yugoslavia 75 N9
Ibarra Ecuador 44 C8
Ibb Yemen 108 I16
Iberian Pen. Physical region SW Europe 54
Ibiza Ibiza, Balearic Islands, Spain 61 P10
Ibiza Island Balearic Islands, Spain 61 P10
Ibotirama Brazil 47 L11
Ibrī Oman 109 O12
Ica Peru 45 E14
Iceland Country Atlantic Ocean 51, 52 J7

Iceland 52

a Icelandic · **≋** Krona · **♦** 7 · **♥** 78 · **●** £2.72 · **✚** (m) 100% (f) 100% · **⌨** 320 · **✚** 376 · **❀** No · **⌂** 91% · **⌿** 3611

Iceland Island Atlantic Ocean 8, 10, 20, 103
Icosium see Algiers
Idaho State USA 32
Idaho Falls Idaho, USA 32 H8
Idfu Egypt 90 G8
Ieper Belgium 65 C15
Iglesias Sardinia 73 C15
Igoumenitsa Greece 78 F5

a Language (official or most commonly spoken) · **≋** Currency · **♦** Population density per square mile · **♥** Average life expectancy · **●** Price of 1 dozen hen's eggs · **⌨** Literacy · **⌨** Number of TVs per 1,000 people · **✚** Number of people per doctor · **❀** Death penalty · **⌂** Percentage of urban-based population · **⌿** Average number of calories consumed daily per person

145

Kampuchea *see* Cambodia
Kam'yanets'-Podil's'kyy (var. Kamenets-Podol'skiy) Ukraine 84 G6
Kananga (prev. Luluabourg) Zaire 95 K15
Kanazawa Japan 122 H10
Kanchanaburi Thailand 125 I12
Kandahar *see* Qandahār
Kandi Benin 93 N10
Kandla India 116 H7
Kandy Sri Lanka 117 L16
Kangaroo I. *Island* South Australia, Australia 133 L14
Kangchenjunga *Mountain* China 115
Kangean *Island* Indonesia 126 J14
Kanggye North Korea 121 P6
Kangnŭng South Korea 121 Q7
Kanjiža Serbia, Yugoslavia 75 M3
Kankakee Illinois, USA 31 L11
Kankan Guinea 92 I10
Kano Nigeria 93 P10
Kanpur India 117 L6
Kansas *State* USA 33
Kansas City Kansas, USA 33 Q11
Kansas City Missouri, USA 33 Q11
Kansk Russian Federation 113 K10
Kao-hsiung Taiwan 121 O14
Kaolack Senegal 92 F8
Kap Farvel *see* Farvel, Cape
Kapchagay Kazakhstan 112 H13
Kapfenberg Austria 69 Q7
Kapos *River* Hungary 71 K15
Kapuas *River* Borneo, Indonesia 126 I11
Kara Togo 93 M11
Kara-Balta Kyrgyzstan 111 Q4
Kara-Bogaz-Gol, Zaliv *Bay* Turkmenistan 110 F5
Kara Deniz *see* Black Sea
Kara Kum *Desert region* Turkmenistan 11, 103
Kara Sea Russian Federation 51 S11, 54, 82 O5, 103, 112 I5
Kara Strait *Channel* Russian Federation 82 N6
Karabük Turkey 105 K5
Karachi Pakistan 100 H5, 116 G6
Karaganda (var. Qaraghandy) Kazakhstan 112 G11
Karaginskiy Is. *Island Group* Russian Federation 113 Q5
Karagiya Depression *Physical region* Asia 103
Karaj Iran 109 N4
Karakaya Barrage *Dam* Turkey 105 P8
Karakinit Gulf *Sea feature* Ukraine 84 J9
Karakorum Mts. *Mountain range* C Asia 118 E9
Karaköse *see* Ağri
Karakum Canal *Waterway* Turkmenistan 111 K9
Karaman Turkey 105 K9
Karamay China 118 H5
Karasburg Namibia 98 I13
Karasjok Norway 57 O2
Karbala Iraq 109 K5
Karditsa Greece 78 I6
Kariba Dam *Dam* Zambia/Zimbabwe 97 K15
Kariba, L. *Reservoir* Zambia/Zimbabwe 87, 97 K15, 99 L8
Karimata *Island* Indonesia 126 H12
Karisimbi, Mt. *Volcano* Zaire 87
Karlovac Croatia 74 H4
Karlovy Vary Czech Republic 70 G8
Karlskrona Sweden 57 K15
Karlsruhe Germany 67 F14
Karlstad Sweden 57 K12
Karpathos *Island* Dodecanese, Greece 79 Q15
Kars Turkey 105 R5
Karshi Uzbekistan 111 L8
Karymskaya Sopka *Volcano* Siberia 103
Karystos Greece 79 L9
Kasai *River* Angola/Zaire 95 J14
Kasama Zambia 97 M11
Kasese Uganda 97 L4
Kāshān Iran 109 N5
Kashgar *see* Kashi
Kashi (var. Kashgar) China 118 E8
Kashmir *Region* S Asia 117 K2
Kaskaskia *River* Illinois, USA 31 K13
Kasongo Zaire 95 N14
Kassala Sudan 91 I12
Kassandra, Gulf of *Sea feature* Greece 79 K4
Kassel Germany 67 H11
Kastamonu Turkey 105 L5
Kastoria Greece 78 H3
Kastorias, L. *Lake* Greece 78 H3
Kasumi Lagoon *Coastal feature* Japan 122 L10
Kasungu *National park* Malawi 97 M13
Kasur Pakistan 116 J3
Katakolo Greece 78 H10
Katar *see* Qatar
Katavi *National park* Tanzania 97 M9
Katerini Greece 78 I4
Katha Burma 124 G6
Kathmandu Nepal 117 N5
Katowice Poland 71 L9
Katsberg Tunnel *Tunnel* Austria 69 O9
Katsina Nigeria 93 P9
Kattegat *Channel* Denmark/Sweden 56 I14
Kaub *Castle* Germany 67 E12
Kaufmann Peak *see* Lenin Peak
Kaunas Lithuania 80 I9
Kavadarci Macedonia 75 O12
Kavala Greece 79 L2
Kawa *Archaeological site* Sudan 91 F11
Kawasaki Japan 123 K11
Kayan *River* Borneo, Indonesia 127 K10
Kayes Mali 92 H8
Kayseri Turkey 105 M8
Kazakh Uplands *Physical region* Kazakhstan 112 G11

Kazakhstan *Country* C Asia 112

Kazakhstan 112

a Kazakh • 🗪 Afghani • ♦ 16 • ♥ 69 • ◔ N/A • ♥ N/A • 🏚 58%

Kazan' Russian Federation 83 J11
Kazanlŭk Bulgaria 77 L13
Kéa *Island* Cyclades, Greece 79 L10
Keban Barrage *Dam* Turkey 105 O7
Kecskemét Hungary 71 M14
Kėdainiai Lithuania 80 I9
Kediri Java, Indonesia 126 I15
Keetmanshoop Namibia 98 I12
Keewatin *Region* Northwest Territories, Canada 23 N9
Kefallonia *Island* Ionian Is. Greece 78 G8
Kegon Falls *Waterfall* Japan 115
Kelang Malaysia 125 J19
Kelkit *River* Turkey 105 P6
Kellett, Cape *Cape* Canada 51 N8
Kelmė Lithuania 80 H8
Kelud *Volcano* Java, Indonesia 115
Kem' Russian Federation 82 I6
Kemerovo Russian Federation 112 I10
Kemi Finland 57 O6
Kemi *River* Finland 57 O5
Kemijärvi Finland 57 P5
Kenai Alaska, USA 22 G8
Kendari Celebes, Indonesia 127 M13
Kenema Sierra Leone 92 H12
Kenge Zaire 95 I14
Kénitra Morocco 88 I5
Kennebec *River* Maine, USA 27 P5
Kennedy Space Center Florida, USA 29 O12
Kennewick Washington, USA 36 K8
Kenora Ontario, Canada 24 F9
Kenosha Wisconsin, USA 31 L9
Kentucky *River* Kentucky, USA 29 N3
Kentucky *State* USA 29
Kenya *Country* E Africa 97

Kenya 97

a Swahili • 🗪 Shilling • ♦ 114 • ♥ 59 • ◔ £0.46 • ♥ (m) 80% (f) 59% • 🖵 9 • ✚ 6552 • ❦ Yes • 🏚 24% • 🍴 2163

Kenya, Mt. *National park* Kenya 97 P5
Kerch Ukraine 85 L9
Kerch Strait (var. Kerchens'ka Protoka) *Channel* Russian Federation/Ukraine 54, 83 C14, 85 L9
Kerchens'ka Protoka *see* Kerch Strait
Kerguelen *Island group* Indian Ocean 101 H14
Kerguelen I. *Island* Indian Ocean, Antarctica 50 I7
Kerguelen Plateau *Sea feature* Indian Ocean 101 H14
Kermadec Is. *Island group* Polynesia, Pacific Ocean 128 I11
Kermadec Trench *Sea feature* Pacific Ocean 128 J11
Kermān Iran 109 P8
Kermanshah *see* Bakhtarān
Kerulen (var. Herlen Gol) *River* Mongolia/China 103, 114, 119 N4
Ket' *River* Russian Federation 112 I10
Ketchikan Alaska, USA 22 I12
Kewanee Illinois, USA 30 J11
Keweenaw Bay *Physical feature* Michigan, USA 31 L4
Key West Florida, USA 29 N16
Khabarovsk Russian Federation 113 P11
Khambhat, Gulf of *Sea feature* India 116 I9
Khamīs Mushayṭ Saudi Arabia 108 I13
Khān Yūnis Gaza Strip 107 K11
Khānaqīn Iraq 109 L4
Khanka, Lake *Lake* 115
Khankendy *see* Xankändi
Kharkiv (var. Kharkov) Ukraine 85 L5
Kharkov *see* Kharkiv
Khartoum (var. El Khartûm) Sudan 91 G12
Khartoum North Sudan 91 G12
Khasab Oman 109 O10
Khashm el Girba Dam *Dam* Sudan 91 I12
Khaskovo Bulgaria 77 L14
Khatanga *River* Russian Federation 113 K6
Khaybar Saudi Arabia 108 I13
Kherson Ukraine 84 J8
Khmel'nyts'kyy Ukraine 84 G5
Khodzheyli Uzbekistan 110 I5
Khon Kaen Thailand 125 K11
Khorog Tajikistan 111 P9
Khorramshahr Iran 109 L7
Khouribga Morocco 88 H5
Khudzhand (prev. Leninabad) Tajikistan 111 O7
Khulna Bangladesh 117 P8
Khyber Pass *Physical feature* Afghanistan/Pakistan 111 O12
Kičevo Macedonia 75 N12
Kidepo *National park* Uganda 97 N2
Kiel Germany 66 H6
Kiel Canal *Waterway* Germany 66 G6
Kielce Poland 71 M7
Kieta Bougainville, Papua New Guinea 133 Q2
Kiev (var. Kiyiv) Ukraine 84 I4
Kiev Res. *Reservoir* Ukraine 84 I4
Kiffa Mauritania 92 H7
Kigali Rwanda 97 L6
Kigoma Tanzania 97 L8
Kikwit Zaire 95 J14
Kilimanjaro *National park* Kenya/Tanzania 97 P6

Kilimanjaro *Volcano* Tanzania 87
Kilis Turkey 105 N10
Kilkis Greece 78 J2
Killarney Ireland 59 B14
Kilwa Masoko Tanzania 97 Q10
Kimberley South Africa 99 K13
Kimberley Plateau *Physical region* Western Australia, Australia 131, 132 I6
Kimito *Island* Finland 57 N11
Kindu Zaire 95 M13
King I. *Island* Tasmania, Australia 133 M15
King Leopold Ranges *Mountain range* Western Australia, Australia 132 H7
King William I. *Island* Northwest Territories, Canada 23 N7
King's Lynn England, UK 59 L14
Kingman Reef *Dependent territory* Polynesia, Pacific Ocean 129 K7
Kingston Jamaica 42 J8
Kingston New York, USA 27 L10
Kingston Ontario, Canada 25 L14
Kingston-upon-Hull England, UK 59 K13
Kingstown St Vincent & The Grenadines 43 T14
Kinshasa (prev. Léopoldville) Zaire 95 H14
Kintyre *Peninsula* Scotland, UK 58 F10
Kirghiz Range *Mountain range* Kazakhstan/Kyrgyzstan 111 P5
Kirghiz Steppe *Physical Region* Kazakhstan 103, 112 F10
Kiribati *Country* Micronesia/Polynesia, Pacific Ocean 128 J8

Kiribati 128

a English, I Kiribati • 🗪 Dollar • ♦ 259 • ♥ 56 • ◔ £2.45 • ♥ (av.) 10% • 🏚 36%

Kirikkale Turkey 105 L6
Kirinyaga *Volcano* Kenya 87
Kiritimati (var. Christmas Island) *Dependent territory* Pacific Ocean 128 L8
Kirkenes Norway 57 P2
Kirklareli Turkey 104 G4
Kirksville Missouri, USA 33 R10
Kirkuk Iraq 109 K3
Kirkwall Orkney Scotland, UK 58 J6
Kirov Russian Federation 82 J10
Kirovabad *see* Gäncä
Kirovakan *see* Vanadzor
Kirovohrad (var. Yelyzavethrad) Ukraine 84 J6
Kirşehir Turkey 105 L7
Kisangani (prev. Stanleyville) Zaire 95 M12
Kishinev *see* Chişinău
Kiska I. *Island* Aleutian Is. Alaska, USA 22 A5
Kismaayo Somalia 91 L18
Kisumu Kenya 97 N4
Kitakyūshū Japan 123 C13
Kitale Kenya 97 N4
Kitami Japan 122 M3
Kitchener Ontario, Canada 25 K14
Kīthnos *Island* Cyclades, Greece 79 L11
Kitikmeot *Region* Northwest Territories, Canada 23 M7
Kitimat British Columbia, Canada 23 I12
Kitwe Zambia 97 K13
Kitzbühel Austria 69 M8
Kiunga Marine Reserve *Nature reserve* Kenya 97 R6
Kivu, L. *Lake* Rwanda/Zaire 95 O13, 97 L6
Kiyiv *see* Kiev
Kizilirmak *River* Turkey 105 M7
Kizyl-Arbat Turkmenistan 110 H7
Kizyl-Atrek Turkmenistan 110 G8
Kjølen Mts. *Mountain range* Norway/Sweden 54, 57 K6
Klagenfurt Austria 69 P9
Klaipėda Lithuania 80 G8
Klamath Falls Oregon, USA 37 H11
Klerksdorp South Africa 99 K12
Ključ Bosnia and Herzegovina 74 I6
Klosterneuburg Austria 69 S4
Kluane L. *Lake* Yukon Territory, Canada 22 H9
Klyuchevskaya Sopka *Volcano* Siberia 103
Knin Croatia 74 I6
Knittelfeld Austria 69 Q8
Knossos *Archaeological site* Crete, Greece 79 M16
Knoxville Tennessee, USA 29 N5
Knud Rasmussen Land *Physical region* Greenland 51 O12
Ko Phangan *see* Phangan I.
Ko Phuket *see* Phuket I.
Ko Samui *see* Samui I.
Kōbe Japan 15, 123 G12, 128 G5
Koblenz Germany 67 E12
Kobryn Belarus 80 I14
Kočani Macedonia 75 P11
Kōchi Japan 123 F13
Kodiak Kodiak I. Alaska, USA 22 F9
Kodiak I. *Island* Alaska, USA 20, 22 F9
Kohima India 117 Q7
Kohtla-Järve Estonia 81 L2
Kokand Uzbekistan 111 O6
Kokchetav (var. Kökshetaū) Kazakhstan 112 G10
Kokkola Finland 57 N8
Kokomo Indiana, USA 31 M11
Kokshaal-Tau Mts. *Mountain range* China/Kyrgyzstan 111 S5
Kökshetaū *see* Kokchetav
Kola Peninsula *Physical feature* Russian Federation 54, 82 J6
Kolda Senegal 92 G8
Kolguyev I. *Island* Russian Federation 82 M6
Kolka Latvia 80 H4

Köln *see* Cologne
Kolonia *see* Palikir
Kolubara *River* Serbia, Yugoslavia 75 M6
Kolwezi Zaire 95 M17
Kolyma *River* Russian Federation 113 O5
Kolyma Range *Mountain range* Russian Federation 113 P6
Kom Ombo *Archaeological site* Egypt 90 G9
Kommunizma, Pik *see* Communism Peak
Komoé *River* Ivory Coast 93 K11
Komoran *Island* Indonesia 127 T15
Komotini Greece 79 N2
Komsomol'sk-na-Amure Russian Federation 113 P10
Kongolo Zaire 95 N14
Kongsberg Norway 56 I11
Königsberg *see* Kaliningrad
Konjic Bosnia and Herzegovina 75 K7
Konstanz Germany 67 G16
Konya Turkey 105 K9
Kopaonik *Mountain range* Serbia, Yugoslavia 75 N8
Koper Slovenia 74 F3
Koprivnica Croatia 74 J2
Korarnikhon Tajikistan 111 N8
Korčula *Island* Croatia 74 I9
Korçë Albania 75 N13
Korčulanski Kanal *Channel* Croatia 74 I8
Korea *Region* E Asia 115
Korea Bay *Sea feature* Korea/China 121 O7
Korea Strait *Channel* Korea/Japan 115, 121 Q9, 123 B13
Korhogo Ivory Coast 92 J11
Kōriyama Japan 122 K9
Korkodon *River* Russian Federation 113 P5
Korla China 118 H7
Kornat *Island* Croatia 74 H7
Koror Palau, Pacific Ocean 128 G8
Körös *River* Hungary 71 M14
Korosten' Ukraine 84 H4
Kortrijk (var. Courtrai) Belgium 65 D15
Koryak Range *Mountain range* Russian Federation 113 Q4
Kos Kos, Greece 79 Q12
Kos *Island* Dodecanese, Greece 79 Q12
Kosciusko, Mt. *Mountain* Australia 131
Košice Slovakia 71 N11
Kossou, L. de *Lake* Ivory Coast 92 J12
Kosti Sudan 91 G13
Kostroma Russian Federation 82 H9
Koszalin Poland 70 J2
Kota India 116 J6
Kota Baharu Malaysia 125 J17
Kota Kinabalu Borneo, Malaysia 126 J8
Kotka Finland 57 P11
Kotlas Russian Federation 82 J9
Kotto *River* Central African Republic/Zaire 94 L9
Kotzebue Alaska, USA 22 G5
Kotzebue Sound *Sea feature* Alaska, USA 22 F4
Koudougou Burkina 93 L9
Kourou French Guiana 44 P6
Kousseri (prev. Fort-Foureau) Cameroon 94 H7
Kouvola Finland 57 P11
Kowl-e-Namaksār *Salt pan* Afghanistan/Iran 110 J12
Kowloon Hong Kong 121 M14
Kozani Greece 78 H4
Kra, Isthmus of *Physical region* Thailand 115, 125 H15
Krâcheh Cambodia 125 M13
Kragujevac Serbia, Yugoslavia 75 N7
Krak des Chevaliers Syria 107 M5
Krakatau *Volcano* Indonesia 9, 114
Kraków (var. Cracow) Poland 71 M9
Kralendijk Netherlands Antilles 43 O14
Kraljevo Serbia, Yugoslavia 75 N7
Kramators'k Ukraine 85 L6
Kranj Slovenia 74 G2
Krāslava Latvia 81 K8
Krasnoarmeysk Russian Federation 82 H13
Krasnodar Russian Federation 83 D14
Krasnovodsk Turkmenistan 110 F6
Krasnoyarsk Russian Federation 112 J10
Krefeld Germany 67 D11
Kremenchuk Ukraine 84 J6
Kremenchuk Res. *Reservoir* Ukraine 84 J5
Krems Austria 69 Q4
Kretinga Lithuania 80 G7
Kribi Cameroon 95 E11
Krichev *see* Krychaw
Krishna *River* India 115, 116 J11
Kristiansand Norway 56 H12
Kristianstad Sweden 57 K15
Kristiansund Norway 52 I7
Krivoy Rog *see* Kryvyy Rih
Krk *Island* Croatia 74 G4
Krka *River* Croatia 74 H7
Krŏng Kaôh Kŏng Cambodia 125 K14
Kruger N.P. *National park* South Africa 99 M11
Krung Thep *see* Bangkok
Kruševac Serbia, Yugoslavia 75 O8
Krychaw (var. Krichev) Belarus 81 O12
Krym *see* Crimea
Kryvyy Rih (var. Krivoy Rog) Ukraine 84 J7
Krzna *River* Belarus/Poland 71 O5
Kuala Belait Brunei 126 J9
Kuala Lumpur Malaysia 125 J19
Kuala Terengganu Malaysia 125 K18
Kualakapuas Borneo, Indonesia 126 J13
Kuantan Malaysia 125 K18
Kuba *see* Quba
Kuban *River* Russian Federation 83 E14
Kuching Borneo, Malaysia 126 H10
Kudat Borneo, Malaysia 127 K8
Kufstein Austria 69 M7
Kuito Angola 98 H6

a Language (official or most commonly spoken) • 🗪 Currency • ♦ Population density per square mile • ♥ Average life expectancy • ◔ Price of 1 dozen hen's eggs • ♥ Literacy • 🖵 Number of TVs per 1,000 people • ✚ Number of people per doctor • ❦ Death penalty • 🏚 Percentage of urban-based population • 🍴 Average number of calories consumed daily per person

147

Londinium see London
London (anc. Londinium) England, UK 14, 59 K16
London Ontario, Canada 24 J15
Londonderry Northern Ireland, UK 58 E10
Londonderry, C. *Cape* Western Australia, Australia 132 H5
Londrina Brazil 47 I14
Long Beach California, USA 37 K19, 129 N5
Long Branch New Jersey, USA 27 L13
Long I. *Island* Bahamas 43 L4
Long I. *Island* New York, USA 27 N12
Long Xuyen Vietnam 125 M15
Longmont Colorado, USA 35 M4
Longreach Queensland, Australia 133 N9
Longview Washington, USA 36 H8
Longyearbyen Svalbard, Arctic Ocean 51 Q13
Lop Nur *Lake* China 115, 118 I8
Lopatka, C. *Cape* Russian Federation 113 R8
Lord Howe I. *Island* Australia, Pacific Ocean 128 I11
Lord Howe Rise *Sea feature* Pacific Ocean 128 I12, 131
Lord Howe Seamounts *Sea feature* Pacific Ocean 131
Lorengau Admiralty Is. Papua New Guinea 133 O1
Lorient France 52 K8, 62 G7
Los Alamos New Mexico, USA 35 L7
Los Angeles California, USA 14, 37 K18
Los Angeles Chile 49 G12
Los Mochis Mexico 38 I7
Lošinj *Island* Croatia 74 G5
Lot *River* France 63 K12
Lötschberg Tunnel *Tunnel* Switzerland 68 F11
Louang Namtha Laos 124 J8
Louang Phrabang Laos 124 K9
Loubomo Congo 95 G14
Louga Senegal 92 F8
Louise, L. *Lake* Alberta, Canada 23 L14
Louisiade Archipelago *Island group* Papua New Guinea 133 P4
Louisiana *State* USA 28
Louisville Kentucky, USA 29 M3
Lourenço Marques see Maputo
Loutra Aidipsou Greece 78 J7
Louvain see Leuven
Lovech Bulgaria 77 K12
Lowell Massachusetts, USA 27 O9
Lower Red L. *Lake* Minnesota, USA 30 G3
Lower Tunguska *River* Russian Federation 113 L9
Lower Zambezi *National park* Zambia 97 L14
Loznica Serbia, Yugoslavia 75 L6
Lualaba *River* Zaire 95 M13
Luanda (prev. Loanda) Angola 98 G4
Luang Lagoon *Coastal feature* Thailand 125 I16
Luangwa *River* Zambia 97 M12
Luangwa, N. *National park* Zambia 97 M12
Luangwa, S. *National park* Zambia 97 M13
Luanshya Zambia 97 K13
Lubana, L. *Lake* Latvia 81 K6
Lubango Angola 98 G7
Lubbock Texas, USA 35 O9
Lübeck Germany 66 I7
Lublin Poland 71 O7
Lubumbashi (prev. Elisabethville) Zaire 95 N17
Lucapa Angola 98 I4
Lucca Italy 72 F9
Lucena Luzon, Philippines 127 L4
Lučenec Slovakia 71 L12
Lucerne (var. Luzern) Switzerland 68 G10
Lucerne, L. of *Lake* Switzerland 68 G10
Lucknow India 117 L6
Lüderitz Namibia 53 M14, 98 H12
Ludhiana India 117 K4
Ludza Latvia 81 L7
Lugano Switzerland 68 H12
Lugano, L. *Lake* Italy/Switzerland 68 H12
Lugansk see Luhans'k
Lugenda *River* Mozambique 99 O6
Lugo Spain 60 G3
Luhans'k (var. Lugansk; prev. Voroshilovgrad) Ukraine 85 M6
Luik see Liège
Luke Air Force Range *Military center* Arizona, USA 34 H10
Lukusuzi *National park* Zambia 97 M13
Lule *River* Sweden 57 M4
Luleå Sweden 57 N6
Lulonga *River* Zaire 95 J12
Lulua *River* Angola/Zaire 95 L16
Luluabourg see Kananga
Lumbala N'guimbo Angola 98 J6
Lumphat Cambodia 125 N13
Lundazi Zambia 97 N13
Lundy *Island* England, UK 59 F16
Lüneburg Germany 66 I8
Luninyets Belarus 81 K14
Luoyang China 121 L9
Lusaka Zambia 97 K15
Lusambo Zaire 95 L14
Luton England, UK 59 K15
Luts'k Ukraine 84 F4
Lutzow-Holm Bay *Sea feature* Indian Ocean Coast, Antarctica 50 G6
Luxembourg *Country* W Europe 65

Luxembourg 65

a French, German, Litzebuergish · 🏛 Franc · ♦ 379 · ● 75 · ◒ £1.67 · ♥ (m) 100% (f) 100% · ⊡ 255 · ✚ 529 · ❊ No · ⌂ 84% · ⑪ 3902

Luxor Egypt 90 G8
Luzern see Lucerne
Luzon *Island* Philippines 127 M3
Luzon Strait *Channel* Philippines 127 L1
Lužnice *River* Czech Republic 70 H10
L'viv (var. L'vov) Ukraine 84 F5
L'vov see L'viv
Lyepyel' ('var. Lepel') Belarus 81 M10
Lyme Bay *Sea feature* England, UK 59 H17
Lynchburg Virginia, USA 29 Q4
Lynn Massachusetts, USA 27 O9
Lynn Lake Manitoba, Canada 23 N12
Lyon France 63 N10

M

Ma'ān Jordan 107 M12
Maarianhamina Finland 57 M11
Maas *River* Germany/Netherlands 65 L12
Maastricht Netherlands 65 K15
Mabaruma Guyana 44 L5
Macao *Dependent territory* SE China 121 M14
Macao Macao, SE China 121 M14
Macapá Brazil 46 I7
Macdonald Is. *Island group* Indian Ocean 101 H15
Macdonnell Ranges *Mountain range* Northern Territory, Australia 131, 132 J9
Macedonia (var. Makedonija) *Country* SE Europe 75

Macedonia 75

a Macedonian · 🏛 Denar · ♦ 191 · ● 72 · ◒ N/A · ♥ (av.) 93% · ⌂ 54%

Maceió Brazil 46 O10
Machakos Kenya 97 P5
Machala Ecuador 44 B9
Machu Picchu *Archaeological site* Peru 45 F13
Mackay Queensland, Australia 133 O8
Mackay, L. *Lake* Northern Territory/Western Australia, Australia 131, 132 I9
Mackenzie *River* Northwest Territories, Canada 10, 20, 23 K9
Mackenzie *River basin* N America 11
Mackenzie Bay *Sea feature* Indian Ocean Coast, Antarctica 50 G8
Mackenzie Bay *Sea feature* Northwest territories/Yukon Territory, Canada 22 J6
Mackenzie King I. *Island* Northwest Territories, Canada 23 L4
Mackenzie Mts. *Mountain range* Northwest Territories, Canada 22 J9
Mackinac, Strait of *Channel* Michigan, USA 31 N5
Macleod, L. *Lake* Western Australia, Australia 132 E9
Macomb Illinois, USA 30 J12
Mâcon France 63 N9
Macon Georgia, USA 29 N8
Macoraba see Mecca
Macquarie I *Island* Pacific Ocean 128 I13
Macquarie Ridge *Sea feature* Pacific Ocean 128 I13, 131
Madagascár *Country* Indian Ocean 100

Madagascar 100

a French, Malagasy · 🏛 Franc · ♦ 54 · ● 51 · ◒ £1.09 · ♥ (m) 88% (f) 73% · ⌂ 24%

Madagascar *Island* Indian Ocean 87
Madagascar Basin *Sea feature* Indian Ocean 87, 101 F11
Madagascar Ridge *Sea feature* Indian Ocean 87, 101 E12
Madang Papua New Guinea 133 N2
Madeira *Island* Atlantic Ocean 52 J9
Madeira *Island group* Atlantic Ocean 87
Madeira *River* Bolivia/Brazil 41, 46 F8
Madeira Ridge *Sea feature* Atlantic Ocean 54, 87
Madeleine, Îles de la (var. Magdalen Is.) *Island group* Quebec, Canada 26 Q10
Madison Wisconsin, USA 31 K8
Madona Latvia 81 K6
Madras India 100 I7, 117 L13
Madre de Dios *River* Bolivia/Peru 45 H13
Madrid Spain 61 K8
Madura *Island* Indonesia 126 I14
Madurai India 117 K15
Mae Khlong (var. Meklong) *River* Thailand 125 H12
Maebashi Japan 122 J10
Mafeteng Lesotho 99 L14
Mafia I. *Island* Tanzania 97 Q10
Magadan Russian Federation 113 P7
Magdalen Is. see Madeleine, Îles de la
Magdalena *River* Colombia 41, 44 E5
Magdeburg Germany 66 J9
Magellan, Strait of *Channel* Chile 41, 49 I20
Magerøy *Island* Norway 57 P1
Maggiore, L. *Lake* Italy/Switzerland 68 G12, 72 F6
Magnitogorsk Russian Federation 112 F9
Mahabalipuram India 117 L13
Mahajanga Madagascar 100 E10
Mahalapye Botswana 99 L10
Mahanadi *River* India 117 N9
Mahé *Island* Seychelles 100 F9
Mahilyow (var. Mogilev) Belarus 81 N11
Mahón Minorca, Spain 61 S8

Mai-Ndombe, L *Lake* Zaire 95 J13
Maiduguri Nigeria 93 R10
Main *River* Germany 67 G13
Maine *State* USA 27 P4
Mainz Germany 67 F13
Maitland New South Wales, Australia 133 P12
Majorca (var. Mallorca) *Island* Balearic Islands, Spain 61 R8
Majuro Marshall Islands, Pacific Ocean 128 I8
Makarikari see Makgadikgadi Pans
Makassar see Ujung Pandang
Makassar Strait *Channel* Borneo/Celebes, Indonesia 127 K13
Makedonija see Macedonia
Makeni Sierra Leone 92 H11
Makeyevka see Makiyivka
Makgadikgadi Pans (var. Makarikari, Soa Salt Pan) *Salt basin* Botswana 99 K9
Makhachkala Russian Federation 83 F16
Makiyivka (var. Makeyevka) Ukraine 85 M7
Makkah see Mecca
Makkovik Newfoundland, Canada 25 Q6
Makokou Gabon 95 G12
Makran *Physical region* Pakistan 116 F5
Makurdi Nigeria 93 P12
Malabar Coast *Coastal region* India 116 I14
Malabo Equatorial Guinea 95 E11
Malacca see Melaka
Malacca, Strait of *Channel* SE Asia 100 L8, 115, 130
Maladzyechna (var. Molodechno) Belarus 81 K11
Málaga Spain 60 J14
Malakal Sudan 91 G15
Malang Java, Indonesia 126 I15
Malanje Angola 98 H4
Malatya Turkey 105 O8
Malawi *Country* C Africa 97

Malawi 97

a English · 🏛 Kwacha · ♦ 242 · ● 46 · ◒ £0.68 · ♥ (m) 34% (f) 12% · ⌂ 12%

Malay Pen. *Peninsula* SE Asia 115
Malaya see Malaysia
Malaysia (prev. Malaya) *Country* SE Asia 125

Malaysia 125

a Malay · 🏛 Ringgit · ♦ 144 · ● 70 · ◒ £0.65 · ♥ (m) 87% (f) 70% · ⊡ 148 · ✚ 2708 · ❊ Yes · ⌂ 43% · ⑪ 2774

Malaysia (East) Borneo, SE Asia 126
Maldive Ridge *Sea feature* Indian Ocean 100 H9
Maldives *Country* Indian Ocean 100 I8

Maldives 100

a Divehi · 🏛 Rufiyya · ♦ 1908 · ● 62 · ◒ £1.33 · ♥ (m) 91% (f) 92% · ⌂ 30%

Male Maldives 100 I8
Malheur L. *Lake* Oregon, USA 36 K10
Mali (prev. French Sudan) *Country* W Africa 92-93

Mali 92-93

a French · 🏛 Franc · ♦ 18 · ● 48 · ◒ £1.41 · ♥ (m) 41% (f) 24% · ⌂ 19%

Mali Hka *River* Burma 115
Malindi Kenya 97 Q7
Malines see Mechelen
Mallaig Scotland, UK 58 G8
Mallorca see Majorca
Malmédy Belgium 65 L16
Malmö Sweden 56 J15
Malta (var. Melita) *Country* Europe 73

Malta 73

a Maltese, English · 🏛 Lira · ♦ 2881 · ● 74 · ◒ £0.78 · ♥ (m) 96% (f) 96% · ⌂ 87%

Maltahöhe Namibia 98 H11
Maluku see Moluccas
Mamberamo *River* Indonesia 127 S12
Mamoré *River* Bolivia 45 J14
Mamry, L. *Lake* Poland 71 N3
Man Ivory Coast 92 I12
Man, Isle of *Dependent territory* W Europe 59 G12
Manado Celebes, Indonesia 127 N10
Managua Nicaragua 42 D11
Managua, L. *Lake* Nicaragua 42 D10
Manam *Volcano* New Guinea 131
Manama (var. Al Manamah) Bahrain 100 F5, 109 M9
Manaslu *Mountain* China 115
Manaus Brazil 46 F8
Manchester England, UK 59 I13
Manchester New Hampshire, USA 27 N9
Manchuria *Region* China 121 P4
Manchurian Plain *Physical region* China 115
Mandalay Burma 124 G7
Mandera Kenya 97 R2
Mangalia Romania 77 P10
Mangalore India 116 I13
Mangla Res. *Reservoir* India/Pakistan 116 J2

Manguéni, Plateau du *Physical region* Niger 93 R5
Manhattan Kansas, USA 33 P11
Manicouagan Res. *Reservoir* Quebec, Canada 25 N9
Manila Philippines 15, 127 L4, 128 F7
Manisa Turkey 104 G8
Manistee Michigan, USA 31 M7
Manistee *River* Michigan, USA 31 M7
Manitoba *Province* Canada 23
Manitoba, L. *Lake* Manitoba, Canada 20
Manitowoc Wisconsin, USA 31 L7
Manizales Colombia 44 E6
Mankato Minnesota, USA 30 H7
Mannar Sri Lanka 117 K15
Mannheim Germany 67 F13
Mannu *River* Sardinia 73 D15
Manokwari Irian Jaya, Indonesia 127 Q11
Manono Zaire 95 N15
Mansa Zambia 97 K12
Mansel I. *Island* Canada 25 K2
Mansfield Ohio, USA 31 P11
Manta Ecuador 44 B9
Mantova (var. Mantua) Italy 72 F7
Mantua see Mantova
Manyara *National park* Tanzania 97 O7
Manyara, L. *Lake* Tanzania 97 O7
Manzanillo Mexico 39 K12
Manzhouli China 119 P5
Manzini Swaziland 99 M12
Mao Chad 94 H7
Maoke Mts. New Guinea 115
Maputo (prev. Lourenço Marques) Mozambique 99 N12
Mar Chiquita, L. *Salt lake* Argentina 48 K8
Mar del Plata Argentina 49 N12, 53 F14
Maracaibo Venezuela 44 G4
Maracaibo, L. *Sea feature* Venezuela 41, 44 G5
Maracay Venezuela 44 I4
Maradi Niger 93 O9
Marajó I. *Island* Brazil 41
Maramba see Livingstone
Maranhão Res. *Reservoir* Portugal 60 G10
Marañón *River* Peru 41, 44 D10
Marathon *Archaeological site* Greece 79 L9
Marbella Spain 60 J14
Marche-en-Famenne Belgium 65 J17
Mardan Pakistan 116 I2
Mardin Turkey 105 Q9
Margarita Island *Island* Venezuela 44 J4
Margherita Peak *Volcano* Uganda 87
Mariana Trench *Sea feature* Pacific Ocean 8, 128 G6
Marías Is. *Island group* Mexico 38 J10
Ma'rib *Archaeological site* Yemen 109 I15
Maribor Slovenia 74 H2
Marie Byrd Land *Region* Antarctica 50 C10
Marie Galante *Island* Guadeloupe 43 T12
Mariental Namibia 98 I11
Mariestad Sweden 57 K12
Marijampolė Lithuania 80 H10
Marinette Wisconsin, USA 31 L6
Marion Indiana, USA 31 N11
Marion Ohio, USA 31 P11
Marion, L. *Lake* South Carolina, USA 29 P8
Maritsa *River* SE Europe 77 M14
Mariupol' Ukraine 85 L8
Marka Somalia 91 M18
Marmara, Sea of Turkey 104 H5
Marmaris Turkey 104 H10
Marne *River* France 63 M4
Maroua Cameroon 94 H8
Marowijne *River* French Guiana/Suriname 44 O7
Marquesas Is. *Island group* French Polynesia, Pacific Ocean 129 M9
Marquette Michigan, USA 31 L4
Marrakesh Morocco 88 H6
Marsá al Burayqah Libya 89 Q7
Marsa Matrûh Egypt 90 E6
Marsabit *National park* Kenya 97 P3
Marseille France 52 L8, 63 O14
Marsh I. *Island* Louisiana, USA 28 H10
Marshall Islands *Country* Micronesia, Pacific Ocean 128 I7

Marshall Islands 128

a English, Marshallese · 🏛 Dollar · ♦ 687 · ● 65 · ◒ £1.28 · ♥ (av.) 7% · ⌂ N/A

Marshfield Wisconsin, USA 30 J7
Martaban, Gulf of *Sea feature* Burma 125 G11
Martha's Vineyard *Island* Massachusetts, USA 27 O11
Martigny Switzerland 68 E12
Martin Slovakia 71 L10
Martinique *Dependent territory* Caribbean Sea 43 T13
Martre, Lac la *Lake* Northwest Territories, Canada 23 K9
Mary (prev. Merv) Turkmenistan 110 J9
Maryland *State* USA 29
Maryville Missouri, USA 33 Q10
Masada Israel 107 L11
Masai Mara *Nature reserve* Kenya 97 N5
Masai Steppe *Physical region* Tanzania 97 O8
Masaka Uganda 97 M5
Masbate Masbate, Philippines 127 M5
Masbate *Island* Philippines 127 M5
Mascarene Is. *Island group* Indian Ocean 101 G11
Mascarene Plateau *Sea feature* Indian Ocean 100 G10
Maseru Lesotho 99 L13
Mashhad Iran 109 Q4

a Language (official or most commonly spoken) · 🏛 Currency · ♦ Population density per square mile · ● Average life expectancy · ◒ Price of 1 dozen hen's eggs · ♥ Literacy · ⊡ Number of TVs per 1,000 people · ✚ Number of people per doctor · ❊ Death penalty · ⌂ Percentage of urban-based population · ⑪ Average number of calories consumed daily per person

149

Mozyr' *see* Mazyr
Mpika Zambia 97 M12
Mtwara Tanzania 97 Q11
Muang Khammouan (var. Thakhek) Laos 124 M10
Muang Không Laos 125 M12
Muang Lampang Thailand 124 I10
Muang Loei Thailand 124 K10
Muang Nan Thailand 124 J9
Muang Pakxan Laos 124 L10
Muang Phetchabun Thailand 125 J11
Muang Phitsanulok Thailand 125 I11
Muang Xaignabouri Laos 124 K9
Muang Yasothon Thailand 125 L11
Muchinga Mts. *Mountain range* Zambia 97 L13
Muck *Island* Scotland, UK 58 F8
Mufulira Zambia 97 K13
Muğla Turkey 104 H9
Mühlhausen Germany 67 I11
Mulhouse France 63 P6
Mull *Island* Scotland, UK 58 F9
Muller Mts. *Mountain range* Indonesia 126 I11
Multan Pakistan 116 I4
Mun, Mae Nam *River* Thailand 125 K12
Muna *Island* Indonesia 127 M13
München *see* Munich
Muncie Indiana, USA 31 N12
Munich (var. München) Germany 67 J16
Münster Germany 66 E10
Munzur Mts. *Mountain range* Turkey 105 P7
Muonio *River* Sweden 57 N3
Mupa N.P. *National park* Angola 98 H7
Muqdisho *see* Mogadishu
Mur (var. Mura) *River* Austria 69 P8
Mura (var. Mur) *River* Slovenia 74 I1
Murat *River* Turkey 105 Q7
Murchison *River* Western Australia, Australia 132 F10
Murchison Falls *National park* Uganda 97 M3
Murcia Spain 61 M12
Mureş Romania 76 H6
Murfreesboro Tennessee, USA 29 L5
Murgab *River* Turkmenistan 111 K10
Müritz, L. *Lake* Germany 66 L7
Murmansk Russian Federation 52 M7, 82 J5
Murmansk Rise *Sea feature* Barents Sea 54
Muroroa *Island* French Polynesia, Pacific Ocean 129 L10
Murray *River* New South Wales/South Australia, Australia 131, 133 L13
Murray Fracture Zone *Sea feature* Pacific Ocean 129 L5
Murrumbidgee *River* New South Wales, Australia 133 N13
Murzuq Libya 89 O9
Muş Turkey 105 R7
Muscat (var. Masqat) Oman 109 P12
Muscat and Oman *see* Oman
Muskegon Michigan, USA 31 M8
Muskegon *River* Michigan, USA 31 N7
Muskogee Oklahoma, USA 33 Q14
Musoma Tanzania 97 N5
Mussau I. *Island* Papua New Guinea 133 O1
Mutare (prev. Umtali) Zimbabwe 99 N9
Muynak Uzbekistan 110 I3
Mwanza Tanzania 97 M6
Mweru, L. *Lake* Zaire/Zambia 87, 95 O16, 97 K10
Mwene-Ditu Zaire 95 L15
Mweru Wantipa *National park* Zambia 97 K11
Myanmar *see* Burma
Mycenae *Archaeological site* Greece 78 J10
Myingyan Burma 124 F8
Myitkyina Burma 124 H5
Mykolayiv (var. Nikolayev) Ukraine 84 J8
Mykonos *Island* Cyclades, Greece 79 N10
Mymensingh Bangladesh 117 P7
Mysore India 116 J13
Mytilini Lesvos, Greece 79 O7
Mzuzu Malawi 97 N12

N

Naberezhnyye Chelny Russian Federation 83K11
Nacala Mozambique 99 Q7
Naestved Denmark 56 I16
Nafplio Greece 78 J10
Naga Cebu, Philippines 127 M4
Nagano Japan 122 J10
Nagarjuna Res. *Reservoir* India 117 K11
Nagasaki Japan 123 B14, 128 F6
Nagercoil India 116 J16
Nagorno-Karabakh *Region* Azerbaijan 85 R14
Nagoya Japan 123 I11
Nagpur India 117 K9
Nagqu China 118 I12
Nagykanizsa Hungary 70 J15
Naha Okinawa, Japan 123 A20
Nahuel Huapí, L. *Lake* Argentina 49 H14
Nain Newfoundland, Canada 25 P5
Nairobi Kenya 97 O5
Naissaar *Island* Estonia 80 I1
Najrān Saudi Arabia 108 I14
Nakamura Japan 123 E14
Nakhichevan' *see* Naxçivan
Nakhodka Russian Federation 112 I7
Nakhon Ratchasima Thailand 125 K12
Nakhon Sawan Thailand 125 I11
Nakhon Si Thammarat Thailand 125 I16
Nakina Ontario, Canada 24 H10
Nakskov Denmark 56 I16
Nakuru Kenya 97 O4
Nal'chik Russian Federation 83 E15
Nam Co *Lake* China 118 I12
Nam Dinh Vietnam 124 N9

Nam Ngum Dam Laos 124 K10
Nam Theun *River* Laos 124 M10
Namangan Uzbekistan 111 O6
Namen *see* Namur
Namib Desert *Desert region* SW Africa 11, 87, 98 H11
Namibe Angola 98 F7
Namibia (prev. South-West Africa) *Country* Southern Africa 98

Namibia 98

a English · **☷** Rand · **♦** 6 · **♥** 58 · **⌖** £2.44 ·
♆ (m) 74% (f) 71% · **⌂** 28%

Nampa Idaho, USA 32 F8
Namp'o North Korea 121 P7
Nampula Mozambique 99 P7
Namur (var. Namen) Belgium 65 H16
Nan Ling *Mountain range* 115
Nan'ao China 128 E6
Nanchang China 121 M12
Nancy France 63 O5
Nanded India 117 K10
Nanjing China 121 N10
Nanning China 121 K14
Nanping China 121 N12
Nansen Basin *Sea feature* Arctic Ocean 54, 103
Nantes France 62 H8
Nantucket I. *Island* Massachusetts, USA 27 P11
Napa Valley *Physical feature* California, USA 37 H14
Napier New Zealand 134 H7
Naples (var. Napoli) Italy 52 L9 73 K13
Naples, Bay of *Sea feature* Italy 73 K13
Napo *River* Ecuador/Peru 44 E9
Napoli *see* Naples
Narach, L. *Lake* Belarus 81 K10
Narathiwat Thailand 125 J17
Nares Plain *Sea feature* Atlantic Ocean 20
Nares Strait *Channel* Northwest Territories, Canada 23 O1
Narew *River* Poland/Belarus 71 N4
Narmada *River* India 115, 116 J8
Narsarsuaq Greenland 51 M15
Narva Estonia 81 L2
Narva *River* Estonia/Russian Federation 81 L2
Narvik Norway 57 M3
Naryn Kyrgyzstan 111 R5
Naryn *River* Kyrgyzstan 111 Q5
Nashua New Hampshire, USA 27 N9
Nashville Tennessee, USA 29 L4
Nasik India 116 I9
Nassau Bahamas 43 K2
Nasser, L. *Reservoir* Egypt/Sudan 87, 90 G9
Natal Brazil 46 O9
Natal *Region* South Africa 99 M13
Natal Basin *Sea feature* Indian Ocean 87
Natitingou Benin 93 M11
Natuna *Island* Natuna Is. Indonesia 126 H9
Natuna Is. *Island group* Indonesia 126 G10
Naturaliste, C. *Cape* Western Australia, Australia 132 F13
Naukuuft Park *National park* Namibia 98 H12
Nauru *Country* Micronesia, Pacific Ocean 128 I9

Nauru 128

a Nauruan · **☷** Dollar · **♦** 1122 · **♥** 67 · **⌖** £1.68 ·
♆ (m) 99% (f) 99% · **⌂** 100%

Navajo Dam *Dam* New Mexico, USA 35 L7
Navajo Indian Reservation *Reservation* USA 35 K8
Navapolatsk (var. Novopolotsk) Belarus 81 M8
Navarin, C. *Cape* Russian Federation 113 Q3, 128 J3
Navoi Uzbekistan 111 L7
Nawabshah Pakistan 116 H6
Naxçivan (var. Nakhichevan') Azerbaijan 85 Q15
Naxos *Island* Cyclades, Greece 79 N12
Nazareth Israel 107 L8
Nazca *Archaeological site* Peru 45 E14
Nazca Plate *Physical feature* 41
Nazilli Turkey 104 H9
N'Dalatando Angola 98 G4
Ndélé Central African Republic 94 K9
N'Djamena (prev. Fort Lamy) Chad 94 H7
Ndola Zambia 97 K13
Neagh, Lough *Lake* Northern Ireland, UK 59 E11
Neapoli Greece 78 J13
Nebitdag Turkmenistan 110 G7
Nebraska *State* USA 33
Nechako *River* Alberta/British Columbia, Canada 22 J13
Neches *River* Texas, USA 35 S11
Neckar *River* Germany 67 G15
Necochea Argentina 49 M12
Negev Desert *Desert region* Israel 107 L12
Negrais, Cape *Cape* Burma 125 E11
Negro *River* Argentina 49 K13
Negro *River* Brazil/Uruguay 48 O9
Negro, Rio *River* S America 41, 46 D7
Negros *Island* Philippines 127 M6
Nei Mongol *see* Inner Mongolia
Neiva Colombia 44 E7
Nejd *Region* Saudi Arabia 108 I9
Nekemte Ethiopia 91 I15
Nellis Air Force Range *Military center* Nevada, USA 34 G5
Nellore India 117 L12
Nelson New Zealand 134 F9

Nelson *River* Manitoba, Canada 23 O12
Néma Mauritania 92 J7
Neman (var. Nemunas) *River* Belarus/Lithuania 80 G9
Nemunas *see* Neman
Nemuro Japan 122 O3
Neosho *River* Kansas/Oklahoma, USA 33 P12
Nepal *Country* S Asia 117

Nepal 117

a Nepali · **☷** Rupee · **♦** 367 · **♥** 52 · **⌖** £0.38 ·
♆ (m) 38% (f) 13% · **⌂** 10%

Nepalganj Nepal 117 M5
Neretva *River* Bosnia and Herzegovina 75 K8
Neris *River* Belarus/Lithuania 80 I9
Nesebŭr Bulgaria 77 O13
Ness, Loch *Lake* Scotland, UK 58 H8
Netherlands *Country* Europe 64-65

Netherlands 64-65

a Dutch · **☷** Guilder · **♦** 1147 · **♥** 77 · **⌖** £1.08 ·
♆ (m) 99% (f) 99% · **⬚** 495 · **♣** 414 · **☠** No ·
⌂ 89% · **†⌐** 3151

Netherlands Antilles *Dependent territory* Caribbean Sea 20, 43 O14
Neubrandenburg Germany 66 L7
Neuchâtel Switzerland 68 E10
Neuchâtel, L. of *Lake* Switzerland 68 D10
Neufchâteau Belgium 65 J18
Neumünster Germany 66 H6
Neunkirchen Austria 69 R6
Neuquén Argentina 49 I13
Neuschwanstein *Castle* Germany 67 I16
Neusiedler L. *Lake* Austria/Hungary 69 S5
Nevada *State* USA 34
Nevada, Sierra *Mountain range* Spain 61 K13
Nevada Test Site *Military center* Nevada, USA 34 G6
Nevel' Russian Federation 82 E9
Nevers France 63 M8
Nevşehir Turkey 105 M8
New Albany Indiana, USA 31 N14
New Amsterdam Guyana 44 N6
New Amsterdam *see* New York City
New Bedford Massachusetts, USA 27 O11
New Britain *Island* Papua New Guinea 131, 133 P2
New Britain Trench *Sea feature* Pacific Ocean 131
New Brunswick New Jersey, USA 27 L12
New Brunswick *Province* Canada 25
New Caledonia *Dependent territory* Melanesia, Pacific Ocean 128 H10
New Caledonia *Island* Melanesia, Pacific Ocean 131
New Caledonia Basin *Sea feature* Pacific Ocean 131
New Castle Pennsylvania, USA 26 G11
New Delhi India 117 K5
New England *Physical region* USA 27 O6
New Guinea *Island* Indonesia/Papua New Guinea 115, 128 G9, 131, 133 M2
New Hampshire *State* USA 27
New Hanover *Island* Papua New Guinea 133 O1
New Haven Connecticut, USA 27 M11
New Hebrides Trench *Sea feature* Pacific Ocean 131
New Ireland *Island* Papua New Guinea 131, 133 P1
New Jersey *State* USA 27
New London Connecticut, USA 27 N11
New Mexico *State* USA 35
New Orleans Louisiana, USA 28 I9, 52 C9
New Plymouth New Zealand 134 G6
New Providence *Island* Bahamas 43 K2
New R. *River* Virginia/West Virginia, USA 29 P3
New Siberian Is. (var. Novosibirskiye Ostrova) *Island group* Russian Federation 51 R7, 103, 113 N4
New South Wales *State* Australia 133
New Ulm Minnesota, USA 30 G7
New York *State* NE USA 27 K9
New York City (prev. New Amsterdam) New York, USA 14, 52 E9, 27 L12
New Zealand *Country* Polynesia, Pacific Ocean 8, 131, 134

New Zealand 134

a English, Maori · **☷** Dollar · **♦** 33 · **♥** 76 ·
⌖ £0.88 · **♆** (m) 99% (f) 99% · **⬚** 442 · **♣** 373 ·
☠ No · **⌂** 84% · **†⌐** 3362

Newark Delaware, USA 27 K14
Newark New Jersey, USA 27 L12
Newark Ohio, USA 31 P12
Newburgh New York, USA 27 L11
Newcastle New South Wales, Australia 133 O12
Newcastle upon Tyne England, UK 59 J11
Newfoundland *Island* Newfoundland, Canada 10, 20, 25 R9, 52 F8
Newfoundland *Province* Canada 25
Newfoundland Basin *Sea feature* Atlantic Ocean 52 G8
Newport Isle of Wight, England, UK 59 J17
Newport Oregon, USA 36 G9
Newport Rhode Island, USA 27 N11
Newport Wales, UK 59 H15
Newport News Virginia, USA 29 S5
Newry Northern Ireland, UK 59 E12

Neyshābūr Iran 109 Q4
Ngaoundéré Cameroon 94 G9
Ngauruhoe, Mt. *Volcano* North Island, New Zealand 134 H6
Ngorongoro *Conservation area* Tanzania 97 O6
Ngorongoro Crater *Physical feature* Tanzania 87
Nguigmi Niger 93 R8
Nguru Nigeria 93 P9
Nha Trang Vietnam 125 P14
Niagara Falls New York, USA 26 H8
Niagara Falls Ontario, Canada 25 K14
Niagara Falls *Waterfall* Canada/USA 20
Niagara Peninsula *Physical feature* Canada 25 K15
Niamey Niger 93 M9
Niangay, L. *Lake* Mali 92 L8
Nias *Island* Indonesia 126 C11
Nicaragua *Country* C America 42

Nicaragua 42

a Spanish · **☷** Cordoba · **♦** 87 · **♥** 65 · **⌖** £0.64 ·
♆ (av.) 66% · **⌂** 60%

Nicaragua, L. *Lake* Nicaragua 41, 42 D11
Nice France 63 Q13
Nicobar Is. *Island group* India, Indian Ocean 100 K7, 115
Nicosia (var. Lefkosa; prev. Levkosia) Cyprus 105 L12
Nicoya, Gulf of *Sea feature* Costa Rica 42 D13
Niedere Tauern *Mountain range* Austria 69 P7
Nifa *Archaeological site* Italy 73 I12
Niğde Turkey 105 M9
Niger *Country* W Africa 93

Niger 93

a French · **☷** Franc · **♦** 16 · **♥** 46 · **⌖** £1.72 ·
♆ (m) 40% (f) 17% · **⌂** 20%

Niger (var. Joliba, Kworra) *River* W Africa 53 F11, 87, 93 M9
Niger Delta *Delta* Nigeria 87, 93 O14
Nigeria *Country* W Africa 93

Nigeria 93

a English · **☷** Naira · **♦** 252 · **♥** 52 · **⌖** £0.39 ·
♆ (m) 62% (f) 40% · **⬚** 32 · **♣** 6134 · **☠** Yes ·
⌂ 35% · **†⌐** 2312

Nihon *see* Japan
Niigata Japan 122 J9
Nijmegen Netherlands 65 K11
Nikolayev *see* Mykolayiv
Nikopol' Ukraine 85 K7
Nikšić Montenegro, Yugoslavia 75 L9
Nile *River* Africa 52 N10, 87, 91 G11, 100 C5
Nile *River basin* Africa 11
Nile Delta *Delta* Egypt 87
Niles Michigan, USA 31 M10
Nîmes France 63 N13
Ninety East Ridge *Sea feature* Indian Ocean 100 J10, 115, 131
Nineveh *Archaeological site* Iraq 109 K2
Ningbo China 121 O11, 128 F6
Ningxia Hui Autonomous Region China 120 J8
Ninigo Group *Island Group* Papua New Guinea 133 M1
Niobrara *River* Nebraska, USA 33 M9
Nioro Mali 92 I8
Nipigon, L. *Lake* Ontario, Canada 24 H10
Nippon *see* Japan
Niš Serbia, Yugoslavia 75 O8
Nissan I. *Island* Papua New Guinea 133 Q1
Nitra Slovakia 71 K12
Nitra *River* Slovakia 71 K11
Niue *Dependent territory* Polynesia, Pacific Ocean 129 K10
Nivelles Belgium 65 G16
Nizhnevartovsk Russian Federation 112 I9
Nizhniy Novgorod Russian Federation 82 H10
Nizhniy Tagil Russian Federation 112 G8
Nizwā Oman 109 O12
Njombe Tanzania 97 N10
Nkhotakota Malawi 97 N13
Nkongsamba Cameroon 94 E10
Nobeoka Japan 123 D14
Nogales Mexico 38 H3
Nome Alaska, USA 22 F5
Nonacho L. *Lake* Northwest Territories, Canada 23 M10
Nordfjord *Coastal feature* Norway 56 H9
Nordhausen Germany 66 I10
Nordstrand *Island* North Frisian Is. Germany 66 G6
Nordvik *Research center* Russian Federation 51 T9
Norfolk Nebraska, USA 33 O9
Norfolk Virginia, USA 29 S5
Norfolk I. *Dependent territory* Pacific Ocean 128 I11
Norge *see* Norway
Noril'sk Russian Federation 112 J7
Norman Oklahoma, USA 33 O15
Normandy *Region* France 62 J5
Norman Wells Northwest Territories, Canada 22 J8
Norrköping Sweden 57 L13
Norrtälje Sweden 57 M12
North Albanian Alps *Mountain range* Albania/Yugoslavia 75 M10

a Language (official or most commonly spoken) · **☷** Currency · **♦** Population density per square mile · **♥** Average life expectancy · **⌖** Price of 1 dozen hen's eggs · **♆** Literacy · **⬚** Number of TVs per 1,000 people · **♣** Number of people per doctor · **☠** Death penalty · **⌂** Percentage of urban-based population · **†⌐** Average number of calories consumed daily per person

151

ⓐ Language (official or most commonly spoken) · 🖹 Currency · ♦ Population density per square mile · ❶ Average life expectancy · ◔ Price of 1 dozen hen's eggs · 📺 Literacy · ⊡ Number of TVs per 1,000 people · ✚ Number of people per doctor · ❀ Death penalty · 🏛 Percentage of urban-based population · ⑪ Average number of calories consumed daily per person

153

---

a Language (official or most commonly spoken) • **☼** Currency • **♦** Population density per square mile • **♥** Average life expectancy • **◉** Price of 1 dozen hen's eggs • **☙** Literacy • **⌸** Number of TVs per 1,000 people • **✚** Number of people per doctor • **☠** Death penalty • **⌂** Percentage of urban-based population • **¶** Average number of calories consumed daily per person

Sumbu *National park* Zambia 97 L10
Sumgait *see* Sumqayıt
Summer L. *Lake* Oregon, USA 36 I10
Sumqayıt (var. Sumgait) Azerbaijan 85 T13
Sumy Ukraine 85 K4
Sun City South Africa 99 L12
Sunbury Pennsylvania, USA 26 J12
Sunda Shelf *Sea feature* South China Sea 115, 130
Sunderland England, UK 59 J11
Sundsvall Sweden 57 L9
Suntar Russian Federation 113 M8
Sunyani Ghana 93 L12
Superior Wisconsin, USA 30 I4
Superior, L. *Lake* Canada/USA 20, 24 H11, 31 L3
Supiori *Island* Indonesia 127 R11
Sur Oman 109 P13
Surabaya Java, Indonesia 126 I15
Surat India 116 I9
Surat Thani Thailand 125 H15
Sûre *River* Belgium/Luxembourg 65 L18
Surigao Mindanao, Philippines 127 N6
Suriname (prev. Dutch Guiana) *Country* S America 44

Suriname 44

a Dutch • 🖱 Gulden • ♦ 7 • ● 68 • ◔ £3.77 •
🖱 (m) 5% (f) 5% • 🏠 47%

Surkhob *River* Tajikistan 111 O7
Surt Libya 89 P7
Susquehanna *River* USA 26 J11
Sutherland Falls *Waterfall* New Zealand 131
Suva Fiji 128 J10
Suwałki Poland 71 O2
Suwannee *River* Florida, USA 29 N11
Svalbard *Island group* Arctic Ocean 51 Q12, 54, 103
Svay Riêng Cambodia 125 M14
Sverdlovsk *see* Yekaterinburg
Sverige *see* Sweden
Svetlogorsk *see* Svyetlahorsk
Svobodnyy ICBM Base *Military center* Russian Federation 113 O11
Svyatahorsk (var. Svetlogorsk) Belarus 81 N14
Swabian Jura *Mountain range* Germany 67 G16
Swakopmund Namibia 98 G10
Swansea Wales, UK 59 G15
Swaziland *Country* Southern Africa 99

Swaziland 99

a English, Swazi • 🖱 Lilangeni • ♦ 124 • ● 57 •
◔ £0.84 • 🖱 (m) 70% (f) 66% • 🏠 33%

Sweden (var. Sverige) *Country* Scandinavia 56-57

Sweden 56-57

a Swedish • 🖱 Krona • ♦ 54 • ● 78 • ◔ £1.98 •
🖱 (m) 99% (f) 99% • 🖵 474 • ✚ 355 • ❂ No •
🏠 84% • ⫿ 2960

Sweetwater Texas, USA 35 P10
Swift Current Saskatchewan, Canada 23 M15
Swindon England, UK 59 I16
Switzerland *Country* C Europe 68

Switzerland 68

a French, German, Italian • 🖱 Franc • ♦ 439 •
● 78 • ◔ £3.03 • 🖱 (m) 99% (f) 99% • 🖵 407 •
✚ 584 • ❂ No • 🏠 60% • ⫿ 3562

Sydney New South Wales, Australia 15, 128 H11, 133 O13
Sydney Nova Scotia, Canada 25 R11
Syktyvkar Russian Federation 82 K9
Sylhet Bangladesh 117 P7
Sylt *Island* North Frisian Is. Germany 66 G5
Syowa *Research center* Antarctica 50 F7
Syr Darya *River* C Asia 103, 112 F13
Syracuse New York, USA 27 K8
Syracuse *see* Siracusa
Syria (var. Aram) *Country* SW Asia 107

Syria 107

a Arabic • 🖱 Pound • ♦ 180 • ● 66 • ◔ £0.97 •
🖱 (m) 78% (f) 51% • 🖵 59 • ✚ 1347 • ❂ Yes •
🏠 50% • ⫿ 3003

Syrian Desert (var. Bādiyat ash Shām) *Desert region* SW Asia 103, 107 P9, 108 I5
Szczecin Poland 70 H3
Szeged Hungary 71 M15
Székesfehérvár Hungary 71 K13
Szekszárd Hungary 71 L15
Szolnok Hungary 71 M14
Szombathely Hungary 70 J13

T

Tabar Is. *Island group* Papua New Guinea 133 P1
Tabasco Mexico 39 L10

Table Bay *Sea feature* South Africa 98 I15
Table Mt. *Mountain* South Africa 98 I16
Tábor Czech Republic 70 H10
Tabora Tanzania 97 M8
Tabríz Iran 109 L2
Tabúk Saudi Arabia 108 G6
Tacloban Leyte, Philippines 127 N6
Tacna Peru 45 G15
Tacoma Washington, USA 36 H7
Tacuarembó Uruguay 48 O9
Taegu South Korea 121 Q8
Taejŏn South Korea 121 P8
Tagula I. *Island* Papua New Guinea 133 P4
Tagus (var. Tajo, Tejo) *River* Portugal/Spain 54, 60 G9
Tahiti *Island* French Polynesia, Pacific Ocean 129 L10
Tahoe, L. *Lake* California/Nevada, USA 34 E3, 37 J14
Tahoua Niger 93 O8
Tai'an China 121 N8
Taieri *River* New Zealand 134 D13
Ṭā'if Saudi Arabia 108 H11
Taipei Taiwan 121 O13
Taiping Malaysia 125 I18
Taiwan *Country* E Asia 115, 121, 128 F6

Taiwan 121

a Mandarin • 🖱 Dollar • ♦ 1670 • ● 74 • ◔ £0.62 •
🖱 (m) 96% (f) 87% • 🖵 387 • ✚ 913 • ❂ Yes •
🏠 N/A • ⫿ 2875

Taiwan Strait *Channel* China/Taiwan 115, 121 N14
Taiyuan China 121 L8
Ta'izz Yemen 108 I16
Tajikistan *Country* C Asia 111

Tajikistan 111

a Tajik • 🖱 Ruble • ♦ 98 • ● 69 • ◔ N/A •
🖱 N/A • 🏠 31%

Tajo *see* Tagus
Tak Thailand 124 I10
Takamatsu Japan 123 F12
Takêv Cambodia 125 M14
Takla Makan Desert *Desert region* China 11, 118 F9
Talak *Desert region* Niger 93 O6
Talas Kyrgyzstan 111 P5
Talaud Is. *Island group* Indonesia 127 N9
Talca Chile 49 G11
Talcahuano Chile 49 G12
Taldy-Kurgan (var. Taldyqorghan) Kazakhstan 112 H13
Taldyqorghan *see* Taldy-Kurgan
Tallahassee Florida, USA 29 M10
Tallinn (prev. Revel) Estonia 52 M7, 80 J1
Talsi Latvia 80 H5
Tamabo Range *Mountain range* Borneo, Malaysia 126 J10
Tamale Ghana 93 L11
Tamanrasset Algeria 89 L11
Tambacounda Senegal 92 G9
Tambov Russian Federation 83 G11
Tambora *Volcano* Sumbawa, Indonesia 9, 115
Tampa Florida, USA 29 N13
Tampere Finland 57 O10
Tampico Mexico 39 O10
Tamworth New South Wales, Australia 133 O12
Tan-Tan Morocco 88 G7
Tana *River* Kenya 97 Q4
Tana *River* Norway 57 O3
Tana, L. *Lake* Ethiopia 87, 91 I14
Tanami Desert *Desert region* Australia 131
Tanana *River* Alaska, USA 22 H8
Tanega-shima *Island* Japan 123 D16
Tanga Tanzania 97 Q8
Tanganyika, L. *Lake* C Africa 87, 95 O15, 97 L9
Tanggula Mountains *Mountain range* China 118 I11
Tangier Morocco 88 I4
Tangra Yumco *Lake* China 118 H12
Tangshan China 121 N7
Tanimbar Is. *Island group* Indonesia 127 Q14
Tanjungkarang Sumatra, Indonesia 126 F14
Tanjungpinang Bitan, Indonesia 126 F11
Tanta Egypt 90 F6
Tanzam Railway *Railway* Tanzania 97 N10
Tanzania *Country* E Africa 97

Tanzania 97

a English, Swahili • 🖱 Shilling • ♦ 74 • ● 47 •
◔ £0.60 • 🖱 (m) 62% (f) 31% • 🏠 33%

Taormina Italy 73 L17
Taos New Mexico, USA 35 M7
Tapachula Mexico 39 R15
Tapajós *River* Brazil 41, 46 G8
Tapti *River* India 116 I8
Taraba *River* Nigeria 93 Q12
Tarabulus *see* Tripoli
Taranto Italy 73 O14
Taranto, Gulf of *Sea feature* Italy 73 O14
Tarawa *Island* Kiribati, Pacific Ocean 128 J8
Tarbela Dam *Dam* Pakistan 116 J2
Tarbela Res. *Reservoir* Pakistan 116 J1
Tarbes France 62 J14
Taree New South Wales, Australia 133 P12
Târgovişte Romania 77 L8

Târgu Jiu Romania 76 I8
Târgu Mureş Romania 77 K5
Tarija Bolivia 45 J17
Tarim *River* China 115, 118 G8
Tarim Basin *Physical region* China 118 G8
Tarn *River* France 63 L13
Tarnów Poland 71 N9
Tarragona Spain 61 P7
Tarsus Turkey 105 M10
Tartu Estonia 81 K3
Ṭarṭús Syria 107 M5
Tashauz *see* Dashkhovuz
Tashkent (var. Toshkent) Uzbekistan 111 N6
Tasman Bay *Sea feature* New Zealand 134 F8
Tasman Sea Australia/New Zealand 128 I12, 131, 133 O15, 134 D11
Tasmania *Island* Australia 131
Tasmania *State* Australia 133
Tassili n'Ajjer *Mountain range* Algeria 87, 89 M9
Tatvan Turkey 105 R7
Tauern Tunnel *Tunnel* Austria 69 N9
Taunggyi Burma 124 G8
Taunton England, UK 59 H16
Taupo New Zealand 134 H6
Taupo, L. *Lake* New Zealand 131, 134 H6
Tauragė Lithuania 80 G9
Tauranga New Zealand 134 H5
Taurus Mts. *Mountain range* Turkey 103, 105 L10
Tavoy Burma 125 H12
Tawakoni, L. *Lake* Texas, USA 35 R10
Tawau Borneo, Malaysia 127 K9
Tawitawi *Island* Philippines 127 L8
Taxco Mexico 39 N13
Tay Ninh Vietnam 125 M1
Taymyr, L. *Lake* Russian Federation 113 K5
Taymyr Peninsula *Physical feature* Russian Federation 51 T9, 103, 113 K5
Taz *River* Russian Federation 112 I8
Tbilisi (var. T'bilisi) Georgia 85 Q12
T'bilisi *see* Tbilisi
Tchibanga Gabon 95 F13
Tchien (var. Zwedru) Liberia 92 I13
Te Anau, L. *Lake* New Zealand 134 C13
Tébessa Algeria 89 M5
Tedzhen Turkmenistan 110 J9
Tedzhen *River* Iran/Turkmenistan 110 J9
Tegucigalpa Honduras 42 D9
Tehran Iran 109 N4
Tehuantepec Mexico 39 P14
Tehuantepec, Gulf of *Sea feature* Mexico 39 P15
Tejo *see* Tagus
Tekirdağ Turkey 104 G5
Tel Aviv-Yafo Israel 107 L9
Teles Pires *River* Brazil 46 G9
Telluride Colorado, USA 35 L5
Telok Intan Malaysia 125 I18
Temuco Chile 49 G13
Tengiz, L. *Lake* Kazakhstan 112 G11
Tennessee *River* SE USA 20, 29 K4
Tennessee *State* USA 28-29
Teotihuacán *Archaeological site* Mexico 39 N12
Tepic Mexico 39 K10
Tequila Mexico 39 K11
Teresina Brazil 46 M8
Termez Uzbekistan 111 M9
Terneuzen Netherlands 65 F13
Terni Italy 73 I11
Ternopil' (var. Ternopol') Ukraine 84 F5
Ternopol' *see* Ternopil'
Terrassa Spain 61 Q6
Terre Haute Indiana, USA 31 L13
Terschelling *Island* West Frisian Is. Netherlands 64 J6
Teruel Spain 61 N8
Teslin L. *Lake* Yukon Territory, Canada 22 I10
Tete Mozambique 99 N7
Tétouan Morocco 88 I4
Tetovo Macedonia 75 N11
Tevere *see* Tiber
Texas *State* USA 35
Texas City Texas, USA 35 S13
Texcoco, L. *Lake* Mexico 39 N12
Texel *Island* West Frisian Is. Netherlands 64 H7
Thac Ba, L. *Lake* Vietnam 124 M8
Thai Nguyen Vietnam 124 M9
Thailand *Country* SE Asia 124-125

Thailand 124-125

a Thai • 🖱 Baht • ♦ 287 • ● 66 • ◔ £0.54 •
🖱 (m) 96% (f) 90% • 🖵 112 • ✚ 4843 • ❂ Yes •
🏠 23% • ⫿ 2316

Thailand, Gulf of *Sea feature* Thailand 100 L7, 115, 125 J15
Thakhek *see* Muang Khammouan
Thames New Zealand 134 H4
Thames *River* England, UK 54, 59 I15
Thane India 116 I9
Thanh Hoa Vietnam 124 M9
Thar Desert (var. Indian Desert) *Desert region* India/Pakistan 11, 115, 116 I5
Tharthár, L. *Lake* Iraq 109 K4
Thasos *Island* Greece 79 M3
Thaton Burma 124 G10
Thayetmyo Burma 124 F9
Thebes *Archaeological site* Egypt 90 G8
Theodore Roosevelt L. *Lake* Arizona, USA 34 I9
Thermaic Gulf *Sea feature* Greece 78 J4
Thessaloníki (var. Salonika) Greece 78 J3
Thika Kenya 97 P5
Thimphu Bhutan 117 P6

Thionville France 63 O4
Thira *Island* Cyclades, Greece 79 N13
Thiruvananthapuram *see* Trivandrum
Thohoyandou South Africa 99 M10
Thompson Manitoba, Canada 23 O12
Thrace *Region* Greece 79 N2
Thule (var. Qaanaaq) Greenland 51 O11
Thun Switzerland 68 F11
Thun, L. of *Lake* Switzerland 68 F11
Thunder Bay Ontario, Canada 24 G11
Thüringer Wald *see* Thuringian Forest
Thuringia *Region* Germany 67 I12
Thuringian Forest (var. Thüringer Wald) *Physical region* Germany 67 I12
Thurso Scotland, UK 58 I6
Tianjin China 121 N7, 128 F5
Tiaret Algeria 89 K5
Tiber (var. Tevere) *River* Italy 73 H11
Tiberias, L. (var. Sea of Galilee) *Lake* Israel 107 M8
Tibesti *Mountain range* Chad/Libya 87, 94 I4
Tibet, Plateau of *Physical feature* China 15
Tibetan Autonomous Region *Region* China 118 H12
Tiburón I. *Island* Mexico 38 G4
Tidjikdja Mauritania 92 H6
Tien Shan *Mountain range* Kyrgyzstan/China 103, 111 R6, 115, 118 G7
Tienen Belgium 65 I15
Tierra del Fuego *Island* Argentina/Chile 41, 49 K20
Tighina (var. Bendery) Moldavia 84 H8
Tigris (var. Dijlah) *River* SW Asia 100 E4, 103, 105 Q8, 107 T1, 109 K3
Tijuana Mexico 38 F1
Tikal *Archaeological site* Guatemala 42 C6
Tikrít Iraq 109 K4
Tiksi Russian Federation 51 T7, 113 M6
Tikveško, L. *Lake* Macedonia 75 O12
Tilburg Netherlands 65 I12
Tillabéry Niger 93 M8
Timaru New Zealand 134 E12
Timbuktu (var. Tombouctou) Mali 93 K7
Timgad *Archaeological site* Morocco 89 M5
Timirist, Râs *Cape* Mauritania 92 F6
Timiş *River* Romania/Serbia 76 H7
Timişoara Romania 77 G6
Timmins Ontario, Canada 24 J11
Timor *Island* Indonesia 115, 127 N16, 131
Timor Sea Australia/Indonesia 127 O16, 131, 133 I4
Tindouf Algeria 88 H8
Tinos *Island* Cyclades, Greece 79 M10
Tirana (var. Tiranë) Albania 75 M12
Tiranë *see* Tirana
Tiraspol Moldavia 84 H8
Tiree *Island* Scotland, UK 58 E8
Tirso *River* Sardinia 73 D14
Tiruchchirappalli India 117 K14
Tisza *River* Hungary 54, 71 M14
Titicaca, L. *Lake* Peru/Bolivia 41, 45 H14
Titograd *see* Podgorica
Titov Veles Macedonia 75 O11
Titova Mitrovica Serbia, Yugoslavia 75 N9
Tiznit Morocco 88 G6
Tlaxcala Mexico 39 N12
Tlemcen Algeria 88 J5
Toamasina Madagascar 100 E10
Toba, L. *Lake* Sumatra, Indonesia 126 C10
Tobago *Island* Trinidad & Tobago 20, 41, 43 T16
Tobakakar Range *Mountain range* Pakistan/Afghanistan 116 H3
Tobruk Libya 89 R6
Tocantins *River* Brazil 41, 46 J10
Tocopilla Chile 48 F5
Togian Is. *Island group* Indonesia 127 M11
Togo (prev. French Togo) *Country* W Africa 93

Togo 93

a French • 🖱 Franc • ♦ 179 • ● 54 • ◔ £1.43 •
🖱 (m) 56% (f) 31% • 🏠 26%

Tokara Is. *Island group* Japan 123 C17
Tokat Turkey 105 N6
Tokelau *Dependent territory* Polynesia, Pacific Ocean 128 J9
Tokmak Kyrgyzstan 111 Q4
Tokuno-shima *Island* Amami Is. Japan 123 B19
Tokushima Japan 123 G13
Tokyo Japan 15, 123 K11
Tol'yatti Russian Federation 83 I12
Toledo Ohio, USA 31 O10
Toledo Spain 61 K9
Toledo Bend Res. *Reservoir* Louisiana/Texas, USA 35 T11
Toliara Madagascar 101 E11
Tomakomai Japan 122 K4
Tombigbee *River* Alabama 29 K8
Tombouctou *see* Timbuktu
Tomé Chile 48 G12
Tomini, Gulf of *Sea feature* Celebes, Indonesia 127 L11
Tomsk Russian Federation 112 I10
Tonga *Country* Polynesia, Pacific Ocean 128 J10

Tonga 128

a English, Tongan • 🖱 Pa'anga • ♦ 360 • ● 67 •
◔ £1.83 • 🖱 (m) 93% (f) 93% • 🏠 31%

Tongking, Gulf of (var. Tonkin, Gulf of) *Sea feature* China/Vietnam 115, 121 K15, 124 O9

---

a Language (official or most commonly spoken) • 🖱 Currency • ♦ Population density per square mile • ● Average life expectancy • ◔ Price of 1 dozen hen's eggs • 🖱 Literacy • 🖵 Number of TVs per 1,000 people • ✚ Number of people per doctor • ❂ Death penalty • 🏠 Percentage of urban-based population • ⫿ Average number of calories consumed daily per person

Vatican City *Country* Rome, Italy 73 H12

Vatican City 73

a Latin, Italian • 🖩 Lira • ♦ 5886 • 🌡 78 • ⬤ £1.32 • 🌒 (m) 100% • 🏠 100%

Vatter, L. *Lake* Sweden 57 K13
Vawkavysk (var. Volkovysk) Belarus 80 I13
Växjö Sweden 57 K14
Vaygach I. *Island* Russian Federation 82 O6
Vega *Island* Norway 57 K6
Vegoritis, L. *Lake* Greece 78 I3
Vejle Denmark 56 I15
Velenje Slovenia 74 H2
Velika Plana Serbia, Yugoslavia 75 N6
Velingrad Bulgaria 76 J14
Velsen Netherlands 64 H9
Venezia *see* Venice
Venezuela *Country* S America 44

Venezuela S America 44

a Spanish • 🖩 Bolivar • ♦ 59 • 🌡 70 • ⬤ £0.52 • 🌒 (m) 87% (f) 90% • 📺 167 • ✚ 590 • ☻ Yes • 🏠 91% • ⳾ 2582

Venezuela, Gulf of *Sea feature* Venezuela 44 G4
Venezuelan Basin *Sea feature* Caribbean Sea 51
Venice (var. Venezia) Italy 72 H7
Venice, Gulf of *Sea feature* Italy 72 I7
Venlo Netherlands 65 L13
Venta *River* Latvia/Lithuania 80 G5
Ventspils Latvia 80 G5
Ventura California, USA 37 J18
Vera Argentina 48 L8
Veracruz Mexico 39 P12
Verde, C. *Cape* W Africa 87
Verdun France 63 O4
Vereeniging South Africa 99 L12
Verkhoyansk Range *Mountain range* Russian Federation 103, 113 M7
Vermont *State* USA 27
Vernon British Columbia, Canada 23 K14
Vernon Texas, USA 35 P9
Veroia Greece 78 I3
Verona Italy 72 G7
Versailles France 63 L5
Verviers Belgium 65 K16
Vesoul France 63 O7
Vesterålen *Island group* Norway 57 L3
Vestfjorden *Coastal feature* Norway 57 L4
Vesuvius *Volcano* Italy 9, 54
Veszprém Hungary 71 K14
Vetluga *River* Russian Federation 82 J9
Veurne Belgium 65 B14
Viana do Castelo Portugal 60 F6
Vianden Luxembourg 65 L18
Viangchan *see* Vientiane
Viareggio Italy 72 F9
Vicenza Italy 72 G7
Vichy France 63 M9
Victoria Seychelles 100 F9
Victoria *State* Australia 133
Victoria Vancouver I. British Columbia, Canada 22 J15
Victoria *see* Limbe
Victoria *River* Northern Territory, Australia 131, 132 J6
Victoria de las Tunas Cuba 43 K5
Victoria Falls *Waterfall* Zambia/Zimbabwe 87, 96 J16
Victoria Falls Zimbabwe 99 K8
Victoria I. *Island* Northwest Territories, Canada 20, 23 M6
Victoria Land *Physical region* Antarctica 50 E11
Victoria Nile *River* Uganda 97 M3
Victoria, L. *Lake* E Africa 87, 97 M5
Vidin Bulgaria 76 I10
Viedma Argentina 49 L13
Viedma, L. *Lake* Argentina 49 I18
Vienna (var. Wien) Austria 69 S4
Vientiane (var. Viangchan) Laos 124 K10
Viet Tri Vietnam 124 M8
Vietnam (anc. Annam) *Country* SE Asia 124-125

Vietnam 124-125

a Vietnamese • 🖩 Dong • ♦ 540 • 🌡 67 • ⬤ £0.59 • 🌒 (m) 92% (f) 83% • 📺 39 • ✚ 2882 • ☻ Yes • 🏠 22% • ⳾ 2233

Vigan Luzon, Philippines 127 L3
Vigo Spain 60 F5
Vijayawada India 117 L11
Vikna *Island* Norway 56 J6
Vila Vanuatu Melanesia, Pacific Ocean 128 I10
Viljandi Estonia 80 J3
Villa Maria Argentina 48 K9
Villach Austria 69 O10
Villahermosa Mexico 39 Q13
Villarica Paraguay 48 N6
Villarrica *Volcano* Chile 41
Villavicencio Colombia 44 F7
Vilnius (var. Wilno) Lithuania 80 J10
Vilyuy *River* Russian Federation 113 M8
Viña del Mar Chile 48 G10
Vincennes Indiana, USA 31 L14
Vincennes Bay *Sea feature* Wilkes Land, Antarctica 50 H10

Vindel *River* Sweden 57 M6
Vineland New Jersey, USA 27 K14
Vinh Vietnam 124 M10
Vinnitsa *see* Vinnytsya
Vinnytsya (var. Vinnitsa) Ukraine 84 H5
Virgin Islands (US) *Dependent territory* Caribbean Sea 43 R9
Virginia Minnesota, USA 30 I3
Virginia *State* USA 29
Virovitica Croatia 74 J3
Virtsu Estonia 80 I3
Vis *Island* Croatia 74 I8
Visayan Sea Philippines 127 M5
Visby Sweden 57 L14
Viscount Melville Sound *Sea feature* Northwest Territories, Canada 23 M5
Viseu Portugal 60 G7
Vishakhapatnam India 100 J6, 117 M11
Visoko Bosnia and Herzegovina 75 K7
Vistula (var. Wisła) *River* Poland 54, 71 N8
Vitava, L. *Lake* Czech Republic 70 H10
Vitebsk *see* Vitsyebsk
Vitim *River* Russian Federation 113 M10
Vitória Brazil 47 M13
Vitoria Spain 61 L4
Vitsyebsk (var. Vitebsk) Belarus 81 N9
Vladikavkaz Russian Federation 83 E16
Vladimir Russian Federation 82 G10
Vladivostok Russian Federation 113 P12, 128 F5
Vlieland *Island* West Frisian Is. Netherlands 64 I6
Vlissingen *see* Flushing
Vlorë Albania 75 L14
Vöcklabruck Austria 69 O6
Vohimena, C. (var. Cap Sainte Marie) *Cape* Madagascar 101 E11
Voinjama Liberia 92 I11
Volga *River* Russian Federation 54, 83 G14
Volga Delta *Delta* Russian Federation 54
Volga-Don Canal *Waterway* Russian Federation 83 F14
Volgograd (prev. Stalingrad) Russian Federation 83 G13
Volkovysk *see* Vawkavysk
Vologda Russian Federation 82 H9
Volos Greece 78 J6
Volta, L. *Reservoir* Ghana 87, 93 L12
Voring Plateau *Sea feature* Atlantic Ocean 54
Vorkuta Russian Federation 82 O7
Vormsi *Island* Estonia 80 I2
Voronezh Russian Federation 83 F12
Voroshilovgrad *see* Luhans'k
Võrtsjärv *Lake* Estonia 81 K4
Võru Estonia 81 K4
Vosges *Mountain range* France 63 P6
Vostochnyy Russian Federation 113 P9
Vostok *Research center* Antarctica 50 F10
Vratsa Bulgaria 76 I12
Vrbas *River* Bosnia and Herzegovina 74 J5
Vršac Serbia, Yugoslavia 75 O5
Vryburg South Africa 99 K12
Vukovar Croatia 75 L4
Vulcano *Island* Lipari Is. Italy 73 L17
Vulci *Archaeological site* Italy 73 G11
Vyatka *River* Russian Federation 83 J11

W

Wa Ghana 93 K11
Waal *River* Netherlands 65 J11
Waalwijk Netherlands 65 I12
Wabash *River* Illinois/Indiana, USA 31 M12
Waco Texas, USA 35 R11
Wad Medani Sudan 91 G13
Waddenzee *Sea feature* Netherlands 64 I7
Wādi Banā *Seasonal watercourse* Yemen 108 I16
Wadi Halfa Sudan 90 F10
Wādī Hajir *Seasonal watercourse* Yemen 109 K16
Wagadugu *see* Ouagadougou
Wagga Wagga New South Wales, Australia 133 N13
Waigeo *Island* Indonesia 127 Q11
Waipapakauri New Zealand 134 F2
Wairau *River* New Zealand 134 F9
Waitaki *River* New Zealand 134 E12
Wajir Kenya 97 Q3
Wakasa Bay (var. Wakasa-wan) *Sea feature* Japan 123 H11
Wakasa-wan *see* Wakasa Bay
Wakatipu, L. *Lake* New Zealand 134 C13
Wakayama Japan 123 G12
Wake I. *Dependent territory* Micronesia, Pacific Ocean 128 I7
Wakkanai Japan 122 K2
Wałbrzych Poland 70 J8
Wales *Country* UK 59
Walker L. *Lake* Nevada, USA 34 F4
Walla Walla Washington, USA 36 K8
Wallenstadt, L. of *Lake* Switzerland 88 H9
Wallis & Futuna *Dependent territory* Polynesia, Pacific Ocean 128 I9
Walvis Bay Namibia 53 M13, 98 G11
Walvis Ridge *Sea feature* Atlantic Ocean 53 K14, 87
Wanganui New Zealand 134 G7
Wankie *see* Hwange
Wanxian China 121 K11
Warren Ohio, USA 31 Q10
Warrnambool Victoria, Austalia 133 M15
Warsaw (var. Warszawa) Poland 71 N5
Warszawa *see* Warsaw
Warta *River* Poland 70 I5

Wartburg *Castle* Germany 67 H11
Wash, The *Sea feature* England, UK 59 L14
Washington Pennsylvania, USA 26 G13
Washington *State* USA 36
Washington D.C. USA 29 R3
Waterbury Connecticut, USA 27 M11
Waterford Ireland 59 D14
Waterloo Iowa, USA 33 R8
Watertown New York, USA 27 K7
Watertown South Dakota, USA 33 O7
Waterville Maine, USA 27 P6
Watford England, UK 59 K16
Watson Lake Yukon Territory, Canada 22 J10
Wau Sudan 91 E15
Waukegan Illinois, USA 31 L9
Wausau Wisconsin, USA 31 K6
Wauwatosa Wisconsin, USA 31 L8
Wawa Ontario, Canada 24 I11
Wda *River* Poland 71 K3
Weda, Gulf of *Sea feature* Halmahera, Indonesia 127 O11
Weddell Sea Antarctica 50 C7, 53 G17
Weed California, USA 37 H12
Weert Netherlands 65 K13
Wei He *River* China 115
Wellesley Is. *Island group* Queensland, Australia 133 L6
Wellington New Zealand 128 J12, 134 G9
Wells, L. *Lake* Western Australia, Australia 132 H10
Wels Austria 69 O5
Wembere *River* Tanzania 97 N7
Wenzhou China 121 O12
Weser *River* Germany 66 G9
Wessel Is. *Island group* Northern Territory, Australia 133 K4
West Australia Basin *Sea feature* Indian Ocean 101 K10
West Australia current *Ocean current* IndianOcean/Pacific Ocean 14
West Bank *Occupied by Israel* SW Asia 107 L9
West Fiji Basin *Sea feature* Pacific Ocean 131
West Frisian Is. *Island Group* Netherlands 64 I6
West Grand L. *Lake* Maine, USA 27 Q5
West Ice Shelf *Coastal feature* Indian Ocean Coast, Antarctica 50 H9
West Indies *Island group* Atlantic Ocean 10, 20, 52 E10
West Lunga *National park* Zambia 96 I13
West Palm Beach Florida, USA 29 O14
West Siberian Plain *Physical region* Russian Federation 103, 112 H8
West Virginia *State* USA 29 P3
Western Australia *State* Australia 132
Western Ghats *Mountain range* India 116 J3
Western Sahara *Disputed territory* Africa 88
Western Samoa *Country* Polynesia, Pacific Ocean 128 J9

Western Samoa 128

a Samoan • 🖩 Tala • ♦ 154 • 🌡 66 • ⬤ £1.25 • 🌒 (m) 98% (f) 98% • 🏠 21%

Westerschelde *Estuary* Netherlands 65 F13
Westport New Zealand 134 E9
Wetar *Island* Indonesia 127 O14
Wetaskiwin Alberta, Canada 23 L14
Wewak Papua New Guinea 133 M1
Wexford Ireland 59 E14
Weyburn Saskatchewan, Canada 23 N15
Whangarei New Zealand 134 G3
Wharton Basin *Sea feature* Indian Ocean 115
White Mts. *Mountain range* New Hampshire, USA 27 N7
White Nile (var. Bahr el Jebel) *River* E Africa 87, 91 G14
White Plains New York, USA 27 M12
White R. *River* Arkansas/Missouri, USA 28 I4
White R. *River* Colorado/Utah, USA 35 L3
White R. *River* Indiana, USA 31 M13
White R. *River* Nebraska/South Dakota, USA 33 N8
White Sands Missile Range *Military center* New Mexico, USA 35 M10
White Sea Russian Federation 82 J6
White Volta *River* Burkina/Ghana 93 L11
Whitehaven England, UK 59 H11
Whitehorse Yukon Territory, Canada 22 I9
Whitney, Mt. *Mountain* California, USA 20
Whyalla South Australia 133 L13
Wichita Kansas, USA 33 O13
Wichita Falls Texas, USA 35 Q9
Wicklow Mts. *Mountain range* Ireland, UK 59 E13
Wien *see* Vienna
Wiener Neustadt Austria 69 S5
Wiesbaden Germany 67 F13
Wight, Isle of *Island* England, UK 59 J17
Wilhelm, Mt. *Mountain* Papua New Guinea 131
Wilhelmshaven Germany 66 F7
Wilkes-Barre Pennsylvania, USA 27 K11
Wilkes Land *Physical region* Antarctica 50 G11
Willemstad Netherlands Antilles 43 O14
Williamsport Pennsylvania, USA 26 J11
Williston North Dakota, USA 33 L4
Willmar Minnesota, USA 30 G6
Wilmington Delaware, USA 27 K14
Wilmington North Carolina, USA 29 Q7
Wilno *see* Vilnius
Wilson North Carolina, USA 29 R6
Wind *River* Wyoming, USA 32 I8
Wind River Range *Mountain range* Wyoming, USA 32 I8

Windhoek Namibia 98 H10
Windsor Ontario, Canada 24 J15
Windward Islands *Island group* Caribbean Sea 41, 43 S13
Windward Passage *Channel* Cuba/Haiti 43 L7
Winisk *River* Ontario, Canada 24 I7
Winnebago, L. *Lake* Wisconsin, USA 31 L7
Winnemucca Nevada, USA 34 G2
Winnipeg Manitoba, Canada 23 O14
Winnipeg, L. *Lake* Manitoba, Canada 20, 23 O13
Winnipegosis, L. *Lake* Manitoba, Canada 23 O14
Winona Minnesota, USA 30 I7
Winschoten Netherlands 64 N7
Winston-Salem North Carolina, USA 29 P5
Winterthur Switzerland 68 G8
Wisconsin *River* Wisconsin, USA 30 J8
Wisconsin *State* USA 30-31
Wisconsin Rapids Wisconsin, USA 30 J7
Wisła *see* Vistula
Wisłoka *River* Poland 71 N9
Wismar Germany 66 J7
Wittenberg Germany 66 K10
Włocławek Poland 71 L5
Włocławskie, L. *Lake* Poland 71 L5
Wodonga Victoria, Australia 133 N14
Wolf *River* Wisconsin, USA 31 K6
Wolfsberg Austria 69 Q9
Wolfsburg Germany 66 I9
Wollaston L. *Lake* Saskatchewan, Canada 23 M11
Wollongong Victoria, Australia 133 O13
Wolverhampton England, UK 59 I14
Wönsan North Korea 121 P7
Woodlark I. *Island* Papua New Guinea 133 P3
Woods, L. of the *Lake* Canada/USA 20, 24 F10
Worcester England, UK 59 I15
Worcester Massachusetts, USA 27 N10
Worland Wyoming, USA 32 J8
Wörther, Lake *Lake* Austria 69 P9
Wowoni *Island* Indonesia 127 M13
Wrangel I. *Island* Russian Federation 51 Q6, 113 P2
Wrangell Alaska, USA 22 I11
Wrath, C. *Cape* Scotland, UK 58 G6
Wrocław (var. Breslau) Poland 70 J7
Wuhai China 119 M8
Wuhan China 121 M11
Wuppertal Germany 67 E11
Würzburg Germany 67 H13
Wuwei China 120 I7
Wuxi China 121 O10
Wuzhou China 121 L14
Wyndham Western Australia, Australia 132 I6
Wyoming *State* USA 32-33
Wyzyna Małopolska *Region* Poland 71 M9

X

Xaafuun, C. *Cape* Somalia 100 F7
Xai-Xai Mozambique 99 N12
Xam Nua Laos 125 L9
Xankändi (var. Stepanakert, Khankendy) Azerbaijan 85 R14
Xanthi Greece 79 M2
Xiamen China 121 N13
Xi'an China 121 L10
Xiangfan China 121 L10
Xiangkhoang Laos 124 L9
Xiao Hinggan Ling *see* Lesser Khingan Mts.
Xichang China 120 I12
Xigazê China 118 H13
Xilinhot China 119 P6
Xingu *River* Brazil 41, 46 I8
Xining China 119 L10
Xinjiang Uighur Autonomous Region *Region* China 118 H6
Xinyang China 121 M10
Xuwen China 121 K15
Xuzhou China 121 N9

Y

Yafran Libya 89 O6
Yakeshi China 119 P3
Yakima Washington, USA 36 J7
Yakima *River* Washington, USA 36 J7
Yaku-shima *Island* Japan 123 C17
Yakutsk Russian Federation 113 M10
Yala Thailand 125 J17
Yalong *River* China 120 H10
Yalta Ukraine 85 K10
Yamagata Japan 122 K8
Yamaguchi Japan 123 D13
Yamal Peninsula *Physical feature* Russian Federation 103, 112 I6
Yambol Bulgaria 77 M13
Yamoussoukro Ivory Coast 92 J12
Yampa *River* Colorado, USA 35 L3
Yamuna *River* India 117 L6
Yamzho Yumco *Lake* China 118 I13
Yana *River* Russian Federation 113 N6
Yanbu' al Bahr Saudi Arabia 108 G9
Yangon *see* Rangoon
Yangtze (var. Chiang Jiang) *River* China 115, 121 K10
Yankton South Dakota, USA 33 O8
Yantai China 121 O8
Yaoundé Cameroon 95 F11
Yap Trench *Sea feature* Pacific Ocean 115, 131
Yapen *Island* Indonesia 127 R11

a Language (official or most commonly spoken) • 🖩 Currency • ♦ Population density per square mile • 🌡 Average life expectancy • ⬤ Price of 1 dozen hen's eggs • 🌒 Literacy • 📺 Number of TVs per 1,000 people • ✚ Number of people per doctor • ☻ Death penalty • 🏠 Percentage of urban-based population • ⳾ Average number of calories consumed daily per person

159

NORTH AMERICA

CANADA
PAGES 22-25

UNITED STATES OF AMERICA
PAGES 26-37

MEXICO
PAGES 38-39

CENTRAL AND SOUTH AMERICA

ANTIGUA & BARBUDA
PAGES 42-43

BAHAMAS
PAGES 42-43

BARBADOS
PAGES 42-43

BELIZE
PAGES 42-43

COSTA R
PAGES 4

JAMAICA
PAGES 42-43

NICARAGUA
PAGES 42-43

PANAMA
PAGES 42-43

ST. CHRISTOPHER & NEVIS
PAGES 42-43

ST. LUCIA
PAGES 42-43

ST. VINCENT & THE GRENADINES
PAGES 42-43

TRINIDAD & TOBAGO
PAGES 42-43

BOLIV
PAGES 4

THE ATLANTIC OCEAN

EUROPE

CHILE
PAGES 48-49

PARAGUAY
PAGES 48-49

URUGUAY
PAGES 48-49

CAPE VERDE
PAGES 52-53

ICELAND
PAGES 52-53

DENMARK
PAGES 56-57

FINLAND
PAGES 56-57

NORW
PAGES 5

BELGIUM
PAGES 64-65

LUXEMBOURG
PAGES 64-65

THE NETHERLANDS
PAGES 64-65

GERMANY
PAGES 66-67

AUSTRIA
PAGES 68-69

LIECHTENSTEIN
PAGES 68-69

SWITZERLAND
PAGES 68-69

CZECH RE
PAGES 7

BOSNIA & HERZEGOVINA
PAGES 74-75

CROATIA
PAGES 74-75

MACEDONIA
PAGES 74-75

SLOVENIA
PAGES 74-75

YUGOSLAVIA
PAGES 74-75

BULGARIA
PAGES 76-77

ROMANIA
PAGES 76-77

GREE
PAGES 7

AFRICA

MOLDAVIA
PAGES 84-85

UKRAINE
PAGES 84-85

ALGERIA
PAGES 88-89

LIBYA
PAGES 88-89

MOROCCO
PAGES 88-89

TUNISIA
PAGES 88-89

WESTERN SAHARA
PAGES 88-89

DJIBO
PAGES 9

GHANA
PAGES 92-93

GUINEA
PAGES 92-93

GUINEA-BISSAU
PAGES 92-93

IVORY COAST
PAGES 92-93

LIBERIA
PAGES 92-93

MALI
PAGES 92-93

MAURITANIA
PAGES 92-93

NIGE
PAGES 9

EQUATORIAL GUINEA
PAGES 94-95

GABON
PAGES 94-95

SAO TOME & PRINCIPE
PAGES 94-95

ZAIRE
PAGES 94-95

BURUNDI
PAGES 96-97

KENYA
PAGES 96-97

MALAWI
PAGES 96-97

RWAN
PAGES 9

THE INDIAN OCEAN

SOUTH AFRICA
PAGES 98-99

SWAZILAND
PAGES 98-99

ZIMBABWE
PAGES 98-99

COMOROS
PAGES 100-101

MADAGASCAR
PAGES 100-101

MALDIVES
PAGES 100-101

MAURITIUS
PAGES 100-101

SEYCHE
PAGES 10

IRAN
PAGES 108-109

KUWAIT
PAGES 108-109

OMAN
PAGES 108-109

QATAR
PAGES 108-109

SAUDI ARABIA
PAGES 108-109

UNITED ARAB EMIRATES
PAGES 108-109

YEMEN
PAGES 108-109

AFGHAN
PAGES 1

PAKISTAN
PAGES 116-117

NEPAL
PAGES 116-117

SRI LANKA
PAGES 116-117

CHINA
PAGES 118-121

MONGOLIA
PAGES 118-119

NORTH KOREA
PAGES 120-121

SOUTH KOREA
PAGES 120-121

TAIWA
PAGES 12

THE PACIFIC OCEAN

BRUNEI
PAGES 126-127

INDONESIA
PAGES 126-127

PHILIPPINES
PAGES 126-127

FIJI
PAGES 128-129

KIRIBATI
PAGES 128-129

MARSHALL ISLANDS
PAGES 128-129

MICRONESIA
PAGES 128-129

NAUR